T0135863

# Agent Technology
## Theory and Application

Band 5

# Agent Technology

## Theory and Application

Band 5

Daniel Moldt (Ed.)

Lawrence Cabac

# Modeling Petri Net-Based Multi-Agent Applications

Logos Verlag Berlin

λογος

# Agent Technology. Theory and Application

Daniel Moldt (Ed.)

Universität Hamburg
Fachbereich für Informatik
Vogt-Kölln-Str. 30
D-22527 Hamburg

moldt@informatik.uni-hamburg.de

Bibliografische Information der Deutschen Nationalbibliothek

Die Deutsche Nationalbibliothek verzeichnet diese Publikation in der
Deutschen Nationalbibliografie; detaillierte bibliografische Daten sind
im Internet über http://dnb.d-nb.de abrufbar.

ISBN 978-3-8325-2673-3
ISSN 1614-676X

Logos Verlag Berlin GmbH
Comeniushof, Gubener Str. 47,
10243 Berlin

Tel.:    +49 (0)30 / 42 85 10 90
Fax:    +49 (0)30 / 42 85 10 92
http://www.logos-verlag.de

# Modeling
# Petri Net-Based
# Multi-Agent Applications

by

## Lawrence Cabac

Dissertation

for the attainment of the degree
Doctor of Natural Sciences
(Dr. rer. nat.)

University of Hamburg
Faculty of Mathematics, Informatics and Natural Sciences
Department of Informatics

Hamburg 2010

"Experience is the result, the sign, and the reward of that interaction of organism and environment which, when it is carried to the full, is transformation of interaction into participation and communication."

John Dewey, *Art as Experience* (1934, p. 22)

## Acknowledgements

First of all I would like to thank my supervisors, Dr. Daniel Moldt and Prof. Dr. Rüdiger Valk, for their help and support. The help and ideas of Daniel and his confidence in my work were a great support. I thank Prof. Dr. Kees van Hee, who acted as external referee of the presented work.

I would also like to thank my colleagues and affiliates of the Theoretical Foundations Group of the Department of Informatics, University of Hamburg, for their cooperation and assistance. It is a pleasure to work with them. These are: Till Dörges, Michael Duvigneau, Frank Heitmann, Michael Köhler-Bußmeier, Kolja Markwardt, Jan Ortmann, Christine Reese, Heiko Rölke and Matthias Wester-Ebbinghaus. Special thanks goes to Michael Duvigneau for the cooperatation on the work for the plugin concept model, RENEW and MULAN and other publications as well as for his patient answers to all my requests.

Furthermore, I thank all the people that have proofread this work and gave me good advice on my language and the consistency of my argumentation. These persons are: Frédérique Revuz-Cabac, Dagmara Dowbor, Eva Müller and Thomas Wagner.

I also thank all persons who were involved in the AOSE teaching projects: students, tutors and teachers who worked on the concepts and implementations of applications and tools. Of all these, special thanks for their direct involvement in contributions to the presented work go to: Hannes Ahrens, Tobias Betz, Eugene Brin, Nicolas Denz, Ragna Dirkner, Marcin Hewelt, Yvonne Küstermann, Alexander Lehning Eva Müller, Sven Offermann, Florian Plähn, Tobias Rathjen, Benjamin Schleinzer, Jan Schlüter, Felix Simmendinger, Volker Tell, Benjamin Teuber, and Thomas Wagner.

Finally, I would like to thank my family. I thank my father George Cabac for his support, love and trust. I especially thank my mother Jutta Cabac and my grandmother Ilse Schneider for their love and trust in my abilities as well as their patience with me. A special thanks goes to my wife Frédérique Revuz-Cabac and my children Lucienne and Maxim who endured the times of work with patience and support. I love you.

Hamburg, June 2010

L. Cabac

vi

# Abstract

For the construction of software systems, it is essential for the developers to have a profound understanding of the nature of the system. Modeling is the essential means for the understanding of complex systems. This is true for the construction as well as for the comprehension. The understanding of a system is a collective process, in which the whole development team participates. In order to integrate the models into this process, the models have to be made explicit: i.e. explicit representations (e.g. diagrams), which are the ground for communication, have to be provided.

Petri net-based Agent-Oriented Software Engineering (PAOSE) is the systematic approach for the development of multi-agent systems on the basis of the MULAN reference model developed in the Theoretical Foundations Group (TGI) at the University of Hamburg. In the context of this approach, I present a set of modeling techniques that are able to support developers during design, construction and debugging of multi-agent applications built with the MULAN/CAPA framework. For the organization of the development team, I provide the *multi-agent system of developers* as suitable guiding metaphor. I also present a tool set that provides the support for the developers to employ the presented techniques and I present a second tool set that helps the developers to analyze the systems at runtime and in their code base.

The modeling techniques for the constructive modeling span all aspects of the framework and constitute a central part of the PAOSE approach. They facilitate the modeling of the system's overview in coarse (Coarse Design Diagrams, CDD), the application-specific agent ontology (Concept Diagrams, CD), the organizational structures in multi-agent applications (Dependency Diagrams, DD and R/D Diagrams), the agent interactions (Agent Interaction Protocol Diagrams, AIP) and the agent-internal processes as decision components (as reference nets).

The set of supporting tools – one tool for each technique – is integrated in the development environment RENEW as plugins. These tools provide the modeling facilities and additionally allow to generate design artifacts from the produced models. These generated artifacts are the system's initial project code base (from CDD), *Java* classes for the ontology (CD), the initial knowledge bases (DD and R/D) and the protocol net skeletons (AIP). For the agent-internal processes, *Java* classes are generated from abstract interface descriptions.

The set of techniques and tools for the analysis are able to provide explicit models for the examination of the multi-agent applications. Some of these explicit models are diagrams and some of them make use of the original design artifacts.

Finally, I describe and evaluate the AOSE projects, in which the techniques and tools have been applied and in which context they have been developed. All techniques and tools are integrated into the PAOSE approach through the *multi-agent system* metaphor. Within the approach, they further the integration and awareness of concurrency and distribution in the developed system as well as in the development system.

By providing modeling techniques and supporting tools, I substantially improve the development of multi-agent applications with the PAOSE approach on a conceptual as well as on a technical level. On the conceptual level, improvements include support for the systematic development, structuring of models and means for the comprehension of the systems. On the technical level, they include the improvement of quality in the development and the observability through explicit representations.

# Zusammenfassung

Bei der Konstruktion von Softwaresystemen ist es essenziell, dass die Entwickler zu einem gemeinsamen, tiefgreifenden Verständnis des Systems gelangen. Modellieren ist das grundlegende Mittel, um komplexe Systeme zu verstehen. Dieses gilt genauso für das Erstellen sowie für das Verständnis dieser Systeme. Um die Modelle für den Verstehensprozess des Entwicklerteams nutzbar machen zu können, müssen diese explizit gemacht werden. Das heißt, es müssen die – für die Kommunikation erforderlichen – expliziten Repräsentationen der Modelle (Diagramme) bereitgestellt werden.

Die petrinetzbasierte Agentenorientierte Softwareentwicklung (PAOSE) ist der systematische Ansatz, der von der Arbeitsgruppe Theoretische Grundlagen der Informatik (TGI) an der Universität Hamburg für die Konstruktion von Multiagentenanwendungen entwickelt wird. Im Kontext dieses Ansatzes stelle ich Modellierungstechniken vor, die die systematische Konstruktion von Multiagentenanwendungen, auf der Grundlage des MULAN/CAPA Rahmenwerks ermöglichen. Für die Organisation des Entwicklerteams stelle ich ein geeignetes Leitbild zur Verfügung. Weiterhin präsentiere ich einen Werkzeugsatz, der den Einsatz der Techniken ermöglicht und einen weiteren, der die Entwickler darin unterstützt, die Systeme sowohl im laufenden Betrieb als auch im Quelltext zu analysieren.

Die vorgestellten Modellierungstechniken berücksichtigen alle Aspekte des Rahmenwerks und stellen eine Kernkomponente des PAOSE-Ansatzes dar. Sie ermöglichen das Modellieren des groben Systemüberblicks (Grobentwurf, CDD), der anwendungsspezifischen Ontologie (Konzeptdiagramme, CD), der organisatorischen Struktur der Systeme (Abhängigkeitsdiagramme, DD und Rollen/Abhängigkeitsdiagramme, R/D), der Agenteninteraktionen (Agenteninteraktionsdiagramme, AID) und der internen Prozesse der Agenten (mit Referenznetzen).

Die bereitgestellten Werkzeuge zu den Techniken sind in das Entwicklungssystem RENEW als Plugins integriert. Sie ermöglichen den werkzeugbasierten Einsatz der Modellierungstechniken und ermöglichen das Erstellen von entwicklungsspezifischen Artefakten aus den erstellten Modellen. Die generierten Artefakte umfassen die initiale Quelltextbasis (aus den CDD), *Java* Klassen der Ontologie (CD), initiale Wissensbasen (DD und R/D) und Protokollnetzskelette (AIP). Für die internen Prozesse können *Java* Klassen aus abstrakten Schnittstellenbeschreibungen generiert werden.

Die Techniken und Werkzeuge für die Analyse sind in der Lage, die beobachteten Systeme durch explizite Modelle darzustellen. Dabei benutzen diese zum Teil die vorgestellten Techniken oder sie integrieren Designartefakte für ihre Zwecke.

Schließlich beschreibe und evaluiere ich die AOSE Projekte, in denen die Werkzeuge und Techniken eingesetzt wurden und in deren Kontext diese entwickelt wurden.

Alle Techniken und Werkzeuge sind durch die Metapher des *Multiagentensystems der Entwickler* in den PAOSE-Ansatz, den Entwicklungsprozess und die Teamorganisation eingebettet. Sie fördern die Integration von Nebenläufigkeit und Dezentralisierung in das entwickelte System und das Entwicklersystem.

Durch die Bereitstellung der Modellierungstechniken und Werkzeuge verbessere ich substantiell die Entwicklung von Multiagentenanwendungen auf der Basis von PAOSE und dies sowohl auf der konzeptionellen, wie auch auf der technischen Ebene. Verbesserungen auf der konzeptionellen Ebene beinhalten die Unterstützung einer systematischen Herangehensweise, besser strukturierte Modelle und die Unterstützung für das Systemverständnis. Auf der technischen Ebene liegen die Vorteile insbesondere in der Qualitätsverbesserung der Entwicklung und der Beobachtbarkeit der Systeme durch explizite Repräsentationen.

# Brief Contents

# Contents

# 1 Introduction

The high complexity of software systems is one of the most challenging problems in nowadays research and development in computer science. In that matter, concurrent and distributed systems are especially hard to handle. This is true in terms of administration and control of executed systems as well as in terms of carrying out their construction or analysis. The means to cope with the complexity of systems are manifold. For example, modeling techniques are employed, systematic approaches developed, architectures proposed and paradigms created. Among the underlying principles applied in the course of system design and analysis, common ones are the use of abstractions, pattern-based design, structuring of technical and application-specific domains, decomposition of systems and models and modularization. Even so, the task of designing, constructing and analyzing concurrent and distributed systems remains a difficult one.

Here Petri nets can step into the breach and provide intuitive and powerful concepts for the modeling of those systems. However, even though many expressive high-level Petri net formalisms exist, there is no design and development approach that explicitly addresses the construction of software systems implemented with Petri net models. Moreover, Petri nets are often not regarded as suitable target languages for system implementation. On the one hand they are considered as modeling languages that do not need abstract design/modeling support but are suitable for system analysis. On the other hand they are not considered apt for system implementation after a system is specified, for instance with the Unified Modeling Language.

In the range of Petri net formalisms, from formal to intuitive ones, the object-oriented formalism of reference nets lies in the center and can be best classified as executable formalism (i.e. having an operational semantics). Although the mathematics are not sufficiently examined to allow for advanced verification techniques, they are still suitable for the modeling and execution of arbitrarily structured and complex systems. As a particular kind of nets-within-nets (see Valk (1998)[1]), reference nets (see Kummer (2002)) also offer specific advantages, such as dynamically changeable structures, instance creation, synchronous channels and a tight *Java* integration. These are valuable advantages when it comes to the modeling of complex systems. The MULAN/CAPA multi-agent system framework (Multi-Agent Nets, see Rölke (2004); Concurrent Agent Platform Architecture, see Duvigneau (2002)) benefits from these advantages. The framework has proven that large, concurrent and distributed systems can be built as Petri net models and executed just like any other software system. This approach has been coined *implementation by specification*. Moreover, through the specification and implementation as Petri net system, concurrency-awareness and synchronization handling are inherent to these systems and their development. In addition, the MULAN/CAPA framework provides the

---

[1] The idea of active tokens / token refinement can be traced back to a proposition by Valk in 1987.

concepts and implementation for the distributed aspects of these systems.

However, there exists no approach, methodology or modeling language that expressively addresses the needs and attributes of such systems. Conventional modeling languages often neglect the concern of concurrency. Even agent-oriented methodologies have a deficit in this matter. The PAOSE approach (Petri net-based Agent-Oriented Software Engineering, see Moldt (2006b)) fills this gap. It offers the concepts, methods and principles that lead to a systematic Petri net-based software development for multi-agent applications.

In this work, I present a set of modeling techniques that are employed in the PAOSE approach. By this, I offer a large contribution to the development of an approach, which explicitly aims at the design of concurrent and distributed multi-agent applications on the basis of Petri nets (i.e. reference nets), while I do not address verification of the models in this work. Integrated in the development approach, the modeling techniques are designed in order to systematize the processes of development. They are specifically designed for the target platform MULAN/CAPA and backed up by a set of tools that are integrated in the existing development framework RENEW (The Reference Net Workshop, see Kummer et al. (2009a)).

## 1.1 Context

Three areas of computer science constitute the context of the presented work: *Petri nets*, *agent-orientation* and *software engineering*. The common aspect that unites the three disciplines is that modeling is used in all areas to cope with the high complexity of system design and analysis.

### 1.1.1 Petri Nets

Petri nets are a thoroughly examined family of formalisms for the modeling of systems. Their main advantages are the support for concurrency and the dual representation as graphs. The models derive their power from the fact that Petri nets offer both operational semantics (for their execution) and formal semantics (for analysis). Moreover, there exist numerous powerful tools for an efficient simulation or analysis of those models, as well as dialects with specialized advantages. While low-level nets offer powerful and efficient analysis possibilities, high-level nets allow to model systems of higher complexity. Advanced verification techniques can be applied to low-level or restricted formalisms, but they depend on a mathematically precise semantics. Among the high-level Petri net formalisms, the colored Petri nets (CPN) and object-oriented Petri net formalisms, such as *reference nets*, are well examined and offer expressive modeling features. RENEW[2] offers an efficient execution environment (virtual machine, VM) for the formalism of reference nets, which is the formalism used in this work.

---

[2]The Reference Net Workshop; in fact, RENEW is a multi-formalism simulator. This, however, will not be in the focus of this work.

## 1.1.2 Agent-Orientation

Agent-orientation is one of the most promising approaches/paradigms to the development of complex systems. The combination of a strict encapsulation of data and behavior in agents, together with a highly structured organization of the system, offers the means to develop highly complex, flexible, distributed and adaptable systems. The fascination with agent technologies lies in part in the fact that here several areas of computer science converge. The main contributing areas are artificial intelligence (AI), distributed systems (DS) and software engineering (SWE). Other fields also contribute to agent-orientation, for instance sociology, Petri nets, robotics and semantic web. Agent-orientation is the underlying paradigm followed in this work.

## 1.1.3 Software Engineering

Software engineering offers sets of well-established approaches to develop complex systems that are backed up with sophisticated methods and techniques. These approaches comprise several areas of the development process, from the analysis to the shipping and maintaining of software. The list of well-established concepts is extensive, but their means are often common, well known and widely in use, such as structuring, modularization or object-orientation. These concepts are supported by the methods, techniques and tools that form the basis – technical and conceptual – for the approaches. The paradigm of object-orientation, for instance, is the underlying concept in approaches such as the Unified Process (UP) or extreme programming (XP). The former utilizes UML (Unified Modeling Language) to specify systems as diagrammatic models. One outstanding feature of UML/UP is that the system's specification is divided into several views. For each view there exists a precise technique. The latter can be regarded as the prototype of the agile approaches. Here the agility of the development process is at the focus of the approach. This work, which focuses on the modeling of systems, bears the mark of a strong influence of UML and related techniques.

## 1.1.4 Modeling and Modeling Techniques

Modeling is *the* means to cope with the high complexity of systems and their design or analysis. Large and complex software systems – especially distributed, concurrent and dynamic ones – are hard to understand, design, build and manage. In a constantly increasing size and complexity, modeling and the ability to find the right abstractions are essential to meet the challenges of distributed and concurrent systems. However, given its purpose, modeling is not a trivial task. It requires and it has also to support creativity. This creative modeling process is backed up by systematic, methodological approaches.

Models – especially diagrammatic ones – are written in a well-defined language. Although there are many methodologies, thus languages, nowadays the de-facto standard for object-oriented software in software development is UML. However, the modeling techniques lack a formal semantics. Petri nets, on the contrary, offer a formal semantics for developed models and offer in addition concepts for the modeling of concurrency.

Each of the above mentioned areas offers advantages for the processes of design and analysis of complex systems. To summarize, the main advantages of each area in the context of this work are:

- Petri nets offer formal semantics as well as operational semantics for the models, a high level of concurrency (locality, distribution) and powerful abstractions such as refinement/coarsening, folding/unfolding.

- Agent-orientation offers the high level concepts of system organization, flexibility of components and systems as well as a high degree of structuring useful to develop complex and distributed systems.

- Software engineering offers well-established methodologies and modeling techniques to systematize and formalize the process of developing a (complex) system. Two of its main features are the decomposition of system elements into independent parts (objects, components) and the multi-perspective approach in system modeling.

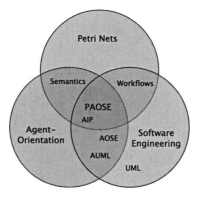

Figure 1.1: Context of PAOSE.

Figure 1.1 gives an informal overview of the context of this work. The three mentioned areas of informatics are displayed. While the three areas overlap, the presented work lies in their intersection. The Petri net-based Agent-Oriented Software Engineering is located in this intersection (PAOSE[3], see Moldt (2005) and Moldt (2006b)). Some of the main aspects of the respective disciplines – or overlapping areas – also appear in Figure 1.1. The Unified Modeling Language (UML) is the standard for object-oriented modeling. The Agent Unified Modeling Language (AUML, see Section 6.3) is an extension to UML that provides support for matters inherent to multi-agent systems and not provided by UML. Agent Interaction Protocol Diagrams (AIP, see Chapter 13) are a dialect of Interaction Protocols defined within AUML that have been developed in the PAOSE context. The other two elements are contributions of the field of Petri nets. Here, Petri nets provide a formal semantics for numerous kind of aspects in multi-agent

---

[3]Note that the *P* in PAOSE mostly stands for *Petri net*. However, other interpretations are sometimes also valid, such as *process*, *prototype* or *perspective*.

systems and offer formalizations for workflows – e.g. in the form of workflow nets – which are used in the context of business process management (BPM).

## 1.2 Motivation and Objective

Petri nets are often used for system specification. Above the expressive power of the resulting models, they offer formal as well as operational semantics. Thus, Petri net models enable the developer to use verification techniques (static and dynamic) on the models as well as to explore the model through direct execution (also called simulation).

Nowadays, high-level Petri net models – even large models – can be efficiently executed on state-of-the-art machines (personal computers). With reference nets (see Kummer (2002)) a formalism that follows the nets-within-nets paradigm (see Valk (1998)) and with RENEW (Reference Net Workshop, http://www.renew.de) an efficient virtual machine exist that offer modularization of large models together with the integration of modern object-oriented concepts and functional libraries through the *Java* context. Rölke (2004) showed that it is possible to build large executable systems on the basis of reference nets that follow the agent paradigm. He presented the MULAN reference model (Multi-Agent Nets, see also Köhler et al. (2003) and Köhler et al. (2001)) that not only allows to model but also to execute multi-agent systems as Petri nets, i.e. reference nets. Duvigneau (2002) extended the MULAN reference model by adding a tight *Java* integration as well as a compliant and efficient message transport system that allows not only inter-platform communication but also communication with other FIPA-compliant platforms, such as *Jade*. The resulting platform named CAPA (Concurrent Agent Platform Architecture, see also Duvigneau et al. (2003)) is a full-fledged FIPA-compliant agent platform.

RENEW offers an efficient runtime environment for systems modeled in reference nets. MULAN/CAPA is a framework, realized as reference net system, that makes it possible to build highly structured applications that form FIPA-compliant multi-agent systems. The systems modeled with reference nets within MULAN have proven their prototypical practicability in the *Settler*[4] projects, presented by Rölke (2004), Cabac et al. (2005a), Willmott et al. (2005) and also in the *WFMS*[4] projects, presented by Cabac et al. (2007), Reese et al. (2007) and Reese et al. (2008). Although the approach of the system development, within the context of the projects, was – at first – ad hoc, experimental and depended on the modeling expertise of the developers, it rapidly developed into a systematic process. Best practices became standard procedures or conventions of the team. Techniques from related areas (UML, AUML) also entered the development process.

In the context of the emerging and quickly developing software development approach PAOSE, the modeling techniques established themselves as parts of the approach and also as driving forces for its further advancement. These modeling techniques are presented in this work. In addition, the essential parts of the PAOSE approach – the context for the modeling techniques – are also addressed in this work.

I formulate the central question of this thesis as follows:

---

[4]The AOSE projects (Settler and WFMS) are also presented in detail in Chapter 22.

**How can the development of systems with the PAOSE approach be adequately supported by (abstract) modeling techniques?**

From this central question I derive two subsequent questions:

- How can the constructive design process of PAOSE-based systems be supported by modeling techniques?

- How can modeling techniques support the analysis[5] of executed PAOSE-based systems?

The approach taken to answer these questions in this work is a constructive, prototyping, iterative, incremental and experimental one. During several teaching projects of agent-oriented software development, re-occurring problems, challenges and solutions were identified and several proposals were made to improve the specification process. The most promising approaches, concepts and techniques from ad hoc solutions as well as from standard approaches and research proposals were integrated into the overall approach as prototypes. Also prototypical tools were built to evaluate the proposed techniques. Then mostly a pragmatic position was taken and qualitative evaluation led to improvements of techniques and tool support. The constant extension of tools and techniques was made possible through the extensible architecture of the tool base RENEW. Since version 2, RENEW has featured a dynamic architecture that is conceptualized by the MULAN reference model. The technical details are presented by Schumacher (2003) and Kummer et al. (2004). Duvigneau (2009) provides a far more detailed conceptual investigation into dynamic architectures on the basis of Petri nets, which is rooted in previous joint work (see Cabac et al. (2005) and Cabac et al. (2006a)). Through the dynamic architecture it is possible to extend RENEW with plugins, such as those plugins presented in this work.

I give answers to the central and the derived questions in the following parts by presenting adequate modeling techniques for the PAOSE approach that are not only backed up by effective tool support but have also proven their usefulness and suitability for the approach in several teaching projects. This work deals with the modeling techniques and approaches that support the systematic construction of multi-agent models, embedded in the context of PAOSE, on the basis of MULAN as reference model, CAPA as FIPA-compliant multi-agent framework and RENEW as execution engine (virtual machine).[6]

## 1.3 Content and Outline

The work presented has been in parts published and presented to the research community on several occasions. It consists of modeling techniques, tools and procedures that help develop concurrent agent-based systems with Petri nets, more precisely with reference nets and the MULAN/CAPA framework.

---

[5]Note that *analysis* does not imply any form of verification technique in this work. Instead, *analysis* is merely the process – or the prerequisite – to support and promote the understanding of complex systems.

[6]In fact, RENEW is also an extensible development environment that includes a plugin system core, which enables the extensions through plugins.

## 1.3.1 Previous and Related Work

This work builds on and embraces previous works such as my *Diplomarbeit* (diploma thesis, (2003)) and my *Studienarbeit* (bachelor's thesis equivalent, (2002)). The foundation Chapters 3, 4 and 6 of this work have been adapted from Cabac (2003, *diploma thesis, Chapters 2–4*). All these chapters have been thoroughly modified and extended. Chapter 4 reflects the evolution of the MULAN framework, Chapters 3 has been extended and revised and Chapter 6 has been substantially modified and extended. Early versions of the net components concept and the Agent Interaction Protocol Diagrams as well as their corresponding tools were also topic in (Cabac 2003) and the initial idea of net components was already presented in (Cabac 2002).

Other parts of the presented work have been previously published. The main publications are, besides those mentioned above, an overview of the modeling of agent applications with MULAN (Cabac et al. 2007b), the description of a suitable guiding metaphor for the approach (Cabac 2007), the presentation of the net components concept as one of the basic structuring means (Cabac 2009), the presentation of a formal concept to model plugin systems with Petri nets and as agent system (Cabac et al. 2005; Cabac et al. 2006a), presentations of modeling techniques (Cabac and Markwardt 2009; Cabac and Moldt 2009; Cabac et al. 2008c; Cabac and Moldt 2005; Cabac et al. 2003), integration of mining techniques for the analysis of multi-agent system (Cabac et al. 2006d; Cabac et al. 2006; Cabac and Denz 2008) and tools to support the development and debugging (Cabac and Dörges 2007; Cabac et al. 2009a).

## 1.3.2 Outline

Part I presents an overview of the state of the art of Petri nets, software modeling, agent-technology and modeling in agent approaches. Part II deals with constructive modeling techniques for the PAOSE approach. Part III presents techniques and tools for the analytical modeling in the context of the MULAN/CAPA framework. Part IV presents example applications, the models created during the development of the examples and discusses the improvements that have been achieved through the use of the presented modeling techniques. Part V concludes the work with a summary and a discussion.

Part I, after a brief introduction into modeling and abstractions, introduces the state of the art in the reference net formalism, that is to say the Petri net formalism used in this work. It also introduces agents and multi-agent systems in general and presents the MULAN reference model in detail, followed by the introduction of the net components concept. The latter is the basic structuring means for the Petri net models presented throughout this work. A chapter about modeling in UML and in agent-oriented approaches concludes, together with a brief summary, this part.

Part II begins with an outline of the guiding metaphor for the orientation of the development team during the development process so as to give the reader a notion about how the modeling techniques are embedded in the approach. Then the modeling techniques for the development of MULAN applications within the PAOSE approach (constructive modeling) are presented in an overview. After that, all modeling techniques are explained in detail: Coarse Design Diagram (overview), R/D Diagram (Roles &

Dependencies), Concept Diagram (ontology) and Agent Interaction Protocol Diagrams (interactions). This part concludes with a description of the modeling of agent-internal process as decision components and a brief summary of the whole part.

Part III shows how the presented techniques can be used to achieve analytical models from the running system. This is, even in conventional, monolithic, local systems, not a trivial task and for deterministic systems of little interest. However, when analyzing the structure and processes of an adaptive, distributed system, the need to determine the state of the system increases rapidly. Thus, several approaches to trace the processes and to observe the behavior of the involved agents are presented. Additionally, the developer's need to investigate and understand the system's specification – i.e. the code base/model base– is also supported and the underlying techniques and tools are presented.

Part IV finally presents example applications. First, a small example is presented in detail, which allows the reader to focus on the techniques.[7] Second, the AOSE (agent-oriented software engineering) projects and their target implementation systems are presented. The presentation of the projects comprises 8 iterations of the series of teaching projects and the target implementations are a distributed multi-user board game (*Settler*) and a distributed agent-based workflow management system (WFMS).

Part V presents the summary of results. This includes a descriptions of my contributions in the respective contexts. Additionally, this part also presents a discusses and provides an outlook.

## 1.4 Terminology

In the context of the PAOSE approach the terminology uses mostly widely accepted interpretations. In some cases, where the term differs from the usual meaning, it will be made explicit. Nevertheless, this section briefly introduces some terminology, in order to provide a foundation definition of terms. This does not mean that the terminology is free of ambiguity, which is – in my opinion – not possible to achieve. There always exists a space for differences in interpretation.

In addition, some of the terms – like *protocol*, which is used differently in the MULAN reference model and in usual agent frameworks/methodologies (see Section 4.3.4) – have different meanings in different contexts. For the experienced reader, the disambiguation is, on ground of the context, mostly obvious. Instead of defining artificially a new terminology, I rather stick to the terminology commonly used for each term in its own context and point out the different meanings where necessary.

The following brief description of terms constitutes a foundation of a terminology for this work. The description is backed up by a Class Diagram in Figure 1.2, which should be interpreted pragmatically, not dogmatically. It is an idealization that shows only a part (fragment) of the whole and is also just one valid view on the terminology.[8]

---

[7]The Producer/Consumer example can be described as a HelloWorld example for multi-agent systems.

[8]For instance, the terms *organization* and *role* do not appear in the diagram but are essential parts for an approach. Here however, I wanted to show the relations in regard to the term *model* and even for this goal some details are missing. For instance it is not shown that an approach is also a model.

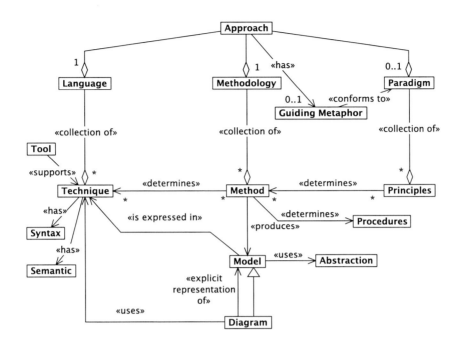

Figure 1.2: Terminology as Class Diagram.

In this work I distinguish between *developed system* and *development system*. While the former is the outcome of the creative process that is called *modeling* and is conceived as part of the *(software) engineering*, the latter describes the system (developers, resources, environment, organization) that executes the process of developing the (software) system.

We conceive *models* as abstractions of systems (technical or social). They represent images of the system in a defined *view* (perspective). Models are often explicated as *diagrams*. Each diagram (and also each model) is created using a modeling *technique* – either formal, semi-formal or intuitive. The processes of achieving models are characterized as *analysis* or *design*. Thus, a model can be *analytical* or *constructive*. The detailed prescribed proceedings that include the actions that lead to a model – together with the resources, the underlying paradigm, etc. – is called *approach*. To achieve models in *languages* that are well defined by the techniques, the approaches have to be supported by *tools*. These tools are often – and in this work this will be assumed – software tools that allow to draw diagrams, but they can also be instruments and resources such as pens and paper. The languages should be intuitive and consistent with common, conventionalized languages. For these reasons, they use common tropes such as similes and metaphors but also conventional symbols.

*1 Introduction*

# Part I

# Multi-Agent Systems and Reference Nets

This part introduces several foundations of this work. In the following sections of this part, system design and modeling of systems as well as the foundation for agent-orientation are presented under the consideration of the basic concepts presented in this chapter. The main aspects are Petri nets, agent technology and the modeling of software systems.

The terms *abstraction* and *model* in general and related topics are discussed in Chapter 2. Chapter 3 introduces reference nets and RENEW, i.e. the modeling technique of reference nets and the tool set that supports the modeling and the execution of the developed models. The formalism of reference nets enables the developer to model complex, concurrency-aware systems that are executable in RENEW. Chapter 4 presents the agent-oriented paradigm – abstract architectural model – and MULAN, which is a reference model (reference architecture) for multi-agent systems modeled in the formalism of reference nets. Due to the fact that MULAN is modeled with reference nets, it can be executed directly within the virtual machine of RENEW. In this chapter, an agent platform is formalized as a Petri net (i.e. reference net) model, which integrates the key feature of concurrency and offers a nested hierarchical structure of nested agent elements (infrastructure, platforms, agents, protocols, knowledge bases and internal processes). Chapter 5 introduces a pattern-based approach that enables the developers/modelers of Petri net-based system to systematically develop structured Petri net models. This can be regarded as the introduction of an engineering approach into Petri net modeling on a very basic level. The net component concept allows through its pattern-based approach for code reuse and structuring of Petri net models. Chapter 6, finally, presents the state of the art of system modeling in the area of object-orientation and agent-orientation. As a representative of modeling in object-orientation, the Unified Modeling Language (UML) is outlined and several modeling techniques used within a variety of agent-orientation approaches are presented.

# 2 Abstractions, Models and Views

In the following, this work adopts the concepts and notions of the terms *abstraction*, *model* and *views* according to Moldt (1996, Chapter III), to which Laue and Liedtke (2000) have contributed in parts. This chapter gives a summary of most of the relevant terms for this work. In particular the notions for the above terms and others like *modeling* and *approach* are presented and discussed.

Section 2.1 commences by introducing the general notion of the term *abstraction*, which leads to the terms *model* and *diagram* introduced and discussed in Section 2.2. Section 2.3 presents as a general concept the term *views*. In Section 2.4 the general term *approach* – as a model for a prescription for the development of systems – is discussed in detail. Section 2.5 considers several practical aspects of modeling, in particular the necessity for tool support and Section 2.6 summarizes this chapter.

This work focuses on the modeling of software systems. This section introduces the terms *model, modeling* and *abstraction* as they are used in this work and discusses the practical impact and the usages of models, as well as the modeling itself. The practical application of modeling and the impact of computer tools on modeling are also discussed.

## 2.1 Abstraction

Abstraction is one of the most common and basic principles (phenomenon, concept, activity) used in computer science. The general process of solving a problem or finding a solution is a deviation of the original challenge through the transformation into a reduced form. In this reduced form the solution can be applied and re-transferred (concretion) to the original settings. Figure 2.1 shows the deviation process. The sought solution (dashed arrow) is achieved through the reduction of the main features of the problem (abstraction). Thus the problem is transferred to an idealized world (or model), in which the non-essential features of the phenomenon are removed. The re-transfer of the solution into the world indirectly solves the original problem. The re-transfer is labeled *concretion* as the antonym of *abstraction*, however, here could also be used the term *implementation* or *application* depending on the context of the abstraction. Obviously, this simple process can be nested and the model further abstracted to an even abstracter (more reduced) model.

The nature of the abstraction is a reduction to the essential parts of the information of the representation of the phenomenon – here the problem. Thus *abstraction* in the context of this work can be expressed as the reduction to the essence. Obviously, the form of the reduction is not independent of the cause or context. Instead, the form and the level of abstraction are highly subjective and experience is needed to find the *right*

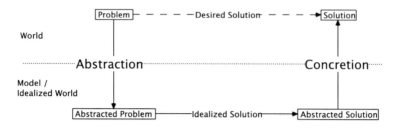

Figure 2.1: Deviation of the solution process using abstractions.

abstraction.

Several types of abstractions can be identified. Reduction by decomposition (or modularization) is a common one. In this case a system or a model will be separated into parts (modules) to form sub-systems. The application of standard solutions can also be described as a form of abstraction. A problem is then categorized and the standard solution applied. These standard solutions are usually called patterns when they concern *small* objectives and architectures when the addressed object is a (*large*) system as a whole. Examples of patterns are the design patterns of Gamma et al. (1995) or workflow patterns of van der Aalst et al. (2000a). Examples of architectures are layered architectures, interface-based architectures or reference architectures (see for instance Lilienthal (2008)).

Moldt (1996, p. 66) lists types of abstractions in the context of Petri net modeling. He considers the antonyms *abstraction* and *concretion* as a continuum or a scale, along which the movement towards one side represents a loss of information (reduction) in the representation while the movement in the opposite direction represents an addition of information in the representation (the model). Those antonyms are presented in Table 2.1.

| Abstraction | Concretion |
| --- | --- |
| Folding | Unfolding |
| Coarsening | Refinement |
| Merging | Splitting |
| Omission | Extension |
| more information in presentation $\longrightarrow$ | |
| less information in presentation $\longleftarrow$ | |

Table 2.1: Types of Abstractions.[1]

While many types of *abstraction* exist, the underlying nature of each abstraction is the formation of a model. The model thus represents a reduced form of a system. It can even represent a reduced form of another model, if the process of abstraction described in Figure 2.1 is nested, i.e. is a model of a model.

---

[1]Table adapted from (Moldt 1996, p. 66, translated from German).

## 2.2 The Model

*Model* is a term that is widely used in computer science.[2] There exist many definitions by many authors. This section introduces the applied notion of the term *model* for the context of this work, which follows the notion of Moldt (1996).

### 2.2.1 Model and Diagram

Moldt (1996, p. 28) describes a model after Lehner (1995a), Lehner (1995b) as a representation of *'something else'* (a part of the world/reality – envisioned or existing) in a certain context. It is developed by humans for a precise purpose.

**Definition 2.1 *Model***
  *A representation of a part of the world.*

In this definition the term *representation* already includes a form of reduction (abstraction). The two terms *model* and *abstraction* are tightly coupled. Models can be a representation of parts of the world that already exist or of parts that do not exist (yet). The former can be determined as *analytical model*, since a part of the world is analyzed.[3] The latter can be described as *constructive model* (also creative model). It is often used during constructions of systems in computer science as well as in other disciplines. Moldt (1996, p. 62) explains that both types of models are used to further the *understanding* of systems. For the two types of models he (1996, p. 63) uses the terms *descriptive* and *prescriptive*. This notion of *model* is also conform to the concepts of Hitz et al. (2005) and Hesse and Mayr (2008).

In computer science models are often made explicit by using a modeling technique. An explicit representation of a model in a defined graphical language is called a diagram.

**Definition 2.2 *Diagram***
  *Graphical representation of a model using a defined (diagrammatic) language or technique. The technique can be formal, semi-formal or informal. A diagram is a concrete or explicit model.*

It is obvious that there are other ways of making models explicit than using diagrams. In architecture, for instance, to represent a building with a 3D model – built from paper or other materials – is a commonly used technique. Again the definition is conform with the one given by Hitz et al. (2005). From Definitions 2.1 and 2.2 follows directly that diagrams are (explicit) models of models.

Hesse and Mayr (2008) identify in this context three types of models. The *mental model* (German: *Denkmodell*), the *linguistic model* (expressed in a language; e.g. a

---

[2]Note that, outside the context of computer science, this term is in much broader use. However, this is not relevant for this work.

[3]Note that this notion of the term *analysis* differs slightly from the usage in software development or in Petri net modeling. In software engineering, *analysis* often denotes the phase of the development process that determines the status quo of a system and the requirements. In Petri net modeling, analysis often indicates a form of verification or validation.

diagram) and the *physical model* (e.g. the small size 3D model of a building). The first one corresponds to Definition 2.1, the second to Definition 2.2. The third kind of model does not come into focus in the presented work. Although the diagram and the physical model can both be regarded as an explication[4] of a mental model.

Petri (2003, p. 3) offers in the context of modeling yet a finer distinction of the mental model. He talks of *informal* and *formal mental image*. The former depends on ("contain") experience, conventions, traditions, preferences and (even) illusions. This kind of model carries the danger of paradoxes. The latter requires deductive power, possibilities of verification, definiteness and the possibility to be shared ("share-ability"). The net is one of the possibilities to express the formal mental model. Petri call this *combinatorial modeling.*

Stachowiak (1973, pp. 131–132) defines (within a set of eighteen concepts) three main attributes of models. These are the attributes of *illustration, reduction* and *pragmatics*.[5] These three attributes are also the foundation of the examination of the concept *model* in software engineering of Hesse and Mayr (2008, pp. 380 ff.).

Stachowiak (1973, p. 56) also expresses that all kinds of knowledge acquisition (German: *Erkenntniss*; also awareness, cognition, insight) is only possible in models or through models. The model and modeling are obviously crucial for the understanding of an entity, e.g. a system or a process.

## 2.2.2 Modeling

The development of models can be described as the action of *modeling*. However, one can distinguish between the development of an (abstract) representation of a part of the world and the creation of a concrete representation. This work uses the term *modeling* for the former (mental or implicit model, see Laue and Liedtke (2000, p. 23)) and *explication* for the latter (explicit model, diagram). The former process is constructive or analytical while the latter process is a transformation from a model to a diagram. Nevertheless, when the distinction is clear, the term *modeling* is often used for both actions. It can also describe a combination of both actions. In any case, in practice of software modeling the two processes (or actions) are tightly coupled. The development of a model is often connected to and depends on the construction of a diagram. Due to the complexity of the model, it can be necessary to make parts of the model explicit before other parts of the model can be developed, made explicit and connected with the already existing parts of the model. This process of modeling and explication can thus be described as cyclic and iterative. When a group of modelers are involved in the development of the model, the explicit representation (e.g. diagram) becomes even more important for the modeling process (development of the model) as the explicit representation (diagram) becomes a

---

[4]With *explication* usually the process of making something explicit is denoted, sometimes also the outcome of the process. In this work the explication of a (mental) model is achieved by transforming it into a diagram.

[5]Translated from the German words *Abbildungsmerkmal, Verkürzungsmerkmal* and *Pragmatisches Merkmal*. Note that the German term *Abbildung* can be translated by *illustration, image, map, mapping, copy, reproduction, interpretation*, etc. many terms of which are adequate translations (source: Leo, `http://dict.leo.org`).

necessity for the communication between developers.

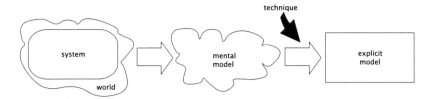

Figure 2.2: System, mental model, explicit model and technique.[6]

Laue and Liedtke (2000, Figure 2.1, p. 23) present a simple (and very abstract) informal model of the process of modeling. Figure 2.2 shows how a part of the world – a system – is transferred into a mental model (by the developer). The mental model is then transferred into an explicit model by using a defined technique. In fact, just like thoughts are often formed in a language, an experienced modeler will already use the technique (of his choice) to form his mental model. This improves the efficiency of modeling. However, it shows that the presented model is not quite accurate. The model can already be mentally modeled using a technique. The explication of the model is a copying, the explicit model a mere reproduction of the mental model.

Due to the degree of abstractness of the presented model, it does not show any information about the iterations of cycles in the process – as mentioned above. However, a more refined (or concrete) version of the model might show this information. Moreover, the presented model only represents the manual, analytical modeling. The authors did not provide other possibilities of modeling. But with the help of tools and techniques also an explicit model (e.g. diagram) can be extracted from an existing system. This form of modeling, which can be described as automatic and analytical[7] (or *descriptive* after Moldt (1996)) reverses the creation of mental and explicit model. Thus, the explicit model that has been directly extracted from a system (or process) by applying a technique, leads to the observer's understanding of the objective as a mental model. This is expressed in Figure 2.3.

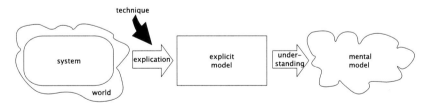

Figure 2.3: Automatic analytical modeling to support understanding of a system.

Both models of Figures 2.2 and 2.3 do not take into account that modeling can be

---

[6]Diagram adapted from Laue and Liedtke (2000, Figure 2.1, p. 23).

[7]Examples for automatic analytical modeling in the context of this work are presented in in Part III.

solely constructive as well. An envisioned object (also phenomenon or system) is often modeled before construction. This means that the object does not exist in the real world, yet. However, a vision exists – a mental model is created from which an explicit model is derived using a technique.

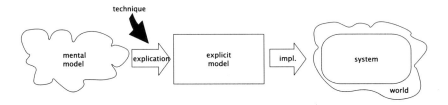

Figure 2.4: Manual constructive modeling to support understanding of a system.

In computer science the process of transforming the (explicit) model into a system is usually called implementation. Here many varieties exist. The implemented system is also often called model (compare with Züllighoven (2005)) and the explication of the model as diagram can be omitted (e.g. in extreme programming, see Beck and Andres (2005)). The implementation can be manual, automatic or assisted. One of the main features of a system in computer science is that the system has an operational semantics. If, however, the explicit model already owns an operational semantics – as it is the case with Petri net models – then the distinction between explicit model and system becomes vague.

### 2.2.3 The Purpose of Modeling

Modeling gives the developers the possibility to design the software systems they are about to build before they are actually constructed. This becomes more important as the complexity of software systems increases. A good model represents the system and parts of it at different levels of abstraction. Not only detailed information about parts is revealed but an overview over the whole system is also given. Essentially, modeling is a means of specification, information, documentation, communication and visualization. As mentioned above, models and their explication are essential for the communication in development teams. However, the visualization of a system is also crucial for its construction. If the developers can visualize the system and its structure, then they can grasp and manage its complexity. *"Developing a model for an industrial-strength software system prior to its construction or renovation is as essential as having a blueprint for large buildings"* (UML Q & A 2009, web-site). Diagrams are a way for developers to visualize the architecture and behavior of the software system. They are the blueprints of software design. The visualization of the models as diagrams, i.e. the explication of the model, is the fundamental action that is necessary for the understanding of the system.

# 2.3 Views

Views are important means for the handling of complex systems during design and construction. The term is rather vague in the literature and various opinions exist about what the term denotes (compare with Moldt (1996, p. 65 ff.) and Laue and Liedtke (2000, p. 24 ff.)). However, it seems to be agreed on that the use of multiple views for the description of complex (software) systems has its advantages. The decomposition of a model into sub-models that describe different aspects (views) of the system is obviously useful for the reduction of the complexity and thus for the understanding of the model. Kruchten (1995, p. 42) explains that the use of multiple concurrent *"views allows to address separately the concerns of the various 'stakeholders' of the architecture: end-users, developers, system engineers, project managers, etc., and to handle separately the functional and non-functional requirements."* Views highlight some elements/aspects of a system, while they intentionally hide other aspects. Balzert (1982) describes the necessity to address only a small part of the attributes of a system at a time – those of importance in the opinion of the observer– in order to understand the system.

Moldt (1996, p. 61) explains that views are means for the structuring of systems. The views rely on classification criteria (sorting patterns) which enable them to structure the addressed aspect or part of the system.

## 2.3.1 Types of Views

The possibility to regard a system under a certain view represents an effective and strong form of abstraction. UML views are represented in different techniques for different aspects of the system. Views in the 4 + 1 view model are the logical view, the development view, the process view, the physical view and the scenarios.

Moldt (1996) also distinguishes between several types of views, but he has a more general perspective. He presents the following views: techniques, methods, parts of the system/subsystems, applications, tasks of development, roles in development, layers, scenarios, errors and exceptions, chronology and specific views. Moldt also stresses the fact that, depending on the context, numerous related terms or simply alternative terms may also be used. Some of them are: *layer, pane, section, cut-out, perspective, interface, model, part, scope, aspect*[8], *projection* or *dimension*.

Although the different views are supposed to be independent from each another, there exist areas where they overlap. This can be problematic when specifications change. However, an overlapping of views is often intended as it is the case for overviews, which are important for the integration of views.

## 2.3.2 Integration

Just like parts of the system have to be assembled to form the system as a whole, views of the model also have to be assembled. This is called *integration*. Apart from the simple merging of the views in order to form a model, the coherence also plays an

---

[8]Translated from the German terms: Schicht, Scheibe, Ausschnitt, Perspektive, Schnittstelle, Modell, Teil, Betrachtungsebene, Aspekt.

important role. Models that are developed with formal techniques make it possible to verify whether views conform to each another (integration/verification/testing). In order to allow the representation of the views' relations, special overviews can be used. They offer information of the system that spans several other views, sometimes even all views.

## 2.4 Approach

In order to apply the modeling techniques to model a system, the developers have to follow a certain process and use certain methods. It is also in the interest of a cooperative development that the means should be used in a similar and comprehensible way for all developers (and other participants) in the development process. For this purpose, a model of the whole development system is usually defined that is called approach or methodology.

### 2.4.1 A Methodology Meta-Model

Shehory and Sturm (2001, 2003) present a concise meta-model for methodologies with the focus on agent-oriented development. Moreover, since it is a general approach, their results can also be applied to conventional methodologies.

Figure 2.5 shows the proposed meta-model as coarse Class Diagram. A methodology consists of three parts: a *technique set*, a *modeling language* and a *life cycle process*.

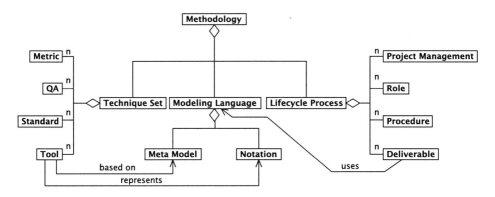

Figure 2.5: A meta-model for multi-agent system development methodologies.[10]

Each of these parts are composed of several other parts. For the *technique set* those are *metrics*, techniques for *quality assurance*, *standards* and a set of *tools*. The *life cycle process* consists of *project management* processes, *role* definitions and affiliations, several ways to follow *procedures* in the development and a multitude of artifacts, which are the results of the methodological approach (*deliverables*, i.e. models and possibly implementation artifacts). As for the *modeling language*, it consists of *meta-model* (for

---

[10]Adapted from Sturm and Shehory (2003, p. 95)

the modeling techniques – semantic) and *notation* (syntax). The modeling language is tightly coupled with the supporting tool set and the modeling tools are based on the meta-models and support models in the defined notation.

Not only in this chapter but also in Shehory and Sturm's meta-model the focus lies on the modeling language, which is in the center of their investigation. They are aware that the embedding in the technique set and the life cycle processes are crucial. Especially the tool set is of importance in a complex agent-oriented setting.

The meta-model of Shehory and Sturm is an exact formalization of the concept *methodology* as a general foundation for methodologies. However, it expands over the initial meaning of the term by engulfing several aspects that are normally not attributed to the term. The meta-model suits the reason to give a formalization in order to be able to evaluate methodological frameworks.

In opposition to the meta-model presented above, Costello (1996, Meriam-Webster) defines *methodology* as follows:

> methodology
>
> 1 : a body of methods, rules, and postulates employed by a discipline : a particular procedure or set of procedures
>
> 2 : the analysis of the principles or procedures of inquiry in a particular field

As described before, models – and thus also this meta-model – are idealizations of the described systems/the real world. Alternatively, the term *approach* is often used for the same – or similar – phenomenon.

## 2.4.2 An Approach Meta-Model

Moldt (1996, p. 30) defines an approach consisting of five facets: *resources*, *tools*, *applications*, *techniques* and *methods*. The five facets are embedded into *principles*, *paradigms*. An approach is applied within a certain *context*.

The facets comprise the methods, techniques,[12] tools and resources, which can be found in the methodology meta-model as procedures, modeling language, tools and roles/project management/technique set. Moldt expressively includes the developed application into the framework since the application is embedded in a human context (socio-technical system).

## 2.4.3 Approach

Following the initial disambiguation from Section 1.4 (Figure 1.2) we investigate the nature of an approach.

Obviously, a description of an approach is an idealized version of the setting in the real world of a development system. Thus, the first observation is that an approach is

---

[11]Diagram adapted from Moldt (1996, p. 30).

[12]Here the term *technique* is used in the sense of *modeling technique*, while the *technique set* of the methodology meta-model is included in the *resources*.

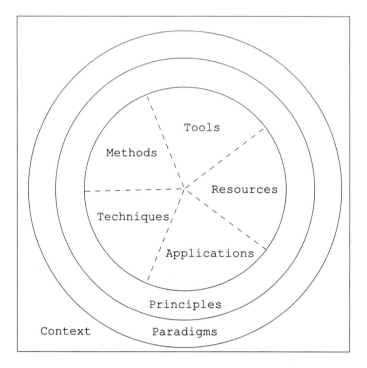

Figure 2.6: Facets of an approach by Moldt.[11]

a model of such a system. For this work we attribute following elements to the term *approach* offering a more intuitive albeit not more precise notion. The elements of an approach/methodology for an (agent-oriented) development system are:

- modeling techniques (syntax, semantic/meta-model)

- tools (modeling, generation, verification, project management)

- methods (procedures, processes, rules, principles, management)

- guidance (paradigm, guiding metaphor, workflows)

- organization (paradigm, principles, conventions, roles)

- documentation (strategy, generation)

The main focus in this work lies on the modeling techniques, which only constitute one (important) part of the approach/methodology. However, the modeling techniques are embedded in the approach through the procedures, the guidance and the tools. Thus, these aspects have to be addressed as well.

# 2.5 Modeling in Praxis

Models are the result of creative processes (compare with Hesse and Mayr (2008)). Developed for a cause, which is usually system design, models are the result of creative processes that are supported by several factors. However, the value of a model depends on the preciseness and the adequateness of the resulting explicit models. This is why the results should be unambiguous and easily understandable and the process should be systematic, coordinated and supported by adequate means.

## 2.5.1 Formal Techniques and Intuitive Understanding

Formal techniques are described through precise syntax and semantics – often in mathematical form. Besides the preciseness they have some general advantages over informal techniques, which are usually described in natural language. Some of the advantages are syntax checks, integration support, simulation and verification possibilities. Precise syntax and semantics allow the reduction of ambiguousness. Thus a formal technique enables correct understanding of a model.

The techniques used in UML, which are called *semi-formal*, remain on the border (even with UML 2). Although the urge to reach a higher level of formality is great, still many elements and features are questioned by a number of authors and are subjected to the interpretation of tool designers. However, the degree of formality varies from low (e.g. Use Case Diagrams) to high (e.g. State Charts).

In order to be understandable, models also need to be intuitive. Here many concepts enter the representations of diagrammatic models that help the reader to understand the model. These concepts are well-known in linguistics. The used symbols and grammar of the techniques follow analogies, similes and metaphors. For instance time is displayed in message sequence charts as distances in vertical (analogy) and a message sent from one entity to another is displayed as an arrow (metaphor). The metaphor especially enables intuitive understanding of models.

## 2.5.2 The Metaphor

A metaphor is a symbol that transfers meaning from one domain to another. It conveys a secondary meaning which gives some insight to the referred entity. For example the symbol of the arrow (e.g. $\rightarrow$) can convey the direction of the information flow of a message. Also the box (e.g. $\Box$) can signify a closure of a class, module, component or system.

### Guiding Metaphor (Leitbild)

The metaphor as extended metaphor also exists for the intuitive classification of approaches. Here the extended nature of the guiding metaphor makes it possible to apply all kinds of metaphors deriving from the extended metaphor (compare with Züllighoven (2005, p. 59 ff.)).

In the context of commerce, a popular translation for the term *Leitbild* is *mission statement* or *vision statement*. An article in Wikipedia (2010, German) discusses the differences of terminology and presents the main functions of a Leitbild for this context.

*"The following functions and matters can be distinguished:*

- *orientation values, norms, policies and paradigms*
- *integration: identification, corporate identity, style of communications*
- *decisions: rules for crisis management, scope of decision-making*
- *coordination: staff, executives, mediation, public relations"*

(Wikipedia – Leitbild 2010, translated from German)

**Approach and Guiding Metaphor**

An approach is a model of the process for the construction of a (software) system. It is a model since it is an idealization of the actual procedure. Usually, an approach is expressed informally and abstractly. A guiding metaphor is a simple way of harnessing an approach into a frame. Thus a very abstract and informal description of the approach is achieved without the need to give a full (and/or formal) definition of the approach. Typical examples of approaches are the waterfall model, cyclic or iterative models and prototyping approaches.[13]

## 2.5.3 Model Life Cycle

In its lifetime a model serves different purposes. It is used to understand an existing system or as a means of construction. A software model is usually developed in the design phase. During the development process it grows in size and maturity (specificity). Then it is used to communicate about features and interfaces with other developers and to remember some early decisions or it will be changed to reflect a change in the design. The distribution of the model, i.e. the explication and availability of the model, is essential for the communication among the developers.

The model can also be used to generate code or code skeletons to support the transition from design/modeling to implementation, if appropriate tools are used. For later access and to serve some documentation purposes the model is archived. It can also be included in an application programming interface (API) documentation to improve the navigation of artifacts and the overview of the information intended for other programmers.

## 2.5.4 Tool Support

The complexity of systems and system design has reached such a level that models themselves have become too complex to be comfortably handled. For complex (software) systems this means that tool support becomes essential. Moldt (1996, p. 32) remarks that tool support embraces means of development support in the form of hardware and

---

[13]The guiding metaphor for the PAOSE approach and also some examples of other guiding metaphors are described in detail in Chapter 8.

software. The possibility to use tools for the modeling of software systems offers several advantages – not only for the creation of the models but also for all other activities related to the models. The following list shows some requirements of tool support concerning models of the development process.

For software development the creation of models has to be supported by adequate tools that allow the application of the techniques. The artifacts have to be shared among the developers and at the same time they have to reside persistently in a repository. This can be achieved through a source code management system (SCM).

## 2.6 Summary

Modeling is an important means of system design. Models can be formal, informal or semi-formal. Techniques with precise syntax and semantics are useful to receive unambiguous models. However, intuitiveness also helps to easily understand the models. A systematic approach and adequate tool support enable efficient and effective development of models for software systems.

Table 2.2 sums up the terminology introduced in this chapter as it is also used throughout the whole work.

| Term | Brief Description |
|---|---|
| abstraction | reduction to the essential |
| model | representation of a part of the world |
| diagram | explicit model |
| modeling | creation of a model / applying abstraction |
| · constructive | modeling with the purpose of creating a system |
| · analytical | extracting an explicit model from an existing system |
| explication | turning a model into an explicit model (e.g. diagram) |
| technique | means of (explicit) modeling |
| · formal | precise syntax and semantics |
| · intuitive | easily understandable / uses well-known concepts |
| metaphor | symbol / transfers meaning from source to target |
| guiding metaphor | extended metaphor / gives guidance to a project team |
| approach | model of an ideal process of developing a system |
| model life cycle | stages of models during the process |

Table 2.2: Brief descriptions of terminology used in this work.

# 3 Reference Nets and Renew

The formalism of Petri nets has the advantage of a dual representation. Petri nets can be formulated as graph or as text. As graph, humans and as text, machines can easily read Petri nets. As a benefit of the textual representation machines cannot only read the code but also execute it. The benefit of the graphical representation is that the structure of the net is revealed to humans and that the execution (or simulation) of the nets can be visualized as a token game, which is an animation of the tokens in Petri nets.

After briefly introducing P/T-nets in Section 3.1, Section 3.2 describes informally but in detail the reference net formalism. Section 3.3 is dedicated to RENEW and Section 3.4 describes the development of RENEW. Section 3.5 summarizes this chapter.

## 3.1 P/T-Nets

Jessen and Valk (1987) define nets as tuples of sets. Those sets are the places, the transitions and the flow relation. Together these sets form a directed, bipartite graph. A basic P/T-net (Place/Transition-net) is a net that also includes capacities for places, weights for arcs and an initial marking. While the abstract textual descriptions seem quite unintuitive, the corresponding graphical representation can be very comprehensive. Figure 3.1 shows an example[1] of a Petri net with the basic net elements: transitions, places and arcs. The figure also displays some transition and place inscriptions.

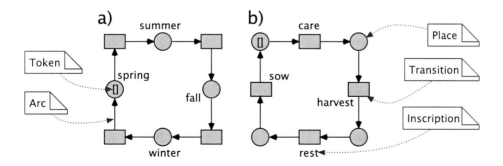

Figure 3.1: The seasons modeled as a Petri net in two different views: The view of the meteorologist (a) that focuses on the states of the seasons and the view of the farmer (b) that focuses on his activities during the seasons.[1]

In the example of Figure 3.1 inscriptions of places and transitions are names or labels for the net elements and have no influence on the execution of the net. Transitions are enabled (activated, firable), if the pre-conditions and the post-conditions are satisfied. To satisfy the pre-conditions enough tokens have to be in the input places. To satisfy the post-conditions the capacity of the output places should not be exceeded.

For detailed descriptions of the Petri net formalism see Girault and Valk (2003), Jensen (1996) or Reisig (1982).

## 3.2 Reference Nets

Reference nets (see Kummer (2002)) are object-oriented high-level Petri nets, in which tokens can be nets again. For these nets-within-nets (see Valk (1995) and Valk (1987)[2]), reference semantics is used. Tokens in one net can be references to other nets. In a simple setting of a single nesting of nets, the outer net is called system net while a token in the system net refers to an object net. Nevertheless, object nets themselves can again contain tokens that represent nets, and so a hierarchy of nested nets can be obtained. The benefit of this feature is that the modeled system is modular and extensible. Furthermore, transitions in nets can activate and trigger the firing of transitions in other nets, just like method calls of objects, by using synchronous channels (see Kummer (2002) and Christensen and Hansen (1992)).

RENEW (The Reference Net Workshop, see Kummer (2002) and Kummer et al. (2009a)) combines the nets-within-nets paradigm of reference nets with the implementation power of *Java*. Here tokens can also be *Java*-objects and nets can be regarded as objects. Objects are instantiations of classes; in a similar way reference nets are instantiated, thus many instances of a net can be produced dynamically while their structure and initial marking are defined in a net template - corresponding to the class defining the structure of an object.

In addition to the net elements of P/T-nets, reference nets offer several additional elements that increase the modeling power as well as the convenience of modeling. These additional elements include some new arc types, virtual places and a declaration. Several inscriptions have been added to the net elements providing functionality for the different net elements. Places can be typed and transitions can be augmented with expressions, actions, guards, synchronous channels and creation inscriptions. All these features are described in the following sections.

### 3.2.1 Types

P/T-nets only deal with black (anonymous) tokens that are indistinguishable from each another. In reference nets tokens can also be of any data type that is available in *Java*. So tokens can be primitive numerical data types like `int` or `long` as well as any object. Reference nets themselves are objects of the type `de.renew.simulator.NetInstance`.

---

[1]The example is an adapted version of a net from Petri (2003, p. 8)

[2]First ideas of including active tokens as token refinements in Petri net models was expressed through the *task-flow nets* by Valk (1987), which contained task systems as tokens.

Nevertheless anonymous (black) tokens are also available in RENEW. The notation for a black token is: '[]'.

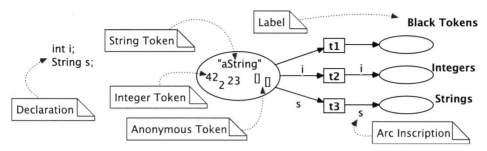

Figure 3.2: Tokens can be objects, primitive data types or anonymous. Objects can only be moved by inscribed arcs, anonymous tokens by arcs without inscription only.

Arcs without inscription can only move black tokens. Variables or expressions in arc inscriptions are required to move other tokens, i.e. tokens that refer to objects, primitive types or net instances. In a simple example an object can be removed from a place and put into another place by adding inscriptions to the two arcs that move the token. This is illustrated in Figure 3.2.

If, for instance, a transition moves object tokens from an input place to an output place, the inscriptions of input and output arcs have to be identical. This is the case in the simple net of Figure 3.2. The firing of the transition t2 or t3 moves objects but not anonymous tokens. The binding of the variable to the object is locally restricted to the neighborhood of the transition.

After the transitions in the example of Figure 3.2 have fired six times, all tokens have been removed from their initial place by the three transitions and sorted by their type into the places labeled accordingly (see Figure 3.3). The transition t1 can only move anonymous tokens, transition t2 only integers (int) and transition t3 only objects of the type java.lang.String.

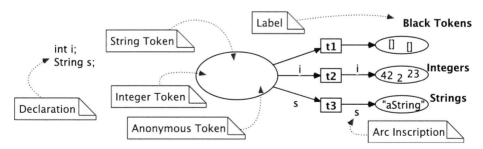

Figure 3.3: After execution of the net, the objects are sorted by type.

An inscribed arc can move any type of object. However, if the variable in the inscription is declared in the declaration, then the arc can only move objects of the type of the variable. In the example, the two variables s and i are declared as String and int, so t2 only moves integers and t3 only strings. By defining the type of the variables, the sorting (by types) of the tokens is achieved.

## 3.2.2 Inscriptions

Several sorts of inscriptions are available for places, transitions and arcs in reference nets. Place inscriptions do not only define the initial marking of a net, but also the type of a place. A typed place can only hold tokens of the appropriate type.

Arc inscriptions can be constants or variables. Furthermore, expressions are allowed in output arcs inscriptions. Figure 3.4 shows the type inscription of a place and an expression on an output arc.

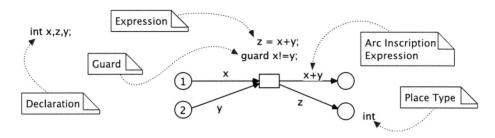

Figure 3.4: Several inscription types.

There is a variety of transition inscriptions: expressions, guards, actions, creation inscriptions and inscriptions for synchronous channels. Expressions are unlabeled, while guards and actions are prefixed with the keywords guard or action.

For the firing of a transition, several conditions have to be satisfied. Firstly, the transition has to be activated. This is the case when there is a sufficient number of tokens of the appropriate type – i.e. compatible to the arc inscription – in the input places of that transition. And secondly, the guards have to be satisfied, i.e. the expressions in the guards have to evaluate to true.

Expressions on a transition are evaluated while the simulator searches for the binding of the transition. The result of the evaluation of an expression is discarded, if it is not bound to a variable by using the unification operator '='. In contrast to expressions, actions are guaranteed to evaluate only once during firing of the transition. They should be used instead of expressions when these contain *Java* method calls that have side effects. Expressions on arcs have the same effect as those on transitions, but in contrast to transition expressions, the result is not lost and is moved to the output place.

The other two kinds of inscriptions for net creation and synchronous channels are presented in Section 3.2.4.

### 3.2.3 Virtual Places

A virtual place is a reference to a place. For any place there can be numerous virtual places that act like place holders for the original place. An arc connected to the virtual place has the same effect as an arc being connected to the original place. So a token that is on the place can be retrieved from any virtual place corresponding to the original place. A token in the net template in an original place or in a virtual place, thus, appears in the net instance in the original place and in every virtual place corresponding to the original. It is, nevertheless, only one token.

Virtual places can only be used within one net, not across different nets or net instances. So they basically are a matter of convenience. Especially, if places have many connecting arcs[3] or if they are connected in different areas of the net, the use of virtual places offers advantages. In other high-level Petri net formalisms, like colored Petri nets (CPN, see Jensen (1996)), a similar concept is known as fusion places. Figure 3.5 displays a simple example for virtual places. A token that resides on the original place can be retrieved from either virtual place by firing t2 or t3, but not from both.

Figure 3.5: Original and virtual places.

Virtual places are identified in RENEW by a double outline. Additionally, they display the same color as the original place to which they belong. However, for humans it is sometimes difficult to map the virtual places to the originals when more than one original place exist.[4]

### 3.2.4 Net Instances and Synchronous Channels

Reference nets are object-oriented nets. Similar to objects in object-oriented programming languages, where objects are instantiations of classes, net instances are instantiations of net templates. Net templates define the type of nets just like classes define the type of objects. While the net instance has a marking that determines its status, the net template determines only the behavior that is common to all net instances of one type.

The paradigm of *nets-within-nets* introduced by Valk (1995) allows tokens to be nets again. In reference nets, tokens can be anonymous, basic data types, *Java* objects or reference nets. The tokens representing the reference nets in nets are references to net instances. Any net instance can create new net instances similar to an object creating new objects. The new net instance is marked with the initial marking according to the marking of the net template. Usually, the new net instance that is created should be

---

[3]Compare with the net for the knowledge base of the MULAN agent in Figure 4.10

[4]In RENEW the original place can be found in the net template by double clicking on the virtual place. This selects the appropriate original place.

bound to a variable of the correct type (`de.renew.simulator.NetInstance`) so that it can be transferred to an output place.

The notation of the creation inscription with the usage of the keyword `new`, to create a new instance, is displayed in Figure 3.6. In this example the system net has an initial marking of three integer tokens. Thus the transition can fire three times, creating three new net instances.

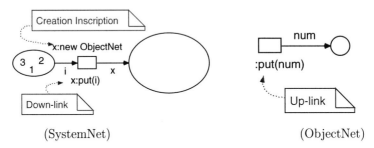

(SystemNet)                                        (ObjectNet)

Figure 3.6: Example system net and object net.

The three new net instances are bound to the variable x and put into the output place. This is displayed in Figure 3.7, in which the net templates (in the back of the image) and the net instances for both nets are displayed. There is one instance of the system net and three instances of the object net (front).[5]

The different net instances are each created during one firing of the transition of the system net that has the creation inscription. The tokens referring to the net instances are put into the output place. In the net instance `SystemNet[0]` in Figure 3.7, these three tokens are displayed in the output place.

For the communication between net instances, synchronous channels are used. A synchronous channel consists of two (or more) inscribed transitions. There are two types of transition inscriptions: *down-links* and *up-links*. Two transitions that form a synchronous channel can only fire simultaneously and only if both transitions are activated. *Down-link* and *up-link* belong to a single net or to different nets. In both cases any object can be transferred from either transition to the other. If two different net instances are involved, it is thus possible to synchronize these two nets and to transfer objects in either direction through the synchronous channel. For this the system nets must hold the reference to the object nets as tokens.

The example of figures 3.6 and 3.7 does not only show the creation of net instances, but also the application of synchronous channels. A synchronous channel `put(.)` connects the two transitions of system net and object net. The system net holds the reference to the object net instance x that is created during the firing of the transitions. The *down-link* `x:put(i)` calls the *up-link* in the object net `:put(num)`. The integers are taken from

---

[5]In RENEW net instances can be identified by the names of the windows and the window background colors. Net templates have a white background color and net instances have an integer number attached to their window title bars that identifies the distinct instances. The identifying numbers are also attached to the tokens.

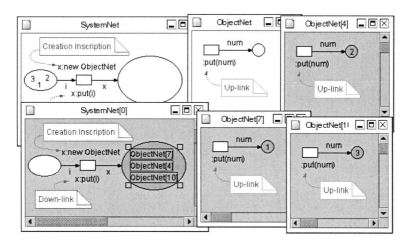

Figure 3.7: A screen shot of a system net and an object net;
the templates (white background) and several net instances (blue background).

the input place of the system net and bound to the variable i used as an argument in the channel inscription. Both transitions fire simultaneously and the two variables i and num are unified. Thus num is bound to the same integer as i, which finally is put into the output place of the object net. So the different numbers in the output places can distinguish the different net instances of the object net.

## 3.2.5 Arcs

In addition to the simple unidirectional arc of P/T-nets, reference nets also offer three other kinds of arcs. *Reserve arcs* are equivalent to two arcs connecting the same two nodes in opposite directions. *Test arcs* are very similar to *reserve arcs*, but instead of removing the token at the start of firing and returning it at the end of firing, as it is the case for reserve arcs, they just test whether there exists a token on the connected place without removing it. This means that the main difference between the two is that, while the transition is firing, the token can be used by another test arc concurrently. As shown in Figure 3.8, the arc types are distinguished by their arrows tips. The reserve arc has one arrow tip at each end of the arc while the test arc has no arrow tip at all.

Figure 3.8: Additional arc types in reference nets.

The last arc types, that are special in reference nets, are the *flexible arcs*. The implementation in RENEW (Kummer et al. 2009b) is based on the proposal of Reisig (1997). Flexible arcs are displayed with two arrow tips at one end of the arc. These arcs represent a dynamically changing (flexible) number of arcs. The number of tokens transported are determined at runtime – to be more precise at the time of firing.

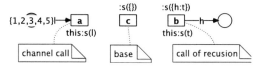

Figure 3.9: Semantics of the flexible arc described with recursive channels.

The incoming arc withdraws all elements of a `Collection` object that reside on a place from this place. The transition can only fire if all elements of the `Collection` are on the place, and only those elements are withdrawn concurrently. Although this only works if the objects in the `Collection` are already known, this mechanism still provides a powerful method for modeling. By using the flexible output arc, all elements of a *Java* `Collection` object can be put into a place. As an example for the usage of the flexible arc, compare with the net component *NC forall* in Section 5.3.

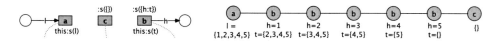

Figure 3.10: Firing of transitions *a,b*, *c* and synchronization graph.

The semantics of the outgoing flexible arc in RENEW is defined through the model shown in Figure 3.9. The reference net model consists of a recursive channel chain $:s(\cdot)$ realized by three transitions (*a*, *b* and *c*). Transition *a* calls the channel chain with a collection of elements (a list), which is recursively decomposed by pattern matching at transition *b*. Transition *b* calls the same channel $:s(\cdot)$ with the reduced list (the tail) until the argument is an empty list, which does not match the pattern $\{h{:}t\}$ any more. It however matches with the *base* case of the up-link of transition *c*. All transitions fire concurrently; i.e. in the example shown *a* one time, *b* five times and *c* one time. The firing of the net instance and the synchronization graph including the bindings are presented in Figure 3.10.

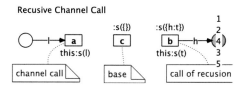

Figure 3.11: Release of single tokens of list after firing of *a*, *b*, *c*.

By the five times concurrently fired transition *b*, five elements are put concurrently onto the output place presented in Figure 3.11. Note that the Figures 3.9, 3.10 and 3.11

show the executed net instance in RENEW, where list tokens are depicted as horizontal heaps and multiple single tokens are depicted as vertical heaps on the places.

Figure 3.12 shows the reference net model for the incoming flexible arc. Note that only tokens matching the list are removed from the input place.

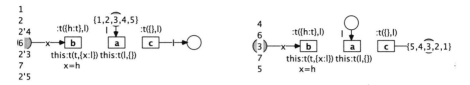

Figure 3.12: Effects of the incoming flexible arc (before and after firing).

# 3.3 Renew

With RENEW it is possible to draw and simulate Petri nets and reference nets. The simulation engine can execute a net that is loaded in the editor. For this the simulator creates an instance of the net. Any simulated net can instantiate other nets. Hence it is possible to produce many instances of different nets. The relationship between net template, also simply called net, and net instance can be compared to the relationship of class and object (see Section 3.2).

## 3.3.1 Editor

Figure 3.13 shows the graphical user interface (GUI) of RENEW, a simple Petri net in the back and a net instance.

The user interface consists of the menu bar, two palettes and a status line. The menu bar offers menus for general operations, attribute manipulations, layout adjustment and Petri net-specific operations. It also provides the possibility to control the simulation. Of the two palettes the first one consists of usual drawing tools while the second one holds the Petri net drawing tools. The latter palette provides the tools for creating transitions, places, virtual places, arcs, test arcs, reserve arcs, inscriptions, names and declarations. In addition to these tools, the editor reacts in a context-sensitive manner to facilitate the drawing of nets. One example is the dropping of arcs on the background that creates a new place if the arc starts at a transition and vice versa. Another example is the right click on inscribable elements that produces an inscription for this element with a context-sensitive default value.

## 3.3.2 Simulator

Net templates hold the initial marking while net instances hold the current marking. In Figure 3.13 the producer-consumer example has been started. In the net template (background) one of two black tokens ('[]') of the initial marking can be seen in the

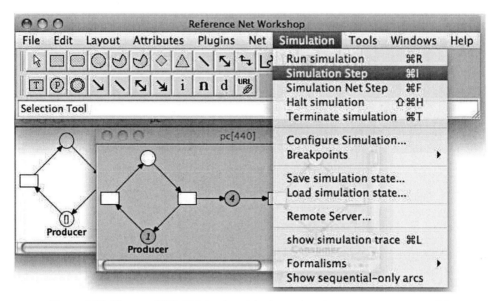

Figure 3.13: RENEW GUI, Petri net and instance (producer-consumer example).

place labeled `Producer`. While the net instance by default only shows the number of tokens in a place, it is also possible to show the contents of the places by clicking on the numbers (compare with Figure 3.7).

RENEW can operate in different modes. This can be achieved by exchanging the net compiler. Modes are available for P/T-nets, reference nets, feature structure nets, provided by Wienberg (2001), timed Petri nets, boolean Petri nets and workflow nets (see Jacob (2002) and Kummer et al. (2009b)). In the *Java* mode, which is the basic mode for reference nets, it is possible to use any kind of *Java* objects as tokens. In fact, transition inscriptions can also hold method calls of objects.

### 3.3.3 Plugins

RENEW is implemented in *Java* and, since version 1.7, extensible through a plugin mechanism that is presented by Schumacher (2003). The plugin mechanism allows to extend the functionality of RENEW in a way that special requirements can be satisfied without the need to change the application system itself.

Plugins can be included in RENEW by providing the classes; i.e. placing the plugin's *Java* archive (*jar*-file) in the 'plugins' folder. The plugin has to be present at starting time. An approach that would allow to include plugins dynamically would be preferable for flexibility reasons, but this is not supported yet.

Schumacher (2003, p. 34) gives a general definition of a plugin, which is the basis for the notion of a RENEW plugin. In his view a system is composed of components, and plugins are special components that extend the behavior of the system.

**Definition 3.1** *Plugin plugins are components that change the behavior of one or more other components in the system. This is done by using the provided interface of the components.*[6]

In this work several plugins for RENEW are presented. One is the Net Components Plugin, described in detail in (Cabac 2002), presented in Section 5.2.5. This plugin provides the functionality of including subnets – net components (see Chapter 5) – into a Petri net by offering the net components as new drawing elements to the developer. The fact that net components are held in adaptable repositories adds to the flexibility of this approach.

Another plugin provides the possibility of drawing Agent Interaction Protocol Diagrams in RENEW. This plugin is presented in (Cabac et al. 2003) and described in Chapter 13. It allows for the generation of Petri net skeletons by facilitating the net components as templates.

## 3.4 Development of Renew

Related work for the RENEW tool is presented by Kummer (2002). In the close context of the RENEW development, however, many improvements have been applied to the system by many people.

### 3.4.1 Improvements

#### Schumacher & Duvigneau

Schumacher (2003) realized in his diploma thesis the redesign of RENEW that resulted in the 2.x branch of the framework. The architecture of RENEW has been refactored to a flexible plugin system. The prototypical realization has been further enhanced by Duvigneau and several other developers.

#### Schleinzer & Duvigneau

In the course of his diploma thesis, Schleinzer (2007) – together with Duvigneau – improved version 2.1 of RENEW. Most notably is the decoupling of the graphical user interface and the simulator as well as the replacement of a proprietary `Graphics` implementation by `Graphics2D`.

### 3.4.2 Contribution to the Renew Development

I contributed to the plugin concept, which is applied to the RENEW architecture since version 2.0 (development version 1.7). Especially the conceptual modeling of the plugin

---

[6]Translated from the German original: "Plugins sind Komponenten, die das Verhalten einer oder mehrerer anderer Komponenten im System verändern. Dies geschieht über von diesen zur Verfügung gestellte Schnittstellen."

system and plugins (see Cabac et al. (2005), Cabac et al. (2006a), Cabac et al. (2007c) and Schleinzer et al. (2008)).

Beside the development of several plugins such as Net Components Plugin (see Chapter 5.2), AIP Diagram Plugin (see Section 13.4), Use Case Plugin (see Section 10.5) and Image Net Diff Plugin (see Chapter 18), I have also contributed to improvements and extensions of the RENEW framework.

I also proposed a redesign of the export functionality and implemented a prototypical SVG export functionality based on the Batik framework[7]. that also allowed displaying of images on the fly. The intention was also to enable zooming for large scale net models. The Batik framework has been replaced by Schleinzer in favor of the FreeHep[8] framework, which was – at the time – more mature than Batik.

The following list presents – in short – some other of my contributions to the development of RENEW.

- Introduction of a file type management.
- Usability: added modifier keys for figure handling.
- Improvements of the ant build environment (plugin info, versions)
- Added prototypical template-based plugin development support.
- Added diverse figure frame border styles.
- Added PNG Export.
- Added command line export features.
- Improved error messages suggestions.

## 3.5 Summary

Reference nets are high-level Petri nets that are extensions of P/T-nets. They offer the possibility to nest net instances as token references in hierarchies of nets, applying the nets-within-nets paradigm. Tokens can be anonymous, basic data types, *Java* objects and instances of nets. New net instances can be created during execution in a manner comparable to objects. The relationship of net template and net instance can be compared to that of class and object. Reference nets offer synchronous channels to provide communication and synchronization between different net instances (or within one net).

RENEW is an editor and simulator for reference nets and other (Petri net) formalisms. It is implemented in *Java* and has an inscription language that is *Java* oriented. Nets can be drawn comfortably in RENEW using the graphical user interface and loaded nets can be executed directly in RENEW.

RENEW serves as the virtual machine for multi-agent applications developed on the basis of the MULAN/CAPA framework, which is presented in the following chapter. Additionally, it serves as graphical IDE (integrated development environment) for the development of reference nets-based systems.

---

[7]The Batik framework, see `http://xmlgraphics.apache.org/batik/status.html`.
[8]The FreeHep framework, see `http://java.freehep.org/`.

# 4 Mulan

This chapter introduces agents and agent-oriented software engineering in general. The basic concepts of software agents, agent-oriented software development and multi-agent systems are discussed. Then a specific model for multi-agent system MULAN (Multi-Agent Nets) is presented. MULAN was first described by Rölke (1999), Köhler et al. (2001). It is a reference model (reference architecture, compare with Lilienthal (2008, p. 34 ff.)) for a multi-agent system that complies with the Foundation for Intelligent Physical Agents (FIPA 2009) specification for multi-agent systems. It provides a framework modeled with reference nets that runs within the Petri net editor and simulator RENEW (Reference Net Workshop, see Kummer et al. (2009a) and see the previous chapter). CAPA (Concurrent Agent Platform Architecture, see Duvigneau et al. (2003)), an extension to MULAN, provides FIPA-compliant communication and agent management. More detailed information about agents, multi-agent systems and MULAN are given by Rölke (2004). This chapter describes the current version of 2009 of the MULAN framework, which has been enhanced and thus differs in several conceptual and technical aspects from the one presented in Rölke (2004).

Section 4.1 introduces the topic of agent technology with a focus on the notion of agents. Multi-agent systems are introduced in Section 4.2. The MULAN architecture is presented in Section 4.3. Section 4.4 describes how agent systems can be built with MULAN. Section 4.5 provides information about work done in the close context of MULAN, and Section 4.6 summarizes the chapter.

## 4.1 Software Agents

While the object-oriented paradigm is still state of the art, some limitations of the object-oriented view lead developers and researchers towards new technologies. One – still very new – approach is the agent-oriented view. It can be understood as a natural extension of object-orientation.

### 4.1.1 Object-Orientation

In object-orientation, an object is an encapsulated entity that has a clearly defined interface. It represents a concrete or abstract object of the real world or the modeled world. The interface of the object defines methods that can be accessed by other objects. Internal representation and data structures are usually not revealed to the outside world in order to hide the implementation details. The static structure of objects is defined in classes that can be seen as templates for a type of objects. This is why classes determine the type of objects. In the object-oriented view, a relation is defined on the objects, which is called generalization or inheritance. Objects are in some ways specializations of other objects and thus categorized. In this relation objects form a hierarchy of inheritance. For example, in *Java* the most general object is Object as the root of the hierarchy.

There are numerous reasons why the object-oriented approach had so much success in recent years. For example, due to inheritance, it is possible to build new objects by extending existing ones. This saves much development time and effort. All kinds of functionalities are implemented in frameworks and toolkits that are used to build application software on their basis, without reinventing or reimplementing the same functionality over again. Re-use driven development is the key to efficient programming that has become possible because it is based on object-oriented programming languages like *C++* or *Java*. However, some limitations and shortcomings exist that demand a more sophisticated view. Designing software using a metaphor of active entities is one of them.

## 4.1.2 Informal Approach to Agents

As described in this chapter, agent-oriented software engineering is influenced by the areas of software engineering and artificial intelligence. There are also influences of areas like distributed systems and social science. All together this leads to a view on systems that emerge from (self) organizing structures.

An agent can be seen as an even more abstract version of an encapsulated entity than an object. While objects export methods as interface to offer functionality to other objects, agents only communicate via messages. These messages are basically strings that have a certain form, i.e. a language. Instead of being used by another object the agent receives messages and 'decides' what to do in response.

The agent, in opposition to the object, can decide to react and may reply to that message or just ignore it. This introduces a notion of autonomy. Another ability, besides the ability to decide, is connected to making decisions. To be able to decide, the agent has to have some criteria on which it can base its decisions. From this follows that an agent has to possess some knowledge. This knowledge includes facts and beliefs about itself, its environment – the world it is situated in – and also other agents. In the agent-oriented view, this knowledge can only be partial.

Agents can be physical or virtual. The difference is that physical agents have representations in the real world, e.g. robots. The physical agent can thus interact directly with its environment by using its effectors and sensors. Virtual or software agents have no manifestation in the real world and are often compared to software objects or components.[1]

Figure 4.1 visualizes the difference between the physical and the virtual agent in their environments. In addition to its communication channels, the physical agent also has sensors that serve cognition and effectors that can manipulate the environment. The only connection of software agents with the environment and thus with other agents,

---

[1]The possibility of simulating a physical agent through a virtual one exists and so the difference is of theoretical nature.

lies in their communication channels. Ferber (1999) distinguished between the purely situated and the purely communicating (software) agents. On the following pages, we always refer to software agents.

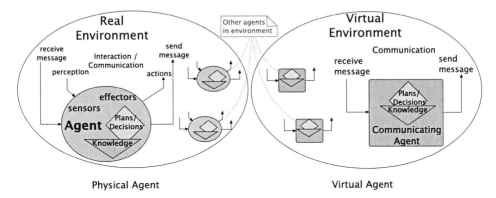

Figure 4.1: Abstract model of an agent and its environment.

### 4.1.3 Agent Definitions

Agents are, so far, independent software components that can decide on their actions on the basis of their knowledge and communicate with other agents. However, to be able to achieve some results they also have to have some goal or interest. Since they 'live' in an environment that is populated with other agents, the agents' goals obviously coincide or differ from each other. Therefore the agents have to coordinate, cooperate or compete with other agents. This means they have to act within a social system.

In a social system, in which agents exist, adaptability seems to be essential. They have to adapt to conventions, protocols and exceptional events. This means that agents have to possess a certain kind of intelligence (Russell and Norvig 1995). So while objects just react to their input (always in a predictable way), agents can act and even decide on their actions.

To sum this up: A software agent is an adaptive, intelligent and independent software component that has a certain goal or interest, some knowledge about itself and its surroundings and can communicate with other agents.

Here are some definitions of various authors. Surely, the aspects that cover their topic of interest bias their view. Researchers of artificial intelligence focus on intelligence and social behavior of the agents while software engineers discuss agents as an extension to object-orientation. Ferber (1999) provides a general definition that can be broadly applied and lists the characteristics of agents.

**Definition 4.1 (Agent)** *"An agent is a physical or virtual entity*

*which is capable of acting in an environment,*

*which can communicate with other agents,*

*which is driven by a set of tendencies . . . ,*

*which possesses resources of its own,*

*which is capable of perceiving its environment . . . ,*

*which has only partial representation of its environment . . . ,*

*which possesses skills and can offer services,*

*which may be able to reproduce itself,*

*whose behavior tends towards satisfying its objectives, taking account of the resources and skills available to it and depending on its perception, its representations and the communications it receives." (Ferber 1999, p. 9).*

Bergenti et al. (2003) stress the differences between the two views – artificial intelligence and software engineering – and offer two different definitions.

**Definition 4.2 (Agent)** *"An Agent must be proactive, intelligent, and it must conversate [sic] instead of doing client-server computing. . . "*
*"An agent is a software component with internal (either reactive or proactive) threads of execution, . . . that can be engaged in complex and stateful interactions [sic] protocols." (Bergenti et al. 2003, p. 127, slide 14).*

Russell and Norvig (1995) offer a very short definition of agents, which can be viewed as a first notion.

**Definition 4.3 (Agent)** *"An agent is just something that perceives and acts." (Russell and Norvig 1995, p. 7).*

An often quoted definition of agents is given by Jennings and Wooldridge (1998). It is a pragmatic view on agents in the agent-oriented software development and varies only slightly from the one given by Ferber (Definition 4.1).

**Definition 4.4 (Agent)** *"An Agent is an encapsulated computer system, situated in some environment, and capable of flexible autonomous action in that environment in order to meet its design objectives." (Jennings and Wooldridge 1998, p. 5).*

These definitions, as already mentioned above, are biased by the authors' perspective. Furthermore, many of the words used in these definitions require further explanation. But the main point here is to present a general notion of the concepts to the reader and not a full discussion of all terms. The latter is not intended within this work and would also exceed its extent. Since the authors in their publications go into further detail, we leave the definitions as they are without further examination.

Generally, it can be said that the definitions vary but do not contradict each other. They merely show different viewpoints. It should just be stated that the agent concept in software engineering is more general than that of the artificial intelligence. In software engineering, objects can be considered to be very simple reactive agents, whereas artificial intelligence demands from an agent approaches that are intelligent.

In this work we will abide by the software engineering view, which is related to the Definitions 4.1 by Ferber and 4.4 by Jennings and Wooldridge.

# 4.2 Multi-Agent Systems

Agents do not only act, but also interact with each another. On the one hand, they communicate with other agents by receiving or giving information, they can send orders, requests or demands to other agents. On the other hand, they have to follow their own interests or goals that can be in opposition to the goals of other agents. Nevertheless, the goals of two agents can also coincide, giving the two agents a chance for cooperation. It is also possible that agents which have different goals can support each other for the benefit of both agents. Precisely this fact can possibly enable the agents to reach their goals in cooperation, when they would have failed on their own. Thus agents have to have mechanisms of coordination, competition and cooperation.

## 4.2.1 Informal Approach to Multi-Agent Systems

Social behavior is somehow necessary to achieve a consensus between different parties. This means that agents not only have to coordinate their actions but also negotiate with other agents about those actions. In fact, the agents are situated in a somehow organized environment. Sometimes such an organization of agents is also called group, society or population.

The term multi-agent system is strongly connected to the term agent as seen in Ferber's Definition 4.1, in which he uses the term multi-agent system to define the term agent. Just as with the term agent, the multi-agent system is used in many different ways according to the point of view.

Reese (2003) describes three views on multi-agent systems, which are all valid but differently motivated. The first point of view focuses on the discrimination of the agent-oriented view from other technologies, like object-orientation or distributed systems. The second point of view focuses on the infrastructure for the agents. Here a multi-agent system is the technical basis on which the implementation is built. This could be regarded as the middleware and the motivation for this lies in software engineering (SWE). The third point of view focuses on the aspect that a network of agents together with the infrastructure forms a system of loosely connected agents that could possibly interact. This satisfies the notion of agents in artificial intelligence (AI). Reese pleads for the following distinction of these views.

- An **agent network** connects agent platforms to a system on which distributed agents can form multi-agent systems (AI).

- An **agent platform** is the technical realization of infrastructure for the agents (SWE).

- A **multi-agent system** is oriented towards the application. It is a coordinated system of agents with a common purpose.

Figure 4.2 shows this distinction again. Agents reside on agent platforms while some agents across platforms can form a multi-agent system. The agent network consists of three platforms. It is also possible to build other multi-agent systems within this network by connecting other agents. So multiple multi-agent systems can coexist on the same agent network. Since the term *multi-agent system* is used for all three distinct views throughout the literature, it is sometimes hard to decide which notion is intended. To get an even better distinction, this work uses the term **multi-agent application** for a purposeful designed system of agents that act together in coordination to achieve a common goal. This is comparable to the notion of a multi-agent system in Reese's terminology.

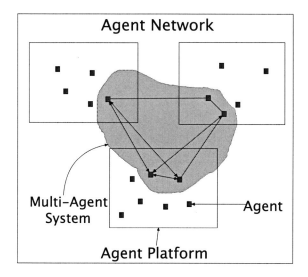

Figure 4.2: Agent network versus multi-agent system.[2]

## 4.2.2 Definitions of Multi-Agent Systems

In this section as well as in the sections about definitions for the term *agent*, the intention is to show the approaches to multi-agent systems. However, a full discussion of the term is not provided. A good introduction to multi-agent systems is done by Ferber (1999). It is a broad definition that covers all aspects of a multi-agent system and also tries to remain very general.

**Definition 4.5 (Multi-Agent System)** *"The term 'multi-agent system' (or MAS) is applied to a system comprising the following elements:*

*(1) An environment, E, that is, a space which generally has a volume.*

*(2) A set of objects, O. These objects are situated, that is to say, it is possible at a given moment to associate any object with a position in E. These objects are passive, that is, they can be perceived, created, destroyed and modified by the agents.*

*(3) An assembly of agents, A, which are specific objects (A ⊆ O), representing the active entities of the system.*

*(4) An assembly of relations, R, which link objects (and thus agents) to each other.*

*(5) An assembly of operations, O, making it possible for the agents of A to perceive, produce, consume, transform and manipulate objects from O.*

*(6) Operators with the task of representing the application of these operations and the reaction of the world to this attempt at modification, which we shall call the laws of the universe (...)" (Ferber 1999, p. 11).*

In contrast to this formal approach, Bergenti, Shehory and Sturm (2003) offer two views on multi-agent systems that are influenced by their different perspectives. Again these are the perspective of artificial intelligence and the perspective of software engineering.

**Definition 4.6 (Multi-Agent System)** *"A multiagent system is a society of individual (AI software agents) that interact by exchanging knowledge and by negotiating with each other to achieve either their own interest or some global goal..."*

*"A multiagent system is a software systems [sic] made up of multiple independent and encapsulated loci of control (i.e. the agents) interacting with each other in the context of a specific application viewpoint." (Bergenti et al. 2003, p. 127, slide 15).*

The different definitions show that different positions exist about the notion of a multi-agent system. The artificial intelligence focuses on the social activities of agents and intelligent solutions, while software engineering focuses on the technical solutions. Ferber manages to give a broadly applicable definition.

In the next section the agent platform MULAN is described as a realization of an operational Petri net-based multi-agent system.

## 4.3 Mulan Architecture

MULAN is a multi-agent system that is modeled in reference nets. One advantage of Petri nets is the fact that the coarse model of a system can be refined to a detailed model that is executable. This concretion can be called *implementing through refinement* or *implementation through specification*. The advantage of this approach is that the gap between modeling and implementation is eliminated. Instead the model is further refined within each stage of development.

The MULAN reference model structures a multi-agent system in four layers, namely *infrastructure, platform, agent* and *protocol*[3] (see Köhler et al. (2001), Rölke (2004)).

---

[2]Diagram adapted from (Reese 2003).

[3]Although the fourth layer actually consists of the agent parts (namely protocols, knowledge base, factory and decision components), we stick here to the original conceptual model. It can also be argued that all agent parts are specialized protocols.

In the reference model (Figure 4.3), the first net is the infrastructure that describes an abstract communication system consisting of locations and communication paths.

The locations can be seen as real world locations, i.e. they can be visualized as different computers. The locations are modeled as places on which the platforms (layer 2, compare with Figure 4.3) reside as reference nets. These nets provide the communication channels for the agents' internal and external communication. Communication is internal when the two communicating parties are resident on the same platform and external if not. In the case of external communication, the platform provides the message transport service (MTS) that transfers the messages across locations. In addition to this, platforms offer the possibility for agents to enter or leave the platform.

MULAN agents reside on a platform. One place of a platform holds all agents that are present on this particular platform. Again MULAN agents are reference nets. These agents have incoming and outgoing communication channels that enable them to communicate over the platform with other agents. They also have the possibility to access services offered by the platform. In the same manner as the platform holds the agent nets in one place, the agents hold their protocol nets for their conversations in one place.

Similar to the platform providing communication channels to the agents, the MULAN agents provide channels for the initialization, destruction and communication between agent and protocol.

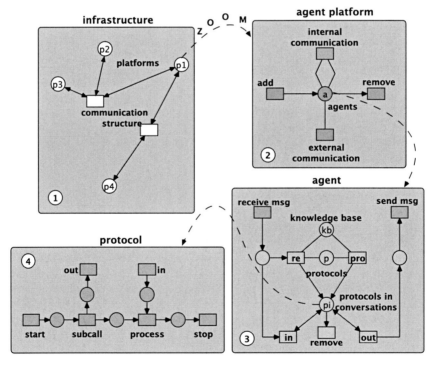

Figure 4.3: The structure of MULAN.[4]

All these channels mentioned above are modeled and implemented as synchronous channels. Thus by synchronizing the different nets over platforms or over different layers of the nested nets, the communication between these nets is provided. This is illustrated in Figure 4.3. The figure shows the net within a net hierarchy of the system. Agents are nets that exist on platforms. The platforms are also nets. There can be many platforms and the agents can communicate with each another within and across platforms. Protocols are nets within the agents and control their behavior.[5]

### 4.3.1 Mulan Agents

Agents are complex entities. They have to provide functionality for communication, interaction, knowledge acquisition, storage and retrieval, decision-making and conversation handling. All this is realized in MULAN agents by a modular, hierarchical design. All components of the MULAN agents are realized as reference nets. This means that all modules are, in fact, nets and the modularity is provided by the nets-within-nets paradigm (see Section 3.2).

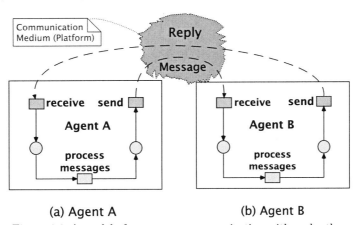

(a) Agent A                    (b) Agent B

Figure 4.4: A model of two agents communicating with each other.

From an outside viewpoint the agents can be seen as black boxes that communicate with each other. They have two channels to send and receive messages. In this very simple model, as shown in Figure 4.4, the internal processes of the agents are hidden. Of course, the messages have to be transported by a medium that is provided by the MULAN Platform. To achieve a more detailed model, the Petri nets have to be refined. This leads to the model of an agent, as shown in the architecture overview in Figure 4.3. Figure 4.5 shows the refinement of the model as a step to reveal more details of the agent.

---

[4]Diagram adapted from (Köhler et al. 2001).

[5]The terminology in the MULAN reference model differs slightly from the FIPA terminology, where the conversation is called protocol. They are described in interaction protocols, while the protocol nets, as described here, have no equivalent. They can be seen as the role-specific part of the interaction.

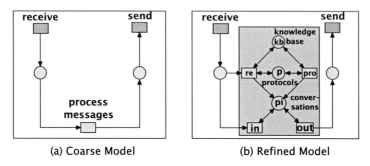

Figure 4.5: Abstract model of the MULAN agent (b as a refinement of a).

Besides the main part of the MULAN agent, often also simply referred to as the agent, the *complete* agent also consists of the knowledge base, the factory and its behavior. The latter is defined as protocol nets and decision components (DC). This is already indicated in Figure 4.3 (agent net, layer 3) where the knowledge base kb and the factory p are inserted as tokens on similarly labeled places. Active protocol nets pi are held in the conversation place. Protocols can be initialized, i.e. conversations can be started pro-actively as well as reactively, and messages leave and enter the agent over the synchronous channels labeled `receive` and `send`.

All the elements shown in this first refinement of the model are also present in the second refinement in Figure 4.6 and in the implementation in Figure 4.7. Actually, the implementation is a refinement of the model that includes some additions. These additions (white net elements) consist in the initialization of the agent with the generation of the initial knowledge and some semaphores, which allow to check whether the agent is idle or busy.

The communication between the different nets (vertical communication) is realized through synchronous channels labeled `access` in the net for the access to the knowledge base, `proactive` and `reactive` for initializing the MULAN protocols and finally `start`, `stop`, `in` and `out` for the interaction of the agent with the protocols. Regarding the communication channels, only the distinction between new and running conversations has to be made, deciding on the conflict of the two transitions `reactive` and `in`.

Figure 4.6 shows a schematic net model of a MULAN agent. Several parts of the operational model, such as inscriptions, synchronous channels and initialization, are omitted for clearness. Instead, descriptive names have been given to the net elements representing synchronous channels or place contents. The model stresses that the agent is a communicating agent being able to `receive` and `send` messages. The labeled places store references to net instances that provide or refine the main functionality of the agent. These are the *factory*, the *knowledge base*, the *decision components* and the *protocols*. Protocol and decision component nets comprise parts of the domain-specific agent behavior. The two corresponding places in the agent net may contain numerous net instances (compare with the *nets-within-nets* paradigm of Valk (1998)).

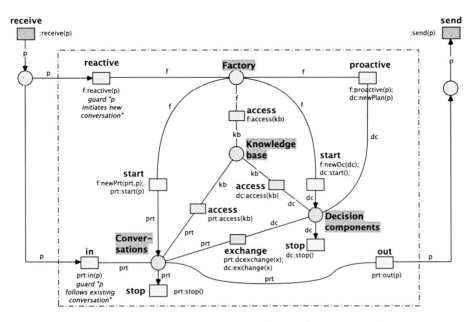

Figure 4.6: The MULAN agent, striped of some administrative elements.

**The factory** produces net instances from net patterns of protocols and decision components. It realizes reactive and pro-active behavior by examining incoming messages and the agent's knowledge.

**The knowledge base** offers database functionality including operations such as atomic *query, create, remove* and *modify* to other subnets of the agent. It is used to store persistent information to be shared by protocol nets and decision components, for example the agent's representation of the environment. The knowledge base also stores the agent's configuration. It holds information about provided and required services as well as a mapping of incoming messages to protocol nets.

**Protocol nets** implement domain-specific agent behavior. Each protocol net template models the participation of an agent role in a multi-agent interaction protocol. Instantiated protocol nets reside on the place *Conversations*[6] of the agent, handle the processing of received messages and may generate outgoing messages. Protocol net instances are the manifestations of the agent's involvement in an interaction with one or more other agents. They can access the knowledge base and exchange information with decision components through the *exchange* channel.

---

[6]The place is called *Protocol nets* in Figure 4.7.

**Decision components** implement domain-specific agent behavior similar to protocol nets. However, in contrast to protocol nets, this *internal* agent behavior is not responsible for the communication. Instead, these processes can be interpreted as internal services offered to protocol nets.

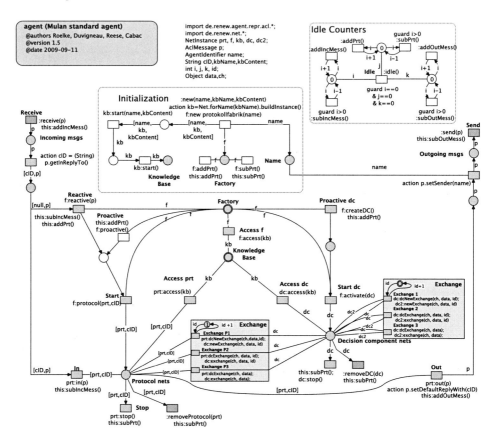

Figure 4.7: An overview of the MULAN agent model.

Software agents communicate by exchanging messages. In fact, this is their only way of interaction with their environment or other agents. MULAN agents accomplish this by synchronization with the platform net over synchronous channels (see Section 3.2.4). These communication channels are labeled *receive* and *send*. Table 4.1 lists the full external interface of the agent.

Agents have to store their knowledge or belief in order to be able to make decisions and to reach their goals. They also have to act in certain adaptable ways. In MULAN, the former is realized through the implementation of the knowledge base as a reference net. The factory and the protocols accomplish the latter – together with the adaptable

| Channel | Description |
|---|---|
| new | initialization of the agent |
| idle | idle flag |
| receive | receiving a message |
| send | sending a message |
| removeProtocol | (debugging) removing of an active protocol instance |
| removeDC | (debugging) removing of an active decision component |

Table 4.1: The external interface of the agent.

mapping from message patterns to protocols also stored in the knowledge base. The following section describes the knowledge base and the factory. After that, a detailed description of the protocol nets is given in Section 4.3.4 and decision components are described in Section 4.3.5.

In the same manner as the presentation of the agent in this section, each section contains a schematic (abstract) model of the main functionality of the net types, the implementation as a refined net[7] and the interface of the presented net types in a table similar to the one given for the agent net (Table 4.1).

## 4.3.2 Knowledge Base

The knowledge base is an important part of a MULAN agent. It is realized as a reference net and provides the possibility of storing, retrieving and modifying information as key-value tuples. Thus the agent may build a representation of the world. Basic functionality is provided for the creation of new entities, checking for existence of a key and retrieving, replacing and removing entries. Additional functionality regarding protocols is provided for reasons of convenience.

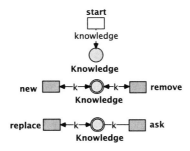

Figure 4.8: A scheme of a knowledge base of the MULAN agent.

---

[7]Note that the refined implementation reference net model is usually too complex to be depicted on one page for close examination. However, close examination of these models is not intended. Instead, these models are presented for completeness and as overview. The main functionality of the nets can be comprehended through the schematic models.

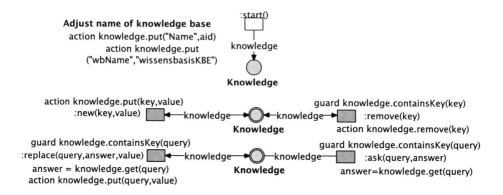

Figure 4.9: An extract from the knowledge base net of the MULAN agent.

The functionality is signified by the names of the synchronous channels. For instance: :ask($\cdot$,$\cdot$) retrieves a value for a given key from knowledge base. The knowledge k is accessed through a test arc because other actions can be concurrently performed. In contrast, the creation of a new entry (:new($\cdot$,$\cdot$)) is synchronized by using a reserve arc.

Figure 4.8 shows a scheme of the knowledge base displaying the knowledge containing place and the basic interfaces (accessibility) as transitions. Like in the complete refined model the knowledge container is displayed three times as one original and two virtual places (compare with Section 3.2.3). This is only done for convenient net layout. The interface consists of the basic functionalities to handle information in the knowledge base: creation, adding, replacing, removing and retrieving knowledge.

The initialization of the knowledge base is abstracted, reduced to one transition and the interface (white net element). Before the knowledge base can be used, the initial knowledge is read from a file and put into the knowledge base (**start**). Note that synchronization is done by the net. Knowledge retrieval (**ask**) can be used concurrently, since the interface is connected by a test arc. The other presented interfaces use an exclusive access to the knowledge by using a reserve arc (comparable to a locking mechanism).

Figure 4.9 shows – as a fragment of the complete net – the refined features for the basic interfaces. The knowledge itself is described as key-value tuples and stored in a hash table of which a reference is held on the central place **Knowledge**. The refining inscriptions include up-links (the actual interface), actions (the manipulation of the knowledge) and guards.

Figure 4.10 shows the complete refined net of the MULAN agent's knowledge base. The net consists in the initialization (white net elements) of the knowledge base, the knowledge containing place with several virtual places, the interface for the initialization of the pro-active protocols and decision components (DC) and the complete interface for knowledge manipulation. The interface of the knowledge base is summarized in Table 4.2.

---

[8]Interface also exists as ˜*Prt* to handle protocol-message mappings.

[9]Interface also exists as ˜*Postfix* to handle multiple entries with the same postfix.

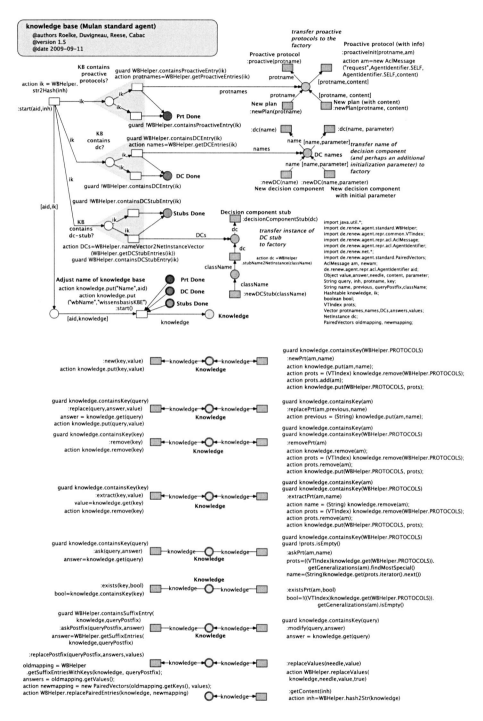

Figure 4.10: Overview of the MULAN agent's knowledge base.

| Channel | Description |
|---|---|
| start | initialization of the knowledge base |
| new[8] | creation of a new entry |
| exists[8] | query for a key |
| ask[89] | retrieving knowledge |
| modify | modifying a value |
| replace[89] | replacing a value by another |
| remove[8] | removing an entry completely |
| extract[8] | removing an entry and retrieving the value |
| replaceValues | replaces all occurrences of a value object by another |
| getContent | retrieves the complete content of the knowledge base |
| newPlan | initialization of a protocol |
| newDC(Stub) | initialization of a decision component |

Table 4.2: The interface of the knowledge base.

### 4.3.3 Factory

The factory is responsible for the initialization and the start of the protocol nets and decision components (DC). This can be done reactively or pro-actively. If an agent receives a message for which no conversation is already active, an appropriate response has to be found. By consulting the knowledge base, a protocol is chosen that can handle the processing of the message as well as the possible following conversation. The factory has the task to instantiate and start the protocol. Furthermore, the factory produces a conversation identifier `cID` (compare with Figure 4.7) to map the conversation to the protocol.

Similarly, decision components are instantiated with or without initial parameter or as net stub.[10] The actual initialization of a net is a linear process which consists in the call (which is parameterized with the name of the net template), the resolution of the net (`Net.forName(·)`), the construction of the net instance (`tempNet.buildInstance()`) and the activation (transfer to the agent net). If the net is a protocol or if a parameter

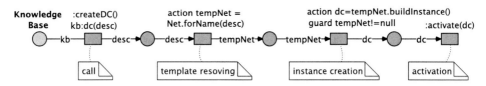

Figure 4.11: The process of net initialization (Example DC).

for a DC is provided, also the parameter (or message) is transferred to the net before the net is transferred to the agent net. For each type of net initialization the sub-process is modeled as a vertical sequence, resulting in four strands recognizable in the refined and

---

[10]Information about net stubs is given in the RENEW User Guide (Kummer et al. 2009b).

complete model of the factory. Note that pro-active and reactive protocol instantiations share a strand. Figure 4.11 exemplifies the process of initializing a DC without parameter (here in a horizontal layout).

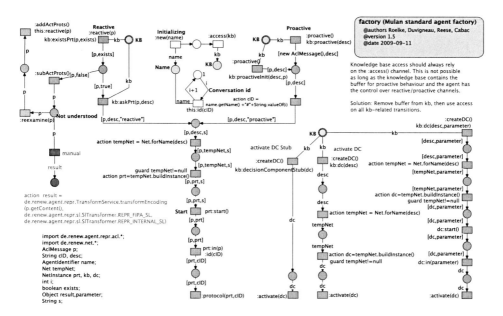

Figure 4.12: The factory of the MULAN agent.

Finally, the protocol net instance is put into the conversations place or the DC net instance is put into the active DCs place of the agent. Figure 4.12 shows the factory with the reactive part in the top/left corner, the pro-active part on the right side, the initialization of the factory and identifier counter in the middle (white net elements) and the protocol initialization, start and release at the bottom (left strand). With the last transition, a tuple of the protocol and the conversation identifier is put into the conversations place of the agent (Figure 4.7). Table 4.3 lists the full interface of the factory.

The actual activities of the agents are handled by the MULAN protocol nets and the DCs. These nets control the agents' parts of the conversations and their internal activities.

## 4.3.4 Mulan Protocol

A conversation consists in a series of related messages exchanged by a set of agents. In a simple setting including only two agents, two MULAN protocols, one for each agent, are sufficient to determine and control the conversation. In a more complex setting, the control over the conversation is distributed over the participating agents.

| Channel | Description |
|---------|-------------|
| new | initialization of the factory |
| access | getting the reference of the knowledge base |
| reactive | reactive creation of a protocol net instance |
| proactive | pro-active creation of a protocol net instance |
| createDC | creation of a decision component |
| reexamine | (debugging) reexamine a message that was not understood |
| protocol | transfer created protocol to agent net |
| activate | transfer created decision component into agent net |

Table 4.3: The interface of the factory.

Each agent holds only the information for its part of the conversation in its protocol net, and the conversation describes the agents' interactions whereas one or more MULAN protocols describe the behavior of one agent during the conversation.[11]

A protocol defines a certain behavior during an interaction. By following the protocol, it is ensured that the interaction between the interacting parties is possible. In the agent-oriented view, a protocol determines the communicational behavior of agents.

Protocols can be compared to workflow-like processes. The protocol defines the actions or activities of the agent at a certain time. It defines sequences, concurrency or decisions. The goal is that the communicating agent can follow the whole conversation successfully until the end is reached. Protocol nets are – just like MULAN agents – Petri nets. An agent can use numerous protocols and instantiate multiple instances of various protocols at the same time. Petri nets are an appropriate method to model workflow-like processes (see van der Aalst and ter Hofstede (2002)) because they directly show the dynamic behavior.

The abstract Petri net model for MULAN, displayed in Figure 4.13, illustrates a simple scenario that is refined later just like the model for the agent. Two MULAN agents that communicate have to instantiate a protocol net each (at least one each). The interaction or communication takes place between the two agents, but the messages are passed from one protocol to the other. Of course, the transportation of the messages has to be accomplished via a medium. This medium is provided by the agents. The agent itself is using the communication medium of the platform.

This leads to the communication layers presented in Figure 4.14. Each layer – except for the physical – accomplishes its communication (vertical) through the next higher level. However, when the two agents reside on one platform, the two top levels, the TCP/IP layer and the physical layer, are not used. Instead there exists only one platform that handles the communication internally.[12] In this model of communication, we identify vertical and horizontal communication. Vertical communication takes place between (vertical) layers, e.g. between the agent and the protocols or between the agent and the

---

[11] As mentioned before the terminology differs slightly from the FIPA terminology, where the conversation is called protocol. Here protocols (i.e. protocol nets) are the role-specific parts of the interactions. Conversations are instantiated interactions.

[12] This is actually achieved through a synchronous channel chain (compare Figure 4.3).

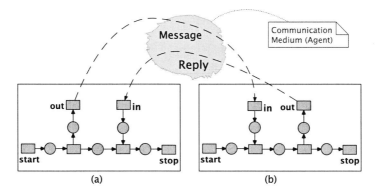

Figure 4.13: Two protocols exchanging messages. Protocol (a) initiates the conversation and protocol (b) replies. Together these two protocols form a conversation.

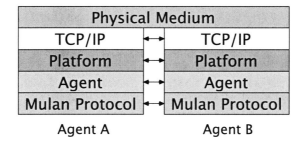

Figure 4.14: Layers of message transportation in MULAN for external communication across platforms.

platform on which it resides. Horizontal communication is the communication of layers of the same level, e.g. the communication between two agents. Of course, horizontal communication has to be realized by vertical communication, if no physical connection exists. The full interface for protocols is listed in Table 4.4.

| Channel | Description |
|---|---|
| start | starting of the protocol |
| stop | stopping of the protocol |
| in | receiving a message |
| out | sending a message |
| access | getting the reference of the knowledge base |
| dc(New)Exchange | communication with decision components |

Table 4.4: The interface of the protocols.

### 4.3.5 Decision Components

Similar to protocol nets, decision components implement domain-specific agent-internal behavior that is, however, not responsible for the communication. Services offered by DCs can be queried by protocol net instances (or other DCs) to add flexibility to the static, workflow-like character of protocol nets. Decision components can also initiate pro-active agent behavior by requesting the factory to instantiate protocol nets via the respective knowledge base interface. Thus an AI-like planning component can be attached to an agent as a decision component or the functionality can be modeled directly as reference nets. Decision components may also encapsulate external tools or legacy code as well as a graphical user interface whereby the external feedback is transformed into pro-active agent behavior. The full interface for decision components is listed in Table 4.5.

| Channel | Description |
|---|---|
| start | starting of the DC |
| stop | stopping of the DC |
| access | getting the reference of the knowledge base |
| (new)exchange | communication with protocols and decision components |
| dc(New)Exchange | communication with decision components |

Table 4.5: The interface of the decision components.

### 4.3.6 Concepts within Mulan

The concepts introduced in this chapter are presented as Concept Diagram (a form of Class Diagram) in Figure 4.15. The diagram shows that in the MULAN framework the agent net, the decision components, the factory, the knowledge base and the protocol nets are reference nets. An instantiated MULAN agent is an agent (as defined in Section 4.1.3) that consists of the agent net, the factory, the knowledge base, several decision components and several protocol nets. MULAN protocol nets as well as Agent Interaction Protocol Diagrams (AIP) are described as protocols. The first is the description of the communicative behavior of one agent. The second is the notion used in the FIPA

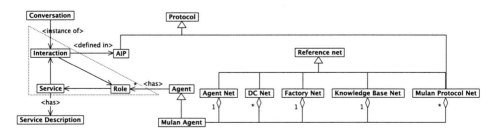

Figure 4.15: Concepts in the MULAN/PAOSE context.

context, where a (interaction) protocol describes the interaction between participating agents. In this work the term protocol is used for both specializations, but the meaning is usually unambiguous. An AIP is a description of an interaction. An instance of an interaction is described as conversation. The participants of the interaction have to play a certain role in the interaction. If a role offers a service, it will be performed within an interaction. These services, which are described by service descriptions, can be published for other agents.

## 4.4 Modeling Individual Agents

For the definition of an application-specific MULAN agent, its behavior and initial state has to be defined. As described in the previous section, the behavior of an agent is modeled by protocol nets for interacting processes with other agents and by decision components (DC) for internal processes such as planning and interaction-spanning synchronizations or for the connection of other resources (e.g. database access, graphical user interfaces). The initial state of the agent is defined as the initial knowledge base definition, which is loaded into the generic knowledge base net (Section 4.3.2) during agent initialization.

### 4.4.1 Description of Mulan Protocols

Protocol nets are Petri nets, more specifically they are reference nets. These protocols possess a clear, control flow-oriented character. They have a starting transition (inscription: `:start()`) and one or more ending transitions (`:stop()`). These transitions define the life cycle of the protocol instances. There are input and output transitions (`:in(p)`, `:out(p)`) which allow the protocol to pass messages from and to agents. These transitions contain *up-links* that constitute, together with the corresponding *down-links* in the agent nets, the synchronous channels that are the means of communication between reference net instances.

   The messages received by an agent through the communication system are passed on to the responsible protocol net through the synchronous channels. It is further processed by the protocol and its content can be extracted. Another message, e.g. a reply, can be formulated by the protocol and passed back to the agent, which sends it through the communication system to the new receiver.

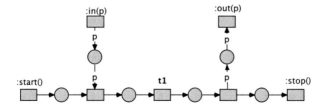

Figure 4.16: A scheme of a protocol.

The protocol defines, through its control flow, the behavior of the agent in the conversation for which the protocol is *responsible*. Therefore it decides which message is sent to which agent, how a message is processed and which internal actions are performed. However, the agents receive messages from or send them to other agents. The agents also decide with the knowledge from their knowledge base which protocols are being started to respond to a certain message, i.e. the agents choose the protocol that leads the conversation. Once a protocol is in charge of a conversation, it keeps the responsibility unless it passes the responsibility to another protocol or it finishes the conversation.

Figure 4.16 describes a scheme of a protocol net. The net shows the RENEW-conform inscriptions for the up-links (:start(), :stop(), :in(p), :out(p), p is a message also called performative). The flow of the process is directed from left to right; a protocol net can therefore be read like a sentence. First the protocol has to be started (transition :start()), then a message is received. Now some other actions could be performed which are omitted in the scheme but signified by transition *t1*. Then a message is sent and the protocol is finally stopped, which ends the conversation.

## 4.4.2 Modeling Protocol Nets

The described Petri net model of Figure 4.3 offers an overview of the agents infrastructure, but it cannot be executed in a multi-agent environment. By refining all parts, a concrete executable model or implementation is constructed. To show an implementation of an application on the basis of MULAN, a version of a producer-consumer example is implemented as protocol nets. Figures 4.17 and 4.18 show executable Petri nets for this example. Since protocol nets are reference nets, communication between agents and protocol nets is realized via synchronous channels. This includes the starting and the stopping of the protocol and the message passing between protocols and agents. Protocol nets can be read from start to stop, i.e. from the transition labeled :start() to one of the transition labeled :stop().[13]

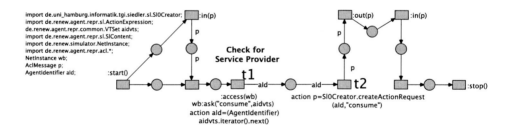

Figure 4.17: Producer-consumer: *produce* protocol as Petri net executable in MULAN.

In this example the producer agent pro-actively starts the *produce* protocol depicted in Figure 4.17 (:start()), a dummy message p is received and ignored. At transition *t1*

---

[13]Usually protocol nets can be read from left to right like a sentence or from top to bottom like a part of an extended Sequence Diagram. In this work most protocol nets are shown in the horizontal version.

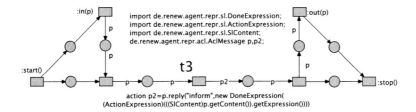

Figure 4.18: Producer-consumer: *consume* protocol as Petri net executable in MULAN.

the knowledge base is queried for an appropriate consumer agent. Assuming that there exists a list of identifiers of consuming agents, one – the first in the list – is chosen and its agent identifier is moved to transition t2. Here a *consume* message is generated with the agent identifier as the receiver's name. This message p is handed to the producer agent for sending, using the synchronous channel :out(p). The *produce* protocol waits for an answer (:in(p)) to terminate the protocol (:stop).

Having received the message, the consumer agent reactively starts the *consume* protocol depicted in Figure 4.18. The message p is then forwarded to the protocol and a reply is produced at transition t3, which is sent back (:out(p)).

In opposition to the presented example, protocol nets and also DCs are usually designed with the help of a pattern-based construction approach. These are called net components and are presented in the following chapter.

### 4.4.3 Description of Decision Components

Decision components are internal processes of the MULAN agents. Unlike protocol nets they lack the ability to communicate (vertically) with the enclosing agent. Because they do not have to abide by any interaction protocol, they may be long running processes, such as planning processes or connections to other software parts (e.g. resources). Active knowledge can also be realized through DCs. Thus they can be regarded as agent internal services.

Decision components offer services via the channels (new)Exchange and they can be accessed by protocols or DCs via the synchronous channel dc(New)Exchange. For this internal communication the agent net offers asymmetric exchange channel chains, each consisting of two down-links as shown in Figure 4.19. There are two possible ways to use the exchange channels. The synchronous way (*simple exchange*, Exchange P3) uses a simple, atomic call of the channel chain. Data can be exchanged synchronously and simultaneously in both directions of the channel chain. This approach, however, does not work if, for example, the called DC functions as an enclosing container for an external software part (e.g. a data base). In this case a synchronous call/response is impossible due to the restrictions of conventional implementations. Thus, an asynchronous approach has to be used.

For the asynchronous exchange channel chain, there exists a pair of channel chains. One for the call, which receives an agent unique identifier (id) and one for the possible

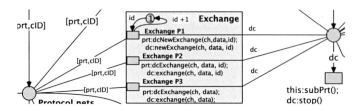

Figure 4.19: Exchange channel chains in the MULAN agent.

responses, in which the identifier has to be provided during the call.

Figure 4.20 shows an example for a decision component: a simple data base lookup realized as key-value tuples. This is very similar to the lookup of the knowledge base.

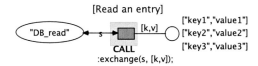

Figure 4.20: A simple decision component for data base lookup.

However, in opposition to the knowledge base, it can be customized to the needs of the application.

The original Producer-Consumer example does not require any decision components.

### 4.4.4 Initial Knowledge Base

The initial knowledge base of an agent defines the agent's initial state in the form of key-value tuples. These key-value tuples comprise the protocol/message mappings service descriptions of required and offered services and other application-specific entries. Protocol/message mappings map patterns of ACLMessages to protocol net template names.

The full list of special entry names is shown in Table 4.6.

| Key | Value |
| --- | --- |
| <protocol name> | <ACLMessage pattern> |
| proactive | list of pro-actively initialized protocols |
| decisionComponent(Stub)s | list of initially started decision components |
| serviceDesc | list of services offered by this agent/role |
| requiredServices | list of services required by this agent |

Table 4.6: Special entries in the knowledge base.

The initial knowledge bases can be defined in two ways. The first and older one is a clear text representation (similar to *Java* properties files); the second is a XML representation. While the first one is already quite powerful, the second one allows for the creation and use of agent roles. Agent role description files can be merged due to their XML representation to form initial knowledge bases. For both representations there exist tools to handle the entries and to model inter-agent (inter-role) dependencies. They and their usage as well as the integration into the development process are presented in Chapter 11.

The initial knowledge bases for the Producer-Consumer example are shown in Listing 4.1 and 4.2.

```
proactive=[generalAgentSetup]
%%%
serviceDesc=[(service-description :name "produce")]
%%%
requiredServices=[(service-description :name "consume")]
%%%
protocol Producer_produce=(request :content "start")
```

Listing 4.1: Initial knowledge base for Producer in *wis*-format.

```
proactive=[generalAgentSetup]
%%%
serviceDesc=[(service-description :name "consume")]
%%%
requiredServices=[]
%%%
protocol Consumer_consume=(request :content "((action_(agent-identifier)_(consume)))" :
    language "FIPA-SL0")
```

Listing 4.2: Initial knowledge base for Consumer in *wis*-format.

An example for a knowledge base in XML representation as agent role description (ARD) is displayed in Figure C.1.

# 4.5 Related Work

Related work in the context of Petri net-based agent modeling has been presented by Rölke (2004, Ch. 5). In the close proximity of MULAN there has been several works that offered either improvements to the MULAN framework, have used the MULAN framework or have constructed MULAN-inspired frameworks in adjacent contexts.

## 4.5.1 Improvements of Mulan

### Duvigneau

The Concurrent Agent Platform Architecture (CAPA, see Duvigneau (2002)) is a partial reimplementation that offers FIPA-compliant agent communication. The FIPA management ontology and CAPA extensions have been implemented. Actually, CAPA and MULAN are often used synonymously.

### Reese

Reese (2003) implemented an extension to MULAN/CAPA that allowed MULAN agents to communicate with other FIPA-compliant agent implementations in the context of

Agentcities (2005) (see also Reese et al. (2003)).

**Seegert**

Seegert (2005) implemented a planning framework for CAPA agents. The original planner integration and interface have been integrated in the main track of CAPA and resulted later in the more flexible and more general concept of decision components.[14]

**Laka**

Laka (2007) implemented a proposal of federated service discovery strategies for MULAN/CAPA and implemented subscription management.

## 4.5.2 Mulan-Related Implementations

### Schleinzer

Schleinzer (2007) reimplemented the MULAN/CAPA framework to achieve a holonic agent system framework. Here agents act as platforms for other agents. This leads to an arbitrary nested structure of the system. The challenges in such a system are the addressing of the agents, the routing of messages and the development of strategies for the re-routing of messages for migrating agents.

Schleinzer also refactored the original CAPA code, applied net components and modularized the components (plugins).

### Müller

Müller (see Cabac et al. (2009b)) implemented a Mobile CAPA (MAPA), which allows to simulate and visualize mobile agents following a prototypical example of a mobile robot by Köhler et al. (2003).

## 4.5.3 Contributions to the Mulan Framework

The reference model MULAN and the implemented framework MULAN/CAPA were developed and influenced by many participants. The original model can be attributed to Köhler et al. (2001) building on earlier ideas from Moldt. The most comprehensive description of MULAN was presented by Rölke (2004). CAPA was originally developed by Duvigneau (2002).

I contributed to the development, refactoring and improvements of the reference model as well as the framework.

- Together with Duvigneau, Reese and Rölke, I introduced the concept and the implementation of the decision components. This caused a redesign of the agent net, the knowledge base and the factory. In the agent net this resulted in the

---

[14]Main contributors to the design and implementation of the DC concept are Cabac, Duvigneau, Reese and Rölke.

currently present communication triangle of protocols, knowledge base and decision components.

- I redesigned and adapted the initialization of the knowledge base net for clearness of the model and to reflect additional DC and DC-stubs entries in the initial knowledge bases.

- I redesigned the agent net, in order to better reflect the architecture, i.e. the four parts of an agent.

- The introduction of the decision component concept allowed the design of a generic (remote) adapter for the agents originally introduced by Markwardt: the RemoteDC. I extended this approach and added several improvements (see Section 14.3.2).

- This chapter explicitly presents, for the first time, the net interfaces shown in Tables 4.1, 4.2, 4.3, 4.4 and 4.5.

In fact, the main conceptual as well as technical improvement in the MULAN/CAPA framework in the recent years, the separation of internal processes and interactions, has made several workarounds and crutches obsolete. Before, protocol nets were often used to express internal processes or functioned as adapter for other software parts. For this they had to run permanently or at least over a long time span, which is in opposition to the notion that protocol net instances should only exist as long as the interaction (conversation) lasts.

The decision component concept also clarified the notion of pro-activeness in the conceptual framework of MULAN. The notion of pro-activity was already present in the original model, but the executing entity $in$[15] the reference model was missing.

## 4.6 Summary

MULAN is a reference architecture for multi-agent systems based on Petri nets, more specifically reference nets. It focuses on the support for concurrency and distribution of processes and offers a highly structured topology. CAPA is a FIPA-compliant agent communication and management extension to MULAN and platform implementation that opens applications designed in MULAN for communication in settings of heterogeneous multi-agent systems.

Together, MULAN and CAPA build a framework (middleware) that enables us to construct concurrency-aware, process-oriented and distributed multi-agent applications. The main parts of the system that have to be modeled during the construction of a multi-agent application are the protocol nets, the decision components and the agents' knowledge bases. Knowledge bases hold the limited knowledge of the agents, containing also a modifiable map of triggers and protocol names to determine reactive behavior. Protocol

---

[15]The pro-activeness can also originate in external components, e.g. attached planning components as it has been done with a Prolog engine.

nets determine the behavior of the agents within conversations. Decision components are able to define agent-internal behavior, such as planning processes.

However, to be able to construct large-scale and complex multi-agent applications on the ground of the MULAN/CAPA framework, we need to follow some kind of approach. This is the PAOSE approach, of which the development process and a suitable guiding metaphor as well as a set of modeling techniques used in this approach are presented in Part II. Additionally, we need to have the possibility to design a large number of application-specific Petri nets – as well as some other design artifacts. In this regard, the next chapter introduces the concept of net components, which is a means to structure nets and accelerate the construction of nets. In fact, net components enable to *engineer*[16] special kinds of Petri nets, e.g. protocol nets.

---

[16]Engineering is seen here as a systematic and structured approach of manufacturing.

# 5 Net Components

This chapter describes the concept and the realization of net components. This instrument accelerates the modeling process through standardized structures of net models and allows at the same time to introduce a pattern-based approach to Petri net modeling.[1] Net components are subnets that are meant to be combined with each another to form a Petri net. By this component-based approach of construction of Petri nets, the drawing of the nets is facilitated and the Petri nets are structured in a unified way – when using the same set of net components – and easily readable. The MULAN net components for protocol nets are presented as an example set of net components. Besides the fact that they provide the basic functionality regarding the communication in protocol nets and protocol management as templates, they also introduce several other patterns.

Section 5.1 outlines the context of the net components concept. In Section 5.2, we introduce the concept of net components and the corresponding tool set. An application-specific set of net components – the MULAN components – serves as an exemplary implementation of the concept in Section 5.3. Section 5.4 is dedicated to experiences in the usage of the net component concept and its tool set earned after several years of use. We also present some related work and other applications in Section 5.5. We conclude with Section 5.6, which summarizes our results and gives an outlook on future work.

## 5.1 Context

High-level Petri net formalisms such as colored Petri nets by Jensen (1996) or reference nets by Kummer (2002) offer modeling constructs and abstractions comparable to basic programming constructs of high-level programming languages: data types and variables, sequences, branches, iterations and code encapsulation with restricted access. Additionally, Petri nets allow an elegant and intuitive modeling of concurrency, which is neglected in most widespread programming languages. Therefore, it is possible to use an appropriate Petri net formalism not only for modeling and analyzing of systems – as it is usually done – but also for implementation. This has the additional advantage that the model can be transformed into an implementation without a change of formalism. Thus the gap between model and implementation can be closed. The Petri net formalism serves as a programming language, and the models at the design stage of the software development

---

[1]Note that *model* and *implementation* fall together through the *implementation through specification* approach. Thus both concepts are used interchangeably in this work. In the context of Petri nets this is rather unusual. Similar work is done, e.g. in the context of CPN tools, where the implementation language is Standard ML (see Jensen (1996)).

process can be directly used – in a refined version – as the implementation of the system.[2] This approach of *implementation through specification* has already been sketched out in previous publications (see Cabac et al. (2005) and Rölke (2004)).

Over the last few years we have used reference nets together with the tool RENEW in several advanced student projects (lasting half a year each) that are related to the main topic of Petri net-based software development. We summarize the efforts and advancements of the pattern-based approach with net components for Petri net-based software development. Several details have already been presented in several publications (see Cabac (2002), Cabac and Knaak (2007) and Cabac et al. (2003)). This chapter focuses on advances of the technique as well as advancements of the supporting tools.

The application domains range from a small *stock exchange game* over our multi-agent system implementation itself to full-scaled multi-agent applications such as an implementation of the *Settler* board game or a distributed workflow management system (WFMS). This leads to a high and continuously growing demand of conceptual, methodological and tool support for the development process. On the conceptual level we are able to employ advanced concepts on the foundation of the intuitive and semantically clear concepts of Petri nets. However, when it comes to implementation, Petri net concepts and their application (i.e. the modeling with Petri nets) can improve from concepts that are common ground in programming languages. Some of these concepts – among many others – are modularization, information hiding, structuring of code, code reuse and pattern-based approaches.[3]

## 5.2 Concept and Design of Net Components

In this section we introduce our general notion and the conceptual background of net components and also describe how a reasonable set of net components can be achieved. Furthermore, we discuss the general attributes of this component-based approach of modeling and point out general advantages that result from the concept itself, as well as special advancements that have been achieved throughout the ongoing development of the net component concepts and tool set.

### 5.2.1 Net Components as Templates

Net components (NC, see Cabac (2002), Cabac et al. (2003), Cabac (2009)) are subnets which can be composed or combined to form (large) composed nets. Net components as a general concept are neither restricted to a special formalism or Petri net dialect nor to

---

[2] In the Petri net formalisms mentioned above, Petri nets are simulated or interpreted, not compiled. Therefore, one has to accept a loss of performance. This is not a problem at the early stages of a software development process, when rapid prototyping means rapid implementation of a prototype that offers as much of the desired functionality as possible. In later design stages performance plays a more important role. Using, for example, the reference net formalism as a modeling formalism, it is possible to switch over to a *Java* implementation in an easy and organized way. This, however, shall not be discussed in depth here.

[3] A strong modularization of our code bases are given through the inherent nesting features of the nets-within-nets paradigm, since reference nets are nets-within-nets.

a special context or means of application. Thus, net component-based approaches of net construction can be applied in various contexts with various specific necessities. In fact, as shown later, the approach of using a component-based approach to modeling can be extended – conceptually and technically – to other areas of model construction.

Net components should not be confused with the software engineering viewpoint on components of large software parts. Instead, the net components presented in this work are parts of Petri nets (subnets). However, the net components may be models for such software components and the system can then be modeled as a composition of net components.

Net components function as templates in the form of ordinary RENEW drawings which are held in a repository that can be shared among developers. We acknowledge the necessity for tool support for the construction of models with net components and the design of sets of net components as well as for the need to share the sets among developers. Net components as subnets are not composable per se (semantically or graphically). Instead, a reasonable set of net components needs to be defined carefully.

In a certain context a well-designed set of net components may provide general functionality that can be commonly used while constructing several similar Petri nets. If many of the same category are produced, the effort of designing a set of net components is rewarded and the benefits of net components are exploitable.

Although it is not necessary, a net component can represent a pattern. Such a net component is a concretion of a pattern as a template.[4]

## 5.2.2 Net Components vs. (Design) Patterns

Patterns and design patterns (see Gamma et al. (1995)), also in the form of workflow patterns by Van der Aalst et al. (2000a), have been discussed extensively in the past. They are useful abstract concepts used during the development of software as well as workflows or business processes. They help developers to name and communicate important (abstract) concepts in the development phase. Patterns are often visualized with graphical methods, e.g. UML for design patterns or Petri nets for workflow patterns. Many patterns are simple, some are complex. Several of the common patterns are omnipresent in current development. For instance the *Observer* design pattern is implemented in the *Java Listener* interface. Other patterns have become so common that they are sometimes not recognized anymore. Nevertheless, there is a widespread agreement that patterns are useful in the development of complex systems.

In the context of Petri net modeling, a pattern can be turned into a template as net component. All kinds of patterns can thus be provided as templates for the developers: commonly known patterns, trivial patterns or even new patterns for a special purpose. In addition to the advantages that are offered by patterns and the fact that net components are available as templates, a set of well-defined net components may offer some other advantages. This results in part from the fact that net components are concretions of patterns and in part from the fact that models and templates are designed in the same language: i.e. Petri nets. Such advantages are:

---

[4]Nevertheless, it can be argued that a net component automatically defines a pattern.

**Concreteness:** In opposition to a pattern a net component is a concrete graphical component that has a fixed graphical representation. A net component can be reused and the fixed form enhances the readability of net models.

**Composability:** Net components can be composed with other net components to form a Petri net. This results partly from their concreteness. However, this has also to be taken into consideration during the design phase of the net components. It accelerates the development and resulting nets are structured in a clear, unified way.

**Convention:** The geometric representation of a net component allows the developers to easily recognize the implemented pattern in a net component in different environments. Thus net components increase the comprehensibility of models. Other (coding/modeling) conventions can easily be established.

**Congenerousness:** Since the pattern and its implementation are modeled in the same graphical language, there exists no breach between model and implementation. This allows flexibility in the design and use of the net component.

From a technical viewpoint, net components also facilitate the generation of code as template implementations together with the predefined layout possibilities and allow to further ease refactorings by simplified graphical reorganization of net code through the weak and flat grouping mechanism.

## 5.2.3 Detailed Design Decisions

Net components should have a certain closeness. For system modeling, for instance, parts of the system can be modeled as net components. Processes can be decomposed into tasks, thus types of tasks can be turned into net components. Net components implementing tasks should be designed in order to be applicable to a broad variety of nets. Furthermore, net components can provide additional help, such as a default inscription or comments. However, for easy integration into Petri net models, it is of advantage to be obliged to customize as few inscriptions as possible.

Every net component has a unique geometrical form and orientation that result from the arrangement of the net elements. This unique form is intended so that each net component can be easily identified and distinguished from the others. The geometrical figure also has the potential to provide a defined structure for the Petri net. If the designed models are workflows or process-like a direction of the control-flow can be enforced by the applied net components.

In the MULAN protocol net components (see Section 5.3) incoming connection points are realized as transitions while outgoing conception points are realized as places (*interface places*) for convenient connection of net components. Only one arc has to be drawn to connect one net component with another. This simple and efficient method also emphasizes the control-flow through the fact that these simple connecting arcs transport by default only black tokens. The connection of net components is provided by this place, which in the example implementation only holds anonymous tokens.

If challenges in model construction frequently re-occur within a context, it is reasonable to introduce a net component for this cause. Functionality that is thus implemented once, can be used frequently without repeating the process of *low-level* implementation again. Altogether these characteristics of net components are summarized in Table 5.1:

| Characteristic | Benefit |
|---|---|
| Generic character | Broad applicability |
| Interconnectivity | Easily composable |
| Closeness | Clear semantics |
| Unique form | Easily identifiable |
| Located in repository | Pre-manufactured but adaptable solutions. |

Table 5.1: Criteria for net components design.

A distinction between different sets of net components for different contexts can be achieved by using different color schemes or unique forms of atomic net elements. Thus the resulting models can easily be categorized by developers.

Especially when nets are produced in large numbers (e.g. while designing Petri net-based applications or other large Petri net models), the advantages of the component-based approach are obvious. The net components contribute not only to a faster development of applications or models, but also to a clear structure of the nets.

## 5.2.4 Structure of Net Components

Net components are subnets that can be composed to form larger Petri nets. As in the case of design patterns their purpose is to provide pre-manufactured solutions to re-occurring challenges. Moreover, they also impose their structure onto the constructed net.

Through their geometric form, net components are easily identified in a larger net. This adds to the readability of the net and the clarity of its overall structure, which as a composition is an accumulation of substructures.

Jensen (1996) describes several design rules for Petri net elements, which are based on work done by Oberquelle (1981). These rules encompass how to draw figures and give general advice for the drawing of Petri net elements such as places, transitions and arcs. They are also concerned with combinations and arrangement of the elements.

Net components extend the rules by giving developer groups the chance to pre-define reusable structures. Although they are open for improvements, these structures are fixed and well-known within the group of developers. Conventions for the design of the code can be introduced into the development process and easily applied, adopted and spread by the developers throughout the net component-based construction. The developing process is consequently simplified and the style of the resulting nets unified. Once a concrete implementation of net components has been incorporated and accepted by the developers, their arrangements (geometrical form) will be recognized as conventional symbols. This makes it easier to read a Petri net that is constructed with these net components. Hence, in order to understand a net component-based net, it is not necessary to read all its net elements, but it is sufficient to read the substructures. This simplifies the review process as well as the refactoring of net code.

## 5.2.5 Realization

Petri nets can be drawn with RENEW in a fast and easy manner. To be able to use net components accordingly, it is desirable to have a seamless integration of net components in RENEW. The drawing tools are provided by simple palettes (Figure 5.1) that are the usual container for the buttons of all drawing tools for net elements.

Renew supports a highly sophisticated plugin architecture (see Schumacher (2003) and Duvigneau (2009)), by which its functionality can be extended through plugins, so that the usual functionality remains available. Thus, the framework for the net components as well as all sets of net components are realized as plugins. Each set of net components offers a palette that holds the tool buttons for the net components, which can be drawn in the same way simple (atomic) drawing elements are drawn, i.e. by selecting the tool from a tool palette and determining the position of the net component by clicking in the drawing. Once a palette is activated, the net components are available for drawing until the palette is deactivated.

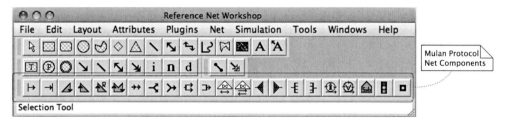

Figure 5.1: Palette for the MULAN net components in RENEW.

All net components are realized as RENEW drawings, so they can easily be adjusted to the need of the programmer by editing within RENEW. The net component drawings are held in repositories[5], thus sets of net components can be shared by a group of programmers. Nevertheless, users can also copy and modify the repository to adjust the net components to their needs, or build new net components with RENEW. It is also possible to use multiple palettes of different repositories.

Net components are added to the drawing in the same way as the usual net elements. The mechanism can be compared to typical IDE (integrated development environment) template mechanisms. As, for instance, in *Eclipse* IDE (`http://www.eclipse.org`), it is possible not only to use predefined templates for all kinds of elements (e.g. *while* loops, *for* loops, *instanceof* statements) but also to modify them or create new templates. RENEW and the Net Components Plugin allow similar handling of net components as templates and, in addition, since sets of net components are usually held in a SCM

---

[5]Repositories hold the drawings of the net components, (optional) images for the tool buttons of the palettes and configuration files that determine the order of the buttons in the palettes.

(source code management system) repository, these modifications can easily be spread among the developers.

## 5.3 Mulan Protocol Net Components

MULAN (Multi-Agent Nets, see Köhler et al. (2003), Rölke (2004)) is a concept model and framework for multi-agent systems designed with reference nets. In order to build a multi-agent application based on MULAN, numerous protocol nets that implement agent behavior and interactions have to be drawn. A Protocol net is an implementation of a part of an agent interaction, usually defined as FIPA-compliant agent interaction protocols.

A set of net components for Protocol nets exists (see Cabac (2002, Chapter 4.3)) that has been successfully tested and used in the frame of teaching projects (*Settler 2–6*, *WFMS 1,2*, see Reese et al. (2007) and Wagner (2009b)) by our group at the University of Hamburg. The set of MULAN net components has been used extensively, and a large number of net component-based Protocol nets have been designed during the projects with them.

The MULAN net components provide the basic functionality to construct protocols (compare with Section 4.3.4 and Köhler et al. (2001)). The protocols that are constructed with the help of the MULAN net components are not restricted to the exclusive use of net components; however, it is unnecessary to use non component-based net elements because the set is self-contained. It provides structures for control flow management that includes alternatives, concurrency, cycles and sequences. In addition, the functionality for exchanging data is provided that allows receiving or sending of messages. Furthermore, some basic protocol-related structures are provided that handle the starting and the stopping of protocols.

### 5.3.1 Requirements for Mulan Net Components

Net components have to be designed for their purpose. In any case, different kinds of nets require different sets of net components. However, within a set of net components that has been designed for a special purpose, we design the net components as generic as possible, so that the net component can be applied to similar (modeling) problems of the same kind. From the perspective of the graphical layout as well as from the semantic perspective, our goal is that net components are easily inter-connectable so that the construction of nets is facilitated and accelerated. Furthermore, to achieve a set of orthogonal net components, each net component is designed to represent one syntactical and semantic entity. This means that a net component is represented in a compact form and represents one task that is not decomposable. Additionally we design our sets of net components so that each net component is easily identifiable to the reader of the net. We achieve this by arranging the net elements in a unique (geometrical) form. The form is either inspired by conventions, intuitiveness or discrimination. Patterns can also be discovered in existing nets and then be extracted to form net components. These patterns might already offer an arrangement that can be adapted to be integrated into the set of existing net components. Examples are: (1) the combination of *conditional* and *merge* that form a rhombus (convention, see activity diagrams), (2) *parallel split* (discrimination from *conditional*), (3) circles for the loops (intuitive form). In the current implementation a *shadow* emphasizes the geometrical form.

One objective in the design of net components presented in the following section is that in common use one inscription at most has to be changed to make an applied net component functional. Thus, for instance, the current version of the conditional, which controls the flow of tokens with pattern matching as arc inscription, has been given preference over an alternative solution using guards on two transitions. Although the alternative is smaller in the number of net elements, for each conditional two transitions have to be inscribed and these inscriptions have to be carefully designed to ensure determinism.

### 5.3.2 Generic Mulan Net Components

A selection of MULAN net components is presented in this section. The goal is to demonstrate what kind of functionality they provide for Protocol nets and how the net components affect the form of the resulting nets. In this section, the essential and most frequent net components for message exchange and for basic flow control are presented. Further net components exist that cover sub-calls and manual synchronization.[6]

#### Control Flow Net Components: Alternatives, Concurrency and Sequences

The conditional, which is shown in Figure 5.2, can be used to add an alternative to the protocol. It provides an *exclusive or* (XOR) situation. To resolve the conflict the `boolean` variable `cond` is adjusted as desired. As a complement to the *NC cond*, the *NC ajoin* (alternative join[7]) merges the two alternative lines of the protocol.

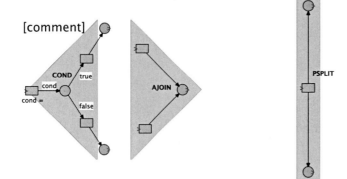

Figure 5.2: Net components for an alternative control-flow: *NC cond, NC ajoin*.

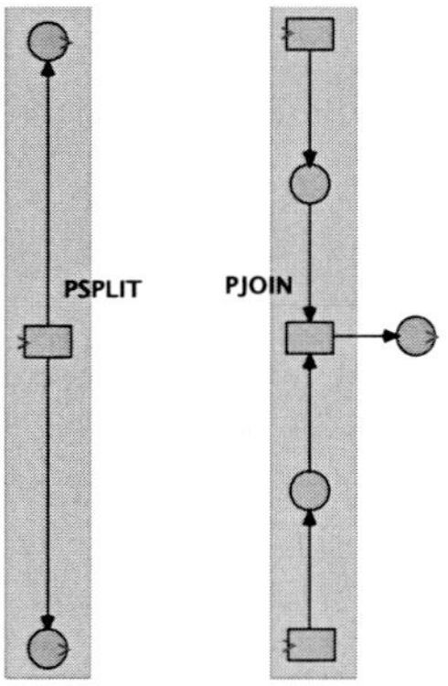

Figure 5.3: Net components for concurrent execution: *NC psplit, NC pjoin*.

---

[6]The full set of net components can be found in (Cabac 2002).

[7]The names of the patterns are inspired by the names of the workflow patterns. See Van der Aalst et al. (2000a) for alternative names of common patterns.

The MULAN protocol net components *NC psplit* (parallel split, see Figure 5.3) and *NC pjoin* (parallel join) are provided to enable concurrent processing within a protocol. Note that the forms of these differ significantly from *NC cond* and *NC ajoin* in order to create a clear separation between concurrency and alternatives within the protocols. We also offer a component for the trivial pattern *sequence* (see Figure 5.4), which already contains an inscription that gets the reference to the agent's knowledge base (a net instance), since it is an often used routine. The accessing of the knowledge base is realized as a synchronous

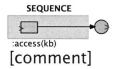

Figure 5.4: Net component for sequential execution: *NC sequence.*

channel. It has to be supplemented with access methods for the data that is stored in or retrieved from the knowledge base. Connectable elements of net components – i.e. the elements that are connected with an arc to an element of another net component or another net element – are marked with '>'. Many net components come with predefined text annotations that are intended as in-line comments. This is a good example for the manifestation of conventions. In order to distinguish between inscriptions and comments, the font color is set to blue and the text is enclosed in square brackets.

**Loops**

Loops are the equivalent of the basic loops in other programming languages. The *NC iterator* provides a loop through all elements of a set described by the `java.util.Iterator`. It processes the base (the iterated parts) of the loop in a sequential order. The *NC forall*

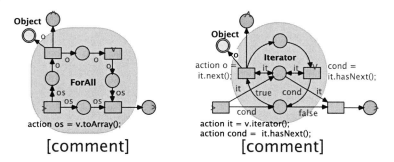

Figure 5.5: Loops: *NC forall* and *NC iterator.*

uses flexible arcs to provide a concurrent processing of all elements of an array. Flexible arcs allow the movement of a flexible number of tokens with one single arc (see Reisig (1997), Kummer et al. (2009a) and Section 3.2.5). The number of tokens moved by the flexible arc may vary for each firing, hence its name. In RENEW double arrowheads indicate the flexible arcs. A flexible arc puts all elements of an array into the output place and removes all elements of a pre-known array from the input place. The bases of both loops, *NC iterator* and *NC forall*, are marked with ∧ (beginning) and ∨ (ending). Data objects are transferred to the main part of the net components with the help of virtual places (labeled *Object*), which are already provided by the net components.

Both net components constitute examples for advanced patterns, offering standard solutions for complex arrangements. The implementation of a loop in a Petri net might already be time consuming. Moreover, the correct usage of specialized elements, as, for instance, the flexible arc, is not trivial – especially for inexperienced developers. The usage of the *NC forall*, however, is simple. It is also an example for the application of the flexible arc.

### 5.3.3 Mulan Protocol Specific Net Components

Some net components for protocol nets are specialized for the use within MULAN protocols. These are net components for protocol management and messaging.

#### Protocol Management Net Components

Beginning (*NC start*) and Ending (*NC stop*) are needed in all protocols (see Figure 5.6). There is exactly one start in every MULAN protocol, but there may be more than one stop. The protocol is started when the transition with the channel inscription `:start()` is fired and stopped when one transition with the inscription `:stop()` is fired. The inscriptions `:start()` and `:stop()` define up-links of synchronous channels. Furthermore, the *NC*

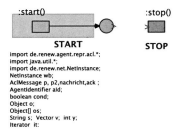

Figure 5.6: Net components for the management of protocols: *NC start* and *NC stop*.

*start* provides a declaration for the net. The declaration already contains the variables that are used in all MULAN net components and the import statements. It can be supplemented with other variables or imports by the developer.

#### Messaging Net Components

Messaging net components are the net components which provide the means of communication (see Figure 5.7). The *NC in* receives a message which is handed to the data block of the net component (above the main part of the net component).

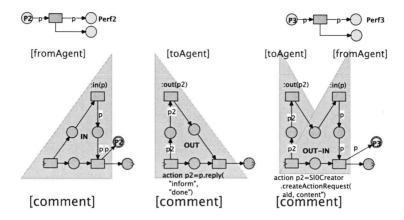

Figure 5.7: Net components for message transport: *NC in, NC out, NC out-in*.

Additional data containing places can be added to the data block as desired. These places can contain elements that were extracted from the messages, for example the name of the sender or the type of the performative. The *NC out* provides the outgoing message task. The *NC out-in* is a short hand implementation for the combination of both *NC out* and *NC in*. It provides a *send-request-and-wait-for-answer* situation, but does not add functionality other than *NC out* and *NC in*. However, it shortens the protocol significantly.

### Agent Internal Communication

The communication between protocol nets and agent internal processes is provided by a chain of synchronous channels called *exchange* channels. The MULAN agent offers three such channels. These channels are used for synchronous – but also bidirectional – calls, asynchronous calls and asynchronous answers (return). Two components are included

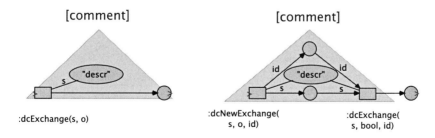

Figure 5.8: Net components for agent internal communication: *NC simple-exchange, NC exchange.*

in the MULAN protocol components (Figure 5.8): *simple-exchange* for synchronous calls and *exchange* for one possibility of asynchronous calls.

# 5.4 Discussion

Net components have been used and are under constant ongoing development since 2002 within our Petri net-based software development projects. In this section, we give an overview of our experiences on how the availability of net components and their tool support influenced the net code created by students in comparison to earlier projects. Furthermore, we present related work and extensions to the concepts and tool set.

## 5.4.1 Experiences with Net Components

To illustrate our experiences, Figure 5.9 shows an example net created by students in a recent project. The net implements a plan of a *User* agent in a workflow management system to obtain addresses of service providers in the system. The plan initiates an instance of the `queryService` Agent Interaction Protocol Diagram for the *WFMS*[8] agent for each required service. We want to stress the point that the net *is* real, executable code from the multi-agent application implementation and that it is shown unmodified[9], as the students drew it.

Note that the nets are not displayed here to be read in all details as Petri nets, although they are fully operational and can be executed in RENEW and MULAN without any changes. Instead, they are presented to give an impression of the structured layout and the application of the net components.

The control flow of the net starts in the lower left corner with an *NC start* and goes in a straight line to the right. In the middle, an *NC forall* splits the control flow in $n$ independent flows, one for each service provider to retrieve. The initiation of the individual Interaction Protocol instances for each queried service and the corresponding result's evaluation are implemented in the shadowed box in the upper part of the net. A protocol instance of another protocol net, which comprises all instance-specific data, is initiated by sending a local message to the agent itself and waits for the response – i.e. the same agent is sending and receiving the messages and also the responses. As the net is a prototype, the reaction to unexpected results is currently not fully implemented.

Due to their graphical nature Petri nets allow the creation of so-called *spaghetti code*. Especially during the modification or refactoring of a net model, code (net elements) is often added in areas that do not offer additional space. The rearrangement of all surrounding net elements is a very time-consuming process that is often skipped when the surrounding elements are not carelessly pushed aside, leaving behind a cluttered net structure. With net components, such situations can be easily handled for several reasons:

- The protocol net components promote a left-to-right net layout, because the components themselves are designed horizontally.

---

[8]WFMS: Workflow Management System.
[9]With the exception that the declaration note (bottom left) has been changed in layout.

## User queries all of his required Services

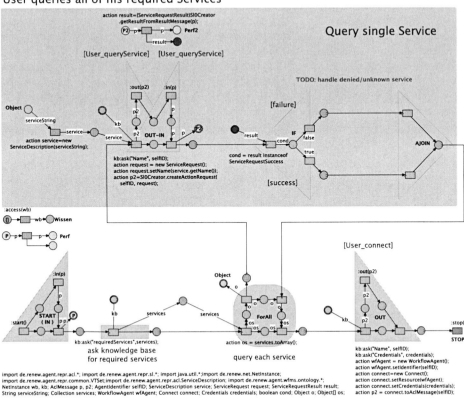

Figure 5.9: Example Protocol net from the WFMS project: *User_queryAllServices*.

- In most net components there is exactly one element to be customized. Therefore, additional data places are forced to be located near this element.

- Ad hoc transitions are not needed because many net components already come with a skeleton for data flow and manipulation.

- Net components are supported in the tool by a weak and flat grouping mechanism.[10] This improvement over early version of the tool set eases the insertion of new elements in the middle of an existing net without destroying the layout of individual net components while it retains full modifiability of net component details.

---

[10]The weak and flat grouping mechanism allows the movement of all elements of the component as a group while individual net elements of the net component are still accessible to any kind of manipulation. There is no hierarchical grouping, instead grouped groups become fused. The classical grouping feature is more restrictive since single elements of a group can not be manipulated nor selected.

- Documentation of nets is promoted by standardized comment templates that are attached to net components.

In general, we observed that nets built with net components are tidier than nets built without. Additionally, the readability of nets is significantly improved. With a little experience the comprehension of the nets is reduced to the reading of two elements per net component: the shape of the component and the customized inscription or comment. Without the need to examine every net element, it is thus possible to understand the described process.

Besides the graphical benefits, the teaching staff observed an increase in code development speed and students' learning curve in Petri net design. There are multiple explanations:

- It is obviously faster to compose a net from larger blocks than to repeat every small step repeatedly (reuse of code); even faster than *copy & paste*.

- The set of net components cover mostly well-known constructs from classic sequential programming languages such as conditionals and loops. Hence the transition from classical programming to Petri net modeling is easier.

- Moreover, net components enable automation of net construction, resulting in generation of nets or round-trip engineering techniques.

- Existing net components come with transitions and places already correctly inscribed and connected, thus showing examples of correct code and inscriptions.

- For the attending teachers and tutors the results of the students' designs are much more easily reviewed due to the structural clarity mentioned above.

- Reuse of concepts and solutions have been intensified. The original set of net components is based on patterns of net elements that have been recognized in Protocol nets. Now, they are commonly used and we detect more advanced patterns that can also become net components. Design patterns become graspable for developers in our pattern-based approach.

- Reuse of concepts is facilitated. It is easy to cut a recognized pattern from an existing net and turn it into a new net component (e.g. by using hot keys).

- The overall acceleration of net design leaves more time to discuss other matters of development, e.g. architectural design.

These benefits do not only apply to software development. Net components have also been applied to other areas. Besides the workflow patterns presented by Moldt and Rölke (2003), a set of net components for the construction of Petri net-based plans, which are automatically assembled during runtime and executed on the fly, has also been developed.

To give an illustration of the qualitative differences, we have carried out some internal tests with experienced members of our group and some of our students. The results, even for most simple example implementations with a given and detailed specification, are already satisfying. Nets drawn without net components tend to be much smaller, due to concise implementation. However, the test persons needed twice to five times as much time to develop the protocol nets.[11] An immediate repetition of the test also showed that the pure coding is at least twice as fast with the use of net components. If we consider that the use of net components helps the developer to avoid many pitfalls in (Petri net) programming/modeling, then the real benefit of using a net component-based approach is obviously much greater.

It has to be admitted that some of the advantages mentioned above entail a trade-off in flexibility of Petri net engineering. The strong form of net components restricts the overall net layout, and – as already mentioned – structured net component-based Petri nets tend to be larger than simple unstructured nets. Moreover, developers tend to stick to the predefined solutions and show themselves sometimes conservative with the introduction of new patterns. Because many net components are oriented along classical sequential programming language constructs, resulting nets include sometimes less concurrency than Petri nets would allow. It could be argued that, depending on the stage of modeling expertise the developers have reached, parts of this flexibility trade-off may also be seen as an advantage rather than a disadvantage. These are very usual and common effects regarded from the perspective of software engineering.

However, some of the original and some of the later proposed net components have been used rarely, if at all. For this, there exist numerous reasons, which are not discussed here, since this is not in the focus of this work. Among possible reasons though, we might name bad integration of net components and extremely specialized purpose.

## 5.4.2 Further Development

We are looking forward to apply the mentioned workflow patterns (see Moldt and Rölke (2003)) – and improve the implementation as net components – to the agent-based distributed workflow engine, which was further improved by Wagner (2009a). The agent-based WFMS integrates a reference net-based workflow engine, which was developed by Jacob et al. (2002), into the multi-agent system MULAN. In this context, net component-based development can improve the development of workflows. A first design of simple net components has already been integrated into the net component tool set (compare with Moldt and Rölke (2003)).

In the future we want to introduce net components into other areas of net development where extensive modeling/coding is undertaken. Net components can be applied to other software development paradigms and besides workflow design they can also improve the construction of large-scale Petri net models in other areas.

Currently, we are experimenting with a collapse (and expand) functionality for net components (similar to coarsening/refinement) that could lead to a rapid prototyping of languages such as workflow languages, e.g. YAWL developed by Hofstede (2005). Figure 5.10 shows an exemplary collapse from a *NC cond* to a YAWL-like notation. New

---

[11]One of our – experienced but skeptical – team members who had claimed he would design faster without net components, was quite surprised that he achieved a speedup of factor five with net components.

graphical language elements can be rapidly defined and directly executed through the underlying operational Petri net semantics.

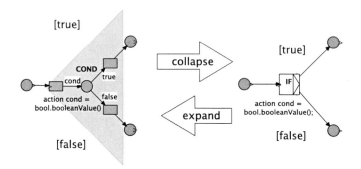

Figure 5.10: Collapsing of net components for rapid graphical language prototyping.

## 5.5 Related Work

Component approaches are not new to the community. There exist many solutions and concepts. This section gives an overview of the research done in this context and presents several related publications and implementations that use net components in particular.

### 5.5.1 Petri Net-Based Components

#### Van Hee

Van Hee (1994) describes elementary and non-elementary processors (similar to Petri net transitions). They are connected to places via connectors. To processors connected places are called *input place* or *output place* depending on the connector's orientation. These places are comparable with the *interface places* described in Section 5.2.3. The notion of non-elementary processor (comparable with a coarsened transition) is then closely related with the notions of the net components as they are provided by the MULAN net components. Moreover, the representation of a collapsed net component in Figure 5.10 comes very close to the representation of the non-elementary processors.

#### Kindler

Kindler (1997) uses Petri net components to model parts of systems (components). The resulting models are used to verify compositional systems. The notion of Petri net components is covered by our general notion on net components. In his approach (in which components are place bounded) the interface places are fused, while in the approach presented in Section 5.3 only one interface place exists between two connecting points of net components. The resulting nets (or net structures) after composition with Kindler's approach are the same as with the approach presented in this chapter. However, no software engineering conceptualizations are discussed in the direction of a set of template implementations.

### Van der Aalst, Ter Hofstede & Barros

Van der Aalst et al. (2000a) present workflow patterns.[12] Although the original intent was directed towards a different goal, this work has strongly influenced the net components, especially the set of MULAN protocol components. The workflow patterns show a comprehensive generic catalog of workflow patterns designed with Petri nets. To our knowledge there exists no tool set that allows their application. However, they have influenced the YAWL language (see Hofstede (2005)) which supports many of the mentioned patterns through direct notations.

### Mulyar & Van der Aalst

Mulyar and van der Aalst (2005) present a realization of workflow patterns in colored Petri nets with CPN Tools (2010) making extensive use of the ML (metalanguage) inscription language. By this, they offer example implementations of the abstract patterns. They do not discuss either the idea of using these patterns as templates in the context of software development.

### Van der Aalst, Van Hee & Van der Toorn

Van der Aalst et al. (2002) provide a framework for the specification and implementation component-based software architectures. They focus on the processes in the specified system and base the component on $\mathcal{C}$-nets (Component nets). These are Petri nets that are labeled and have a unique starting point. The latter fact and the fact that the labeled transitions function as the components interface is very similar to out MULAN protocol nets (and also the other agent components). The labeled transitions that provide the communication channels are comparable to the up-links of the protocol nets (compare with the messaging net components in Figure 5.7). The expressiveness is restricted, since $\mathcal{C}$-nets are based on P/T-nets and the component structure is static.

## 5.5.2 Net Component Plugins

### Moldt & Rölke

In the context of net components other implementations have been done. Moldt and Rölke (2003) have modified the plugin to design and supply advanced workflow patterns implemented through reference nets. This set is merely an example pattern implementation with no practical purpose, but it has a nice conceptual value offering elegant solutions for challenging problems in workflow design.

---

[12]Compare also with the advanced workflow patterns by van der Aalst, Barros, ter Hofstede and Kiepuszewski (2000).

## Braker

Braker (2004) has adopted the *workflow pattern* of van der Aalst et al. (2000a) for reference net-based process definitions in an early modification of the Net Components Plugin. Braker covers a broad variety of advanced workflow patterns in a practical setting. The approach suffers from overloaded, complicated implementations and from the weaknesses of the early version of the Net Components Plugin, such as the missing possibility to group net components. These net components were also meant to *dock* on to each an other, a feature that was however only envisioned.

## Cabac & Denz (formerly Knaak)

Cabac and Knaak (2007) have also presented data-flow components in the context of process mining. In opposition to the pure control-flow net components presented in Section 5.3 (with anonymous tokens in the interface places), the data-flow components focus on the processing of data, which is transported via the interface places through the *mining chain* between processors, filters, sources and sinks (which are specialized net components).

## Hewelt & Wester-Ebbinghaus

Hewelt and Wester-Ebbinghaus (2009) provide an implementation for a unity theoretic approach. Units are dynamic entities that allow several basic features. They are modeled/specified with reference nets and implemented as a net components plugin for RE-NEW.

## Renew

The Net Components Plugin[13] itself has been plugified to respect the fact that several sets of net components have to be supported. Thus the repository can be not only an arbitrary (but suitable) directory but also a plugin that extends the tool set with new sets of net components.

## Use Case Components

As mentioned above the Net Components Plugin and its technical possibilities also allow to use the component-based approach for other modeling techniques. Figure 5.11 shows the RENEW main window and the sub-menu for the net components (sub-)plugins. A set of *modeling components* are shown for the modeling of use cases in an example drawing together with the detached palette for these components. Just as with net components it is possible to quickly group a selection of drawing elements[14] and turn this group into a component by saving it in the repository. A customized image for the palette finalizes the repository and, if no customized image exists, the tool chooses a standard image.

---

[13]The Net Components Plugin and some standard components (also as plugin) can be downloaded from the RENEW home page, see Kummer et al. (2009a).

[14]Compare with the gray elements in the menu shown in Figure 5.11.

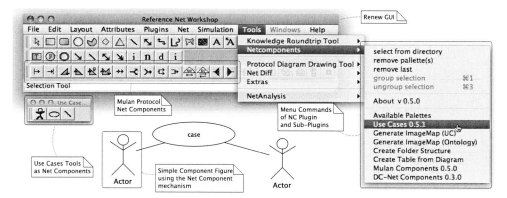

Figure 5.11: Palettes and net components for Use Case Diagrams in RENEW.

Additionally, in the course of the development of the Use Case Plugin, the necessity to include other tool buttons than the ones producing components was identified. The net components framework has been extended to also allow customized palettes as in the case of the shown use cases palette. Figure 5.11 displays a specialized line connection tool. The Use Case Plugin also allows to generate code bases for multi-agent application, image maps and the diagram structure as table in LaTeX (see Chapter 10).

### 5.5.3 Development

Design and development of the Net Components Plugin as well as the design and modeling of all provided net components have been done by me. The MULAN net components are a separate plugin, i.e. the MULAN Components Plugin. Other plugin extensions of the Net Components Plugin are the DC Components Plugin, the Use Case Plugin – also developed and designed by me.

**Development History**

0.2.0 Simple template inclusion of nets in repository folder.

0.3.0 Usability: adding and removing palettes by menu commands.

0.3.1 Consolidated form of NCs (more compact, compatible with each another).

0.3.2 Added support for multiple repositories/palettes.

0.3.3 Decomposition of the Net Components Plugin into framework and domain-specific parts.

0.3.4 Introduction of geometrical 'shadow' figure.

0.3.5 Inclusion of *NC subcall, NC sequence, NC reply.*

0.4.0 Made Net Components Plugin extendible by repository plugins.

0.4.2 Introducing week/flat grouping, grouping (net component figure).

0.5.0 Plugins may provide custom buttons on palette.

## 5.6 Summary

For the construction of Petri net models – as, for instance, in the PAOSE approach – structuring elements, pattern-based development and efficient implementation of Petri net models are needed. We have shown with the presentation of the MULAN protocol net component for the (Petri net-based) agent-oriented paradigm that net components can provide the means for this.

Net components are sub-nets with geometrical arrangements that ease their identification in Petri net models. They can be easily located and discriminated from other components. As a means of structuring, the MULAN net components presented in Section 5.3 are capable of accelerating the development of protocol nets. The readability of net component-based protocol nets is increased significantly as well as the speed of construction of nets in comparison to protocol nets without net components. The net components tool implemented as a plugin for RENEW enables us to use net components for the fast and systematic construction of Petri nets. Net components that are held as Petri net drawings in repositories are directly editable in RENEW, thus adaptable to the needs of the development team. Moreover, the Net Components Plugin itself is extensible by repository plugins that are dynamically pluggable and unpluggable at runtime.

MULAN net components are successfully used since the second teaching project of the ongoing series of multi-agent system development projects (AOSE projects, see Chapter 22) in our research group and have eased the teaching and development of Petri net-based protocol nets.

# 6 Modeling Techniques for Object-Orientation and Agent-Orientation

The great challenge in software development is the handling of complexity. This refers to the complexity of the systems themselves as well as the complexity of the development processes. These systems and processes have grown so large and complex that a single person cannot completely comprehend their nature. Hence, to be able to construct these systems or follow such construction processes especially with large groups, software modeling techniques are employed for the understanding of systems and for the communication among developers.

In this chapter several modeling techniques are presented. Section 6.1 outlines the context of modeling techniques in object-orientation and agent-orientation. Section 6.2 introduces the Unified Modeling Language (UML). An extension to UML, the Agent Unified Modeling Language (AUML), is presented in Section 6.3. Section 6.4 offers an overview of a selection of agent-oriented modeling techniques used in several different approaches/methodologies. Section 6.5 sketches the related work in the matter of comparison or evaluation of agent-oriented methodologies. Section 6.6 summarizes the chapter.

## 6.1 Context

This chapter gives an overview of the state of the art in modeling within object-oriented and agent-oriented methodologies with a strong focus on the proposed modeling techniques. As a representative for object-oriented approaches, the Unified Modeling Language (UML, see OMG 2003) is introduced as a means of modeling. The goal is to handle the complexity of large software systems. This is mainly achieved by using abstractions. Two examples of diagrams used in UML – the Class Diagram and the Sequence Diagram – are presented.

A manifold of methodological approaches to the development of software systems under the agent-oriented paradigm (agent-oriented methodologies) have been proposed. Many of them are inspired by a certain platform, language or specialized alignment. The development of the methodologies have been influenced over the years by conventional methodologies (Unified Process), advancements in techniques (object-orientation) and concepts (extreme programming) including advancements of modeling techniques (UML) and other disciplines. We present the Gaia methodology (see Wooldridge et al. (2000),

Zambonelli et al. (2003) and Bergenti et al. (2004)), a very abstract methodology that can also be regarded as a prototype or foundation for many other (more detailed and focused) methodologies. Then we investigate some modeling techniques of selected agent-oriented methodologies.

## 6.2 Unified Modeling Language

Object-orientation (introductions to object-orientation can be found in Sommerville (1996) or Oestereich (2001)) is the result of the software-engineering community's attempt to cope with the growing complexity of programs and their development over the years. In the object-oriented approach numerous ways of abstractions are used. Objects themselves are instances of classes that are typed and named modules. They are (usually) ordered hierarchically in a tree of dependencies called inheritance. Object-oriented programs are composed of objects that use, create or destroy other objects. Objects are modeled in analogy to the (to be modeled) part of the real world or domain.

Not only the software systems but also the software development processes have been subject to progress. Again, the challenge regarding development processes is how to cope with complexity. Several software process models or paradigms have been developed. For object-oriented development there are the Booch (1993) method, the object-oriented modeling technique (OMT, see Rumbaugh et al. (1991)) and object-oriented software engineering (OOSE, see Jacobson et al. (1992)). These culminated into the Unified Modeling Language (UML, see Booch et al. (1999) and UML (2009)), which was standardized by the Object Management Group (OMG 2003). The current version of UML is version 2.0 (UML 2003b). However, some of the underlying techniques have been adopted from version 1.5 (UML 2003a).

### 6.2.1 Description of UML

The Unified Modeling Language (UML) has established itself as the standard of software modeling especially for object-oriented software development. It provides a large and extensive set of modeling techniques, with which numerous aspects of software systems can be modeled. Each technique offers a diagram style to model the desired functionality. These diagrams can roughly be divided in two sets, one set describing the static structure and the other describing the (dynamic) behavioral characteristics of the system.

In this section only a small part of UML is described. For an introduction to UML see Sommerville (1996), Oestereich (2001) or Booch et al. (1999). A complete description is available online at the OMG web-site (OMG 2003).

Generally spoken, UML diagrams are used to describe software systems. There are different kinds of diagrams for different purposes and for different stages of modeling and implementation. These diagrams cover various views of the system and are meant for diverse actors (developers and users) in the software development process. Use Case Diagrams are used to ease the communication between developers and users. Other diagrams are mainly used by the developers.

**UML – Types of Diagrams**

| Models of Structure | Models of Behavior |
| --- | --- |
| Class Diagram | Use Case Diagram |
| Object Diagram | Activity Diagram |
| Package Diagram | State Machine Diagram |
| Component Diagram | Sequence Diagram[1] |
| Composite Structure Diagram | Communications Diagram[1] |
| Deployment Diagram | Timing Diagram[1] |
| | Interaction Overview Diagram[1] |

Table 6.1: Modeling techniques in UML.

In the following sections two of the available UML diagram types (see Table 6.1) are described to give a notion of the expressiveness. The Class Diagram is used to model the architecture of the software showing the static dependencies of the objects, while Sequence Diagrams describe the behavior of objects in a scenario.

Figure 6.1 repeats the modeling techniques as Class Diagram. In the figure shows the classification of the techniques.

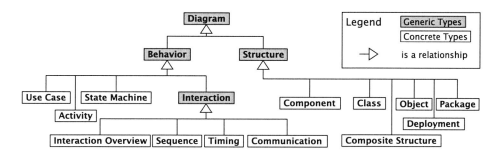

Figure 6.1: Modeling techniques a in UML as Class Diagram.

**Modeling and Implementing**

The Unified Modeling Language (UML) has established itself as the standard language for software modeling. There are many reasons for its great success. These include simplicity, expressiveness, broad applicability and adaptability. One very practical reason is the existence of a broad variety of tools, supporting the design and construction of models.

One of the most important advantages of computer-aided software development is the fact that the tools can generate code from the models. By this the development process is significantly accelerated, leaving more time for the developer to care about

---

[1]Interaction Diagram

design matters or enhancements instead of manually converting graphical specification into code. This approach tries to benefit directly from the fact that the specification, if modeled in the appropriate way, can be transformed into code. The aim is to generate as much code as possible from graphical specification. One could argue that this weakens the borderline between specification and implementation. At least the border is pushed from the concrete implementation as text further towards the abstract graphical description, meaning that more implementation work is now already done during modeling. This could be described as implementing by modeling.

The designed model that used to offer the specification now also holds - at least parts of - the implementation. For a language - and for a programming language especially - the syntax and semantics have to be well-defined to warrant precision and uniqueness. Only then it is possible to transform the description and receive generated code or code structures that can (after manual augmentation) be compiled into executable code. This holds also for graphic modeling using the Unified Modeling Language.

## 6.2.2 Class Diagrams

The structural diagrams are used to model the architecture of systems. They allow the developer to model the software architecture at different levels of abstraction and granularity. A Class Diagram (see Booch et al. (1999, Chapter 8)) displays classes or types and their relationships. It shows the system's structure and the dependencies between the elements. Class Diagrams are the frequently used and common diagrams of UML. They are excessively used to generate code.

### Description

The Class Diagram is very expressive and can convey inheritance and usage relationships between classes as well as objects. Essentially, the Class Diagram is a graph with classes and interfaces as nodes. The relationships between the classes, association, generalization and dependency are displayed as arcs between these nodes. While dependency and generalization are directed, associations can be directed or bidirectional. Associations can exhibit multiplicity and qualifiers and express different kinds of associations such as aggregation or composition, which are indicated by end decorations in the form of diamonds. Classes or interfaces are displayed as boxes with three (interface: two) compartments that are ordered vertically. The top compartment contains the name of the class. The other two compartments are optional and contain fields and methods. The basic elements of a Class Diagram are listed here:

**Class** is a box containing 3 compartments:

   **Name** of the class or interface (in italics or marked «interface»)

   **Fields** of the class (optional)

   **Methods** of the class or of the interface (optional)

**Associations** are displayed as arcs between classes. They can be directed.

**Aggregations** have hollow diamond ends.

**Compositions** have filled diamond ends.

**Multiplicity** (optional) is a number, a range of numbers or a '*'[2].

**Qualifiers** (optional) are rectangles attached to the end of associations.

**Notes** are boxes that have one folded corner and contain a descriptive text.[3]

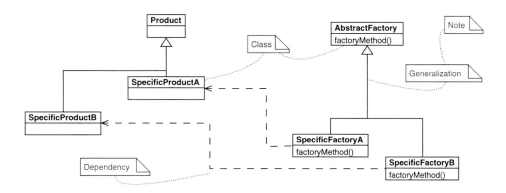

Figure 6.2: The design pattern *factory* as an example for a Class Diagram.

Figure 6.2 shows an example of a Class Diagram that describes the *factory* design pattern (see Gamma et al. (1995)). `SpecificFactoryA` and `SpecificFactoryB` are subclasses of `AbstractFactory`. They implement the abstract method `factoryMethod()`. The diagram is supplemented with note figures that can be used for annotations. In this example they describe the diagram elements.

Dependencies are indicated by dashed lines meaning that `SpecificFactoryA` creates `SpecificProductA` objects in `factoryMethod()` and `SpecificFactoryB` creates objects of the class `SpecificProductB` with its implementation of `factoryMethod()`.

## 6.2.3 Sequence Diagrams

Scenarios are descriptions of processes or sequences of action. They can be modeled with Interaction Diagrams (see Booch et al. (1999, Chapter 18)) that describe the behavior of objects. There are two different kinds of Interaction Diagrams, the Collaboration Diagram and the Sequence Diagram. They are usually used to model the dynamic behavior of objects and the interactions between objects. Especially Sequence Diagrams give a good notion of the procedures because time is directly represented.

---

[2]The asterisk ('*') represents an arbitrary number.
[3]Notes are available in all UML diagram types.

**Description**

In Sequence Diagrams the order of the displayed elements have a meaning: the vertical dimension represents time and the horizontal one represents different instances of objects. Object identifiers, which are located on the top of the diagram next to each other, represent the objects that are involved in the described scenario. The vertical dimension represents the temporal progress (downward) in the process. This orders the diagram sequentially. A life line is a vertical line that starts at an object identifier and extends downwards. The existence of an object is indicated by the life line, which runs downward from the object identifier until the object is destroyed. A cross that is located at the end of the life line indicates the destruction of the object. Times of activity of objects are displayed as activations, which run along the life lines. Method calls are displayed as message arcs that are sent from one object to another. These messages can be decorated by a solid or a stick arrow tip indicating synchronous or asynchronous messaging. If a message is a return statement, the line is dashed. Only an object that is active can send messages, i.e. call methods. Several graphical elements are listed here:

**Object identifiers** describe the objects that are involved in the modeled process.

**Life lines** start at an object identifier and last until the objects are destroyed.

**Activations** mark the active states of the objects. An activated object can act and thus call methods of other objects or of itself.

**Messages** are used to represent the method call.

**Crosses** are used to indicate a destruction of objects.

Figure 6.3 shows an example Sequence Diagram of two objects Object1 and Object2 of the type A and B. Object1 creates a new instance of B (Object2) and calls aMethod() of Object2. After the method is finished, the return statement lets Object1 continue with its activity, which is the destruction of Object2. Finally Object1 destroys itself. Note that the sequence is clearly recognizable by the top-down ordering of the diagram.

In contrast to the Class Diagram that reflects the static architecture of a system, the Sequence Diagram reflects the behavior of it or of parts of it. The Sequence Diagram does not contain any information about the system's structure. Instead it represents the actions of the objects for a certain scenario. Furthermore, it does not reveal any information of the internal actions of the objects. It focuses thus on the communication between objects.

## 6.3 AUML

In AUML (Agent UML) the Foundation for Intelligent Physical Agents (FIPA 2009) developed UML-based enhancements in order to be able to model issues for multi-agent systems. A strong emphasis lies on the improvements of Interaction Diagrams, since the UML Sequence Diagram only allows to model one sequence at a time and does not support concurrency. Specifications of agent interactions protocols at FIPA are defined with AUML. Several proposals as well as many proposed enhancements exist.

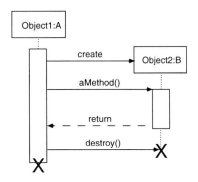

Figure 6.3: Example Sequence Diagram.

## 6.3.1 Agent Interaction Protocol Diagrams

Sequence Diagrams are restricted to show only one scenario each. This is a limitation that can be overcome by introducing control flow elements as supplements in the diagrams. By this, several scenarios can be folded together into one diagram. Proposals have been made by Odell et al. (2000) that cover nested Sequence Diagrams, combinations of Sequence Diagrams with other (nested) diagram types and the introduction of new elements providing the control flow elements mentioned above.

This section focuses on the extensions regarding control flow elements. These elements are presented in the next subsection. The diagram types that use these extensions are called extended Sequence Diagrams, Protocol Diagrams or Agent Interaction Protocols. In order to distinguish the variant of these diagrams that is used in this work, they are here, and furthermore in this work, called *Agent Interaction Protocol Diagrams* (AIP). Since these diagrams are extended Sequence Diagrams it seems appropriate to describe them at this point together with the other UML diagrams. Lets recollect that an agent could be regarded as a generalization of an object, that it communicates with other agents by the means of messages and that it can act proactively.

## 6.3.2 Extending Sequence Diagrams

Agent Interaction Protocol Diagrams are a part of the Agent UML (AUML) (see AUML (2004) and FIPA (2009)) that extends UML with agent related modeling techniques.[4] Extended Sequence Diagrams and Agent Interaction Protocol Diagrams are intended to enhance the modeling capabilities of Sequence Diagrams to model agent protocols.

In extended Sequence Diagrams some additional elements are added to the usual elements of Sequence Diagrams. Those additional elements provide alternative, concurrent and arbitrary splitting in a manner of the three gates AND, XOR and OR.

---

[4]The specifications of the Agent UML are defined and maintained by the Foundation for Intelligent Physical Agents (FIPA 2009).

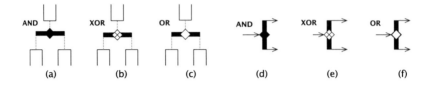

Figure 6.4: New elements of extended Sequence Diagrams.
New elements of extended Sequence Diagrams: AND, XOR, OR splits.

Figure 6.4 displays the new elements in a horizontal and a vertical version. The first elements are used to split the life lines of an agent (a, b and c), the second to split the (vertical) messages (d, e and f).

Odell et al. (2000) propose two different ways of using these elements: an elaborated version and a short version. Both versions are presented in the FIPA interaction protocol library specification (FIPA 2001b). In the elaborated version the two forms are always used together. This means that a split of messages also enforces a split of life lines. In the short version the life line split can be omitted.

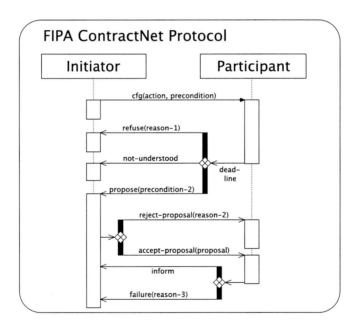

Figure 6.5: The FIPA Contract Net Interaction Protocol Diagram.

Figure 6.5 shows an example Protocol Diagram for the contract net protocol as presented in (FIPA 2001a). It shows the short (abbreviated) variant of presenting alternatives with the additional elements.

In addition to the split figures, FIPA describes the complements of the split figures as a variation of their presentation (FIPA 2001b). These are actually join figures – as pointed out in (Cabac et al. 2003) – matching the according split figures as complements. They are displayed in Figure 6.6.

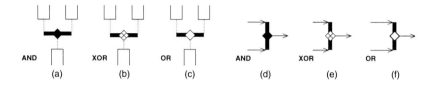

Figure 6.6: New elements of extended Sequence Diagrams: AND, XOR and OR joins.

A split up life line can be rejoined at some point in the diagram. This reflects a synchronization for the AND split and a merge for a XOR or OR split. Since the FIPA defines them as variation of presentation, they look similar to the split figures. However, the appearances of these figures in diagrams as splits or as joins distinguish the two sorts of figures from each other. In this work and in the implementation of the plugin (Chapter 13), a clear distinction is made between the splits and joins.

In this work, only AND and XOR splits and joins are used, since the semantics of OR splits and joins have not been defined properly. Furthermore, most of the diagrams are displayed in the elaborated version. The only exceptions are the diagrams taken or adapted from other sources. However, the elaborated version used in this work differs slightly from the elaborated version of the original proposal.

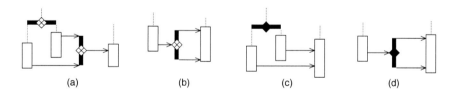

Figure 6.7: Reflecting actual message numbers in diagrams by combining splits and joins. A message sent after a decision results in a single received message (a). Two messages sent concurrently result in two received messages (c); and the short forms (b) and (d).

The difference is, however, only a difference in style or in variation of presentation and thus within the limits of the definition of interaction protocols. The aim in using this style is that especially the number of messages sent from an agent or received by an agent is reflected in the number of message arcs drawn in the diagram. So the messages sent to one agent after a life line XOR split with more than one outgoing message arc is joined by a message join figure. Figure 6.7 illustrates this. For a detailed discussion see section 13. These diagrams, that satisfy the briefly described style, are in this work called Agent Interaction Protocol Diagrams (AIP).

## 6.4 Modeling in AO-Methodologies

Numerous agent-orientation methodologies have been proposed. Many of them are tightly coupled with an agent framework. Others extend and refine generic approaches (such as ROADMAP extend Gaia) or transfer techniques from the outside to agent-orientation, such as Tropos (requirements engineering, $i^*$) and MAS-CommonKADS (knowledge engineering).

### 6.4.1 Gaia – a Methodology Prototype

Several of the currently developed (or maintained / supported) methodologies have a strong focus on modeling techniques and provide specialized and highly developed tool support. In contrast, Gaia (see Wooldridge et al. (2000), Zambonelli et al. (2003) and Bergenti et al. (2004)) provides a general (abstract) approach that can be applied to a variety of methodologies, languages and implementations. However, the frame of Gaia is very narrow. It focuses on the main parts of the analysis and design phase. It is neither concerned with the requirements engineering nor with the implementation staying independent from implementation constraints and details..

The first version of Gaia (see Wooldridge et al. (2000)) already shows the main proposed models. These models and their causal dependencies are depicted in Figure 6.8.

The main stages are described as analysis and design. In the analysis the roles and

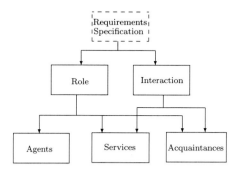

Figure 6.8: The main design artifacts of Gaia[5] (version 1).

the interactions of the system-to-be-designed are defined. For the defined roles abilities, responsibilities and relevant interactions are to be determined. The interactions have to be named and the participating roles have to be defined.

---

[5]Adapted from Wooldridge et al. (2000, p. 287)

During the design phase the roles are aggregated to form agents (agent model). Information about roles and interactions leads to a service model and the acquaintance model. The acquaintance model shows the agents that cooperate with each other. Requirements are outside of the scope of Gaia.

Concepts in Gaia are divided into *abstract* and *concrete* concepts. Abstract concepts are *roles, permissions, responsibilities, protocols, activities, liveness properties* and *safety properties*. Concrete concepts are *agent types, services* and *acquaintances*.

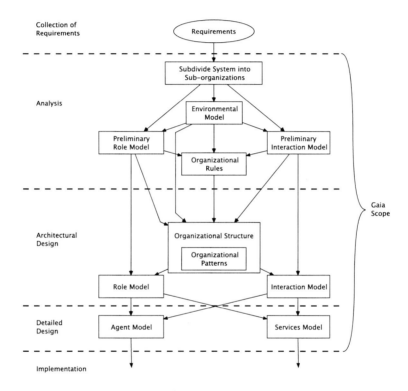

Figure 6.9: Artifacts in Gaia (version 2). The three phases that span the scope of Gaia are the *analysis*, the *architectural design* and the *detailed design*. The collection of requirements and the implementation are not within the scope of Gaia.[6]

The second version of Gaia (see Zambonelli et al. (2003)) is more detailed. Figure 6.9 shows a diagram of the artifacts in Gaia (version 2) and their inter-dependencies. The requirements engineering and the implementation are (still) outside of the scope of Gaia. The phases, however, have developed into three phases: *analysis, architectural design* and *detailed design*. Main improvements are the strong focus on the environmental and the organizational models and the incremental approach through the introduction of preliminary (coarse) models.

---

[6]Adapted from Zambonelli et al. (2003, p. 336)

The preliminary role model consists in descriptions (schemata) of the roles, their protocols and activities, their permissions and responsibilities. The latter is divided in liveness and safety. However, Gaia does not describe any method to define roles (or the preliminary role model) from the gathered requirements. Roles in Gaia are atomic (meaning no subroles) and have no counterpart in the designed systems implementation. Table 6.2 shows a template for a role schema.

| Role Schema | *name of role* |
|---|---|
| Description | *short description of the role* |
| Protocols and Activities | *protocols and activities in which the role plays part* |
| Permissions | *"rights" associated with the role* |
| Responsibilities | |
| Liveness | *liveness responsibilities* |
| Safety | *safety responsibilities* |

Table 6.2: Template for a role schema.[7]

The preliminary interaction model defines the protocol names, the initiator, the participating partners, the inputs, the outputs and a textual description of the interaction. Interactions are defined with abstraction from the implementation. Table 6.3 shows an example for an interaction definition.

| Protocol Name: **Reduce Speed** | |
|---|---|
| Initiator: **Stage[1]** \| Partner: **??** (Stage[1-i] or Controller) | Input: **proposed new speed** |
| Description: When a stage cannot afford the current speed of items, it has to start a protocol to negotiate a new speed | Output: **new speed** |

Table 6.3: Example for an interaction definition.[7]

**Detailed Design**

During the detailed design phase three kinds of models are created: the agent model, the acquaintances model and the services model. The agent model defines agent types and assigns roles to the agent types. It also defines the number of instances of the agent types in the system.

The acquaintance model shows communication relations of agents depending on roles and interactions.

[7]Tables are adapted from Zambonelli et al. (2003, pp. 347,348).

The services model is a "single, coherent block of activity". It defines inputs, outputs, preconditions, postconditions and a description. For the model in-/output definitions are derived from interaction specifications. The preconditions and postconditions depend on role specifications.

### Discussion

Gaia is the basis for many (more detailed) methodologies and it has been extended many times. The reduction to the core of analysis and design of multi-agent systems and the abstract description make it possible to achieve a generality that allows to use it as a prototype for many AOSE methodologies (e.g. ROADMAP, Paose). Thus Gaia provides a common ground for the development of multi-agent systems and for agent-oriented methodologies. The lack of concreteness, however, makes it hard to decide on the practical applicability.

## 6.4.2 Prometheus

Padgham and Winikoff (2002a, 2004) describe the Prometheus methodology, which has been developed at the Royal Melbourne Institute of Technology (RMIT). The Prometheus methodology provides a general approach in early stages and orientation towards BDI (Beliefs, Desire, Intentions, after Bratman (1987)) in later stages. Tool support is provided through the freely available Prometheus Development Tool[8] (PDT).

### Design Artifacts of Prometheus

The methodology comprises a large collection of modeling techniques depicted in Figure 6.10. Most important is the System Overview Diagram, which is both expressive and intuitively understandable.

Figure 6.11 presents a schematic example of a System Overview Diagram. It shows the notation for agents, protocols, messages, percepts, actions and data resources.

Other applied diagram types are simple Interaction Diagrams as UML Sequence Diagrams and as AUML Interaction Protocols. Processes are modeled using an extended version of Activity Diagrams.

### Discussion

Padgham and Winikoff offer with Prometheus a pragmatic, non-dogmatic approach to model agent applications. The modeling techniques are numerous, clear and expressive. The most important, the System Overview Diagram, seems somewhat overloaded though, if it comes to large models. With the PDT, Prometheus offers superb tool support as integrated development environment (IDE) for all supported techniques and some cross checking features to validate the designed models.

---

[8]PDT available at `http://www.cs.rmit.edu.au/agents/pdt/`

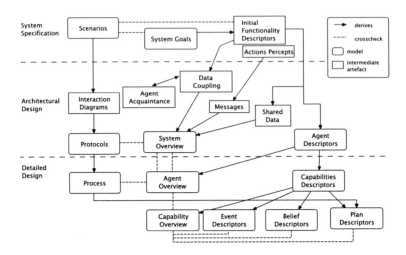

Figure 6.10: Classification of the Prometheus design artifacts in relation to phases.[9]

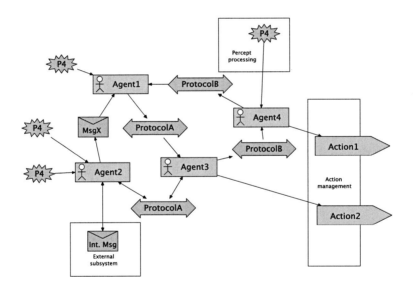

Figure 6.11: System Overview Diagram example in Prometheus.[10]

The methodology does not directly support the modeling of roles. However, it is planned to extend the methodology with social concepts, i.e. teams and roles.

---
[9]Diagram adapted from Padgham and Winikoff (2004, p. 67)
[10]Diagram adapted from Padgham and Winikoff (2004, p. 92)

## 6.4.3 ADEM/AML

Cervenka and Trencansky (2007) describe the Agent Modeling Language (AML). It is developed at Whitestein Technologies (2009).

### General Properties

On the one hand, AML extends the Unified Modeling Language (UML) with a multitude of models, concepts and stereotypes for the modeling of multi-agent systems. On the other hand, it is inspired by several agent methodologies – e.g. Gaia, MESSAGE, ROADMAP, PASSI, Prometheus and others – and other fields, such as web-services and logics. Figure 6.12 depicts the modeling techniques together with their embedding in UML.

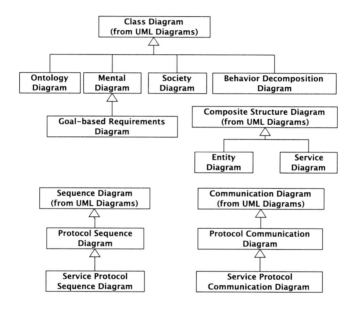

Figure 6.12: Overview of modeling techniques in AML.[11]

From the set of modeling techniques, we present two, the *Ontology Diagram* and the *Protocol Sequence Diagram*.

### Ontology Diagram

The Ontology Diagram resembles a UML Class Diagram. The OntologyClass is depicted with a stereotype «oclass» and/or with an icon (compare with Figure 6.13). OntologyClass objects list attributes, operations, parts and behaviors as slots as well as all kinds

---

[11]Adapted from Cervenka and Trencansky (2007, p. 315)

of commonly known relationships (from UML Class Diagrams) may be included in the Ontology Diagram.

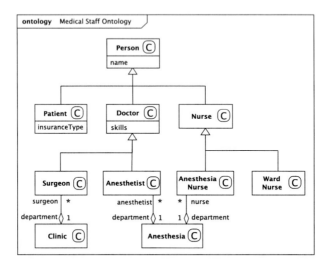

Figure 6.13: Example ontology in AML.[12]

Additionally, Ontology Diagrams may contain objects of the stereotype OntologyUtility («outility» and/or similar icon as OntologyClass but with a $U$), which provides global ontology constants, ontology variables and ontology functions/actions/predicates.

### Protocol Sequence Diagram

Protocol Sequence Diagrams are extended UML Sequence Diagrams. Some of the extensions are communicative interactions, multi-life lines and multi-messages.

Communicative interactions are similar to the communicative acts of AUML. Multi-life lines allow for multiple participants in an interaction as well as for the splitting of life lines, if the participants change groups. Multiplicity is depicted in the head of the life line in brackets (e.g. [m]). Figure 6.14 shows the FIPA contract-net protocol modeled in the AML style. For example the change of group takes place in the case when the participants refuse or accept to propose.

It seems obvious that the participants are either refusers, proponents or, if they do not answer to the *cfp*, they will not appear later in the Protocol Sequence Diagram ($m \leq n+j$). In the presented example the change of groups is exclusive. The participant can become either refuser or proponent but not both. Thus, the multi-life line splitting represents an alternative.

---

[12]Adapted from Cervenka and Trencansky (2007, p. 301)

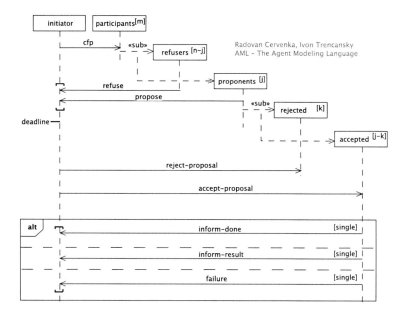

Figure 6.14: Sequence Diagram with multi-life lines in AML (FIPA contract-net).[13]

## ADEM and UML/RUP

Also the development process/approach borrows from UML. The Agent-Oriented Development Methodology (ADEM) extends the Rational Unified Process (RUP) to form a complete multi-agent system development method called *Extended RUP*. The additions of ADEM are in the disciplines *business modeling, requirements* and *analysis & design* as presented in Figure 6.15. They are provided through the techniques defined in the Agent Modeling Language (AML).

## Discussion

AML provides concepts and modeling techniques as extension to the concepts and modeling techniques of UML for the development of multi-agent systems. The methodology makes use of the extensive set of models from UML and adapts them to the needs of agent-oriented development. Besides the mentioned techniques and concepts the methodology considers all kinds of aspects from agent-orientation such as services, roles, social aspects and many others.

It is notable that the methodology does not address concurrency sufficiently. This could result from the fact that they are based on UML or from the fact that the methodology is oriented towards a pragmatic approach, without reaching into details of implementation.

---

[13]Adapted from Cervenka and Trencansky (2007, p. 188)

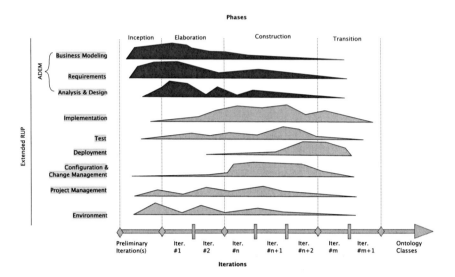

Figure 6.15: Classification of ADEM methods in the UML/RUP approach.[14]

Thus only as much consideration is given to concurrency as it is done by UML (Activity Diagrams, combined fragment *par*) and RUP.

### 6.4.4 AGR – Agents, Groups, Roles

In his introduction to Multi-agent systems, Ferber (1999) proposes and describes several modeling techniques to define structure and behavior of multi-agent systems. In his descriptions he focuses on the architectural structure as intuitive models and the agent behavior modeled as Petri nets. The design of a concrete multi-agent application (concrete organization) is described as analysis.

He distinguishes between functional analysis, structural analysis and instance parameters (see Figure 6.16). For the process-based decomposition Ferber introduces a description language for component-based modeling that allows for an abstraction of internal processes and the compositional aspects (BRIC, Basic Representation of Interactive Components). Components are described by their interfaces, which consist of input and output poles. The internal behavior is again depicted as Petri nets. Thus Ferber mixes formal (Petri nets, high-level Petri nets) and semi-formal modeling techniques (BRIC) with informal ones that can describe organizational structures or dependencies as graph structures.[15] The components of artificial organizations are depicted in Figure 6.16.

The AGR approach (Agents, Groups, Roles; see Ferber et al. (2003)) focuses on organizational matters. As suggested by the name, agents, roles and groups are the central aspects of the methodology. Starting from the meta-model of AGR (Figure 6.17),

---

[14]Adapted from Cervenka and Trencansky (2007, p. 104)

[15]Petri nets have been discarded by the authors due to the lack of expressiveness of the used formalism.

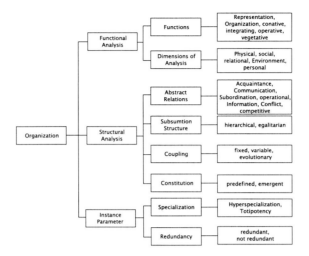

Figure 6.16: Elements of organizational analysis of artificial organizations.[16]

the authors present – besides the techniques mentioned above – three modeling techniques for the system design. These are the *Cheese-Board Diagram*, *Organizational Structure Diagram* and *Organizational Sequence Diagram*.

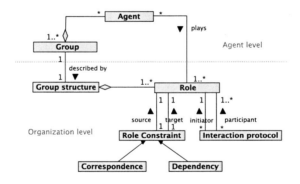

Figure 6.17: The meta-model of AGR.[17]

The Cheese-Board Diagram shows agents with their role affiliation and group memberships. In this diagram type also dynamics of group structures can be expressed. The Organizational Structure Diagram shows the group structures, the roles and interactions in the groups and can express correspondence of roles in different roles. Figure 6.18 shows the layered organization of a program committee as a Cheese-Board Diagram. Again the

---

[16]Diagram adapted from Ferber (1999, p. 120).
[17]Diagram adapted from Ferber, Gutknecht and Michel (2003, p. 222).

multiple membership of agents in several groups is clearly shown in the diagram.

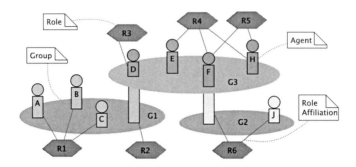

Figure 6.18: Modeling roles and groups in AGR – Cheese-Board Diagram.[18]

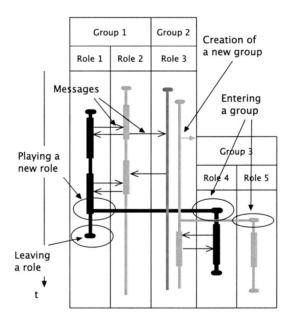

Figure 6.19: Modeling interactions – Organizational Sequence Diagram.[19]

The Organizational Sequence Diagram shows interactions between roles and groups. Arbitrary communications between roles and groups can be expressed as well as creation of groups and changing of group memberships. Similar to the Sequence Diagram with

---

[18]Diagram adapted from Ferber et al. (2003, p. 222).
[19]Diagram adapted from Ferber et al. (2003, p. 224).

multi-life lines in AML (Section 6.4.3), life lines can be split to show simultaneous memberships in several groups. Figure 6.19 shows an abstract example of an Organizational Sequence Diagram. Groups are explicitly modeled as compound elements, which conjoin roles.

### Discussion

AGR is an intuitive approach to model multi-agent systems that is influenced by the framework and the agent platform implementation MadKit. Thus, the modeling techniques take direct account of the inherent concepts, such as roles and groups. The integration of groups and roles as acting entities in the Organizational Sequence Diagram and the explicit representation of agent/group relationships in the Cheese-Board Diagram are powerful extensions to usual modeling techniques. Especially the representation of agents belonging to one or more groups by using a pseudo-perspective viewpoint is intuitive.

## 6.5 Related Work

Comparisons of agent-oriented methodologies have been undertaken in recent years. Most of them appeared during the development of this work. Two of the most comprehensive ones are from Henderson-Sellers and Giorgini (2005) and from Weiß and Jakob (2006).

Henderson-Sellers and Giorgini stress the fact that many agent-oriented methodologies have their root in object-orientation. Figure 6.20 depicts their view of dependencies between several methodologies.

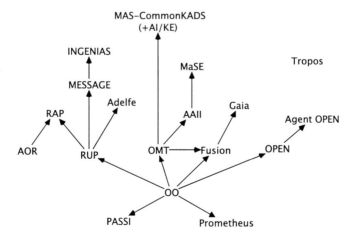

Figure 6.20: Influences of object-oriented and agent-oriented methodologies.[20]

---

[20]Diagram adapted from Henderson-Sellers and Giorgini (2005, p. 7).

### Henderson-Sellers & Giorgini

Henderson-Sellers and Giorgini (2005) include ten detailed presentations of agent-oriented methodologies and present a comparative evaluation of them. The examined methodologies are Gaia, Tropos, MAS-CommonKADS, Prometheus, PASSI, ADELFE, MaSE, RAP, MESSAGE and INGENIAS. The authors argue for a systematic approach methodology design on the basis of a proposed methodology meta-model.

### Weiß & Jakob

Weiß and Jakob (2006, in German) present five methodologies and six agent frameworks together with an evaluation. The evaluated methodologies are Gaia, MASSIVE, Zeus, MaSE and Aalaadin. The compared frameworks consist in FIPA-OS, JADE, Zeus, MadKit, agentTool and Jack.

### Shehory & Sturm

Shehory and Sturm (2001, 2003) present a framework for the evaluation of agent-oriented methodologies and apply this approach to three methodologies: AOM, ADEPT and DESIRE. They also present the investigation into the nature of agent-oriented methodologies and define the term through a meta-model, which is presented also in Section 2.4.1.

### Braubach, Lamersdorf, Pokahr & Sudeikat

Braubach et al. (2004) argue that satisfying evaluations of (agent-oriented) methodologies cannot be undertaken without the consideration of the target platform, i.e. the used agent framework. They present an evaluation framework that takes platform specific criteria into account and provide a comparison of MaSE, Tropos and Prometheus.

### Braubach & Pokahr

Braubach and Pokahr (2009) are the authors of *Jadex*. *Jadex* does not prescribe a fixed set of modeling techniques for the development of agent applications. They use several techniques from other methodologies/languages, such as UML, AUML, Prometheus and Tropos. Braubach (2007, p. 305) presents the evaluation of methodologies for *Jadex* based on the evaluation framework mentioned above. He (2007, p. 160) also provides an extensive and detailed classification of agent frameworks, ranging from agent platforms over languages, architectures and theories to research disciplines. Pokahr (2007, p. 136) stresses the fact that tool support for all activities in software development is essential for the efficiency and effectiveness. He (2007, p. 145) also presents an overview of the interrelationships of modeling tools with methodologies and other artifacts.

### Dam & Winikoff

Dam and Winikoff (2003) provide an attribute-based evaluation of the three methodologies MaSE, Tropos and Prometheus. To promote objectivity, information from the authors of the methodologies are included into the evaluation as well as an experimental evaluation. The authors claim that other evaluations can suffer from subjective views, since the selection of criteria influence the result of the evaluation.

## 6.6 Summary

The Unified Modeling Language (UML) is the de jure standard in object-oriented software modeling. It is also a well-accepted standard. It provides a large set of techniques for the modeling at different stages and for different points of view. A general distinction can be made between structural and behavioral modeling. In the first part of this chapter two diagram types are presented as representatives to show the modeling capabilities of UML. These are the Class Diagrams and the Sequence Diagrams.

Although UML is widely accepted in the context of object-oriented development, this does not imply that it fits also in the context of agent-oriented development, as Padgham and Winikoff (2004) point out.

> Is it not possible to use object-oriented techniques to build agent systems? The short answer is 'Not well!'.
>
> (Padgham and Winikoff 2004, p. 22)

Agent Interaction Protocol Diagrams are an extended variant of Sequence Diagrams. These diagrams, which are part of the Agent UML (AUML), are proposed to overcome the restrictions of Sequence Diagrams by introducing control flow elements.

In Section 6.4 the modeling techniques of several agent-oriented methodologies/approaches are presented. Regarding interactions and organizational structures, there exist many similarities between the presented techniques of the various methodologies. The influences of the two major UML diagram types in the modeling of agent-oriented methodologies/approaches are also clearly observable. This can be regarded as a form of continuation, since the methodologies in agent-oriented software engineering are regarded as extensions to object-oriented software engineering. It is also the declared strategy in AUML to adopt appropriate techniques from other areas (i.e. UML) and develop new techniques if no suitable ones can be found. A similar observation can be made with the other presented methodologies, most obvious in AML.

# 7 Summary

This part presents an introduction to modeling, abstractions and views as the basis to this work. Agent-technology is presented in general and the reference net-based reference architecture MULAN is presented as a formalized version of a FIPA-compliant framework. The basis for the execution and modeling of MULAN is given with RENEW which is presented together with the high-level Petri net formalism *reference nets*. For the engineering of Petri nets, the pattern-based concept of net components is introduced together with its tool integration and an example set of net components. Finally, this part presents an overview of several sets of modeling techniques in the fields of object-orientation and agent-orientation.

In software engineering, various modeling techniques are used throughout a variety of approaches, methodologies and paradigms. For object-orientation, UML is well-established while in the agent-oriented community many variants of modeling techniques exist, most of which are based on UML or likewise languages.

Most of the concrete sets of modeling techniques (modeling language, often defined within a methodology) are tightly coupled with special agent frameworks and inspired by them. In most cases the aim is to support the unique or special features of the agent framework with adapted/suitable modeling techniques.

This work acknowledges that the reference net formalism is strong in regard to the modeling of structured systems. The common attributes of Petri nets, locality of execution and concurrency, are accompanied by the nesting aspect (see the nets-within-nets paradigm by Valk (1998)). Reference nets offer, additionally, the creation of net instances, a powerful synchronization feature for the communication between elements and a tight *Java* integration.

Although the general structuring abilities of reference net models are powerful – or maybe because of their power, the models do not, per se, have a good (clear, useful) structure. Moreover, the dynamics of the structure in reference nets model can lead to uncontrollable effects. Here the MULAN reference model offers an infrastructure that is built after the FIPA specifications and is furthermore strongly influenced by socionics (see v. Lüde et al. (2009), v. Lüde et al. (2003) and the project page Asko (2005)). The reference model harnesses the structuring power of reference nets into a clear and controllable, albeit still very dynamic structure, which is organized in four layers: infrastructure, platforms, agents and agent-internal elements. By this the systems that are built follow a clear and systematic structure, and the structures of these systems become understandable and manageable for the developers. CAPA provides the technical extension that offers inter-platform communication for real world distributed systems. It thus extends MULAN to a full-fletched FIPA-compliant agent platform. With this MULAN/CAPA framework it is possible to construct concurrent and distributed systems as multi-agent applications.

On the micro level, i.e. the internal processes of the agents, the structure and systematized approach of constructing these processes is provided by the concept of net components. They provide a conventionalized structure for designed net models and ease their handling. They enable us to construct a large amount of large-scale application-specific process models, i.e. protocol nets and decision components, in an engineering manner

Missing still, is the systematic and structured approach. With PAOSE an approach is emerging that addresses the concerns of multi-agent application development on the ground of Petri nets within the MULAN/CAPA framework. The approach allows concurrency and distribution in the developed system as well as in the development system. For the MULAN reference model (and the MULAN/CAPA framework) so far no suitable modeling language exists. MULAN offers several unique features, which hinder the direct adoption of a given modeling language. Especially the implementation as high-level Petri net models requires specialized techniques. The two outstanding points are the graphical representation of executable models/implementation artifacts and the integration of true concurrency as first-order concept.

In the following part, a set of modeling techniques for the PAOSE approach is presented and its embedding in the PAOSE approach outlined. Several aspects of the development process as well as the description of the organizational structure of the PAOSE development projects and its guiding metaphor are described as well.

# Part II

# Constructive Modeling and the Design Process

This part presents the PAOSE modeling techniques and the supporting tools. Additionally, in order to embed the presented modeling techniques into the context, some basics of the development approach, the followed principles, the processes that lead to model creation, the team organization and the guiding metaphor suitable for the presented approach are discussed in brief. In this part, the focus lies on the presentation of the modeling techniques and their application in the constructive design process together with the description of the supporting tools.

Chapter 8 proposes the *multi-agent system of developers* metaphor as guiding metaphor for agent-oriented development in general and PAOSE development in particular. The guiding metaphor eases the team integration and coordination and offers a self-image of the development team for the orientation of the individual developer. Chapter 9 introduces the system (matrix) organization and the development team (matrix) organization as well as the modeling techniques applied during the constructive design of a multi-agent application. Modeling techniques for the following purposes are presented: the *coarse design*, the design of the *application structure* and *agents' knowledge*, the *terminology*, the *agent-internal processes* and the *communicative behavior* (*social behavior*). While this chapter introduces the modeling techniques and gives an overview of them, the following chapters describe each modeling technique and present the supporting tools. As the first detailed description of a modeling technique, Chapter 10 introduces the Coarse Design Diagram, which models a coarse overview of the system using the syntax of Use Case Diagram, while applying a different semantics. Chapter 11 presents the R/D Diagram (roles & dependencies) which defines the agent roles' inter-dependencies as well as the agent roles' initial knowledge as agent role descriptions (ARD). These agent role descriptions (fragments of knowledge bases) are merged to form the initial knowledge bases for the agents that own the defined roles. The supporting tool (the KBE, Knowledge Base Editor Plugin) also supports the definition of the agent-roles relationships. In this chapter another similar technique together with a supporting tool is presented as an alternative approach to model agents' service dependencies. The focus of the technique lies on a round-trip engineering approach that allows not only to define knowledge bases but also to extract models from already designed multi-agent applications. Chapter 12 presents the modeling of the application-specific ontology as simplified Class Diagrams. Chapter 13 presents the Agent Interaction Protocol Diagrams (AIP), which are used to model the communicative behavior of the agents. Chapter 14 describes how agent internal processes can be built through decision components.

# 8 Multi-Agent System: A Guiding Metaphor for the Organization of Software Development Projects

This chapter presents a guiding metaphor that is capable to dynamically adapt to the needs of the PAOSE team and development processes. Criteria for a powerful and acceptable metaphor are its simplicity, flexibility and the range of the commonly known concepts. It should take account of the main concepts and design objectives of the developed system; e.g. the multi-agent application concepts such as distribution, concurrency and dynamical structures.

The context of the metaphor the *multi-agent system of developers* is presented in Section 8.1. Section 8.2 introduces the term *guiding metaphor* and explains the guiding metaphor *multi-agent system of developers*[1] for the development of multi-agent-based projects in detail. Section 8.3 describes the application and our experiences with this guiding metaphor. Section 8.4 presents related work, and Section 8.5 summarizes the chapter.

## 8.1 Context

Multi-agent systems are applications based on encapsulated, autonomous software entities that can flexibly achieve their objectives by interacting with one another in terms of high-level interaction protocols and languages. Agents balance their reactive behavior in response to influences from the environment with their proactive behavior towards the achievement of design objectives.

The agent-orientation paradigm demands adapted development techniques that support the unique features of multi-agent systems, such as adaptability, distribution and concurrency. Traditional software development techniques, such as, for example, object-oriented analysis and design, are inadequate to capture the flexibility and autonomy of an agent's problem-solving capabilities, the richness of agent interactions and the (social) organizational structure of a multi-agent system as a whole. Many agent-oriented software development methodologies have been brought forward over the last years, many of them already in mature state.

Agent-oriented development methodologies, such as Gaia (see Wooldridge et al. (2000), Zambonelli et al. (2003)), MaSE (see DeLoach (2005)) or Prometheus (see Padgham

---

[1]We include all participants of a development process, such as programmers, users, supporting staff, etc. We could thus also call the metaphor *multi-agent system of participants* but in the context of system development we regard all participants as developers of the system.

and Winikoff (2002b)), are well-established. Similarities can be found in methods and abstractions such as use cases, system structure (organization) diagrams, role models, interaction diagrams and interaction protocols. However, it is not a trivial task to decide on a suitable implementation platform as pointed out by Braubach et al. (2004).

Similar claims hold for the management of development processes, the organization and guidance of a team as well as for project management. In the same manner as for methodologies and techniques of software development, there exists a necessity to develop approaches for the management of projects that particularly fit the agent-oriented paradigm. As already proposed by Petrie et al. (1999) the organization of projects can be oriented towards the agent concept. The proposal here is to increase even more the symmetry between the project management and the software being built.

## 8.2 Leitbild: MAS

Before we start with our approach, we will elaborate on the notion of the *guiding metaphor*. Then we will describe the guiding metaphor of a *multi-agent system of developers* in regard to three aspects. First, we describe the guiding metaphor in more details in its role as a Leitbild (Züllighoven 2005) regarding orientation, notions, strategies and terminology in the environment of multi-agent application development. Second, we go into details of the guiding metaphor's manifestation in the organizational structure of a (multi-agent application) development project especially in regard to concurrent and distributed development. Third, we focus on communication, coordination, project organization and team management.

### 8.2.1 Guiding Metaphor

A guiding metaphor (German: *Leitbild*) is a strong and well-established concept that can guide the participants of a development team in a general sense. While the term originated in business management, it is also well-established in software engineering. A guiding metaphor should have four functions. It should offer orientation and have a strong integrative force, support decision processes and also be a means of coordination. Züllighoven et al. define a guiding metaphor as follows.

> For our purposes, a *guiding metaphor* is a basic viewpoint that helps us perceive, understand, and design a piece of reality.
>
> In software development, a guiding metaphor provides a common orientation for all participating groups throughout the development process. It supports the design, use, and evaluation of software and is based on value concepts and objectives. A guiding metaphor can have a constructive or an analytical function.

(Züllighoven 2005, p. 59)

An important feature is that the guiding metaphor is so general and common that every potentially involved person has at least a good idea of the organizational concepts, structures, notions and rules. A good guiding metaphor comes with a whole set of other metaphors that do not have to be named explicitly.[2] In the context of developing software we can distinguish three different forms of guiding metaphor. It can be used to characterize the software systems, the development process and also the team organization (or project management).[3]

Examples of guiding metaphors are the *factory* and the *expert work place* in the *Tools & Material* approach (see Lippert et al. (2003) and Züllighoven (2005)) for software systems. Guiding metaphors for team organizations are *the factory, the office, the workshop* or the *free jazz band* (the last by Wikström and Rehn (2002)).

One interesting approach to define a new guiding metaphor for team organization has been done by Mack (2001). He proposes the guiding metaphor of an *expedition* for the development process and derives some aspects that are useful in everyday (work) life of a software developer. Here we will not go into details of this guiding metaphor, but we would like to elaborate on the notions that are instantly linked to this example in order to show the potentials of a guiding metaphor.

For a (development) expedition one will need a team (developers, supporting users and other staff) and resources (computers, software, rooms, paper, etc.). There should be a good notion of how much everyone can carry (individual capabilities of team members) on the way. The organizers need to work out a plan in advance that is detailed enough to take as many aspects as possible into account and flexible enough to allow the team members to react to sudden changes and dangers. In an expedition it seems clear that all members have to support each another and that conflicts that are left unsolved can lead to difficulties that can endanger the expedition (software project). A good communication between members of the team is essential at all stages of the expedition. We know that an expedition is a socially challenging project that can be adventurous as well as hard work. In addition, in the beginning the outcome of an expedition is open.

The example shows that a strong guiding metaphor offers many notions (common in the team) and a multitude of metaphors. These help team members to find orientation in the project and by this the guiding metaphor succeeds in guiding a team.

In the following sections we describe a guiding metaphor that is well-applicable to the development of multi-agent applications and is also well-known in the multi-agent community. It is the multi-agent system.

## 8.2.2 Multi-Agent System of Developers

Our approach of organizing projects for multi-agent application development is described by the guiding metaphor of *multi-agent system of developers*. Developer teams, their members and their actions are characterized by the attributes usually related to agents (see Wooldridge and Jennings (1995)), multi-agent systems (see Ferber (1999)) and also cooperative workflows (WfMC 2005).[4] In the team, members are acting in a self-

---

[2]In this way the guiding metaphor is related to an *extended metaphor* or a *parable* as used in literature.

[3]In this work we focus on the function of the guiding metaphor for the team's organizational structures/project management.

[4]In the following many agent concepts are used to describe behaviors or attributes of members of the development team. These are used for the metaphorical power.

organized, autonomous, independent and cooperative way. They all have individual goals that culminate in a common vision of the system that is to be developed.

Like agents in a multi-agent system, developers are situated in an environment, in which they communicate with other developers and other participants of the development process. Moreover, the environment offers services or restricts the possibilities of action for the developers.

## Multi–Agent System of Developers

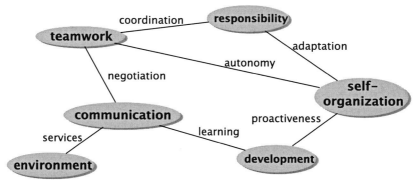

Figure 8.1: Agent concepts used in the context of team organization (selection).

Figure 8.1 shows a selection of typical multi-agent concepts and their inter-relationships that are utilized in the development project context as metaphors. As shown in the figure, Lippert et al. (2003) identify a selection of key metaphors as a metaphor design space.

The agent metaphor leads to dynamic and flexible structures in the team's organization. All members can form (sub-)teams with other members during the development process. This is not only encouraged but also a main aspect of the self-responsible and autonomous actions of team members. The structure of a team is not static. Sub-teams are able to decide their own dissolution and to proactively decide on new alliances. From this point of view concurrent and distributed work is a natural phenomenon.

According to the *multi-agent system of developers* metaphor, control, project management and organizational matters in the development process are managed through mechanisms typically owned by social agents (v. Lüde, Spresny and Valk 2003). Thus, social norms, conventions and motivation become important forces in the team's behavioral patterns.

At first glance it seems odd to re-transfer the concept (metaphor) of a multi-agent system, which has been used to define and organize software systems in the manner of (sociological) organizations, back to an organizational structure of people. However, the metaphor of a multi-agent system has grown so strong in recent years that many developers are well-acquainted with the notions and key elements of agent concepts. Therefore, the multi-agent system is a reasonable, well-established and powerful guiding metaphor. But even for participants of the team that do not share the concepts of multi-agent systems as paradigm – e.g. users with no technical background – still all the concepts are well-known, since they are rooted in social organizations.

In the following two sections we elaborate on two main aspects of agent-oriented development. These are the communication of agents and the concurrency and distribution. Through the guiding metaphor both aspects take a leading role in our vision of the project organization.

### 8.2.3 Matrix Organization

In a multi-agent application development project the organizational structure has to be defined, so that responsibilities for certain aspects can be assumed by team members or sub-teams. The general perspectives in the area of a multi-agent system and – therefore also here – for the development process are *structure*, *behavior* and *terminology*. These perspectives are orthogonal with connecting points at some intersections (compare Figure 8.2).

The structure of a multi-agent system is given by the agents, their roles, knowledge bases and decision components (compare with Chapter 4.3 and Köhler et al. (2001), Rölke (2004)). The behavior of a multi-agent system is given by the interactions of the agents, their communicative acts and the internal actions related to the interactions (see Cabac et al. (2003)). The terminology of a multi-agent system is given as a domain-specific ontology that enables agents to refer to the same objects, actions and facts. The agents' common ontology is crucial for their successful interactions.

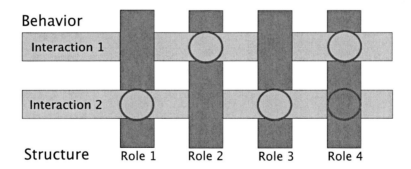

Figure 8.2: Two dimensional matrix showing perspectives (*behavior, structure*).

A schematic two dimensional matrix is depicted in Figure 8.2 showing the independence and interconnections of agent roles and interactions. Neither is there any direct relationship between any pair of agent roles, nor between any pair of interactions. Thus these architectural elements are independent and drawn in parallel to each other. Roles and interactions are orthogonal because each agent is involved in some interactions and vice versa. When an agent role and an interaction are coupled, a circle marks the interconnection point.

The general case for any two structural and/or behavioral elements is independence. In the diagram interconnections are explicitly marked. The ontology, which is omitted in the diagram, is the third dimension of perspectives. This perspective is orthogonal to the other two perspectives, but it tends to have many interconnection points because each interaction and each agent needs parts of the ontology definition to fulfill its purpose.

Since the three perspectives are orthogonal and the elements of a perspective are independent, it is easily possible to divide the tasks of design and implementation into independent perspectives and independent parts. This means that different interactions can be developed by independent sub-teams and different agent roles can be designed by other independent sub-teams. Between agent role teams and interaction teams, coordination is needed for the crucial parts only (circles). Following this method, the different parts of the system can be developed independently and concurrently as long as there is enough coordination/synchronization between intersecting groups.

In general it is not a good idea to assign tasks of orthogonal dimensions to the same sub-team because the responsibilities of the different dimensions might then become blurred. However, developers are well-advised to look for similarities between independent elements of the same dimension, like for example a set of similar interactions. In such a situation, code reuse becomes possible if a sub-team is responsible for multiple parallel elements.

The (agent-based) software system imposes its matrix structure onto the team organization. In the metaphor of *multi-agent system of developers* this is naturally supported.

### 8.2.4 Communication, Coordination and Synchronization

We can identify four main task types when applying the guiding metaphor of a *multi-agent system of developers* to the time schedule: (1) the requirements analysis, (2) the (coarse) design of ontology/roles/interactions, (3) the concurrent and highly interactive implementation of ontology/agents/interactions and (4) an intense and concurrent integration and testing phase. The time schedule is iterative in all task types. However, in normal settings iterations in task types two, three and four would suffice.[5]

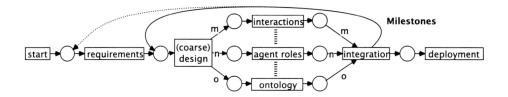

Figure 8.3: Schematic Petri net model of the PAOSE development process.

Figure 8.3 shows a schematic Petri net model of the development process. The design

---

[5]Note that the development process is described in more detail in Section 9.2.1. Here the task types and the process are only presented to describe the context, in which the communication has to take place.

phase results in several independent tasks for interaction, agent and ontology implementation.

The synchronizations between concurrent processes during implementation in the form of communication between the groups have to be supported during development, both through synchronous and asynchronous communication. This is achieved by physical meetings (synchronous), through (web-based) tool support (synchronous and asynchronous) and implicit communication in documentation of activities and code (asynchronous). At the end of the implementation phase a thorough integration phase is necessary to obtain a milestone/running system. Each phase in itself is a process with its own structure.

While the processes of independent activities are concurrent, some synchronizations are necessary during implementation between orthogonal groups (gray arrows). Also phase shifts should be coordinated. This is implied in Figure 8.3 and explicitly shown at integration, which should be entered synchronously by the whole team.

All team members are attributed the sociality of communicating agents. The team structure is self-organized and controlled through participating developers by observation, negotiation, rules and norms.

Awareness of participants is an important factor in avoiding problems resulting from faulty coordination. Unfortunately, the support for user awareness in our tool set is not sufficient yet. Thus, we have to compensate with extensive communication about changes in design and implementation. Nevertheless, some simple elements in our communication platform exist, which enable us to track recent changes. Improvements are being discussed.

# 8.3 MAS of Developers in Project Contexts

The concept of the guiding metaphor has to be backed up with the utilization in the context of a multi-agent application development project. Here the guiding metaphor can unveil its usefulness.

## 8.3.1 Employing the Guiding Metaphor

Following the guiding metaphor of *multi-agent system of developers*, project organizers or initiators will be able to anticipate the needs of the team members during the development. Good equipment, enough resources and an adequate team composition are essential to any project. Here also the means of communication, coordination, learning, reorganization and the possibility to take responsibility are important parts in the development process. These processes have to be supported by adequate means, for example regular meetings for direct communication and teamwork sessions and/or a (web-based) communication system for asynchronous (and synchronous) communication. These communication means have to be integrated into the environment (platform) of the developers (agents).

The organizers have a powerful means to guide the actions, the way of thinking and the general behavior of participants in the context of the project. Here the main responsibility is that the metaphor is well-conveyed to all participants. If all participants have a good notion of agent concepts, everyone will be able to live the metaphor (and the team will profit from that). This means that all participants are aware of the fact that participation (coordination, negotiation) in the development process and in the decision processes of team members as well as the possibility for the team to exercise the sociological prosperity is of importance. The ease of the adaptation to the guiding metaphor – borrowed from sociological theories about organizations – can lead to higher motivation, integration and identification with the group and the common goals which in turn leads to quicker orientation in the project and higher productivity.

In addition to the metaphor's inherent organizational powers, the developers can benefit from a structural organization of the development process that resembles the structure of the developed system.

## 8.3.2 Homomorphic Structure

The advantages to work with a homomorphic – similar – structure in software organization and project organization are manifold. In general, they are the same advantages as those of multi-agent systems over conventional paradigms.

The multi-agent system organization of the development team allows and supports distributed as well as concurrent development. In this context it is important that developers act self-responsibly and consider self-reorganization if necessary. Structures in the team should emerge from the processes during development. Thus independence and flexibility as well as means for communication and mobility are supported in this approach as first-order concepts. One main advantage of the similar structure used for the developed software – and a successful project – is that the same principles, concepts and organization also help the developers to design a truly agent-oriented software system. Distribution, autonomy and concurrency in the organizational structure will automatically foster the same attributes in the designed system.

Figure 8.4 depicts the developed system (e.g. Settler[6]), the development system (e.g. the PAOSE development team) and the (formalized) MAS metaphor. In both systems we identify organizational structures and processes. The process of a software system is obvious, the process of the development team is the development process (here schematically depicted as Petri net). Input of this process is the application model and the requirements, which are produced in the system as well. The output of the development process is the software (here a multi-agent application). By applying the same principles for the organizational structures and for the processes for both systems, we achieve a similar structure in those two quite different systems. Some disadvantages also exist and – not surprisingly – these are the same disadvantages as those of multi-agent systems again. To succeed with the project by employing the *multi-agent system of developers* metaphor, a strong emphasis on communication and adaptive processes has to be made. This leads to a large communication overhead. Due to the flexible and dynamical organization, the inherent concurrency and distribution, the complexity of the project organization is very high. This leads to more management overhead (compared to a

---

[6]The Settler GUI serves as placeholder for an application, see also Chapter 22.

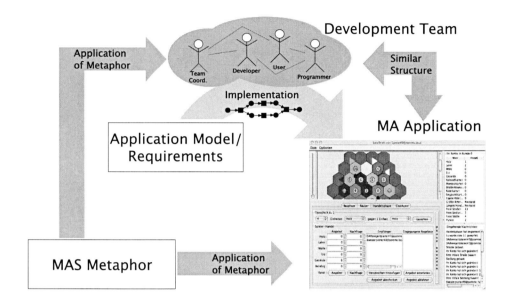

Figure 8.4: Multiple applications of the MAS metaphor to processes/systems.

non-distributed and non-concurrent development).

### 8.3.3 Experiences

Especially in our teaching projects the guiding metaphor of *multi-agent system of developers* works extremely fine. This results to some extent from the fact that our students have a well-founded background knowledge of basic and advanced agent concepts. Usually these concepts are conveyed through conceptualized object Petri net models, which have a strong graphical representation for concurrency, locality and hierarchical nesting.

The main aims of multi-agent system development (concurrent, independent development) are reached with the support of the guiding metaphor. However, it is still useful to gather the source code in a central repository, even if parts of the system are run exclusively in disjunct places. This eases the deployment of system and framework.

In addition, common elements have to be made available to all members. Many documents like overview diagrams (multi-agent system structure) or ontology definitions as well as models are also still designed in a central (non-distributed) fashion. Here, still more flexibility can be added to the development process. However, it is not essential to work concurrently (or independently) on these elements, since the ontology for instance is meant to be common to all agents as well as to all developers. Moreover, these *central* specification elements (especially ontology) can be used by the project leaders in order to actively control the direction of the development. The software MAS ontology becomes a common language for the developer MAS as well.

Many improvements in support of the development team, communication means and increase of flexibility are possible and the extent of the guiding metaphor has not reached its limits yet. We would like to include direct and indirect communication, inline documentation and workflow capabilities into our development environments (RENEW, see Section 3.3 and Kummer et al. (2009a); MULAN, see Chapter 4 and Köhler et al. (2001), Köhler et al. (2003), Rölke (2004); Eclipse, `http://www.eclipse.org`) to better support the interactive means of the developers in their environment. Web-based documentation and groupware features can also be more heavily exploited.

## 8.4 Related Work

### Petrie, Goldmann & Raquet

Petrie et al. (1999) propose agent-oriented project management. They introduce agent concepts and agent technology to cope with the management of distributed and/or large-scale projects, e.g. software development projects. Although the aim is – in particular – to support flexibility, they do not explicitly propose any guiding metaphor for the development process. The agent-orientation manifests itself in the conceptual modeling and the tool support.

### Mack

Mack (2001) describes a novel, powerful and also exotic guiding metaphor for the development of software: the *expedition*. Especially the adventurous aspects of uncertainty but also collaboration and team spirit are required of the team members. There exist several similarities to the *multi-agent system of developers*. The main difference is that the *multi-agent system of developers* is formalized through the multi-agent system model, which is influenced by sociological theories.

### Winkström & Rehn

Wikström and Rehn (2002) offer another exotic guiding metaphor for the project organization: the *playing of live Jazz*. Typical attributes are improvisation and the focus on the performance of the individuals. Most notable, in comparison to the *multi-agent system of developers* metaphor, is that the authors claim as a central point that *order is emergent, not pre-defined*, which fits very nicely the adaptability of agents and the emergence of structure in multi-agent systems.

### Züllighoven

Züllighoven (2005) presents several guiding metaphors in general. From the various explicit and implicit guiding metaphors in software development, the author chooses to present the guiding metaphors *Object Worlds*, *Direct Manipulation*, *Factory* and *Expert Workspace* as examples. He describes the *Expert Workplace* as a suitable guiding metaphor for the *Tools and Material* (*T&M*) approach. It is concretized by a set of design metaphors.

## 8.5 Summary

This chapter presents a guiding metaphor for the organization of (multi-agent) application development projects. The guiding metaphor itself is taken from agent technologies. It is the multi-agent system metaphor applied to the team of developers (and other participants). By this self-reflective view on the organization of development teams, a coherent structure in all parts of the system and all processes is defined.

Guiding metaphors are well-suited to give a common orientation in a development team. Through its origination from socio-organizational structures, its generality, its ease of accessibility and its recognition of distribution, the multi-agent system is well suited to serve as the guiding metaphor for project organization. We believe that it is an especially powerful metaphor when it comes to multi-agent application development. And in the spirit of this guiding metaphor, we believe that the organizational structure and the team notion of the guiding metaphor itself is subject to change, adaptation, self-organization and emergence. Thus the power of the metaphor will improve during the development process.

The principle behind the usage of guiding metaphors can add to the socio-organizational processes in the development team. Thus, the project managers have a powerful concept tool[7] that enables guidance on an abstract level.

With the organization of the development team as a multi-agent system, we have achieved agent-oriented software engineering (AOSE) in two ways. In the original meaning of the term *agent-oriented software engineering*, the software system is the objective. In our approach, the development team is also oriented (guided) by the multi-agent system metaphor.

---

[7]A tool or concept to guide and organize (or even transmit) one's thoughts. The artificial German term *Denkzeug* (Moldt 2005), a mix of *denken* (to think) and *Werkzeug* (tool), fits better.

# 9 Models for the Development of Multi-Agent Applications

The PAOSE (Petri net-based Agent-Oriented Software Engineering) approach facilitates the metaphor of multi-agent systems in a formally precise and coherent way throughout all aspects of software development as well as a concurrency-aware (Petri net-based) modeling and programming language. The metaphor of multi-agent systems is formalized by the MULAN reference architecture presented in Section 4, which is modeled using reference nets (see Section 3). PAOSE integrates several ideas from other methodologies as well as concepts from conventional modeling techniques (UML). The result of those efforts is a development methodology that continuously integrates our philosophy of Petri net-based and model-driven software engineering in the context of multi-agent systems.

This chapter focuses on an overview of the modeling techniques used within the PAOSE approach and its integration in the sketched approach. The following chapters of this part then elaborate on each modeling technique.

Section 9.1 outlines the context of the modeling techniques in the PAOSE approach. In Section 9.2 we introduce the basic conceptual features of multi-agent application development with PAOSE and MULAN/CAPA. The particular techniques, models and tools are introduced in Section 9.3. Section 9.4 provides a brief summary of this chapter.

## 9.1 Context

The agent metaphor is highly abstract and it is necessary to develop software engineering techniques and methodologies that particularly fit the agent-oriented paradigm. They must capture the flexibility and autonomy of an agent's problem-solving capabilities, the richness of agent interactions and the (social) organizational structure of a multi-agent system as a whole.

Many agent-oriented software development methodologies and modeling techniques have been brought forward over the past decade, many of them already in a mature state. The following sections present our contribution to this rapidly evolving field of research by describing agent models and their usage during the development of multi-agent systems with PAOSE/MULAN (Multi-Agent Nets, see Köhler et al. (2001)). As a matter of course there exist many analogies to related agent-oriented development techniques and methodologies like Gaia by Zambonelli et al. (2003), MaSE by DeLoach (2005) or Prometheus by Padgham and Winikoff (2002b). This concerns development methods and abstractions like use cases, system structure (organization) diagrams, role models, interaction diagrams and interaction protocols as well as more fine-grained models of agents' internal events, data structures and decision making capabilities.

Reference nets[1] and thus also MULAN run in the virtual machine provided by RENEW (see Chapter 3), which also includes an editor and runtime support for several kinds of Petri nets. Since reference nets may carry complex *Java* expressions as inscriptions and thereby offer the possibility of Petri net-based programming, the MULAN models have been extended to a fully elaborated and running software architecture, the FIPA[2]-compliant extension CAPA by Duvigneau et al. (2003).

Reference nets can be regarded as a concurrency extension to *Java*, which allows for easy implementation of concurrent systems in regard to modeling (implementation) and synchronization aspects. Those – often tedious – aspects of implementation regarding concurrency are handled by the formalism as well as by the underlying virtual machine. In this aspect lies the advantage of our approach. We rely on a formal background, which is at the same time tightly coupled with the programming environment *Java*. MULAN can be regarded as a reference architecture for concurrent systems providing a highly structured approach using the multi-agent system metaphor.

## 9.2 Concepts of Application Development with Mulan

This section investigates, on the basis of the internal agent components (see Section 4.3), the interrelations between the agent components , which results in the organizational structure of the system. For the details of further aspects of the MULAN architecture see Chapter 4 and Rölke (2004).

### 9.2.1 Development Process

In PAOSE the development process is concurrency aware. This means that not only the developed software but also the development process are carefully designed to allow as much concurrency as possible. Thus the term *phase* – as it is often used to describe different aspects of the development process in other methodologies – does not apply any more, instead we introduce the term task types. The process can then be sketched by six task types. These are:

(1) Requirements analysis
(2) Coarse design
(3) Ontology implementation
(4) Role implementation
(5) Interaction implementation
(6) Integration

---

[1] Reference nets (see Section 3.2 and Kummer (2001)) are high-level Petri nets comparable to colored Petri nets. In addition they implement the nets-within-nets paradigm where tokens are active elements (token refinement). Reference semantics is applied, so tokens are *references* to *net instances*. *Synchronous channels* allow for communication between net instances.

[2] Foundation for Intelligent Physical Agents `http://www.fipa.org`.

Requirements analysis in distributed environment and/or agent-oriented software engineering is a topic that is not investigated in depth in this work. We refer do other works, such as that of Gumm (2008). Instead we acknowledge that there is a desire to build a system that leads to a vision of a system-to-be, which leads into the development process.

These requirements lead initially to a very coarse vision of what should be the parts of the system (system organization) and what are the processes within that system. To concretize these visions of the individual participants and to achieve a common unified image of what is to be done, the developers model a system overview in the coarse design task (type).

The produced model in this phase is the result of a discussion of all participants. It shows the envisioned agent roles and interactions as well as the relationships of these elements, i.e. which role participates in which interaction. In this phase also first design decisions regarding the terminology / ontology, responsibilities and abilities of agent roles are made. The model is concretized as a list of roles, a list of interactions, a list of concepts for the ontology and the interrelations. The interrelations are modeled as a table and as a coarse design diagram.

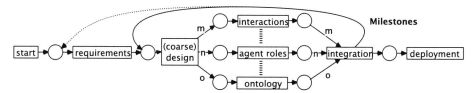

Figure 9.1: The PAOSE development process sketched as a Petri net
(Repetition of Figure 8.3).

The coarse design diagram holds already the organizational structure for the multi-agent application. Thus the tasks can be directly derived. There will be $n$ role modeling tasks $m$ interaction modeling tasks and $o$ ontology related tasks. All tasks can then be approached concurrently. This is sketched in Figure 9.1. Note that all role, interaction and ontology tasks types are independent (concurrent) from other tasks of types roles, interaction and ontology. However, the concurrency is restricted, which is indicated by the dotted lines between interactions, roles and ontology tasks. This means that the implementing developers have to agree on a common interface, e.g. for the roles that participate in an interaction. During integration the independently developed system artifacts are assembled, their inter-connectivity tested and possible errors found, located and fixed (debugged). The outcome of the integration are milestones of prototypes that allow the developers – together with the experience gained during integration – to reconsider their previous design. We conceive the process iterative within each task type as well as over the process (indicated by the backwards arcs in the Petri net).

## 9.2.2 Design Artifacts

The design artifacts (deliverables) are listed in Figure 9.2 subject to the task types and significance of the process.

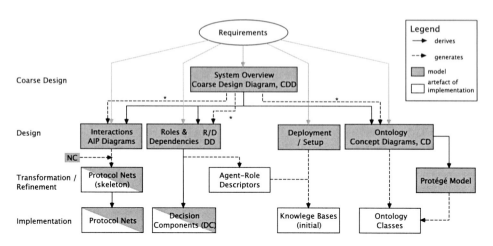

Figure 9.2: The design artifacts in the PAOSE approach and their dependencies.

Models – or to be more precise: diagrams – are displayed with gray boxes while the executables (*Java* code, XML files,... ) are displayed as white boxes. Petri nets are considered executable diagrams, hence the bicolored boxes. Solid arcs indicate artifacts that are derived from other artifacts, dashed lines indicate generated artifacts.

The first diagram will be the coarse design diagram (sometimes also called system overview diagram). It contains already the lists of roles and interactions. From this diagram skeletons for the models for interactions, roles and ontology are generated. Each model then generates either directly usable code (agent role descriptors, ontology classes) or skeletons of Petri net models (protocol nets) that can be modified to receive an executable. Only decision components are designed manually.[3]

For the software deployment or setup there exist several approaches so far. The configuration can be defined within the coarse design diagram, the setup can be coded as startup script, a configuration utility (within the KBE[4]) sets up a XML-based configuration file (or even sets up a running system) or the setup is done by an agent within the system.

---

[3]For the modeling of decision components several proposals exist. However, the techniques are not mature and no supporting tools exist. Thus – for now – DCs are modeled directly in the reference net formalism.

[4]The Knowledge Base Editor will be described together with the R/D diagram modeling technique in Chapter 11.1.

# 9.3  Techniques, Models and Tools

In this section we describe the techniques applied during the various stages of multi-agent application development with MULAN. An agent-based Workflow Management System (WFMS) serves as an example application to provide real world models. However, the WFMS is not the objective in this chapter. It will, together with the Settler application, appear in the other chapters as a resource for example models. In Chapter 22 their development is discussed and several more models are presented.

We present the applied techniques and resulting models starting with the coarse design giving an overview over the system, continuing with the definition of the structure of the multi-agent application, the ontology and the behavior of the agents.

## 9.3.1  Coarse Design

The requirements analysis is done mainly in open discussions. The results are captured in simple lists of system components and agent interactions. This culminates in a Coarse Design Diagram as shown in Figure 9.3. Of course other methods to derive use cases can also be applied.

A Coarse Design Diagram in the form of a Use Case Diagram is especially useful to derive the multi-agent application matrix because we can intuitively depict agent roles in the system as actors in the diagram. In contrast, usually in use case models the actors represent real world users.

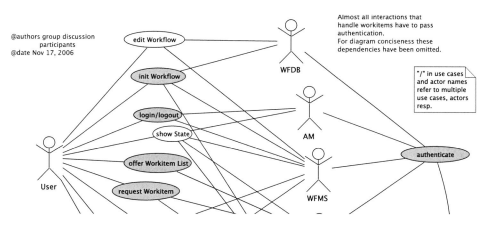

Figure 9.3: Coarse Design Diagram showing the system overview: WFMS.

Figure 9.3 shows a fragment of the Coarse Design Diagram of the agent-based workflow management system (WFMS, see also Figure 10.1). In detail, it shows the Account Manager (AM) role, the Workflow Data Base (WFDB) role, the Workflow Management System (WFMS) role and the User role together with several interactions. Already the Coarse Design Diagram reveals the matrix structure in two dimensions. Agent roles form the multi-agent application structure while interactions form the behavior of the system.

Arcs in the diagram correspond to the matrix interconnection points from Section 8.2.3. Coarse Design Diagrams are drawn directly in RENEW. The Use Case Plugin provides the functionality by adding a palette of drawing tools to the editor.

The Use Case Plugin integrates a generator feature, which generates the complete folder structure of the application necessary for the implementation of a multi-agent application. This includes a standard source package folder structure, skeletons for all agent interactions, role diagram and ontology files as well as configuration files and build / start scripts. The generator utilizes the Velocity[5] template engine.

## 9.3.2 Multi-Agent Application Structure

The structure of the multi-agent application is refined using a R/D Diagram (Roles/Dependencies Diagram). This kind of diagram uses features from Class Diagrams and Component Diagrams. Class Diagrams provide inheritance arcs to denote role hierarchies. Component Diagrams provide explicit nodes for services as well as arcs with *uses* and *offers* semantics to denote dependencies between roles. Initial values for role-specific knowledge bases are included through refinement of nodes.

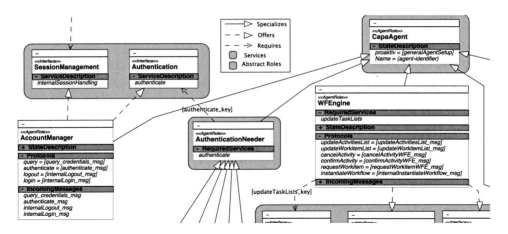

Figure 9.4: Fragment of a R/D Diagram (agents, roles, services).

Figure 9.4 shows a fragment of the WFMS R/D Diagram. The fragment depicts several roles marked «AgentRole»: CapaAgent, AuthenticationNeeder, AccountManager and WFEngine. Also some services marked «Interface» are depicted: SessionManagement, Authentication etc. As an example, the service Authentication is offered by the AccountManager and used by each agent that holds the role AuthenticationNeeder.

The agent role descriptions are automatically generated from the R/D Diagram. Role descriptions are combined to form agent descriptions (initial knowledge bases). Roles can easily be assembled to form the multi-agent application using the graphical user interface.

---

[5]The Apache Velocity Project `http://velocity.apache.org/`

The multi-agent application is started either from within the tool, by a startup script or by a Petri net.

### 9.3.3 Terminology

The terminology of a multi-agent system is used in a twofold way. First, it is used in the form of an ontology definition by the agents to communicate with each another and for their internal representation of the environment. Second, it is used among the developers to communicate about the system and its design.

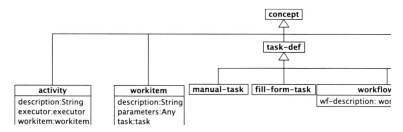

Figure 9.5: Fragment of the WFMS ontology.

To define the ontology of our multi-agent applications we have been using Protégé[6] since 2005. Ontologies are defined in Protégé and then translated by a generator into *Java* classes. Protégé is a very powerful tool, but it features a completely different user interface design than RENEW.

The RENEW feature structure plugin allows to explicitly model the ontology as a Concept Diagram as shown in Figure 9.5. These are Class Diagrams restricted to inheritance and association. The Concept Diagrams can easily be understood by all sub-teams to capture the context of the concepts in use.

The translation of models from the feature structure concepts to Protégé ontologies is a manual task. The Protégé model can then be used to generate the *Java* ontology classes. Alternatively, a prototypical implementation of an ontology classes generator (directly) from Concept Diagrams exists.

### 9.3.4 Knowledge and Decisions

While the agent's interactive behavior is defined in the interaction protocols (see next section), the facts about its environment are located in the agent's knowledge base. The initial knowledge of the agent is defined in its initial knowledge base file, constructed by joining information from the role definitions, which have been defined in the R/D Diagram (introduced in Section 9.3.2). This XML document that can also be customized apart from the R/D Diagram is parsed to build the initial knowledge of the agent during its initialization. Alternatively, a text file in the style of properties files suffices for the same purpose.

---

[6]Protégé http://protege.stanford.edu/.

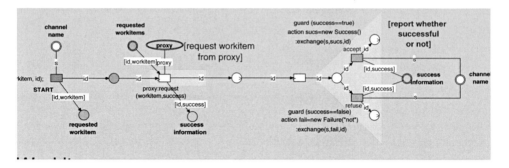

Figure 9.6: Fragment of a decision component net: RequestWorkitemHandling

Decision components (DC) are constructed as reference nets. There exists a generalized form of a DC providing GUI interface connection. Also net components (see Chapter 5 and Cabac et al. (2006e)) for the development of DCs are provided.

Figure 9.6 shows a fragment of the DC net handling the request of a user for a workitem in the workitem dispatcher agent. The net holds the proxy net which implements the interface to the workflow engine. A request starts at the left of the image and is handed over to the proxy, which holds a list of available work items for the given user. The result of the request is handed back to the DC net and passed (via the *exchange* channel) on to the requester, a protocol net, which in turn sends an appropriate message to the requesting agent.

### 9.3.5 Behavior

The interactive behavior of the system components is specified using Agent Interaction Protocol Diagrams (AIP, proposed by Odell et al. (2000), integrated in PAOSE by Cabac et al. (2003)).

Figure 9.7 depicts a fragment of an AIP involving the two roles AccountManager and WorkitemDispatcher in the authenticate interaction. Agent Interaction Protocol Diagrams are integrated in our tool set through the AIP Diagram Plugin which is also capable of generating functional skeletons for protocol nets. As described in Section 9.2, protocol nets are reference nets that directly define the behavior of a MULAN agent. Protocol nets are composed of *net components* (Cabac, Duvigneau and Rölke 2006e). Net components are also used for automatic generation of protocol net skeletons from Agent Interaction Protocol Diagrams. The protocol nets are then refined during the implementation phase by adding inscriptions to the nets. Figure 9.8 shows an example protocol net.[7] Several decisions are made after receiving a request message. Finally, the appropriate answer is sent back.

With the implementation of interactions as protocol nets, the internal processes as decision components and the knowledge bases through the description of the R/D Diagram, the whole multi-agent application is defined.

---

[7]The net components are recognizable and show the structure of the protocol net.

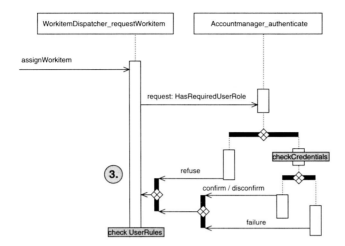

Figure 9.7: Fragment of an Agent Interaction Protocol Diagram.

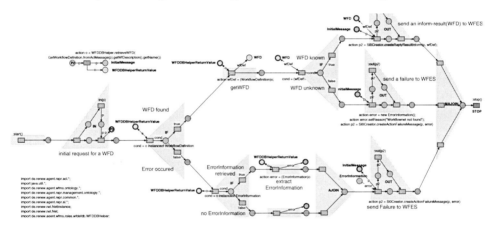

Figure 9.8: A protocol net constructed with net components.

Additionally, all diagrams presented here serve as documentation elements and are included in the API-documentation of the system (Mulandoc, see Chapter 19).

## 9.3.6 Overview of Techniques, Tasks and Tools

In the context of MULAN and PAOSE we can identify three basic dimensions in which the perspectives on the system can be categorized. *Structure* relates to roles and knowledge. *Behavior* relates to interactions and internal processes, which reflects the natural view via Petri nets onto systems with respect to behavior. *Terminology* is covered by ontologies and provides the glue between the different perspectives. Organizational embedding is covered by the matrix-like treatment, which provides the relationships between entities in the organizational context including the involved people. In addition, Table 9.1 shows a table of relations between task types, modeling techniques, applied tools and resulting artifact.

| Task | Technique | Tool | Result |
|---|---|---|---|
| Coarse Design | Coarse Design | Use Case Plugin | Plugin Structure |
| Ontology Design | Concept Diagram | FS-Nets/Protégé | Generated Classes |
| Role Design | R/D Diagram | KBE Plugin | Knowledge Bases |
| Internal Processes | Petri Net[8] | RENEW[8] | Decision components |
| Interaction Design | AIP Diagram | AIP Plugin | Protocol Nets |

Table 9.1: Overview over the contiguous techniques, tasks and tools.

### 9.3.7 Experiences

The presented approach has been applied to several teaching projects consisting of twenty to forty students, tutors and lecturers. The approach has been further developed over the years, which resulted in better tool support and further elaboration of methods and techniques (many of which were presented earlier). After a phase of learning the concepts, methods and techniques, the students were able to design and construct rather complex concurrent and distributed software systems. For example, an agent-based workflow management system (compare with Reese (2009) and Wagner (2009b)) was developed using this approach.

The results of 5 weeks of teaching and 9 weeks of implementation include about 10 agent roles, more than 20 interactions and almost 70 concepts in the ontology. The outcome is a running prototype of an distributed agent-based workflow management system, where a user is represented by an agent and basic interaction is provided through a GUI: Authentication, workflow instantiation, offering of available tasks according to application roles and task rules, accepting, cancellation and conclusion of tasks during the progress of a workflow. Workflows themselves are specified with Petri nets using a special task transition which provides cancellation and activation awareness (compare with Jacob et al. 2002). Thus synchronization and conflict solving are provided by the inherent features of the RENEW simulation engine. This example and our other previous projects show that PAOSE together with the guiding metaphor of a *multi-agent system of developers* (see Chapter 8 and Cabac 2007) enable us to develop multi-agent applications with MULAN. The developed methods and tool support have proven to be effective in supporting the development process.

---

[8]For the internal processes no abstract modeling technique has been presented. Several proposals exist, but have not resulted in tool support, yet. However, those processes can be modeled directly as reference nets in RENEW, either directly or by using the set of net components for DCs (see Section 14.3.1). Processes can also be externalized, for instance by using a generic *Java*/Net adapter (see Section 14.3.2).

# 9.4 Summary

This chapter presents an overview of the modeling techniques used within the PAOSE approach to build agent models. The tools that are used during the development process support all tasks of development with modeling power, code generation and deployment facilities. Still, some of the tools have prototypical character. Specifically, we have presented techniques to model structure, behavior and terminology of concurrent software systems in a coherent way following the multi-agent paradigm. All techniques and tools own semantics built upon the unique, concurrency-oriented modeling and programming language of reference nets, either directly or by referring to the MULAN reference architecture.

The concurrency-awareness in development process and modeling techniques distinguishes our approach from most of the methodologies mentioned in the introduction since they usually do not address true concurrency explicitly (compare with Shehory and Sturm 2001). The advantage of tight integration of abstract modeling techniques with the conceptual framework given through the formal model of MULAN is responsible for the clearness and the effectivity of our approach.

For the future, we follow several directions to refine the approach. On the practical side, we look into further developments, improvements and integration of tools and techniques. On the conceptual side, we work on expanding the multi-agent-oriented approach to other aspects of the development process like project organization and agent-oriented tool support. Following these directions, we want to achieve symmetrical structures in all three aspects of software development: the system, the development process and the project organization as described in Section 8.3.2.

Each of the following chapters presents one of the techniques, which have been introduced in this chapter, together with the corresponding tool support in detail.

# 10 Coarse Architecture of Multi-Agent Applications

Before the system can be modeled in detail the developers have to establish an overview of the system. In the context of PAOSE this has been phrased *coarse design*. For this cause we model the basic elements of the designed system in an application matrix of roles and interactions. On the one hand this matrix shows basically which roles are involved in which interactions and on the other hand it shows the participating roles for the interactions. This is an intuitive coarse perspective on the system since the roles are defined through their behavior, abilities and responsibilities. Definition of interaction behavior is one of the foremost tasks in the design phase of many common agent-oriented approaches.

The representation of the matrix can be done as simple table (spreadsheet) or as diagram. We have opted for a diagrammatic representation, which owns the syntax of Use Case Diagrams, but offers a completely different semantics and application context, i.e. it is not used in the requirements engineering phase but in the analysis/design phase. This *coarse design* allows us to intuitively model the coarse organizational structure of a multi-agent system in the early stages of construction. In addition, through the tool support we are able to generate code base skeletons for the envisioned system.

Section 10.1 outlines the context of coarse design in multi-agent systems. In Section 10.2 we describe the semantics, the approach, its integration into the development process and the resulting models. Section 10.3 offers an extensive example and discusses the presented technique in the context of our experiences and in relation to other approaches. Section 10.4 discusses related work and similar approaches. Section 10.5 introduces the tool support offered by the Use Case Plugin and Section 10.6 summaries, in brief, this chapter.

## 10.1 Context

In opposition to usual engineering approaches, which are usually top-down oriented, the agent-oriented approach is usually a bottom-up process (see Ferber (1999)). From the design of the small, detailed parts and principles, such as rules, goals and concepts of communication, emerges the organizational structure in the fused, composed system of aggregated entities and processes. This effect is often described by the sociological concept of the micro-macro link (see Köhler et al. (2005)). Especially in multi-agent-based simulation these effects are of importance and are often the main target of investigation.

In agent-oriented software engineering, additionally the controlled design of the organizational structure of the designed system is not only of importance but the main cause in the design process. The obvious solution to this challenge is a hybrid approach that incorporates both approaches. A bottom-up design of the system's parts and a controlled top-down design view on the desired organizational structure.

## 10.2 Coarse Design with Use Case Diagrams

The construction of multi-agent application depends in many methodologies on the fact that (earlier) identified requirements are used in an analytical phase to achieve a profound and – among the development team – agreed-on insight of the envisioned system. Then in a design phase this insight is turned – with the help of the artifacts developed in the analysis phase – into a design of the system; usually a set of models representing partitions of the system. Consequently, this design is refined and turned into a detailed design and this is followed by an implementation.

Many currently used methodologies have the goal to transform early models from the analysis into refined, more detailed models in design and implementation. This can be achieved (automatically or – more often – semi-automatically) by transformation or by generation from existing models into refined models or implementation artifacts.

In Gaia and Gaia-like methodologies (Roadmap, Paose, Message/UML, Ingenias) the phases of design are defined as analysis, architectural design and detailed design. Following the Gaia terminology the analysis phase consists of the preliminary or coarse description of the sub-organization, the environment, the roles, the interactions and the rules.

### 10.2.1 System Analysis with Coarse Design Diagrams

Each role is involved in certain interactions as well as each interaction is associated with a number of roles. Thus, this relationship is often referred to as organizational matrix of the application. Moreover, as for in Paose (see Moldt (2006b), Cabac et al. (2007), Cabac (2007) and Cabac et al. (2008a)) the organizational matrix is also sometimes written as a matrix (spreadsheet). In or after the initial start of the architectural design phase, when the first elements (roles, interactions, ontology concepts) of the system are identified, these concepts have to enter the models. Here takes place the first decomposition into sub-organizations (see Zambonelli et al. (2003)) of the system. For the roles, their responsibilities and abilities have to be defined. Consequently, the defined responsibilities also define the organization of the matrix. For the interactions the participants have to be defined. This is done according to the desired objectives and to the abilities and responsibilities of the participating roles. For the reason of these interconnections between roles and interactions we believe that the identification of interactions and roles cannot be achieved separately but only jointly with the identification of them. Instead of a separated approach we propose an incremental one. Here the design is done in a coarse manner and is successively and incrementally refined. The result of the incremental process is a joint coarse model of roles and interactions as well as their relations that resembles a Use Case Diagram but is in fact the multi-agent system overview diagram, called Coarse Design Diagram.

For the coarse design of the organizational matrix of roles and interactions we propose, here, an alternative to the spreadsheet notation, which suits the intuitive modeling in software processes much better. We propose to use the well-known syntax of the Use Case Diagrams for the application matrix with a semantic difference. *Actors* in use cases represent *agent roles* of the designed system. *Use cases* represent the *interactions* in the system – not like in the usual semantics the interactions *with* the system.[1] The matrix is spanned by the arc connections in the diagram.

By using the well-known and very simple syntax it is very easy for developers to intuitively adopt this technique for the development process. Especially when this stage of the development / design is done within the group of developers it is essential that the technique should be lightweight and easily understandable for all participants. In the early stages of analysis, which are usually accompanied by discussions, the technique should also allow for easy manipulation, adaptation, revisions and incremental advances. In this stage the main tasks consist in:

- naming and sketching the roles which define the decomposition of the system, their abilities and responsibilities,

- naming the interactions and sketching their workflow and their triggers and

- associating the participants of the interactions with them.

Additionally, many concepts of the system are already used during discussion. These should be *collected* and directly enter the ontology for the system (or if not used by the agents these concepts can enter the ontology of the development system team: the glossary). Furthermore, already first mappings of agent roles and agents in the system enter the discussion. Although also this does not primarily interest the developers at this stage, these assumptions can enter the later models (agent model). This is sometimes already included in the diagram through clustering of actors/roles or through the connection of several actors/roles to one actor/agent. In the latter case the new actor/agent can be displayed differently to achieve a distinction between roles and agents (color, annotation).

**Alternatives**

There are many possibilities for alternatives to the presented modeling technique of using use case syntax for the application matrix.

**Spreadsheet matrix** → easily generatable.

**UML:** Communication Diagram → fits not so good

**Prometheus:** The System Overview Diagram in Prometheus covers the interactions and the agents. Thus, offering the same possibility as the Coarse Design Diagram. However, it also includes environmental information and is far more detailed and more overloaded.

---

[1] In usual Use Case Diagrams the actors represent real users of the system and use cases represent scenarios of interactions with the system. Use cases are often used to describe existing systems and how they are used by the users.

## 10.2.2 Project Kick-off

Each software development project has to be started at some point. Usually parts of the requirement engineering is done before the *real* start (kick-off) of the process and depending on the type of system either requirements are clear and obvious or they remain to be defined. The question where requirements engineering ends and analysis, coarse design or architectural design start is also not clear and depends on the developers, the techniques they use, the paradigm applied and the personal preference of the participants.[2]

Let's assume that all participants agree on and have a notion of the envisioned system. The development group meets and wants to start the development phase. We are then in the analytical phase (Gaia) or at the coarse design (PAOSE). Now, in an agent-oriented methodology the participants have to define roles, interactions and functional concepts (ontology) in order to get a notion of the to-be-envisioned design. Consequently, the participants have to agree on a design. It seems obvious that, if such a task is done collectively by a group, the process of coarse design is a controversial, time-consuming task that needs elaboration, negotiation, reflection, re-elaboration, re-negotiation and re-reflection for there are several individuals in the team who have possibly competing and developing interests and insight into the system.

This process of competing, cooperating, negotiating individuals that need to be coordinated, self-coordinated or self-organized is exactly the kind of process we attribute to intelligent agent societies. For this reason we have given the development process and the development team the guiding metaphor of the multi-agent system of developers (see Chapter 8).

To support this process and to direct it to a result we want to apply a technique that has the following attributes:

- It is easily understandable for all participants.

- It is unobtrusive and thus does not hinder the discussion.

- It can be applied on the fly during discussion (light-weight).

- It should integrate into the development process (code generation).

With the Use Case Diagrams as coarse design modeling technique we are able to achieve those goals.

# 10.3 Examples: Coarse Design

In this section we present two examples for the modeling of the application matrix. One is a workflow management system and the other one is a multi-agent multi-user game. We use the previously described use case element syntax. However, the semantics and

---

[2]Note that we believe that software development is an incremental, evolutionary, concurrent and dynamic process. Thus, the idealization made here cannot be achieved in a real setting and stages, phases or tasks have to be reiterated during development as necessary.

pragmatics behind the diagrams are different from the usual application of Use Case Diagrams and should not be confused with that. We call this model coarse design.

From the pragmatic point of view the largest difference between usual use case modeling and the coarse design modeling lies in the stage or phase in which the model is used. While Use Case Diagrams are usually created during the requirements engineering phase, coarse design is done after that and starts in the architectural design phase. However, as a system overview of all (or at least a closed partition of all) interactions and roles it comes handy in all stages of development and should be maintained throughout the whole process.

### 10.3.1 A Workflow Management System

Figure 10.1 shows an agent-based workflow management system that follows the definition of the Workflows Management Coalition's (WfMC) reference architecture. The management system is represented by the WFMS agent role. Dependent agents (or sub-

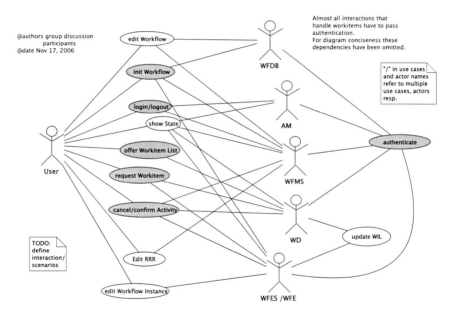

Figure 10.1: Coarse design of an agent-based workflow management system (WFMS).

components) are workflow data base (WFDB), the account manager (AM), the workitem dispatcher (WD), the workflow engines (WFE), the workflow enactment service (WFES) and a user of the workflow management system. An agent owning the *user* role acts as a proxy/placeholder for some real (human) user. Several interactions have been defined; e.g.: login, logout, request workitem, cancel or confirm activity and so on. Many of which (the ones involving the proxy *user*) are interactions that can be interpreted also as interactions with the system. However, most of them require several internal agents and some interactions are solely internal. Although the system has not been built yet, the system's structure is clearly conceivable from the coarse design.

Whether the system is built with exactly this structure is not of importance. What matters is that the development team should have a means to develop a common vision on the system from which further discussions can start. The tool makes it possible to extract a table from the diagram, which can be used to have yet another different view on the system and compare with the existing designed system. Table 10.1 shows the extracted table for the agent-based workflow management system.

| | accountmanager | WIDispatcher | WFES | WFDEFDB | User | WFMS |
|---|---|---|---|---|---|---|
| offerWorkitemList | | × | | | × | |
| edit Workflow Instance | | | × | | × | |
| request Workitem | | × | × | | × | |
| init Workflow | | | × | × | × | × |
| show State | × | × | × | | × | × |
| login | × | | | | × | × |
| Edit RRR | | | | | × | × |
| authenticate | × | × | × | × | | × |
| cancelActivity | | × | × | | × | × |
| n dbEdit | | | | × | × | × |
| updateWorkItemList | | × | × | | | |

Table 10.1: Generated matrix table from diagram (WFMS).

## 10.3.2 A Multi-Agent Multi-User Game

Figure 10.2 shows the coarse design for the multi-user game *Settler*. Again there exists a placeholder agent that represents a real player in the system. However, in this design, the agent is realized through four different roles: *Player, Trader, CurrentPlayerListener* and a *GUI player*. The GUI Role can be exchanged with another role to implement an automated (AI) player/planner. Otherwise the system consists of several agent roles representing the functional decompositions (components) of the system. There is the *game control*, the *bank*, the *board* representation, *controller* for trading and building as well as a role that is responsible for *initialization* (set-up) of the game. Again many of the interactions involve one of the roles assigned to the player agent, which can be human or a system's part (artificial agent). However, the role *CurrentPlayerListener* is assigned to all agents that have to know about the current player of each round, i.e. the bank and the board. The *GameControlAgent* does not need to get information because it is the game control that is to decide on the current player. The *InitAgent* has the *Init* role and initializes the whole game. Thus this role and all agents participate in the *initGame* interaction.

The application matrix as table is presented in Table 10.2. The above mentioned agents sometimes enter the diagram as compound agent roles. This is either achieved as a specialized actor symbol or as a simple grouping through graphical elements, such

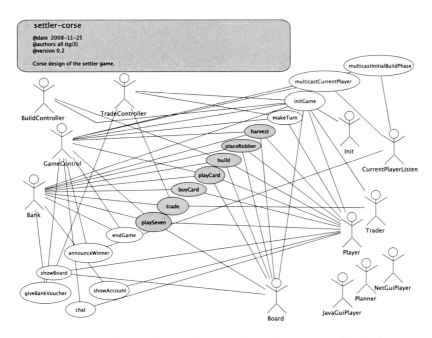

Figure 10.2: Coarse design of an agent-based board game (Settler).

as circles as shown in Figure 10.3. These circles own a distinctive color to identify the agents even if the agent roles are not co-located in the diagram.

| | Bank | Board | GameControl | TradeController | CurrentPlayerL. | Init | Player | BuildController | Trader |
|---|---|---|---|---|---|---|---|---|---|
| showBoard | | × | | × | | | × | | |
| playSeven | × | × | × | | | | × | | |
| playCard | × | × | × | | | | × | | |
| placeRobber | × | × | | | | | × | | |
| initGame | × | × | × | × | | × | × | × | × |
| chat | | | × | | | | × | | |
| showAccount | × | | | | | | × | | |
| multicastInitialBuildPhase | | | × | | × | | | | |
| endGame | × | | × | | | | | | |
| trade | × | | | × | | | | | × |
| build | × | × | | | | | × | × | |
| makeTurn | | | × | × | | | × | | |
| announceWinner | | | × | | × | | | | |
| buyCard | × | | | | | | × | | |
| giveBankVoucher | × | | × | | | | | | |
| multicastCurrentPlayer | | | × | | × | | | | |
| harvest | × | × | × | | | | × | | |

Table 10.2: From the diagram generated table of the *Settler game* matrix.

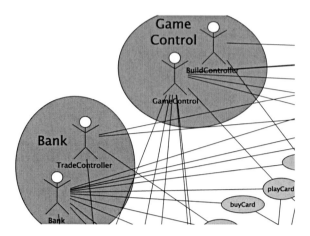

Figure 10.3: Fragment of the Coarse Design Diagram of *Settler* with grouping.

### 10.3.3 Generating Code Bases From Coarse Design Diagrams

The coarse design models are used to generate the applications source code directory as well as model skeletons, code skeletons for the roles, interactions and ontology as well as all configuration and build files needed to compile the project. The diagram is further used at other stages of the development process to add to the API documentation's overview. In the HTML-based API Documentation,[3] which is automatically generated from all design artifacts, the Coarse Design Diagram is integrated and overlaid with hyperlinks that lead from diagram elements directly to the documentations for the represented artifacts.

## 10.4 Related Work

Use Case Diagrams are widely used to model requirements of (software) systems. This is also done in agent-oriented methodologies. "Creating use-cases has proven to be a very effective and sufficient method to discover requirements" (see Juan, Pearce and Sterling (2002, p. 6)). Examples for such a use are ROADMAP and ADELFE. In opposition to this *traditional* use of the use case syntax we redefine the semantics behind the diagram elements and transport the technique from the requirements to the (coarse) design of the system.

Adapting the semantics of Use Case Diagrams or diagram elements has been done frequently in agent-oriented methodologies. It seems the temptation to use a human-like icon for an agent is very high and the effect – the intuitive understanding of the diagram element – is seldom missed.

---

[3]Mulandoc generates a hyperlink document with and from all relevant design artifacts in a Mulan-based multi-agent application including Interaction Diagrams, protocol nets, decision components, knowledge base files and combines those with a generated application matrix as well as the Coarse Design Diagram. Thus it supplements the *Java* API documentation.

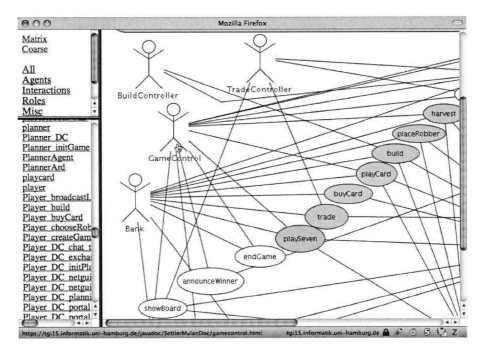

Figure 10.4: Screen-shot of a Coarse Design Diagram with hyperlink overlay.

### Gerd Wagner

In RAP/AOR Wagner (2005) proposes use cases-like models, as an alternative to *interaction frames*, in order to model agent interactions. Agents can be modeled interchangeably as actors or as systems while the cases depict interactions between agent and system (also an agent).

### Iglesias & Garijo

In MAS-CommonKADS (see Iglesias and Garijo (2005)) use cases are used to model interactions/cases of human and artificial agents with a system (also an agent). The notation distinguishes between the human and the artificial (square head) agent. An artificial agent can be depicted as (square headed) actor or as system depending on the focus.

### Cossentino & Potts

In PASSI (see Cossentino and Potts (2001) and Cossentino (2005)) Use Case Diagrams are used for requirements engineering. Here the actors are used in a more traditional sense as human agents / users but also sometimes as external (outside of the system) resources.

**Pavón, Gómez-Sanz & Fuentes**

In INGENIAS (see Pavón et al. (2005)) Use Case Diagrams (with a slight variation in syntax) are used to define the users interactions with the envisioned system. Here user roles, which define the position of the human agents and are outside of the system, are related to use cases.

We can sum up the usage of Use Case Diagrams in agent-oriented requirements engineering as follows. In general, agents are seen as part of the system – depicted by the system border in Use Case Diagrams – and actors are often used to represent users of the system (human agents). However, depending on the grade of abstraction and the focus also agents are sometimes depicted as actors. This reflects the ambiguous definition and the non-fitness into traditional modeling approaches of the agent concept.

In opposition, in our approach we model the application matrix as identified agent roles, their interactions and the connections of both in the stage of analysis or coarse design. However, the application matrix can be found in central models of almost all agent-oriented methodologies.

**Zambonelli, Jennings & Wooldridge**

In Gaia (see Zambonelli et al. (2003)) this information is defined in the preliminary role and interaction model. However, these are abstract descriptions of models that have no syntactic representation.

**Padgham & Winikoff**

In Prometheus (see Padgham and Winikoff (2002a)) the systems model contains the matrix of interactions and agents. However, it is hidden behind several other aspects that are defined in this central diagram (perceptions, data). Instead as an alternative the agent acquaintance models show the *social network* of the agents withholding the information about interactions.

# 10.5 Tool Support

The Use Case Plugin is integrated as plugin into our tool set environment of Petri net-based multi-agent development.

## 10.5.1 Tool Description

The plugin's functionality consists in (1) a palette that provides the tools to draw the basic elements such as actors, cases or arcs and (2) a generator based on Velocity that produces the generated output.[4] Figure 10.5 shows, besides the main window of our development environment, the additional elements provided to the GUI by the plugin:

---

[4]An addition to the plugin responsible for the documentation of the application (Mulandoc, see Chapter 19) allows to integrate the diagram as image map into the web-based API documentation allowing graphical elements to function as hyperlinks.

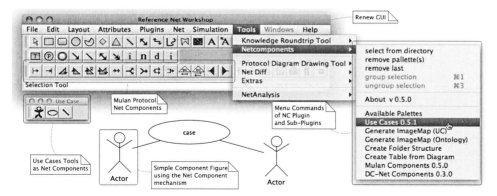

Figure 10.5: The main window of RENEW with the Use Case Plugin, its palette, menu entries and a use case example (repetition of Figure 5.11).

menu entries for the palette, for generation of the image maps and for the creation of an application's folder structure as well as the palette for the basic drawing elements – here detached from the window for better recognition.

## 10.5.2 Tool Development

The Use Case Plugin was designed and developed by me in 2007 and 2008. It extends the Net Components Plugin, using its extension mechanism to draw templates (net components) of drawing elements in an easy way.

Thus it is possible to design the graphical elements for the diagrams as components and include them as tool buttons in a palette without extensive coding. Only the possibility to include non-component elements into the palettes needed some extending of the original Net Components Plugin. In the current version also connection tools (arc connections) can be drawn by using a tool from the same palette as the other tool elements for use cases (compare with *use case tools* in Figure 10.5).

The Use Case Plugin includes several templates and a generator class, which enable the developers to generate a complete setup for a multi-agent application from the Coarse Design Diagram. The generator utilizes the Velocity template engine, which turns the template into context-dependent development artifacts. Listing 10.1 shows all generated files for the example shown in Figure 10.5. The main generated files correspond to the application matrix and the build environment. File skeletons for the designed interactions, roles and ontology are generated. This includes skeletons for the AIPs, which can be used to generate protocol nets (see Chapter 13), simple DC nets and *Helper* classes skeletons for each role as well as basic Protégé files, which include already the FIPA and the CAPA management ontology. Furthermore, an R/D Diagram (RolesDependecies.mad) and a setup file for the system configuration (Test.mas) are created.

The build process which compiles Petri nets, generates classes from ontology descriptions, compiles *Java* classes and constructs the executable archive is based on ant (http://ant.apache.org), thus the generator creates a application-dependent build file

153

```
./build.xml
./etc/plugin.cfg
./src/de/renew/agent/test/agents/projects.xml
./src/de/renew/agent/test/agents/RolesDependencies.mad
./src/de/renew/agent/test/agents/startKBE.sh
./src/de/renew/agent/test/agents/Test.mas
./src/de/renew/agent/test/interactions
./src/de/renew/agent/test/interactions/someinteraction
./src/de/renew/agent/test/interactions/someinteraction/someInteraction.aip
./src/de/renew/agent/test/roles/actor1/Actor1_DC_test.rnw
./src/de/renew/agent/test/roles/actor1/Actor1Helper.java
./src/de/renew/agent/test/roles/actor2/Actor2_DC_test.rnw
./src/de/renew/agent/test/roles/actor2/Actor2Helper.java
./src/de/renew/agent/test/TestPlugin.java
./src/ontology/Test.pins
./src/ontology/Test.pont
./src/ontology/Test.pprj
./testing/start.sh
./testing/startCapa.rnw
```

Listing 10.1: Generated files for the example from Figure 10.5.

(`build.xml`). Multi-agent applications for MULAN/CAPA are compiled to plugins, thus they need a configuration file that describes the plugin (`plugin.cfg`). The start script (`start.sh`) sets up and starts the environment while the start net (`startCapa.rnw`) initializes the execution. Also these two files are provided by the generator.

This code base is immediately compilable and the system can be started after compilation, however to achieve an application-specific behavior it needs to be implemented by the developers. For the modeling of the specific parts of the multi-agent application see the following chapters. The tool also offers the possibility to create tables (LATEX) and HTML image maps from the diagrams. The latter is used as overview diagram for the web-based application programming interface documentation (API), which includes hyperlinks to project documentation artifacts.

## 10.6 Summary

In this chapter we present a simple technique for the modeling of the application matrix in multi-agent systems, which consists in roles and interactions. The resulting models can be facilitated for a variety of purposes throughout the development process from the early stages over generation of code bases to the documentation.

At early stages (coarse design) the lightweight technique presented here provides the possibility to model on-the-fly – during the ongoing developers group discussion – in a coarse manner. Thus the basic system decomposition and the coarse overview are modeled in an intuitive way. It enables the developers to change the model rapidly during development. From the artifact, which also reflects the organization of the development team, a project folder for the system's code can be generated that allows immediate and concurrent beginning of detailed design/coding. Other representations can also be derived from the model; i.e. the matrix as a spreadsheet or table. Additionally, the model is automatically integrated in the hypertext-based API documentation of the multi-agent system, including navigation with hyperlinks in the diagram image.

# 11 Organizational Structures of Multi-Agent Applications

Organizational structures are important for the understanding of the systems, especially if they feature dynamical structures. Section 11.1 introduces the necessity for the modeling of dependencies in multi-agent applications. We point out in this chapter that during the design of agent services, the right level of abstraction and its variation is of great importance for the resulting system design. The distinction between soft and hard dependencies is introduced in Section 11.2. We propose the Dependency Diagram for the modeling of hard service dependencies, which resembles a composite structure diagram in UML 2.0. Section 11.3 presents the Dependency Diagram that clearly shows the dependency hierarchy of agents. With the Knowledge Round-Trip Plugin it is possible to create Dependency Diagrams from existing sources, from scratch or from other sources of information of dependency. The enhancement of the Dependency Diagrams, the Roles/Dependencies Diagrams, is presented in Section 11.4. Section 11.5 provides an overview of related work. We present the tools that support the Dependency Diagram and the R/D Diagram and their capabilities in Section 11.6. As an example of the R/D Diagram we present the model of the plugin structure extracted from the real dependencies of the Renew plugins. Section 11.7 provides a summary.

## 11.1 Context

One key factor for the successful operation of multi-agent systems is the smooth communication between agents. Usually, interactions are modeled in detail using interaction diagrams and agent protocols (see AUML (2004), FIPA (2009), Odell et al. (2000)). Besides the definition of sound interactions, structural aspects are also of major importance for the understanding of the architecture of a multi-agent system. One example of such a structural aspect is the dependency relation that exists between agents (often also referred to as *acquaintance*). In order to attain a goal, most agents have to rely on other agents. Thus, those dependencies exist between agents in almost every multi-agent system.

Especially in multi-agent-based applications, where the global structure (macro level) emerges from local information (micro level), the analytical modeling of resulting dependencies becomes crucial. Here we focus on the dependencies that are related to the services offered and required by the agents in the system. These relationships are often modeled in agent-oriented methodologies as acquaintance models (Prometheus) or service models (Gaia). For the multi-agent architecture Mulan, we provide tool integration for the presented techniques as plugins for Renew (see Kummer et al. (2009a)), the Knowledge Round-Trip Plugin and the Knowledge Base Editor (KBE). In MULAN (see Rölke (2004)), offered and required services are explicitly defined in the agents' configuration files (the agents' initial knowledge bases).

## 11.2 Service Dependencies

In the context of multi-agent systems, we understand services as collections of agent actions that serve a common purpose. A service is realized through one or more agent protocols and through the capabilities of the serving agent. Our notion of a service fits very well with the notion given by Zambonelli, Jennings and Wooldridge (2003, p. 21):

> The [...] services model [...] identifies the main services – intended as coherent blocks of activity in which agents will engage – that are required to realize the agent's roles, and their properties.

In general, the action to perform a service may be requested by any agent. This implies an interaction of (at least) one agent with (at least) one other agent. As a consequence, in order to be able to access a service, the interface (protocol description) and address of the provider has to be published. The user of the service expects that it will be performed under certain conditions (e.g. payment, quality of service, availability). The reactive behavior of an agent is initiated by triggers (sometimes also called events). For this a mapping from (received) message types to predefined behavior exists.

During the design phase of the multi-agent system, the developers have to decide on the level of abstraction of the services and their published interface. As an example we consider an agent that wants to play a board game. In order to play the game, the agent has to be able to access the *board game service*. This may include in its interface description all necessary interaction protocols for the whole game. However, this does not take into account composability or scalability. In opposition, the game services can be implemented as several smaller services, which can be offered by different agents. Thus, in a finer level of abstraction, the developers can decide to design following services for the board game: *board control, accounting, game control, trading*. Now, several distinct parts of the system – and certain responsibilities as well as capabilities – are identified.

The corresponding design artifacts for the (early) structural design in the development of multi-agent systems are roles. They are typically defined as role descriptions. In a flexible way the developers may decide that all roles can be executed by one agent or each role is implemented by one single agent.

The challenge for the developers is to find the right level of abstraction, i.e. abstract enough to get an idea of the offered services as a whole and detailed enough to recognize if two agents perform similar tasks. Through their flexibility in regard to the choice of the level of abstraction, the services are suitable for modeling the overall structure of big as well as small systems without designing too complex or too trivial representations in the models. Most agents use services of other agents to accomplish their goals or even to provide their own services (by delegation). Thus, if an agent requires a service from another agent, we recognize a dependency between agent role (which is responsible for the agents behavior) and offered service. This we call hard dependency because this is defined during design time and is thus of a static nature.[1] Hard dependencies describe a minimum set of services that are required by an agent to fill out a role.

Another dependency exists between agents that are not in a service provider/requester relationship but communicate with each another on a different basis. These agents are on a personal acquaintance level between the two identities of agents. We call these dependencies soft dependencies (sometimes dynamic dependencies).

While soft dependencies are dynamic and thus not modeled a priori, hard dependencies are explicitly specified by the developer. However, information about soft dependencies can easily be gathered during runtime of the multi-agent system and may result in an acquaintance model describing the communication structure and can be presented as a social network.[2]

In MULAN/CAPA applications, hard dependencies (*required services*) are defined in the initial knowledge base file as FIPA[3]-compliant *service descriptions*. These service descriptions are published by the providers at the directory facilitator (DF) and this data can be queried by the requester.[4] Thus, the service provider can be found by the service requester. To request the service, the agent has to abide by well-defined protocols. A typical means to trigger service is to send an *action request*, which tells the receiver to perform a task.

We apprehend protocols as implementations of a complex agent actions that are assigned to one or more services. In many methodologies, as also in MULAN/CAPA, conversation patterns are typically defined as interaction protocols (Cabac 2003).

In this chapter we propose a modeling technique for hard dependencies. We recognize a dependency between an agent and a service that is offered by another agent, if an agent requests another agent to perform a task or an action.

In many cases – but not always – the interactions between requester and provider follow the FIPA Request protocol or a similar one and use an action request as a performative. To illustrate the technique, we use the FIPA Request protocol (FIPA 2002) as a prototypical protocol presented in Figure 11.1. The Participant in the Request protocol offers the service to perform a certain task – let's say the service *participate*. The Requester wishes a task to be performed by the Participant. This implies that the Requester sends a message (action request) to the Participant and waits for an answer if necessary.

The service offered by the Participant is completed with an answer to the initial request. Thus a hard dependency exists, which is modeled in the right part of the figure as a fragment of a Dependency Diagram. Services can be required by several agents and can also be offered by multiple agents. Thus, the dependency does not exist directly between the two agents (or their roles), instead – as pointed out above – the dependency

---

[1]Note that this is a static dependency between agent roles and services and not between roles. The requester can always choose from a number of service providers.

[2]This is done within our tool set by another tool (MULAN-SNIFFER, compare with Section 16.3.3 and Cabac et al. (2008d)) and is not the topic of this chapter.

[3]Foundation for Intelligent Physical Agents, FIPA.

[4]Note that the directory facilitator offers the service of registering and querying information about services in the multi-agent system. However, this is a mandatory service that is always accessible on FIPA-compliant platforms.

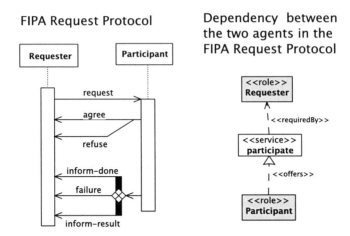

Figure 11.1: FIPA Request protocol and a representation of dependencies.

exists between an agent and an offered service.

In general, we seek for a hierarchical structure in a Dependency Diagram. This allows code reuse in the system, composability and easy reconfiguration. Interdependencies (cyclic dependencies) between agents are undesirable, firstly because they can cause deadlocks in the system's configuration and secondly because they complicate the substitution of agents. Also unmet dependencies usually cause trouble in the system configuration. We believe that through explicit (analytical) modeling, such problematic aspects can be found in a system design, and developers can be supported in the process of eliminating them. Figure 11.2 shows the elements of the diagram as a Class Diagram. A Dependency Diagram consists of role figures, service figures and dependency connections. They own the stereotypes «role»,«service», «offers» and «requiredBy».

## 11.3 Modeling Service Dependencies

For the modeling of service dependencies, we employ UML component diagrams. However, we exclusively use the detailed version, so that the service is explicitly represented in the model and we slightly modify the syntax.

Usually, component diagrams are used to model the constitution of replaceable software constructs and their relationships. Besides the components and the interfaces, classes and objects are also used in component diagrams (UML 2005, p. 139-171). In the agent context, where we deal with agents, services and the dependency relations, we use the elements of the component diagram adapted to those needs.

A service is an abstraction of a set of (complex) agent actions that serve a common purpose. Several services may be provided by one agent and several agents may offer the same services. Our notion of a *service* (see Section 11.2) is very similar to the concept of an *interface* in the UML superstructure (UML 2005, p. 82):

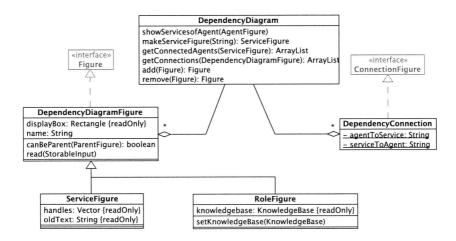

Figure 11.2: Meta model of the Dependency Diagrams.

> An interface is a kind of classifier that represents a declaration of a set of
> coherent public features and obligations. An interface specifies a contract;
> any instance of a classifier that realizes the interface must fulfill that contract.

Thus, it seems straight forward to model services in a way that is similar to the modeling of interfaces. We add the stereotype «service» to the elements in our models. The stereotype is meant to express the differences. First, we model in a completely different context. Second, in contrast to an object, an agent has the ability to break contracts, so services are indeed also an obligation to fulfill a specified task. However, there is no definitive certainty that this will (or can) be done. Third, we like to use classes and interfaces together with agents and services within one model. The introduction of a new stereotype gives us the ability to do so without introducing confusion into the models.

From the software engineering viewpoint, agents are often regarded as special components. If one is to take this position, again it seems straight forward to model agent roles as components together with the offered and required services. We introduce the stereotype «role» for the depicted agent roles.

In the detailed version of the component diagram, the relationship of agents to implemented interfaces is depicted as a dashed arc with a triangle arrow tip. We follow this notation and draw a dashed arc from the agent that offers the service to the service itself. Again, we explicitly distinguish between arcs and provide the stereotype «offers».

Required interfaces are modeled in the component diagram by a dashed arc with an open line arrow tip (stereotype «use»). This arc points at the used interface. In contrast, in Dependency Diagrams we draw the arcs in the opposite direction and – accordingly – offer the stereotype «requiredBy»[5]. By doing so we get a relation chain from offering role to offered service and from the service to the role that requires the service. At first glance

---

[5]Note that we sometimes omit the stereotypes on the arcs, if the context is clear.

this change seems odd, but we achieve the possibility to model hierarchical structures. In Section 11.2 we point out the benefits of hierarchical dependencies.

Figure 11.3 shows an example Dependency Diagram as described above. In order to better distinguish between agents and services, the roles possess a colored background. The figure shows a snapshot of a workflow management system in development, giving

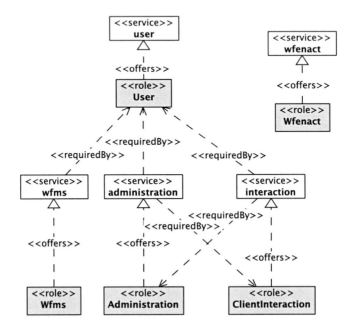

Figure 11.3: Dependencies of a workflow management system in development.

an overview of the agent roles in the system.

In the model, a developer can easily identify potentially problematic areas. Usually, this is a hard task because the information resides distributed in several local property files, the initial knowledge bases, which can be distributed. In this very simple example we are able to identify two problems: First, there exists a cyclic dependency between the roles `Administration` and `ClientInteraction`. A cyclic dependency may indicate that the agent roles could be fused to one role since they are so tightly coupled and can only act as pair or, as in this case, that the developers of one of the roles have a misconception of the tasks of the designed role. Second, the agent `Wfenact` is not connected to the other agents. An isolated agent that offers a service means that this role does not interact with other roles within the service relationship.[6]

Here, since the diagram has been taken during the development phase, the depicted configuration is not final. During analytical examination of the designed structure of the

---

[6]Maybe it interacts on a different basis, e.g. in negotiations or as user.

service dependencies, this means that still some work has to be done by the developers. Both situations are undesirable and should be changed in the further development process. The developers may be automatically supported in finding such structural anomalies by the modeling tool that is described in the next section.

We employ for the purposes of finding anomalies two simple checks (acyclic property check and connectedness property check) from another plugin of RENEW, the NetAnalysis Plugin. For this means we have implemented a conversion of the diagram into a net structure, which can directly be analyzed by the NetAnalysis Plugin. Another possibility – yet to be implemented – is a direct feeding of the graph structure into the checking algorithms.

## 11.4 Roles and Dependencies

Dependencies of agent roles can be nicely modeled with the Knowledge Round-Trip Plugin as a Dependency Diagram. Through the round-trip integration together with the Knowledge Base Editor, we achieve a convenient way to model constructively (during design tasks) and analytically (during evaluation, testing).

The main disadvantage in this approach does not arise from the techniques. It lies in the artifacts that are used to represent the initial knowledge bases. These are simple property files, which are transformed into knowledge base instances by an assisting process during initialization. This process makes use of the reflection mechanism to instantiate runtime objects.

This is a flexible and simple technique to realize instances of knowledge bases. However, since property files are not extensible there is no ground to support the modeling of role hierarchies or even multiple knowledge base files per agent type, which leads to code duplication for agent types that share roles. The relationship of one knowledge base file (agent role descriptors) for one agent type is not feasible for an efficient and scalable implementation. Instead, we prefer to use extensible artifacts, which can be modeled in an inheritance hierarchy similar to class inheritance. The technique of choice for such extensible artifacts is the Extensible Mark-up Language (XML). Thus we are able to make use of composed as well as specialized role types for the agents.

Being able to implement the code for a role hierarchy, we are able to model not only the dependencies of agent roles, but also the hierarchy of roles. Moreover, we are able to model both hierarchy and dependencies in one diagram. This leads to the Roles/Dependencies Diagram (R/D Diagram). Here the different roles appear in a hierarchy of (specialized) role types together with services and the dependencies of the role types. To model these two aspects in one diagram makes sense, since dependencies are also inherited, thus in the combination of both aspects the inherited dependency is easily found and the structure of the dependencies benefits from the clustering of roles through generalization.

A prototypical implementation of a Knowledge Base Editor (Version 2) exists that supports the XML knowledge base format. It incorporates the model in its user interface. The technique is designed to show the dependencies as explained in Section 11.3 as well as the hierarchies of roles.

Role descriptors (initial knowledge base files in XML notation) can be created and edited directly in the tool, which also validates entries on the fly. Models can be centralized as well as fragmented. If fragmented the joining (distributed) elements of the diagrams are the services and the abstract roles. Because of the generality these can be in several models and if the models are distributed those artifacts have to be present in all affected models.

From the initial models (R/D Diagram), which are the main design artifacts, agent role descriptors (ARD in XML notation) can be generated. These artifacts are sufficient to initialize agent types defined with the same tool in a simple agent model, which maps agents to roles (compare with the agent models of Gaia, see Zambonelli et al. (2003)). Alternatively, the merged ARD descriptions can also be created for the convenient use of agent knowledge bases (KB) in other contexts.

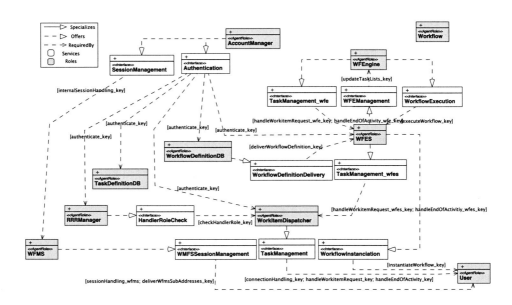

Figure 11.4: Dependencies in the WFMS (version 2).

We return to the example of a workflow management system to illustrate the power and the usage of the R/D Diagram. Figure 11.4 shows the dependencies of the reimplementation of the WFMS done with the enhanced tools. The system features several agent roles to form the WFMS, an agent role for the workflows and an agent role as a placeholder (proxy) for the user of the system. The user can be in different user roles (administrator, executor, initiator, etc.), which is reflected by the fact that user agents also own user roles.

The WFMS core is represented by an agent that owns the role WFMS (the WFMSAgent, which can be regarded as a singleton agent). This agent delegates several tasks of the WFMS to its participants: e.g. agents that own the role WFEngine or WFES (workflow enactment service).[7]

The dependencies in the model reflect the domain specific constraints. For instance the AccountManager is capable to authenticate the permissions of the participants of the WFMS and it offers this as a service. The WFES can thus delegate the task of authentication to the AccountManager.

Note that the agent roles WFES and WFEngine are in a cyclic dependency, meaning that they are tightly coupled. One cannot perform the tasks in the WFMS context without the other. However, this cycle is not resolvable and also those agent roles cannot (normally) be included within one agent as the WFES takes up a manager role for the WFEngine agents, which execute the workflows. Also the WFES could create new agents for the execution of workflows on demand.

Figure 11.5 shows a possibility for generalization of agent roles. Basically all agents that perform a task within the WFMS (and offer services to other WFMS agents) have to be able to use the authentication. Here a generalization is obvious. Also all agents are CapaAgents because we are running a CAPA engine solely with standard agents.

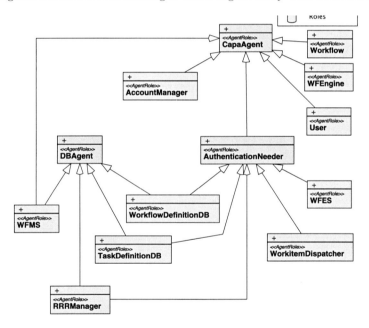

Figure 11.5: Role hierarchy of the model.

Figure 11.6 integrates both into one R/D Diagram. Through the generalization of agent roles we are able to reduce the number of dependency relations considerably. However, much of this improvement is again taken back since we have to add generalization arcs to the diagram. Also the fact that we combine (ideally) two hierarchies in one diagram

---

[7]All notions and qualifiers are directly taken from the definition of a WFMS given by the Workflow Management Coalition (WfMC (2005)).

does not make the layout easier, since the resulting graph is sometimes not even planar. Nevertheless, the diagram shows numerous aspects of a complex system and we are also able to switch to one or the other perspective (hierarchy of roles, or dependencies).

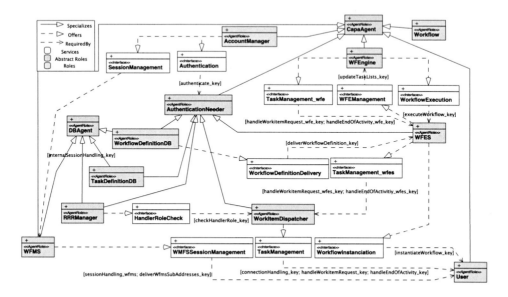

Figure 11.6: R/D Diagram of the WFMS (version 2).

So far we have only discussed the macro structure of the R/D Diagram. To inspect and edit the micro structure the elements can be expanded (the "+" at the top of the figure acts as a handle). The expanded role descriptor in Figure 11.7 reveals several sections (such as RequiredServices, StateDescription, Protocols and IncomingMessages) and in each section several entries. Sections and entries can be directly added, removed or edited within the tool.

The R/D Diagram offers for developers of multi-agent systems the possibility to inspect the system roles and dependencies on a broad level (macro, see Figure 11.6) and on a detailed level as well (micro level, see Figure 11.7). Additionally, the other views (role hierarchy view and dependencies view) are also present in the models.

## 11.5 Related Work

Most software developing methodologies contain a technique for modeling some kind of dependencies between their components. In the following paragraph we consider several examples from the agent oriented context, Tropos, AGR (Agent/Group/Role) and others, and we have a look at how the Dependency Diagram can be used in other component-based domains.

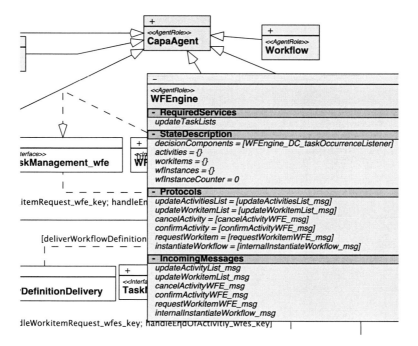

Figure 11.7: Fragment of the R/D Diagram showing the WFEngine role expanded.

### Braubach & al.

Our definition of hard dependencies is comparable with that of service dependencies of Braubach et al. (2005).

### Cossentino & Potts

A definition of soft dependencies can be found in the PASSI method. There a soft dependency exists if a service is not required, but "helpful or desirable" (see Cossentino and Potts (2001, p. 6)). This notion conflicts with ours where soft dependencies subsume the hard dependencies.

### Silva & Castro

The Tropos methodology distinguishes four kinds of dependencies between agents, from hard dependencies (resource) to soft ones (soft-goal). Silva and Castro (2002) shows how Tropos dependency relations can be expressed in UML for real time systems. Hard dependencies in our definition are comparable to resource dependencies, goal dependencies or task dependencies in Tropos, depending on the kind of service. We want to abstract as much as possible from the agent internals to get a clear image of the system structure, so the distinction between different kind of services in terms of the underlying action is not useful for our needs.

### Ferber, Gutknecht & Michel

Another agent oriented modeling technique, that describes dependencies between agents is AGR (Agent/Group/Role). Ferber et al. (2003) show how the organizational structure of an agent-based system can be modeled using the AGR technique. One of the proposed diagrams, the organizational structure diagram, shows roles, interactions and the relations between roles and interactions. This diagram is comparable to the Dependency Diagram. In both diagrams an arc from an agent (or from the agent role) means that the agent starts an interaction. Differences between the diagrams come from additional elements in the organizational structure diagram. First the groups to which the roles belong are also modeled. Second, the situation that every agent in a specific role must be member in another role is modeled as a direct relation between the two roles. In MULAN/CAPA-systems there are (for now) no elements like groups or teams, so the advanced modeling possibilities of an organizational structure diagram is not suitable in this context.

### Eclipse IDE

As well as in the agent context, also in other component-based systems it is important to model the dependencies between components. One example of a well-known component system is the Eclipse framework (`http://www.eclipse.org`) with its numerous plugins. The visualization of the dependencies between different plugins is complex and no sufficient commercial tools exist that can visualize the structure of the whole system appropriately.

### Jennings, Wooldridge & Zambonelli

In Gaia Zambonelli et al. (2003) focus strongly on the organizational modeling. One of the important models is the service model. Our Dependency Diagram can be regarded as an implementation of the Gaia service model. However, Gaia does not recognize hierarchical roles.

### Padgham & Winikoff

Padgham and Winikoff (2004) explicitly model acquaintances in Prometheus. However, from these models they do not derive any agent (role) dependencies. Roles are not modeled in Prometheus, instead the focus lies on agents. The system model in Prometheus gives a good overview of the system comparable with the overview of the R/D Diagram. It is much more detailed but does not explicitly show any dependencies except the interaction protocols or messages that connect agents. The structure of the system model reflects the one of the acquaintances model.

# 11.6 Tool Support

Both techniques, the Dependency Diagrams and the R/D Diagrams, are supported by tools within our tool set, included as plugins in RENEW.

## 11.6.1 Tool Description

Both tools make it possible to model agent service dependencies and to define the content of agent knowledge bases.

### Knowledge Round-Trip Plugin

Dependency Diagrams can directly be drawn in RENEW, they can be synthesized from knowledge base files (text format) in application folder structures and they can be generated from other descriptions, such as plugin dependencies (see Section 11.6.3).

Figure 11.8 shows both GUI elements of the plugins. The Knowledge Round-Trip Plugin offers a round-trip engineering possibility for knowledge base development, i.e. knowledge bases can be transformed into diagrams, which can be adapted and saved again as knowledge base files.

The tool that handles Dependency Diagrams is the Knowledge Round-Trip Plugin for RENEW (see Kummer et al. (2009a)). The plugin has two main functionalities. It generates the Dependency Diagram from existing MULAN knowledge base files and it offers tools for creating and editing Dependency Diagrams.

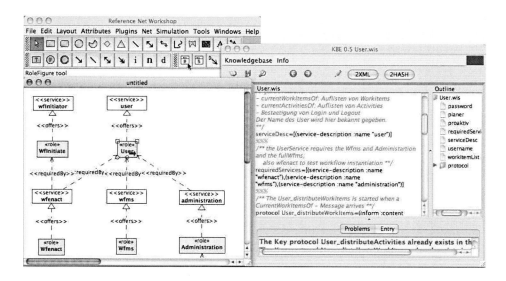

Figure 11.8: Screen shot of the development with the Knowledge Round-Trip Plugin.

Figure 11.8 shows a screen shot of the development of the workflow management system with the Knowledge Round-Trip Plugin with a Dependency Diagram. In the upper left corner is the RENEW menu bar with the standard palettes and the Dependency Diagram palette. Beneath, the Dependency Diagram is shown. In the diagram the role figure User is selected. On the right hand side of the figure the KBE with the knowledge base of the agent User is depicted.

For the generation of a diagram the tool searches (recursively) for knowledge base files in a user-defined directory. For each knowledge base found a role figure is created. A knowledge base contains a list of offered services and a list of the agent's required services. For each service in the lists the corresponding service figure and the role figure are connected. A new service figure is created if the service is not already present in the drawing. For the user's convenience the tool provides a simple automatic layout mechanism.

In addition to the possibility to use all standard drawing tools of RENEW, the plugin offers new editing functions. These are offered as three tools for editing Dependency Diagrams: a *role figure* tool, a *service figure* tool and a *dependency connection* tool (see the last three items in the lower RENEW tool bar in Figure 11.8). The dependency connection tool is used for drawing the arcs between agent role figures and service figures. The arrow type and the inscription depend on the direction of the arc (see Section 11.3). Arrows are adapted automatically while they are drawn so that the same tool draws both arc types.

A special function of the Dependency Diagram is the KBE handle, which is part of the role figure. It connects the Dependency Diagram to the KBE. With a click on the handle (a blue arc in the bottom right corner of the figure that is visible when the figure is selected), the knowledge base of the agent role is opened in the KBE for further inspection or editing. This is especially useful for debugging purposes and during the design of new knowledge base files.

By first generating a Dependency Diagram and then editing it, one faces an inconsistency between the diagram and the code it is generated from. To minimize such conflicts between diagrams and knowledge bases the tool realizes a round-trip engineering system. It preserves the consistency between knowledge bases and Dependency Diagram by automatically transferring to the knowledge bases changes occurring in the Dependency Diagrams. For example, when the service administration is connected to the agent role User via a dependency arc, a new service-description is inserted in the list of the required services in the knowledge base. This also works in the other direction. However, changes in the knowledge base are not transferred immediately to the Dependency Diagram, but as soon as the knowledge base is saved. A detailed description of the Dependency Diagram tool and the round-trip engineering system is presented by Dirkner (2006, German).

**Knowledge Base Editor Plugin**

The Knowledge Base Editor Plugin makes it possible to design complex R/D Diagrams and edit the contents of XML-based knowledge base files (and agent role descriptions). This plugin is an advancement of the first version, however backwards compatibility was lost during development. The main advantages of version 2 are a more flexible representation of knowledge base descriptions and the possibility to describe the agent knowledge on a role-based level. These resulting agent role descriptions are merged during setup to form a compound XML-based knowledge base. By this the possibility of agents supporting multiple roles in a multi-agent system is introduced into MULAN. Klenski and Willner (2007, German) provide more detailed information about the KBE.

## 11.6.2 Tool Development

The development of both tools has been concurrently carried out by independent parties, and although the intentions were slightly different, the results of the two development processes are comparable. However, on the one side, the main focus for the Knowledge Round-Trip Plugin is a round-trip engineering system with a simple and minimal diagrammatic representation. On the other side the Knowledge Base Editor Plugin focuses on an integrated approach of several useful features during the development of knowledge bases in special and multi-agent systems with MULAN/CAPA in general.

### Knowledge Round-Trip Plugin

Dirkner and I designed and developed the Knowledge Round-Trip Plugin. The original implementation was done by Dirkner (2006) (see also Cabac et al. (2006c) and Cabac et al. (2008c)). Since 2007, I have maintained the plugin and adapted it to our increasing demands. I refactored and redesigned several aspects of the implementation. The functionality relies on another plugin, the Knowledge Base Editor Plugin (version 1) developed by Klenski and Willner, which offers convenience editing, syntax highlighting and syntax checking for plain text-based knowledge base files. In 2008, I included the access of structural net analysis features for Dependency Diagrams by translating the diagrams to nets.

### Knowledge Base Editor Plugin

The Knowledge Base Editor Plugin was developed by Klenski and Willner (2007, version 2) on the experiences gained with the first version. Rölke did the main conceptualization and I introduced the concept of service dependencies into the diagrams, as previously proposed in Dependency Diagram modeling. Since 2008 maintenance, bugfixes, redesign of the graphical elements (and syntax) and refactorings were done by me. Together with Wester-Ebbinghaus, I also introduced new features (e.g. entries and parser features for decision components).

R/D Diagrams are drawn directly in the enhanced version of the KBE. The KBE started out as a simple but convenient editor for the original properties of knowledge base files. It included syntax checking for ontology concepts represented in the Semantic Language (SL) by employing the parser as validator.

The enhanced version of the KBE was grounded on three aspects. First, the redefinition of the knowledge base format and by that the possibility to allow specialization/generalization of roles. Second, the implementation of the editor as diagram reflecting the hierarchy of roles (i.e. a Class Diagram-like model). Third, the integration of the representation of the macro level, i.e. the dependencies between agent roles.

The enhanced version features interactive drawing of R/D Diagrams (including role definitions, service definitions, dependencies relations), direct inspection of the XML code, generation of agent role descriptors and initial knowledge bases and the validation of the graphs and entries.

### 11.6.3 Dependency Diagrams for Plugin Systems

The Knowledge Round-Trip Plugin is not bound to agent role dependencies but can also be used to model other component-based, hierarchically structured systems that own inter-dependencies. Another example of such a hierarchical system in our context is the plugin structure of RENEW. Similar to the agents in the MULAN-system, every plugin contains a configuration file in which the required and offered services (among other things) of the plugins are declared. Therefore the Dependency Diagram tool can be used to generate a Dependency Diagram of the plugin structure without much additional effort. A function to remove these transitive arcs in the diagram is therefore very useful but has not been realized yet.

The example in Figure 11.9 shows a fragment of the RENEW plugin structure without transitive arcs (manually beautified). The model shows the connection between the plugins GUI and Simulator as well as several other related extensions. RENEW Util is a plugin that encapsulates basic libraries used throughout the system. The GUI itself is divided into two parts, one is an adaptation of the graphical framework JHotDraw (RENEW JHotDraw) the other (RENEW Gui) offers Petri net specific drawing features.

We can identify some oddities from the diagram. First, RENEW Ant is not connected. This is perfectly all right because this plugin provides build support. None of its functionality is used by any other plugin at runtime. Second, RENEW Prompt and RENEW Gui Prompt implement the same service, which is actually not required by any other plugin but offers a user interface for the user (developer) of RENEW. The only difference is that one provides a command line prompt convenient for remote access and the other is implemented as *Swing* GUI. Third, the Simulator/Formalism and the JHotDraw plugin are independent of each other, meaning one can run the system and use the common drawing features of RENEW JHotDraw without the Simulator plugin loaded, and it is also possible to run a simulation without the GUI.[8] However, if the RENEW Gui plugin is loaded, both sides of the system (Simulator and JHotDraw Gui) have to be loaded.

## 11.7 Summary

In this work we present techniques to explicitly model the dependencies between agent roles and services. The benefit of these techniques are intuitive diagrams, which are close to UML standard diagrams, derived from Component and Class Diagrams, and at the same time suitable for expressive modeling in the context of agent-oriented methodologies. The use of the proposed diagrams helps software developers of multi-agent systems

---

[8]It is actually possible to attach or detach the GUI, while the simulation is running.

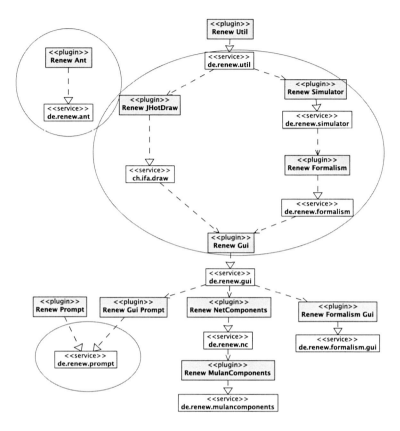

Figure 11.9: Fragment of the RENEW plugin dependencies.

to get an overview of the overall structure of a system and to identify desired or undesired dependencies hidden in the (possibly distributed) source code. The presented techniques can be applied in constructive as well as analytical modeling. Furthermore, the diagrams can also be valuable for presentation and documentation purposes.

Mainly, we have shown that common standard methods of modeling can be successfully applied to system modeling in the agent-oriented context. Moreover, even for this area, where the standard notions, concepts and perspectives fail to be effective, the commonly known techniques can be applied, if they are adapted to the needs apparent in the paradigm of multi-agent system. With the R/D Diagram one perspective that is often addressed in agent-oriented methodologies is covered in a suitable way which is not alien to object-oriented developers either.

With the Knowledge Round-Trip Plugin for Dependency Diagrams, including the round-trip engineering system capabilities, developers can generate and use Dependency Diagrams without additional effort. The Dependency Diagram always shows an up-to-date documentation of the system due to its round-trip engineering integration. The application of the Dependency Diagram technique can be extended to other domains such as component-based, plugin-based or service-based software systems. The current version of the Knowledge Round-Trip Plugin, for example, can generate diagrams that show the RENEW plugin dependencies. Because the RENEW plugins and the plugin system were conceptually based on agent technology, this additional functionality was achieved with only little effort (compare with Cabac et al. (2006a)).

Standard validation techniques can be applied to the generated diagrams directly within our tool set. Thus an analysis of the structure of the diagram is possible, is easily applied and offers valuable additional information about the system. As a presented example, the Net Analysis Plugin allows to check for simple properties in graphs, properties such as the absence of cycles or connectedness.

With the Roles/Dependencies Diagram (R/D Diagram) it is possible to integrate the advantages of dependencies modeling together with the structural modeling of specialization hierarchies of agent roles.

In parts the changing of the implementation language for the design artifacts to XML, which can be merged, played a major role in this improvement. The enhanced version of the Knowledge Base Editor (KBE) includes the diagram in its interface, allows to edit knowledge base entries directly within the diagram and offers on-the-fly syntax checking and validation. However, the analytical modeling, i.e. the round-trip engineering capability of the Knowledge Round-Trip Plugin, is not yet integrated into the KBE. While the tools have been successfully applied in some experimental projects, we currently aim at an integration of the round-trip engineering system of the Knowledge Round-Trip Plugin into the KBE Plugin, which already offers flexible editing and verification power.

Future work aims at an integration of techniques within our tool set. A connection between services as used in the R/D Diagram with the interaction diagrams could fill the gap between service descriptions and service/role implementations, i.e. triggers for certain actions. We would like to apply our techniques to other domains and evaluate them against other agent-oriented methods, for instance Jadex (see Braubach et al. (2005), Braubach and Pokahr (2009)). The work on dependency modeling and roles and dependencies modeling presented in this chapter are examples of the block of a broader approach on agent-oriented software engineering based on Petri nets and other graphical modeling formalisms called PAOSE (Petri net-based Agent-Oriented Software Engineering). Included in this field of research is the MULAN/CAPA framework as well as efforts of the improvements in multi-agent application development with Petri nets (see Duvigneau et al. (2003), Rölke (2004) and Cabac et al. (2005a)).

# 12 Modeling Application-specific Agent Ontologies

Ontologies are essential parts of multi-agent application development. The design, although the basic aspects (*concept, specialization*) are simple, is challenging due to the complexity and the size of ontologies – even in the case of small systems.

In this chapter we provide two modeling techniques for the design of MULAN-based ontologies. The first is based on Protégé as a tool set, which allows to explicate (a-posteriori) as diagrams. The second is integrated as plugin in RENEW and allows to model the ontology directly as Concept Diagram (a limited Class Diagram). Both approaches allow for the generation of *Java* classes for the convenient use of the ontologies.

Section 12.1 outlines the context of ontology modeling. Section 12.2 expresses the special case of ontologies in multi-agent systems. The modeling of application-specific agent ontologies is addressed in Section 12.3. Tool dependent related work is pointed out in Section 12.4, the tool support described in Section 12.5 and a summary provided in Section 12.6.

## 12.1 Context

Two of the main aspects in common system design and analysis are the definition of domain-specific concepts and the definition of programming interfaces. Domain-specific concepts – usually collected in software development as glossary – form a central aspect to support the developers to understand the domain of application as well as to form a common communication basis for different stakeholders in the development process, such as software architects, programmers and users. It is obvious that without a common *language* between these stakeholders, no coherent development can be achieved. For the designed and implemented system, similar necessities can be claimed. Parts of the software have to be able to communicate in an orderly way with other parts of the system. In object-oriented approaches, this is done as interface design.

In the PAOSE approach of modeling MULAN applications, we design the concepts of agent communication – the ontology – in the domain specific language. The ontology concepts thus play the role of interfaces for the agent communication, i.e. the concepts define what can be expressed by agents. Furthermore, not only the system parts that follow the interface definition are thus able to communicate with each another, but also the developers (e.g. programmers) are able to communicate on the basis of a well-defined language.

**Advantage** Since the domain-specific concepts become part of the design artifacts by entering the ontology, they are much more easily adopted by the developers than if the glossary remains a documentation artifact.

In the opposite direction the elements of the developed system (ontology concepts) become elements of the language of the developers. Thus there is no gap between documentation / communication language and programming ontology.

**Challenge** Interface design artifacts have to be maintained, controlled and extended during software projects. Lilienthal (2008, p. 151) shows that this requires high amounts of discipline and frequent reviewing from developers. This statement– although given for object-oriented systems – is also true for the ontology design. The ontology is thus one of the crucial parts of the system design and it requires special care and the attention of all participants.

## 12.2 Ontologies in Agent Applications

In multi-agent systems we are able to integrate both aspects into one domain specific ontology for the designed system. The domain-specific concepts, as defined in a glossary, can directly be included into the agent ontology. Thus the agents are able to communicate about domain-specific objects (or entities) in the same manner as developers and users communicate with each another. This fact adds to the self-reflective nature of agents and agent systems.

In fact, in MULAN even the internals of the multi-agent framework such as the concepts of agent management are designed as ontology, following the FIPA specifications of the FIPA management ontology. Thus concepts like `AgentDescription`, `AgentIdentifier`, `ServiceDescription` or `SearchConstraints` are found in the CAPA management ontology. These elements are defined as *Java* classes, which offer convenient creation of messages and – together with the implemented parser – also convenient message parsing. Following the FIPA specifications, the concepts are defined as key-value tuple or as simple value tuples. In the MULAN/CAPA framework this means their class implementations are classes of the types `KVT` or `VT`. Again for convenience, the framework offers abstract classes in generic form : `GenericKVT` and `GenericVT`.

All framework classes – mainly the CAPA management ontology – are implemented manually. The amount of implemented convenience classes is already hard enough to maintain for the framework, even though the ontology does not undergo large or frequent changes. For the development of multi-agent applications, however, it became quickly clear that this approach was not feasible. The ontology constantly grows during the development of the system and manual repetitive tasks bind resources that can be used for other – more important – tasks.

The obvious solution is the generation of these similarly structured class files from one model (or from several ones).

# 12.3 Modeling of Ontologies

We utilize two means of modeling agent ontologies for MULAN applications. The first one uses Protégé (`http://protege.stanford.edu/`), a powerful and well-known tool in the area of ontology design. The modeled concepts are designed in a hierarchical structure, although Protégé also allows to model multiple inheritance relations. The second means of modeling employs a built-in feature of RENEW. To model concept hierarchies for MULAN applications, we use the type definition features of the Feature Structure Net formalism of RENEW developed by Wienberg (2001).[1]

## 12.3.1 Defining Agent Ontologies with Protégé

Protégé is a powerful tool for the modeling of ontologies in general. It is extensible with plugins. A multitude of plugins exist that offer all kinds of functionality.

Offermann and Orthmann[2] have adapted a plugin for Protégé, originally designed for the generation of ontology classes for *Jade*. The generator plugin for MULAN/CAPA (compare the last tab in Figure 12.1) uses the template engine of Velocity[3].

The modeling of agent ontologies has quite low demands concerning the modeling technique. It follows that many features/capabilities of Protégé and Protégé-based ontologies, such as instances, forms, multiple inheritance, are not used in our ontologies. A more simple technique would be sufficient and would also relieve the amount of attention that developers have to pay to technical aspects.[4]

In Protégé, the creation of concepts and slots is done using the creation tools by adding nodes to the tree (compare with Figure 12.1). Attributes such as abstractness/concreteness, slot entries and comments are defined using a form editor shown on the right side of Figure 12.1. Protégé has also a limitation that forced us to find a work-around. Concepts and slots are not allowed to carry the same name although this is common in our ontology. To avoid this problem, we decided to start all concept names with a capital letter, which is quite odd and against the FIPA-conventions. However, the name of a concept will be the frame descriptor in the SL representation (Semantic Language) of FIPA-compliant communication, which is specified as containing only lower case letters and dashes. Thus, the generator had to be extended to adapt the frame descriptor to our needs.

The high demands on the design abilities of the developers and the limitations of Protégé, together with a slow progress in model creation and an unsatisfying representation of the model for the developers, lead to the search for more simple and flexible techniques.

---

[1]The FS Plugin – offering the Feature Structure Net formalism – is publicly available as additional plugin for RENEW at `http://www.renew.de`.

[2]Offermann participated as student in the AOSE projects. Orthmann is a PhD. candidate.

[3]Velocity, see `http://velocity.apache.org`.

[4]In fact, experience shows that the usage of Protégé is so demanding that many developers need special support and only few of them are able to handle the tool independently.

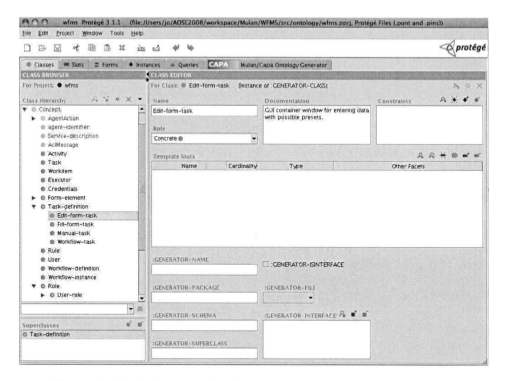

Figure 12.1: Protégé user interface showing an example agent ontology: WFMS.

## 12.3.2 Modeling Ontologies with Concept Diagrams

The type definition in Feature Structure Nets are expressed as Class Diagrams. These diagrams – a simple, efficient and minimalist approach – are directly drawn in RENEW. The original feature has been extended to allow the import of other ontologies and to allow the developers to annotate the diagram elements with API comments – a feature that we value in Protégé. Figure 12.2 shows a Concept Diagram of the WFMS ontology. Concepts are defined by adding text figures to the diagram. The text, once entered and released, is rendered as a typical Class Diagram-like box with the name on top in bold letters and the slots given by their name and their type. Types can be either standard

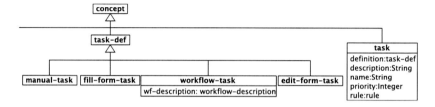

Figure 12.2: A Concept Diagram showing part of the WFMS ontology.

Figure 12.3: A Concept Diagram showing RENEW's edit field with API comment.

*Java* type, inherited types from imported ontologies, or defined concepts in the current ontology. Concepts, in opposition to classes, do not contain any methods. Thus the simplicity of the diagrams. Inheritance arcs and association arcs are either drawn with

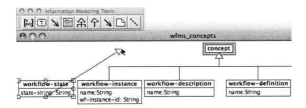

Figure 12.4: Tool palette of the FS formalism; showing the usage of arc handles.

the tools provided by the palette of FS tools or by convenient arc handles of the figures.

### 12.3.3 Concept Hierarchies

Concepts (ontological objects, mental representations, representations of objects) are figures of speech/language. Each concept is identified by its name and its attributes. The main structuring element in agent ontologies is specialization / generalization. In the context of software development, it seems natural and straightforward to define these structures as Class Diagrams. Concepts can be defined by defining the name and the attributes as slots or associations with other concepts. The intuitive *is-a* relationship can be described by inheritance arcs.

## 12.4 Related Work

Protégé, developed by Stanford Center for Biomedical Informatics Research at the Stanford University School of Medicine, available at `http://protege.stanford.edu` is a powerful tool for the modeling of ontologies. Protégé offers visualization of ontologies as diagrams through some plugins. Two of these are the Ontoviz plugin[5] and the Jambalaya plugin[6].

---

[5]Ontoviz, see `http://protegewiki.stanford.edu/index.php/OntoViz`.

[6]Jambalaya, see `http://www.thechiselgroup.org/jambalaya`.

## 12.4.1 Tool Extensions

### AML

Cervenka and Trencansky (2007) describe the Ontology Diagrams in AML (compare with Section 6.4.3). This technique is comparable to the Concept Diagram presented in this chapter. Nevertheless, differences exist. We design our ontologies solely from concept names (frames), fields (slots) and specialization. No operations are defined, since the concepts are concepts of communication. However, the ConceptUtility in AML is again comparable with helper classes for concepts, which provide static (global) methods for information processing of concepts and slots.

### Ontoviz

Ontoviz offers a visualization in a Class Diagram-like fashion based on the basis of Graphviz (see http://www.graphviz.org/). In the framework of Graphviz graphs are generated with an incredibly good layout mechanism, but neither graph nodes nor the layout can be edited.

### Jambalaya

Jambalaya offers several layouts of graphs – also generated from the Protégé ontology – and allows to edit nodes by zooming-in. Graph types include tree layouts and also a tree-map layout. However, the handling of diagrams is time consuming and requires even more familiarization with yet another tool.

### Wienberg

Wienberg (2001) was one of the original developers of RENEW and provided in his dissertation the Feature Structure Net formalism.

### Ortmann

The version of the generator for Protégé was adapted for CAPA by Ortmann and integrated into the *Ant* development environment as a RENEW plugin: Ontology Generator Plugin. Several improvements were since done by Duvigneau, Reese, Teuber and me.[7]

### Teuber

Teuber (see Cabac et al. (2009)) re-implemented the ontology generation feature for Concept Diagrams, i.e. FS type definitions extended by package and import definitions, and the possibility of additional comments in concept figures. Together with Friehe, he also converted the Protégé-based Settler ontology to Concept Diagrams.[7]

---

[7]Teuber and Friehe are students, who participated in the AOSE projects. Ortmann, Duvigneau, Reese are PhD. candidates who participated as tutors or organizers.

## 12.4.2 Contributions

My contribution in this part is the introduction of class models – however ever obvious – into the development process. At first the diagrams were only used for documentation means, since no suitable generator existed.

I supervised the project assignment of Teuber. We originally conceptualized a feature as round-trip system between Protégé and Concept Diagrams. Due to technical problems with Protégé, the dimension of the assignment and the desire for a maintainable lean solution, we opted for a simple generator feature, which was successfully achieved. In order to integrate these diagrams into the ontology package of the *Javadoc* API documentation as navigable image maps, I implemented the generation of image maps for HTML.

Other contributions are the improvement of controlling the necessity of class re-generation during compilation and the easing of the use/setup of Protégé ontologies through the integration of ontology templates in the Use Case Plugin (see Chapter 10).

# 12.5 Tool Support

Protégé is a powerful tool for the modeling of ontologies. The support for the definition of FIPA-compliant ontologies is good, however, some drawbacks exist.

The tool support for the modeling of Concept Diagrams is directly given by Renew. Diagrams are drawn fast and easily, generation of *Java* code is automated and the setup for the *ant* build environment is provided by the project setup done by the Use Case Plugin's generation features.

### Generation of Ontology Classes

Generation of code is provided for Protégé-based ontology models by the OntologyGenerator Plugin and for Concept Diagrams by the FSOntologyGenerator Plugin. Both generation features are based on the Velocity template engine and both plugins are components of the build environment, i.e. they are not functional as runtime plugins for Renew. This can be regarded as degeneration of the plugin concept. However, in the aim to unify all relevant components of a system, it is of advantage to even include components that are solely functional at build-time as plugins. The structure of the source code organization and the build process of the component supporting the build environment is simplified.

The generation of the ontology is fully integrated into the automated build process with *ant* (http://ant.apache.org). Concept code generation is done very early (after net-stubs generation) during the *ant* run of compiling a multi-agent application plugin. Besides the generation of all concepts defined in the ontology model, also a management class is generated that registers all available concepts of the designed ontology at the parser when starting the system. Thus, the handling of ontology matters is fully automatic and developers can concentrate on the design of the ontology as model and other matters of system development.

179

```
package de.renew.agent.wfms.ontology;

import de.renew.agent.repr.common.*;
import de.renew.agent.repr.acl.*;
import java.util.*;
import de.renew.agent.repr.sl.Sl0Creator;
import de.renew.agent.repr.sl.Sl1Parser;
import de.renew.agent.repr.sl.ParseException;

/**
 * <p>
 * Protege name: Workflow-task
 * </p>
 *
 * <p>
 * This class is generated from the concept workflow-task
 * of the Protege ontology WorkflowOntology.
 * </p>
 */
public class WorkflowTask extends TaskDefinition {

    //—————— constants ——————
    /**
     * The name of the concept used in textual representations is
     * {@value} .
     **/
    public static final String TYPE = "workflow-task";
```

Listing 12.1: Class `WorflowTask` (first 29 lines). Compare with Figure 12.1.

Listing 12.1 shows the first lines of a generated class from a Protégé model (a fragment of which is depicted in Figure 12.1). The name of the class (*WorkflowTask*) as well as its frame name (*workflow-task*) is inferred from the model and as in the model it is sub-concept of *TaskDefinition*.

## 12.6 Summary

Ontology design is a major part in the design of multi-agent applications. The design of the ontology controls much of the overall design of the system through the definition of available terms in the development process/team and possible topics of conversation in the multi-agent system itself.

With Protégé a powerful tool exists that is widely used in the community of agent-oriented software development. However, to master the tool in its complexity is a demanding challenge. With the transition to Concept Diagrams we are able to easily design ontologies for MULAN applications by simply drawing the diagram in an intuitive way. Generation of code is achieved from either model, Protégé or Concept Diagram. Still – also with the modeling as Concept Diagram – the complexity of large ontologies makes their design challenging. A decomposition into hierarchical models is supported by both tools. However, neither allows for an overview of the ontologies super structure.

# 13 Modeling Interactions

By offering tool support for the construction and modeling of protocol nets, we have succeeded in accelerating their development. Also, the form and the structure of protocol nets have become unified and easily readable. Another advantage is that the agents' interactions are documented in the Agent Interaction Protocol Diagrams. Therefore, the overview of the system has been simplified and enhanced.

In this chapter we describe one further step towards an integrated development environment for MULAN applications. By combining the two described approaches, we are able to generate Petri net structures from the Agent Interaction Protocol Diagrams.

The following pages briefly recapitulate the modeling of agent conversations with Agent Interaction Protocol Diagrams. Finally, a prototype tool for code generation will be presented together with a simple example. Section 13.1 outlines the modeling of agent interactions in the context of computer aided design. Section 13.2 discusses the AUML Agent Interaction Protocol Diagrams (AIP) and introduces the possibility to define their semantics with Petri nets. Section 13.3 provides the main aspects of the mapping from diagrams to protocol nets, which defines the semantics in the context of MULAN. Section 13.4 describes the AIP Diagram Plugin. Related work is presented in Section 13.5 and a summary concludes the chapter in Section 13.6

## 13.1 Context

Computer aided software engineering (CASE) tools are programs that support the development of large software systems. They provide tools for modeling and constructing applications. Furthermore, they provide the possibility to generate code from models, to facilitate the development and to strip the development process of unnecessary recurrent and error-prone manual tasks. Successful tools for various programming languages exist and are in extensive use.

Especially for the usage of the Agent Unified Modeling Language (AUML) within CASE tools, a well-defined semantics is required. However, the semantics of agent interaction protocols (AIP) is usually defined by the semantics of Sequence Diagrams and descriptions in natural languages. These semantics are usually ambiguous and vague. To address the challenge of defining a formal semantics for agent interaction protocols, we use high-level Petri nets. Since Petri nets do not only offer a well-defined formal, but also and operational semantics, we can by this means, not only provide formal semantics, but also operational semantics to Agent Interaction Protocol Diagrams.

While modeling with Petri nets is common, the idea of programming with Petri nets has not been widely accepted yet. But especially when it comes to concurrent and distributed processes, e.g. multi-agent systems, the advantages of Petri nets are obvious. For this reason, we build concurrent and distributed software systems as multi-agent systems on the basis of reference nets (see Kummer (2002)) – a high-level Petri net formalism, which is enriched with *Java* as inscription language. The framework's reference architecture for the multi-agent system is MULAN[1]/CAPA.[2] It is implemented in reference nets and can be executed efficiently in RENEW.[3]

The process of implementing application software in MULAN requires the construction of protocol nets which define the behavior of the agents. A protocol net is a reference net that describes the communication and the internal behavior of an agent. Since the construction of a large system requires building many protocol nets, which frequently require similar parts of functionality, the need for software engineering methods and techniques becomes evident. This includes standardizations, conventions and tool support.

We have established two methods to handle the complexity of protocol nets and support their construction. First, we use net components (see Chapter 5 and Cabac (2009)) to construct the protocol nets and to achieve a unified and structured form of the protocols. Second, we model the agents' interactions on an abstract level using Agent Interaction Protocol Diagrams (see Cabac et al. (2003)). Agent Interaction Protocol Diagrams are defined by the FIPA (Foundation for Intelligent Physical Agents (FIPA 2009)) in AUML (FIPA 2001b). The advantage of modeling in AUML is its intuitive graphical representation of the processes/scenarios.

## 13.2 AUML and Petri Nets

This section describes how Agent Interaction Protocol Diagram semantics can be defined with the help of Petri nets. Examples for some expressions of the diagrams are given to show the general notion.

Different versions or flavors of AUML have been presented and discussed. See Odell et al. (2000), Odell et al. (2001) and Koning et al. (2002) for the old version (version 1) and their extensions. These are also used by the FIPA to describe the Interaction Protocols (see FIPA (2001b)). The new version (version 2) is still under development (see Odell and Huget (2003) and Huget and Odell (2004)). However, we are not concerned with the different flavors of the AUML Agent Interaction Protocol Diagrams. Since the meaning behind these flavors is basically the same, which makes the graphical representation interchangeable, it is superfluous to discuss this matter here. The shown examples are given in Agent Interaction Protocol Diagrams of the old version (version 1). If a semantics is defined for one of the flavors, it can easily be translated to the other flavors.

### 13.2.1 AUML Flavors

Each of the different flavors of AUML Agent Interaction Protocol Diagrams have advantages and disadvantages. We favor the old version of the AUML Agent Interaction

---

[1]Multi-Agent Nets, (see Köhler, Moldt and Rölke (2001)).

[2]Concurrent Agent Platform Architecture, (see Duvigneau et al. (2003)).

[3]Reference Net Workshop, (see Kummer (2002), Kummer et al. (2009a))

Protocol Diagrams for several reasons. First, we think that the old representation of agent interactions is more intuitive and clearer in appearance than the new style that is oriented towards the UML 2.0 standard. Second, through dropping the threads, the new version of AUML (version 2) does not reflect concurrency in a sufficient way. Third, we have been working with the old version successfully over the last two years in several teaching projects with over one hundred students. The modeling technique - although new to the students - was well accepted and successfully used in the development of multi-agent applications.

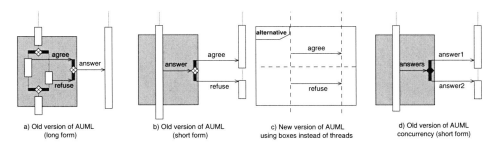

Figure 13.1: Flavors of AUML, representing the alternatives of sending one of two possible (a,b,c) / concurrently sent (d) messages.

Figure 13.1 shows the representation of the alternative to send one message out of two possible messages as an example for the different flavors of AUML Agent Interaction Protocol Diagrams.[4] This example shows another advantage of the old long (or explicit) version (Figure 13.1 a) of Agent Interaction Protocol Diagrams. With the usage of message join figures we are able to represent the fact that only one message is actually received by the receiver of the message. Instead, in the short version (b) and also in the new version (c) of AUML there is no *structural* difference in the representation of receiving one message (of for example two possible messages) and the representation of two concurrently sent / received messages (d), although the syntax itself is unambiguous.

## 13.2.2 Semantics for AUML

By using Petri nets, which offer a well-defined operational semantics, it is possible to describe the operational semantics of Agent Interaction Protocol Diagrams. To demonstrate how this is done, the example of Figure 13.1 (see also Figure 13.2 a) is used and modeled as Petri net in an abstract (or simplified) fashion. Figure 13.2 shows the representation of two alternatively sent messages modeled with a Petri net[5] (b). In addition, Petri nets also offer the possibility of coarsening (respectively refining) nets. The coarsened Petri net is shown in (c) which can be interpreted in the coarsened Agent Interaction Protocol Diagram as shown in (d). This way of modeling offers the possibility to use

---

[4]Only parts of the diagrams are shown in the image.

[5]For the semantics including inscriptions and pattern variations see Cabac (2003).

abstractions that can clarify the models. It also offers the possibility to exchange one agent's behavior with another possible behavior without the need to alter the behavior of the communicating agent. For instance, the sending agent can always reply with an agree and the receiving agent's behavior would not have to be altered.

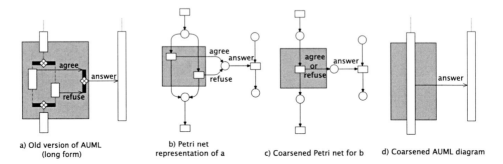

a) Old version of AUML
(long form)

b) Petri net
representation of a

c) Coarsened Petri net for b

d) Coarsened AUML diagram

Figure 13.2: Semantics for the alternative message provided by Petri nets and coarsened descriptions.

By translating AUML Agent Interaction Protocol Diagrams into Petri nets we manage to define the operational semantics of the Agent Interaction Protocol Diagrams, i.e. the semantics of the diagrams is defined through the semantics of Petri nets. However, the translation is not done on the abstract level as shown in Figure 13.2. For a translation into a form of executable Petri nets we need to use more elaborate and concrete methods. These methods are a framework architecture for the execution of the resulting protocols and a mapping from Agent Interaction Protocol Diagram expressions onto (unified) expressions of Petri net code that can be executed in the framework's architecture. The first is given through MULAN/CAPA (see Köhler et al. (2001), Duvigneau et al. (2003)), which offers a Petri net-based infrastructure as a reference model for a FIPA-compliant multi-agent system. In addition, the multi-agent applications built on MULAN/CAPA are also executable within the framework. The second is achieved through mapping the Agent Interaction Protocol Diagram expressions onto net components. Net components (see Chapter 5) as a means of automatically structuring protocol nets are presented in the next section.

## 13.3 Net Structures

This section describes the way we model agent communication with AUML diagrams and presents how Agent Interaction Protocol Diagrams (AIPs) are mapped to Petri net structures using the net components (see Chapter 5) for protocol nets. While AIPs describe the conversations of agents, protocol nets define the behavior of the MULAN agents, and net components are descriptions of basic tasks in the protocol nets.

### 13.3.1 Structured Petri Nets

Petri nets are graphs, i.e. they have a graphical representation. A graphical representation is useful for the understanding of the behavior of a model. A graphical/diagrammatic representation may be more comprehensive than a textual one. However, a diagram can also be very confusing if it does not provide a clear structure or if substructures of similar behavior are displayed in many different ways. One of the greatest advantages of a diagrammatic representation is the fact that reappearing structures can be perceived by the human cognitive system without effort.

The usage of net components enables developers to recognize reappearing net structures in protocol nets effortlessly. Furthermore, a conventionalized style of the developed Petri nets is achieved by using net components for the construction of protocol nets.

### 13.3.2 Modeling Agent Interaction

Modeling agent interaction can be done by using several means. The FIPA (FIPA 2009) uses the AUML Agent Interaction Protocol Diagrams (see FIPA (2001b)) for the modeling of agent interactions. These diagrams are an extension of the Unified Modeling Language (UML) Sequence Diagrams (see Booch et al. (1999)), but they are more powerful in their expressiveness. They can fold several sequences into one diagram by adding additional elements (AND, XOR and OR) to the usual Sequence Diagram. Thus, they are able to describe scenarios. Figure 13.3 shows the FIPA Request Protocol and a compliant Producer-Consumer example.

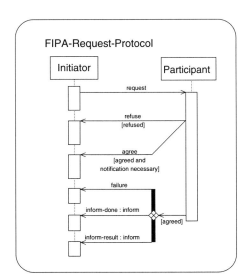
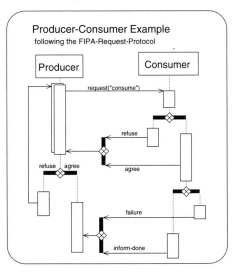

Figure 13.3: Agent Interaction Protocol Diagrams of the FIPA Request Protocol and a compliant Producer-Consumer example.

There are several advantages in the method of modeling agent interactions with Agent Interaction Protocol Diagrams. Three of them are:

- The models are easily readable by all participants because of the similarity to UML.

- Abstract modeling increases the overview over the system.

- A means of communication, specification and documentation is established.

We do not only model the agent interactions with AIP, We also include the interaction models in the source base – for easy access and inclusion into a versions control system – and into the API documentation of the application (see Chapter 19).

### 13.3.3 Mapping Agent Interaction Protocol Diagrams to Mulan Protocols

The tool for the drawing of AIP diagrams, the AIP Diagram Plugin, integrates the net components concept and facilitates an adapted version of the MULAN Net Components for its generation feature. By using Agent Interaction Protocol Diagrams for the modeling of agent communication the structure of the protocol nets can be derived directly from the diagram. This is done by mapping the relating elements in the Agent Interaction Protocol Diagrams to the net components. In detail this means (compare with Figures 13.5 to 13.10):

- A message arc is the abstract representation of the basic messaging net components (*NC out* and *NC in*).

- A split figure is the abstract representation of a conditional (*NC cond*) or a parallel split (*NC psplit*).

- A life line between a role descriptor and an activation marks the start of a protocol (*NC start*).

Several other net components (loops, sub-calls) and also possibilities to handle instances of protocols (indicated by the shadow activation figure in Figure 13.3 in the Producer thread) are not yet represented in our tool for Agent Interaction Protocol Diagrams, since the elements representing that kind of functionality do not exist in the abstract model. It seems that for some of these basic tasks/features the notation of the Agent Interaction Protocol Diagrams has to be extended. However, the possibility to model that kind of functionality exists in Petri net protocols and is applied by using net components. For the following functionality Agent Interaction Protocol Diagram representation offers no equivalent.

**Loops:** Loops are not well-represented yet. Proposals exist for their representation, but so far there has been no way to determine whether a sequential or a concurrent process is desired.

**Sub-calls:** It is possible to nest Agent Interaction Protocol Diagrams, but semantics is ambiguous.

These and some other challenges are for instance addressed in the development of the AUML version 2.0 (see Huget and Odell (2004)). In general, the main problem is the vague semantics of the Agent Interaction Protocol Diagrams. Although the lack of specification of detail within a model that results from abstraction can be of advantage while modeling, the semantics of notation should be clear and well-defined. The process of modeling can be accelerated by postponing the description of details to the implementation or by relying on implicit knowledge that defines the missing semantics. In contrast, if there is the need to define a specific mapping, clear semantics is desired/necessary.

An approach that consecutively enhances/refines the models can be described as implementation through model refinement (*Implementation by Specification*), i.e. the model's details are progressively worked out.

The mapping in Table 13.1 presents the mappings of AIP elements to protocol net elements. Most diagram elements that can be transformed are represented as net components in the protocol nets. The role descriptor figure is the one exception. It is mapped onto a protocol net and can be conceptualized as a reference to this drawing. The role descriptor's name is given to the protocol net, as well.

The current version of the AIP Diagram Plugin uses net components that can be parameterized. This allows to transfer inscriptions from the diagram to the protocol nets. The possibilities of using transferred diagram inscriptions is presented in the lower part of the table. The mapping described in the table 13.1 defines – partially – the operational (transformational) semantics in the context of protocol nets.

| Diagram | Protocol Net / Net Component |
|---|---|
| Role descriptor figure | protocol net drawing |
| First activation figure | *NC start* |
| Message arc figure end | *NC out* |
| Message arc figure tip | *NC in* |
| OR split figure | *NC cond* |
| AND split figure | *NC psplit* |
| OR join figure | *NC ajoin* |
| AND join figure | *NC pjoin* |
| Action text figure | *NC sequence* |
| Exchange text figure | *NC exchange* |
| Exchange text figure "simple" | *NC simple-exchange* |
| **Parameter** | Protocol Net Inscription |
| Action text | *NC sequence* transition inscription |
| Exchange text | *NC exchange* place inscription |
| Message text | *NC out* transition inscription |

Table 13.1: The mapping of diagram elements to protocol net elements.

## 13.4 Tool Support

The AIP Diagram Plugin[6] is designed as a plugin for RENEW and allows to draw AIPs directly with the RENEW user interface. With the help of adapted net components it allows to generate Petri net model skeletons for protocol nets.

This section describes the features of the AIP Diagram Plugin. This includes the tool support for mapping Agent Interaction Protocol Diagrams to protocol net structures. The plugin generates Petri net structures similarly to program source code skeletons generated by other UML CASE tools. To achieve a functional protocol net, the model has to be refined, e.g. the inscriptions have to be adjusted (compare with Section 21.3.4).

### 13.4.1 Tool Description

The Net Components Plugin is included in the release of RENEW[7] since version 2.1 as optional plugin. The AIP Diagram Plugin is available separately.[8] The diagrams are used as means of specification, documentation and communication among the developers of MULAN applications.

Figure 13.4 displays the RENEW GUI including the control elements of the diagram plugin. The last palette contains tool buttons for the drawing of role figures, activations, messages, life lines, split and join figures, note figures, frames and inscriptions.

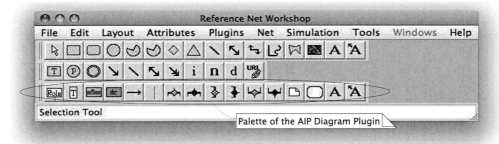

Figure 13.4: RENEW's GUI with the tool support for drawing diagrams.

The process of constructing a protocol net with net components requires the usually manual task of mapping the diagram structures to protocol nets (compare with Section 5). This is done by drawing the net components and connecting them with each other using the functionality of the Net Components Plugin. Many elements in the Agent Interaction Protocol Diagrams are mapped onto net components in a straight forward fashion as described in Section 13.3.3.

---

[6]Since the concepts related to AIPs have been provided by me and the implementation of the AIP Diagram Plugin have been done by me, I summarize mainly the central contributions, without stressing the fact that I am the contributor.

[7]Current version of RENEW is 2.2, see Section 3.3.

[8]The AIP Diagram Plugin is available at http://www.renew.de/plugins.

It seems obvious that this task can be performed automatically by the introduced tool. Since Agent Interaction Protocol Diagrams describe the interactions and the splitting of activities, we decided to implement a prototype that is capable of generating Petri net skeletons from the diagrams that reflect these structures. To be able to execute the generated code, it has to be refactored and adjusted with additional functionality. This is a common approach for code generation: The parts that can be derived from the model are generated and the rest is added manually.

## 13.4.2 Tool Development

I am the author of the original conception and implementation as well as of all improvements to the AIP Diagram Plugin. The first version of the tool allowed to draw simple Agent Interaction Protocol Diagrams for documentation and communication. The general drawing figures of AIPs were included as standardized boxes and lines and provided by tool buttons. Up to the current enhanced version a multitude of improvements have been included. The following list summarizes the efforts of reaching a higher expressiveness, a user friendly behavior, a higher integration into the development process and a powerful feature for the generation of protocol nets.

**Development History**

- Added specialized figures to the JHotDraw framework.
- Improved horizontal message line connections.
- Added UML Note figures to add comments/notes.
- Improved split figures and their connectors (parallel, alternative).
- Added convenient message handles for accelerated model construction.
- Refactored figure compounds to decorated figures.
- Added drawing restrictions that makes automatic drawing of anticipated figures possible; i.e. if during the drawing of a connection the mouse is released on the background of the drawing at the right place the anticipated figure is constructed automatically and the connection is attached.
- Added snap-to-fit of figures.
- Added generation of code by using net components.
- Added automatic layout of generated nets on the basis of diagram arrangement.
- Added automatic arc connections for generated net elements.
- Added message templates to generate adapted inscriptions on the ground of diagram arc inscriptions.
- Added action figures – as attachable figures – to represent simple actions.
- Added life line handles.
- Added text generation for actions.
- Added generation of *NC stop*.

- Added DC exchange figures with text generation.
- Improved generation of texts of messages (three different possibilities).
- Added support for DC simple exchanges.
- Introduced flat/weak grouping for generated net components.
- Added collapsing/expanding feature for action/exchange inscriptions.

Concurrently to the development of the AIP Diagram Plugin several persons worked on enhancements and additions to the concepts. Dirkner and Lehning (2005) designed and implemented a first prototype for AIP/protocol net round-trip engineering. Lehning improved the tool resulting in a second prototype (NDsync) that was capable of drawing peered drawing elements simultaneously in both diagram types: Petri nets and AIPs. However, the (by the time of availability) improved generation features of the AIP Diagram Plugin made a change to the NDsync prototype obsolete.

Gertchikova (2004) implemented together with Deliu a prototype that featured message generation in context of the chosen FIPA protocol. The efforts were fruitful but the result was not feasible in an engineering context due to its generic approach and the protruding representation. A simpler generation of inscriptions in the AIP Diagram Plugin and the generation of ontology objects from Protégé or concept models made the system obsolete.

### 13.4.3 Geometrical Arrangement of Mulan Protocols

In addition to textual code generation, the construction of Petri nets also has to deal with the layout of the generated nets. The structure of nets is crucial to readability. If the code is used as it is generated, there is no need to design the layout of the code. But if the code has to be adjusted, the programmer has to understand the code. Thus, the layout of the nets is an important issue.

Net components provide a structure for Petri nets. This is not only true for the manually constructed nets but also for generated code. For each net component only some additional information is needed that provides the knowledge of how it can be connected to other net components and how this is reflected in the layout. The position can consecutively be determined. By starting with the first net component (*start*) at a convenient place the position of the next connected net component is defined. Thus, net components provide the structure by imposing their own structure onto the net structure. However, the generated Petri net code structures have always the same form due to the automated generation.

Figure 13.6 shows the source of the model for the Producer-Consumer example augmented with the geometrical representation of the corresponding net components and Figures 13.7 and 13.9 show the two parts of the model that match the two protocol nets, rotated counterclockwise by ninety degrees. The resulting skeletons are shown in Figures 13.8 and 13.10.

All augmented models are just presented here to illustrate the matching of diagram elements to net components. They are not necessary for the generation of the protocol nets. The generated protocol net skeletons are shown (Figures 13.8 and 13.10) as they have been generated, without any modification of nets or inscriptions.

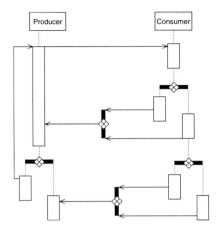

Figure 13.5: Source for generation of the Producer-Consumer example.

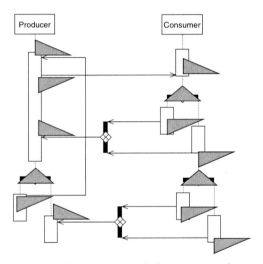

Figure 13.6: The source from Figure 13.5, with the geometrical representation of the corresponding net components.

### 13.4.4 Example: Producer-Consumer

Generating code skeletons from the Producer-Consumer Agent Interaction Protocol Diagram example is possible and results in two protocol net skeletons. Figure 13.5 shows the diagram from which the code is generated.

The results of this simple example are satisfying. The protocol nets do not need to be refactored because the conversation deals only with communication and decisions. However, in order to convert these skeletons into executable protocol nets, we still have to work on them. The relevant data has to be extracted from the messages and from the agents' knowledge bases. Furthermore, we have to define the decisions and the outgoing messages.

It seems that for more complex communication protocols, dealing with internal behavior, loops or sub-calls, this simple approach is not powerful enough. But since most of the used net components deal with message passing, splits, starting and stopping, this approach will already generate more than ninety percent of the Petri net code structure. Only the parts that deal with broadcasting or multi-casting messages, or the parts that deal with internal behavior have to be adjusted manually.

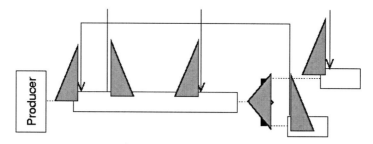

Figure 13.7: The Producer part of the source from Figure 13.5, with the geometrical representation of the corresponding net components. Rotated counterclockwise by ninety degrees to fit the orientation of the resulting protocol net.

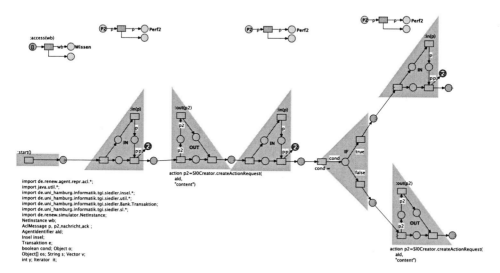

Figure 13.8: Generated Producer protocol net skeleton

192

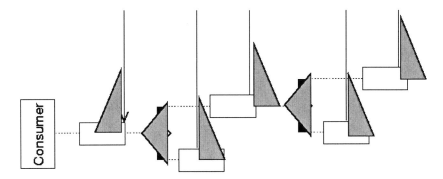

Figure 13.9: The Consumer part of the source from Figure 13.5, with the geometrical representation of the corresponding net components. Rotated by ninety degrees to fit the orientation of the resulting protocol net.

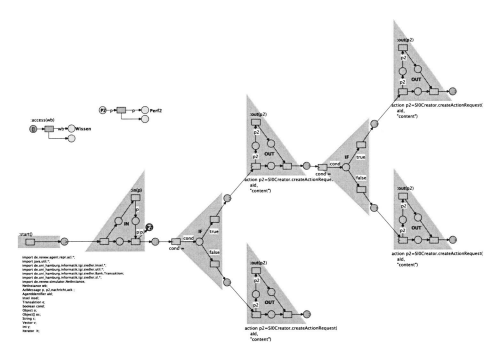

Figure 13.10: Generated Consumer protocol net skeleton.

## 13.5 Related Work

### Odell, Parunak & Bauer

Odell, Parunak and Bauer (2000) propose extensions to UML for the modeling of agents, leading towards AUML. The agent interaction protocols as descendants of Sequence Diagrams are introduced. Splitting and merging of life lines and messages allow for the modeling of scenarios with the Sequence Diagram-like modeling technique.

### Odell & Huget

Odell and Huget (2003) propose a new version of interaction modeling for agents influenced by recent developments in UML 2.0 Interaction Diagrams. Multiple life lines are dropped again in favor of combined fragments. We see this development as a sign that object-oriented concepts are still dominant even in the AOSE community. This reduces the flexibility gained with the first approach and also withdraws the process awareness from the technique. In addition, large diagrams become illegible because of a multitude of parallel lines. For instance, those parallel lines result from messages (solid), splitting separator (dashed) and frames of combined fragments (solid).

### UML 2.0

In UML 2.0 (2005) the combined fragment is introduced in the specification allowing to express scenarios in Sequence Diagrams. The combined fragment's semantics is defined by the keyword identifier. Combined fragments may be alternatives, optional, break, parallel, weak sequencing, strict sequencing, negative or critical region. Keywords are accordingly: *alt, else, opt, break, par, seq, strict, neg* and *critical*. The Sequence Diagram notation of UML 2.0 has gained wide acceptance throughout the object-oriented community. However, the fact that semantic different executions have the same or a similar structure in the diagram is a drawback. Combined fragments can only be understood by reading the keyword.

### Harel & Marelly

Harel and Marelly (2003) propose an alternative approach as extension to Sequence Diagrams or message sequence charts, the life sequence chart (LSC). In LSC, scenarios can be expressed through alternative, optional and conditional parts of the processes. The unique feature is that scenarios can be defined by executing samples of processes, which are manually expressed and the system 'learns' the possible behaviors (play-in). In a different mode the LSCs can then be executed to control the system (play-out).

### AML / ADEM

In the Agent Modeling Language (Cervenka and Trencansky 2007, AML) Sequence Diagrams contain similar elements as in AUML. Life lines can be split into alternative possibilities of execution. Thus scenarios can be represented in AML.

### Ehrler & Cranefield

Ehrler and Cranefield (2004) are using the second version of AUML Interaction Diagrams. Diagrams are enriched with annotations of *Java* code, which is interpreted by the BeanShell interpreter (`http://www.beanshell.org/`). Direct execution of diagrams is one of the advantages. However, the approach is not mature enough. Only one combined fragment is supported (*alternative*), which reduces the richness of the technique to a small subset. In contrast to the annotated diagrams of the direct execution, our approach focuses on a lean, concise representation of the model. In Agent Interaction Protocol Diagrams we try to reduce implementation-specific code to a minimum.[9]

### Dirkner & Lehning

Dirkner and Lehning (2005) implemented an enhancement of the AIP Diagram Plugin – a prototype – that included concepts from round-trip engineering. In fact, the approach was called *live-trip engineering*, meaning that both models, AIPs and protocol nets, were editable concurrently and changes would affect both models simultaneously.

### Padgham, Winikoff & Poutakidis

Padgham and Winikoff (2004) use Interaction Diagrams (comparable to simple Sequence Diagrams) to design agent interactions. These Interaction Diagrams are transformed into Protocol Diagrams (comparable to AUML 2 Interaction Protocols), from which processes are derived. A simple description language enables the developers to model these Protocol Diagrams for the Prometheus methodology. Poutakidis et al. (2002) use these diagrams to identify possible matches of faulty interactions by comparing the design artifacts with observations. In general, this approach of debugging returns a list of possible interactions that could have caused an error, such as a dead-lock. Such an approach is not necessary in MULAN/CAPA, where dead-locked interactions not only manifest themselves as *hanging* protocols in the MULAN-VIEWER (see Chapter 16), but the exact location and cause of the dead-lock can be traced directly in the protocol net – a feature owed to the fact that protocols in MULAN are Petri nets.

## 13.6 Summary

Software engineering methods have been developed to enhance the construction of large software systems and are used and applied successfully. These methods can also be applied for system development based on high-level Petri nets. With more extensive use of these conventional techniques, the process of Petri net-based software development can be improved. The advantages of Petri nets lie in their inherent concurrency, whereas UML is a powerful modeling language that is well-accepted and widely spread. Both – UML and Petri nets – can contribute to the construction of large distributed and / or

---

[9]Note that the introduction of action and exchange inscriptions in the Agent Interaction Protocol Diagrams makes it possible to add application-specific inscriptions to our models.

concurrent systems. Combining their advantages results in a powerful method to develop applications.

A crucial point is the semantics of the used AUML Agent Interaction Protocol Diagrams. It has to be well-defined for the development/design as well as for the generation of code (structures). We showed that the defining of Agent Interaction Protocol Diagram semantics can be achieved by mapping the diagrams onto Petri nets. For this, a net component-based approach was used, which enables the generation Petri net code structures from the diagrams. The net components provide the functionality of syntactic / semantic unities as well as the structure of the resulting protocol nets. However, the definition of semantics is realized in the tool and not explicitly given here.

In addition, by using net components, the protocol nets are structured and their structure is unified. This increases the readability of protocol nets and the software development is accelerated. The integration of UML-based modeling into the developing process has contributed to the clearness of the system and its overall structure. Apart from the development process, the focus of development was also altered by using AUML. The center of focus shifted from the agents' processes to the communication between the agents.

The introduction of AUML-based modeling into the developing process and the unification of net structures turned out to be a successful approach. Nevertheless, the integration of conventional methods (e.g. UML) in the development of software with Petri nets can be driven further.

For the development of large applications on the basis of the Petri net-based multi-agent framework MULAN/CAPA, tool support is needed on different levels of abstraction. This includes the construction of protocol nets, the modeling of agent interaction and the debugging of the system (see Chapter 16) during development. The first two points are covered by the tool support for net components and Agent Interaction Protocol Diagrams. Additionally, we can now also ease the developing process by generating code in the form of Petri net structures from diagrams.

# 14 Modeling Agent-Internal Behavior

This chapter describes the conceptual and technical aspects of decision components. Decision components are agent-internal processes that may function as a service to the protocol nets, as an encapsulation for (other) software resources (e.g. data bases) and as adaptor for eternally attached deliberation engines. The latter includes extensions to the agent as *planner* and can also be – if the agent functions as placeholder agent – the interface for a human user.

Besides the basic concepts and the technical frame, a generic decision component is also presented that provides the adaptor functionality between reference net and *Java* implementations.

The context is briefly sketched in Section 14.1. Section 14.2 introduces the descriptions of internal agent behavior. Section 14.3 describes the modeling of decision components by two means. The first is a set of net components for decision components, the second a generalized decision component that can be used in the context of bridging between reference nets and other software systems. Related work in the close context of decision components is presented in Section 14.4, a brief description of the available tool support is given in Section 14.5 and Section 14.6 summarizes the topic of decision components.

## 14.1 Context

In the original model of MULAN, all processes of the agents are modeled as protocols. For a lean and abstract reference model of a multi-agent system architecture, this approach seems feasible. But on second thought and when designing multi-agent applications, the need for protocol net independent decisions becomes obvious.

The line of communicating – i.e. social – actions is defined by the interactions of the agents. In MULAN/CAPA these are modeled as protocol nets. However, the agent must also be able to decide on *which* line of action or which line of response. As in the case of an independent player agent of a game (e.g. Settler), it is obvious that some entity inside the agent has to plan its strategy, its actions, its willingness to negotiate with other players, and so on. If, however, this software agent represents a human player participating in the game, the user interface has to be connected to the agent. In this case the human player becomes the deciding entity. In a third scenario an agent offers a service that requires a resource, such as a data base, then the bridge to this (other) software system has to be provided independently from any conversation instance.

## 14.2 Internal Behavior

Internal behavior of an agent may include interaction spanning synchronizations (such as needed in advanced negotiations), planning processes, user interface connection or encapsulation of external resources, such as for instance data bases or other (legacy) software systems.

### 14.2.1 Planning

Seegert (2005) developed a planning framework for MULAN agent entirely designed with reference nets. This was the first implementation of a decision component and the first implementation of the interface to the agent existed (still) in the knowledge base. The planning framework generates on-the-fly protocol nets, which perform the intended action of the planner, i.e. the planning component. Generation is automatically done during runtime by the planner. For the construction of the generated protocol nets, Seegert facilitated a set of net components and functionality of the Net Components Plugin (compare with Chapter 5).

Other realized approaches are the integration of simple *Java* code and also a planner in *Prolog*. Brin (2008) integrated the *Jadex* system as planning component into the MULAN/CAPA framework.

### 14.2.2 Connecting User Interfaces

User interfaces have been attached to place-holder agents for the Settler game implementation as well as for the interaction of executors with the WFMS. With the introduction of decision components, the conceptually unclean ad-hoc solutions for the user interface connection has been encapsulated in decision components, which offer a convenient programming interface (see Subsection 14.3.2).

Decision components have been used to provide prototypical user interfaces for interactive testing and for the observation of MULAN-based applications. In Settler 5 a complete user interface has been constructed (compare with the *NetGui* presented in Figure C.11), in which all interaction features of the game are available. The construction of such a prototype is considerably faster than a graphical user interface written in *Java*. Thus, for some time – as long as the *Java*-GUI was not available – the *NetGui* was the only means to control the game and to perform integration tests for interactions.

### 14.2.3 Encapsulating Resources

The first version of the WFMS (see Reese et al. (2008), Reese (2009))uses the underlying workflow engine of RENEW (see Jacob (2002), Jacob et al. (2002)) to execute fragments of the distributed workflow locally. The information of the workflow definitions, the workflow instances, as well as the presentation of workitems and activities have to be exchanged between local WFMS (the 'legacy system') and the framework of the AgentWFMS.

# 14.3 Modeling Decision Components

There are currently two ways for the construction of decision components, apart from modeling without any support. The first one uses the net components for decision component and the second one facilitates the generalized decision component of the RemoteDC. The DC net components (DCNC) are provided by the DC Components Plugin, and the generalized decision component is provided by the RemoteDC Plugin.

## 14.3.1 Net Components for Decision Components

In the context of multi-agent application development with MULAN, a new set of net components has been developed for the construction of decision components (DC). These nets

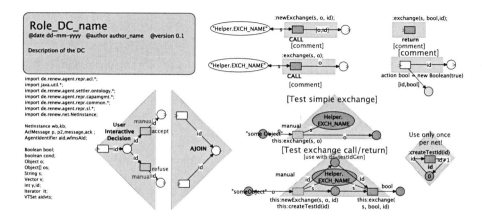

Figure 14.1: The decision component net components.

implement the internal behavior of agents, especially processes that do not control the communication of an agent and internal long running processes, such as planning or interaction spanning synchronizations. For these nets, similar net components as from the set of net components for protocol nets are used (and have accelerated the construction of DCs). However, there are also some differences, such as explicit handling of synchronizations of calls. Each call/return gets its own ID, which has to be handled explicitly in the net. Figure 14.1 shows several proposed components that are currently in use. For instance, the interfaces to the protocol nets: *call* (synchronous), *call/return* (asynchronous). These are the counterparts to *simple-exchange* and *exchange* (see Figure 5.8). Other net components are the manual choice, the merge and some test components with which the functionality of the DC can be tested as a *stand-alone* net instance (manual unit testing). Note that the color scheme differs significantly from the one of MULAN protocol net components.

## 14.3.2 Generalizing Decision Components

An effort to ease the connection of external software systems to agents in an orderly and safe way is offered by the RemoteDC Plugin. A generalized net stub[1] that makes it possible to access synchronous channels as methods from *Java* code.

Figure 14.2 shows a part of the net implementation of the RemoteDC. The system can, with the depicted parts, instantiate new protocol nets by calling the `:newPlan(·)` as the stub method. Note that the behavior of synchronous channels and *Java* method

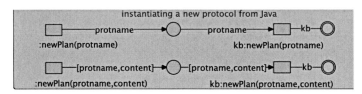

Figure 14.2: Net DCJavaNetInteraction: instantiation of a new protocol net from *Java* (*newPlan*).

calls are significantly different. Synchronous channels are able to transport information in both directions of the channel by using the RENEW unification feature. When calling a synchronous channel from *Java*, this ability is restricted. The `:newPlan(·)` up-link will receive the protocol name and, if so, also the designated message content and the arguments will be passed to the knowledge base calling the channel with the same name. This is typical for an adapter such as the DCJavaNetInteraction net.

Figure 14.3 shows a more complicated part of the net which defines the adapter for the exchange interface in the direction from net to *Java*. The three exchange channels are provided (`EX`, `RET` and `ex`) and the calls are handed over to the respective *Java* class (DCModelManager). The two simple exchange channels are in mutual exclusion, one for

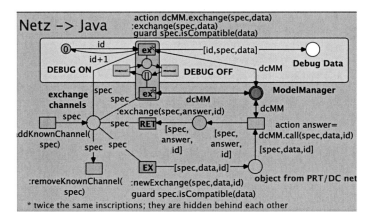

Figure 14.3: Net DCJavaNetInteraction: exchange with *Java* classes.

---

[1]For information about the net stub mechanism please consult the Renew User Guide.

the normal usage, one for debugging purposes.

Figure 14.4 shows the interface of knowledge base access for *Java* classes.

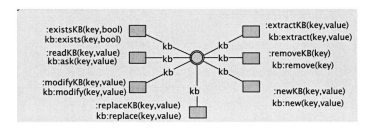

Figure 14.4: Net DCJavaNetInteraction: KB access.

Figure 14.5 depicts an overview of the DCJavaNetInteraction and Table 14.1 lists all interfaces. The net offers a generalized approach of accessing *Java* code from RENEW Petri net models without defining any net stubs.

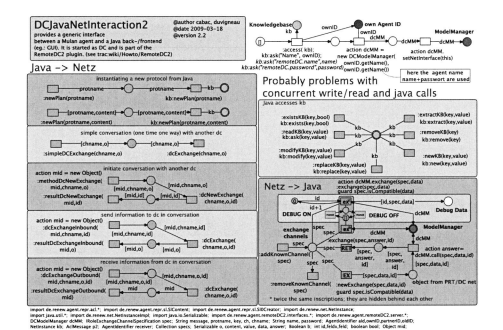

Figure 14.5: The overview of the Net DCJavaNetInteraction.

| Channel | Arity | Description |
|---|---|---|
| Java *calls knowledge base* | | |
| existsKB | 2 | query existence of a key in KB |
| readKB | 2 | read an value from KB |
| newKB | 2 | create new key value tuple in KB |
| removeKB | 1 | remove entry from KB |
| modifyKB | 2 | modify a value in KB |
| replaceKB | 2 | replace a value in KB |
| extractKB | 2 | extract an entry from KB |
| Java *calls net* | | |
| newPlan | 1,2 | proactive instantiation of a protocol |
| simpleDCExchange | 2 | calling a DC from *Java* |
| methodDcNewExchange | 3 | initiating a conversation with a DC |
| dcExchangeInbound | 3 | send information to DC from *Java* |
| dcExchangeOutbound | 4 | receive information from DC in *Java* |
| *Net calls* Java | | |
| newExchange | 3 | initiate a request for *Java* |
| exchange | 3 | fetch answer of request from *Java* |
| exchange | 2 | method call from net |

Table 14.1: The interface of the DCJavaNetInteraction.

## 14.4 Related Work

Several advancements have been made for the concept of modeling internal processes in the form of decision components and the technical realization of these.

### 14.4.1 Advancements

**Rölke**

Rölke provided the first interface in the knowledge base in order to attach a decision making entity: the planner interface. Soon it was established as a first-order concept and part of the agent, when the interface (and container place) was moved to the agent net.

**Markwardt**

Markwardt implemented the first version of the RemoteDC, which offered only a limited interface with a very reduced interaction scenario. He implemented the RemoteDC as a client/server architecture, which is based on RMI (remote method invocations). This allows the actual user of the interface to be located on another machine as the executing engine. However, the connection works – as typically for RMI – also without any problem on a local system.

**Brin**

Brin (2008) used the same interface – the RemoteDC – to integrate a planner, which runs in the *Jadex* system as autonomous player for the Settler game. In fact, he was able to reuse the same interface definition of the human player GUI connection.

### Rathjen

Rathjen (see Cabac et al. (2008b)) re-implemented the RemoteDC as project assignment for several reasons. The programmers support for the connection of the RemoteDC to a *Java* implementation was not supported efficiently in the first version. Too many elements had to be programmed manually. Especially the different behavior of *Java* method calls and synchronous channels create a multitude of possibilities for mistakes on the *Java* side. Some steps had already been done before to ease the programming amount. I implemented an interface definition as array provided by the *Java* side of the interface. This prevented the possible rejection of exchange calls that could not be answered. These rejections resulted either from (1) possible syntax errors or (2) from DCs that were in conflict.[2] I proposed and enforced a second means to increase the reliability of the interface. This was the introduction of class constants for the description of exchange channel names as convention. However, the programming effort was still quite high, which led to the re-implementation. Now channel specifications (*specs*) are declared in a text file, from which the code of the interface connection is generated at compile time.

## 14.4.2 Contributions

Together with Reese and Duvigneau, I furthered the separation of communicating and internal processes as a conceptual advancement in the design of agent processes in MUL-AN. This separation clarified the conceptual and technical basis of the framework. Thus, it is possible to dispense with the conceptually questionable long-running protocol nets – e.g. for synchronizing over several conversations or for the permanently attaching of software resources.

I introduced predefined channel names that reduce the generic interface to prevent calls of unavailable names/parameters and avoid unnecessary conflicts. This solved an error that occurred after the transition from single to multiple decision components. In this coarse, I also introduced the convention to use class constants for exchange names, enabling syntax error detection at compile-time.

By adding several (at first unavailable) knowledge base accessors, I managed to enable checks for the existence before running into deadlocks in the case of a non-existing entry. This fixed a severe bug that occurred when retrieving information from the knowledge base from within *Java* code.

I added a debugging feature to the *DCJavaNetInteraction* net, in order to be able to track and handle increasingly complex interactions. I also redesigned the net completely and added several missing reverse exchange calls (*Java*→Net) together with Duvigneau.

To ease and accelerate the construction of decision components I analyzed the decision components available and – similar to the development of the MULAN net components

---

[2]Actually, the first implementation of the DC interface in the knowledge base allowed only one decision component. Although this was changed quite early, the RemoteDC was not adapted to the new interface.

– I provided a prototypical set of net components that gathered the best solutions as templates.

## 14.5 Tool Support

Modeling of decision components as Petri nets is done directly in RENEW. For the development of these nets a set of net components exists that considerably facilitates their construction. With the set of net components comes a subset of test components, which makes it possible to test the constructed net on a stand-alone basis against the decision component interfaces. These manual tests accelerate the design of *correct* decision components.

Sometimes Agent Interaction Protocol Diagrams have also been used to specify the processes of decision components with some success. However, the form and diversity of decision components make it difficult to define a coherent and unified modeling technique. Also the use of State Charts for the specification is frequently proposed with only little success.

It seems that the range of different application areas leads to a diversity of decision component types that do not make it possible to find *one* modeling technique for all decision components. Moreover, with the existence of the RemoteDC, as generalized approach of connecting any *Java* code / system to an agent, the necessity to find a modeling technique decreases.

The RemoteDC as a generalized decision component is provided as plugin for RENEW. The plugin offers the connection infrastructure for an interface connection between agent and *Java*. The second major version of the plugin offers a task that generates the connection call methods from the *specs* files.

## 14.6 Summary

Decision components are process models that define the internal behavior of agents. They differ from protocol nets in the fact that they do not participate in external communication within agent conversations. Moreover, protocols have a workflow-like character, with a short life span that depends on the respective conversation. Through the independence from such a restricted life time, it is possible to model inter-conversation spanning synchronization to allow planning or negotiation features. Also the diverting of decisions to third entities becomes possible, such as attaching a GUI or encapsulating another software system, such as a data base or a workflow management system.

# 15 Summary

This part presents the PAOSE modeling language, i.e. a set of modeling techniques that enables developers or development teams to systematically engineer multi-agent applications after the multi-agent paradigm with the MULAN/CAPA framework. Additionally, the main aspects and parts of the development process together with the philosophy behind the development of Petri net-bases agent-orientation software are sketched, in order to embed the presented techniques in the development processes and team organizational settings. The jest of the PAOSE approach is best presented through the guiding metaphor of *multi-agent system of developers* and the project team organization as matrix of independent views and elements. Two of the unique features of the PAOSE approach and the development with the MULAN/CAPA framework is the acknowledgment of concurrency as first-order concept and the pervasive application of the multi-agent metaphor. Concurrency-awareness seems obvious at first glance if one considers that Petri nets are the basis for the approach. The ubiquitous application of the multi-agent system as a paradigm to categorize and structure all objects of investigation results from the socionics influence and the belief that the full power of the paradigm can only be exploited if the chains of conventional system engineering can be broken. In PAOSE the integration of concurrency and also the pervasive application of the multi-agent metaphor are observable in all aspects of the approach and in the ongoing research these applications are constantly extended. Thus, concurrency is not only sought in the implementation of the system but also in the design, the system's analysis, the development team's organization, the development processes and the supporting tool set. However, if concurrency is a first-order concept, also the constrain of concurrency becomes important – either in general or also for efficiency.

The *multi-agent system of developers* metaphor and the organizational matrix are models for the software development process organization, the team organization and for the behavior of participants. The power of the guiding metaphor derives from the formalization of social organizations as multi-agent system and its simplicity, which is a common feature of good metaphors. It also builds on the high complexity of the multi-agent system as a model (e.g. MULAN) for the organization of participants, which offers a multitude of other metaphors and the highly structured system organization (environment, platforms, agents, processes, interactions). The participants are agents for software systems and developers for software development systems (i.e. projects).

Another main aspect is that multi-agent systems are distributed systems. Just as the developed system, the development system is naturally distributed in space and time. The former offers more challenges again in design, analysis, testing, debugging, construction, deployment and maintenance. The latter is inevitable for all development teams of complex systems. The more people are involved, the more distributed is the development process and the team organization. Planning and project management have to take distribution of resources and developers into account. Within the multi-agent paradigm and especially with the *multi-agent system of developers* metaphor these aspects are not superimposed onto a team organization but are inherent part of the system.

All these aspects are a challenge within the software as well as the development process. Especially, the distributed and the concurrent aspects together with the high complexity of multi-agent systems are imposing problems to the developers that are not present in conventional approaches. The following part deals with techniques and tools related to the modeling techniques presented in this part for the analysis of MULAN-based applications. The main aspect is to support the developers' understanding of the system. *System* means the design artifacts, the running processes, the organizational structure and the implementation artifacts as well as the development system, i.e. development processes, workflows, project management. The main points in the following part are the analysis of the systems, the tool support for the explication of the system as model and the integration of the activities of developers into the development process. The systems that are analyzed are the executed multi-agent applications as well as the designed systems of source code artifacts.

We conceive the development environment, which can be either integrated (IDE) or loosely coupled, as a socio-technical system itself. For such systems, which contain heterogeneous entities of execution (i.e. software and human beings) the multi-agent metaphor is well-suited (compare with Lehmann et al. (2005)).

# Part III

# Analytical Modeling of Multi-Agent Systems

This part introduces techniques and tools as means of analytical modeling for the support of the understanding of the MULAN-based systems. Tasks that need to be supported are the testing of parts of the systems (unit tests), the debugging of the running system as well as the analysis of source and runtime code and data. Tools are the means that can help the developers in these tasks. They can provide the easy access to the design artifacts of the system as well as to the implementation artifacts. Furthermore, they can provide the possibility to observe the running system, and gathered information can be presented to the developer in processed and concise representation, e.g. as diagram. In addition, the observable artifacts have to be linked with design artifacts to allow for quick and easy navigation between executables and sources.

The focus in this part is on the techniques and tools for analytical modeling of the systems that were developed to enable developers to understand the multi-agent systems. The part is structured as follows. Chapter 16 investigates debugging in the context of multi-agent systems in general and presents two tools, the MULAN-VIEWER and the MULAN-SNIFFER, which allow to analyze the developed system by several means. Chapter 17 presents a means to analyze the observed messages, the Mining Plugin. It extends the MULAN-SNIFFER by adding process mining techniques. The prototypical implementation of the Mining Plugin is capable to aggregate information to more concise process representations. This offers a multitude of possibilities in the multi-agent context, from automatic protocol generation from observed conversations to the introduction of adaptive behavior of agents.

Chapter 18 presents an approach to introduce semi-automatic comparison of versions of diagram. For texts, there exist powerful tools that achieve the tasks of comparing and merging automatically, as long as there are no conflicts. A similar feature for diagrams would be desirable. Although the presented technique does not provide any merging feature, it supports the developers in the process of comparing diagrams on a visual level.

Chapter 19 presents Mulandoc, which is a system for the organized presentation of the design artifacts produced during the development process in the PAOSE approach. It is designed after the *Java* API system *Javadoc*, it is web-based and thus offers comfortable navigation to easily find the presented artifacts.

# 16 Mulan-Viewer, Mulan-Sniffer and Debugging

This chapter presents techniques and tools for debugging of multi-agent systems. This concerns various aspects like inspection, observation and visualization of the structure and the processes in multi-agent systems. The chapter is structured as follows. Section 16.1 briefly outlines the context of debugging multi-agent systems and of the two tools for that cause: MULAN-VIEWER and MULAN-SNIFFER. Section 16.2 presents the basic concepts of the debugging process and classifies the related aspects with respect to three dimensions (*activities*, *scale* and *coupling*). Based on these dimensions, we identify the resulting requirements. Section 16.3 introduces our view on multi-agent system development and the matching tools to support detecting and locating bugs. In Section 16.4 we present related work. Section 16.5 summarizes and provides an overview of the presented tools as table in the context of debugging.

Debugging of multi-agent systems (MAS) is hard due to their distributed, concurrent, adaptive, highly interactive, flexible, mobile and heterogeneous nature. As said above, we identify three dimensions that span across the area of debugging and derive general requirements for a debugging tool set in the multi-agent context. The implemented tool set and the requirements for these, in the context of the MAS reference model MULAN, are presented. This tool set comprises general low level debugging possibilities that are included in the virtual machine (execution engine RENEW), specialized MULAN-dependent debugging facilities that enable debugging on higher agent concepts and independent debugging aspects that rely on publicly available information – i.e. message logs – together with advanced techniques, such as visualization and mining.

## 16.1 Context

Debugging is the process of locating and fixing bugs. Especially the *locating* part is one of the most time consuming and difficult tasks nowadays in software development projects. But before a bug can even be located, its existence needs to be detected. At best, bugs should be detected before the system goes into production. A common approach to check for yet unknown bugs in a project under development is testing (see Sommerville (1996) and Myers (2004)), which is addressed in Section 16.3.4.

In this chapter, we concentrate on detecting and locating bugs within multi-agent systems from a software-engineering point of view. Thus the main emphasis lies on multi-agent system-related metaphors for structure (agents) and processes (interactions). The tasks of detecting and locating bugs are already challenging in the case of distributed and concurrent systems. Here reproduction of events, control over executing entities and causal dependencies are in many cases beyond the control of the developer. But multi-agent systems are not only concurrent and distributed systems, but also composable and adaptable systems where the interfaces of entities (agents) may change during runtime. This fact imposes another challenge onto testing and debugging as the correctness of a system may vary in different configurations. On the other hand, multi-agent system concepts impose a strong structure on a software architecture. It is advisable to try to benefit from this structure in the process of testing and debugging.

We examine the main characteristics of debugging of multi-agent systems by presenting the requirements for the debugging of multi-agent systems based on the fundamental concepts that are present in such systems as well as in their development processes. Tools are the central means for implementation support as well as sufficient concepts, metaphors, techniques etc. in order to create an effective, efficient and productive development setting. For the MULAN/CAPA (see Köhler et al. (2003)) framework we have developed techniques and tools to reduce the time consumption of the debugging phase.

## 16.2 Dimensions of Debugging

The task of detecting and locating bugs involves several *activities* that can be categorized according to their effect within the debugging process. However, activities are not the only dimension to exploit when it comes to MAS debugging. As a multi-agent system uses metaphors both on micro and macro levels to impose a strong structure on the artifacts that make up a software system, the dimension of *scale* needs to be considered as well. Furthermore, MAS are composable, concurrent and distributed systems. We group these properties under the dimension of *coupling*. Depending on the kind of bug, the developer has to or needs not to care about the issues imposed by such properties. Thus, debugging activities are spread along this dimension, too.

### 16.2.1 Activities

As can be seen in Table 16.1, several kinds of activities exist within the tasks of detecting and locating bugs. The system's artifacts have to be compiled, deployed, started, terminated, and tests have to be invoked either manually or automatically. The system has to be observed while running (monitoring). Sometimes it is necessary to freeze the system, watch execution steps one-by-one or deeply inspect the state of a system's artifacts. Manipulation of artifacts, data and code during runtime might speed up the preparation and variation of test cases or validate the appropriateness of proposed bug fixes. This can be described as *hot code replacement* or *hot data replacement*. Last but not least, communication between developers is especially needed when the development team is distributed in time and space.

Each of these kinds of activities requires specific support. We can derive the requirements for supporting tools from the necessary activities during debugging with respect to the other dimensions, scale and coupling. How these can be addressed follows in Section 16.2.4.

Most of the activities mentioned so far are not specific to MAS debugging (with the

| Preparation | Observation | Navigation |
|---|---|---|
| · Loading / Starting | · Observing behavior | · Step-by-step execution |
| · Compiling | · Reading code | · Encounter breakpoints |
| · Invoking tests | · Monitoring artifacts | · Finding source code |
| · Terminating | · Logging | · Exploring artifacts |

| Control | Manipulation | Communication |
|---|---|---|
| · Start agents, protocols | · Runtime code | · Informing other developer |
| · Set breakpoints | · Runtime data | · Asking for Support |
| · Step-by-step execution | · Source code | · Simultaneous debugging |

Table 16.1: Activities in Debugging

obvious exception of *Start agents, protocols, plans*). Nevertheless, each of these activities is well-suited to be performed within some range of the other two dimensions and hard to perform within other ranges. We will mention examples within the following discussion of the other two dimensions.

## 16.2.2 Scale

The second dimension, *scale*, deals with system wide issues vs. local (agent) issues. While the two areas are connected with each other through the micro-macro link, we use this qualification to distinguish between them (Table 16.2).

Lynch and Rajendran (2008) identify two main levels in the classification of tools in a multi-agent system development environment. While on the system level agents are considered to be black boxes, on the agent level the main interest lies in intrinsic agent state or behavior. The system level is more general (i.e. implementation independent), while the agent level depends highly on the agent platform and the applied language.

This kind of classification is useful for the observations in debugging of multi-agent systems. Here, we also distinguish between system wide (general) issues, and agent (local) issues. However, through the micro-macro link these issues are interdependent and sometimes the borders are not defined.

| System wide issues | Agent issues |
|---|---|
| · Organization of agents | · Knowledge |
| · Acquaintances of agents | · Interaction |
| · Deployment of agents | · Message |
| · Platform infrastructure | · Trigger / Events |
| · Ontology issues | · Planning / Goals |

Table 16.2: Classification of *object of investigation*

The objects of investigation **on the agent level** can be for instance faulty knowledge or the lack of appropriate knowledge. Interactions of unfinished conversations need to be identified and dead-locks to be determined. Messages may contain wrong addresses, performatives etc. Also triggers can be missing or matching the wrong message/interaction response pairs. Plans might not lead to the targeted goals and goals can also be wrong. All these objects of investigation can be inspected and undesired behavior or states be corrected once the cause is identified. This, though, requires that the developer has access to the agents under investigation.

While agent level debugging is quite straight forward, i.e. conventional focusing on agent and component matters, system level debugging is difficult and new unconventional approaches have to be taken (see Ndumu et al. (1999)).

**On the system wide level** observation becomes more difficult. In distributed and/or open systems, access to agent information (e.g. organization, acquaintance, deployment) or platform information is not trivial or is sometimes even undesired.

The ontology is usually shared and can be subject to different interpretation as well as changing over time. In concurrent systems faulty behavior might not be reproducible. Observations might not (and usually do not) show the true state of the system. For instance the causes for emergent organizational structures or behavior might remain obscure to the observer.

In general, on the system wide level, information has to be gathered and the *image* of the system has to be composed (visualized) from fragments of information.

## 16.2.3 Coupling

When considering the debugging of multi-agent systems, the question arises whether they are to be treated like other modular, distributed and concurrent systems or not. The following paragraphs differentiate systems with respect to their *coupling*, i.e. whether they are monolithic systems or loosely bound, distributed and/or concurrent. However, since multi-agent systems debugging extends general debugging we look into the monolithic case first. Note that the concepts presented in Table 16.3 do not build upon each another. For instance, distribution and concurrency are orthogonal to each other.

**Coupling of Systems**
· Monolithic, sequential systems
· Composable systems
· Distributed systems
· Concurrent systems

Table 16.3: Coupling of system parts relevant in debugging

**Monolithic, sequential systems** give the debugging developer full control while preparing, observing and manipulating the system's execution. Preparation of system execution is straightforward, testbeds can be created and executed with full control over the system's state as a whole. Pausing the system's execution for inspection will not be noticeable from the view of the system's behavior. Observation, Navigation and Manipulation are supported by conventional debugging tools. Communication with other developers is only needed if the code under review has been created sometime or somewhere else by some other developer.

**Composable systems** have different debugging requirements. Since multi-agent systems are composable systems that are loosely combined, the agents and even their interior components (protocols, knowledge, plans) can be tested and debugged by providing testbeds for each of them.

An important issue of composable systems is that the characteristics assigned to each component may get lost through composition. Liveness is one prominent example for this. Only with severe restrictions will this property of the individual components also hold for the composed system. Therefore, either verification is necessary or, if this is not possible, a good test and debugging environment is needed. Since agents only contain some parts of an overall conversation within a given system, all relevant agents (and their sub parts) need to be included for the tests.

**Distributed Systems** might require access to foreign administrative domains, i.e. remote systems/platforms, for debugging. However, it is not always possible or desirable to allow a remote investigation/control of a part of a system. In the agent-orientation community message inspection is a common method to infer certain information of a remote system. Nevertheless, a (global) state can be assumed but generally not inferred from the observed messages. Lam and Barber (2004) take a different approach by modifying existing multi-agent systems so that the agents report their internal state to a central debugging component. Lynch and Rajendran (2008) take a similar approach, in which the aggregating system is a multi-agent system. Still in both cases a realistic global state representation cannot be assumed in any asynchronous gathering of information.

**Concurrent Systems** can imply that the observation of the global state of the system becomes highly restricted. Actually there might not even exist a representation of a global state because the system is concurrent and distributed as well. Errors might not be reproducible (e.g. race conditions) and step-by-step execution is impossible or at least leads to unsatisfactory observations of one single serialization. The whole set of possible traces is not manageable.

Testbeds mostly fall short of providing information about race-conditions and non-deterministic behavior. Here, verification methods, such as structural analysis or model checking, might lead to satisfactory results.

## 16.2.4 Requirements for Distributed Debugging

Debugging multi-agent systems has many aspects in common with debugging normal modular, distributed and concurrent systems. Since the FIPA standards dictate agent communication via asynchronous message passing, techniques for the debugging of (synchronous) remote procedure calls are not applicable. There is, for example, no such thing as a "distributed thread of control". Furthermore, an agent's roles (comparable to interface declarations or class definitions) are exchangeable during a system's lifetime. No global control or state is present, each agent has incomplete local information and no agent is guaranteed to be able to collect *all* information about a system's current state or behavior. The consequence is that much information available by design in conventional software systems has to be recovered via observation in multi-agent systems or volunteered by the agents (see Lynch and Rajendran (2008)). When information is recovered from observation, techniques such as mining or the exploitation of design artifacts (see Poutakidis et al. (2002)) can be applied. The situation becomes slightly better when we add debugging capabilities to a platform instead of injecting a debugging agent as a peer within the MAS, because the platform can inspect *all local* agents and messages while they are executed or sent. Since many platforms provide a framework for agent implementation, the framework can be enriched to observe or manipulate an agent's internals – of course thus violating the agent's autonomy.

From the three dimensions (*scale, coupling, activities*) given in Section 16.2 the following requirements can be derived:

**Display information** on various levels of detail (*observation*). This is the most basic requirement, it covers the whole dimensions of *scale* and *coupling*.

**Automation** of the debugging cycle[1] – at least as widely as possible. This relates mainly to the *preparation* activity from Table 16.1. The integration of all debugging, testing and development tools helps to satisfy this requirement.

**Logging/Tracing** The course of asynchronous events needs to be recorded to investigate the cause of error conditions.

**Replay** It can be very tedious to manually reproduce an error condition. Therefore a replay mechanism for logged events is desirable.

**Distribution** To cover the whole dimension of coupling, debugging tools should be able to remotely connect to every part of the multi-agent system.

**Linking** information and artifacts enables the activity *"navigation"*. Zooming into an object or out of it means moving along the dimension of *scale*. Being able to analyze distributed objects relates to the domain of *coupling*.

**Message analysis** is crucial, because agents only communicate via messages. This comprises filtering and mining (see Botía et al. (2004), Cabac et al. (2006)).

**Information aggregation** means to be able to condense data as needed. One (simple) example would be to display the number of agents present on a platform rather than each agent individually (see Botía et al. (2004)). See also the Linking and Visualization requirements.

**Visualization** is a feature that displays results from mined data, like for example the communication between a pair of agents or the social network of agents (see Ndumu et al. (1999)).

---

[1]The debugging cycle denotes the process of debugging. This includes starting, observing, finding bugs, determining possible causes, fixing, compiling, restarting etc. of the system. Cabac, Moldt and Schlüter (2008) offer more details as for instance a complete debugging cycle for MULAN applications.

**Manipulation** All the previous requirements did not change the system being debugged. But capabilities for hot code replacement or data manipulation may speed up the debugging cycle (see Cabac et al. (2008)).

Additionally these general requirements exist:

**Security** is very important because systems are likely to be dispersed over different administrative domains. Here, for example, the need for the confidentiality of data will certainly arise.

**Communication** with other developers must be possible in order to facilitate distributed debugging. It has to be assumed that several developers are concurrently and distributedly working on the multi-agent system being debugged.

**Modularity and Portability** are not hard requirements. But they are considered best practice.

# 16.3 Application of Debugging in Mulan

This section introduces the mechanisms and tools for debugging in the context of MULAN. We present the facilities that provide efficient debugging of MULAN-based multi-agent systems. These are the CAPA platform running within the RENEW runtime environment, the MULAN-VIEWER and the MULAN-SNIFFER.

## 16.3.1 Debugging Features in Renew and Mulan

*Java* reference nets (see Section 3.2) are a Petri net-based *Java* extension that enable convenient programming and execution of concurrent systems. *Java*'s threading and object communication facilities are replaced by Petri net facilities. Each Petri net graph is executable code comparable to a class definition. Any statement inscribed on Petri net transitions is executed concurrently, unless restricted by places and arcs. Net instances and *Java* objects can be used interchangeably. Bidirectional synchronous channels provide a powerful communication mechanism.

The virtual machine that executes the code (RENEW, see Section 3.3) has already several built-in features to inspect code at runtime. The Petri net token game can be thought of as a visual debugger that helps to follow the control flow and deeply inspect a system's state. Tokens can be inspected in several ways; as string representation or as UML-like deep inspection (see ellipse highlight in Figure 16.1) of the object's state. Navigation between encapsulated entities is supported through hyperlink-like functionality, where reference tokens function as links. RENEW supports elaborated breakpoints for all relevant entities. However, there are some shortcomings when it comes to the visualization of the overall structure of the (local) system.

MULAN is specified in *java reference nets*. The specification serves as implementation due to the operational semantics of Petri nets. CAPA adds an efficient and elaborated platform implementation to MULAN that supports FIPA-compliant message communication via TCP/IP.

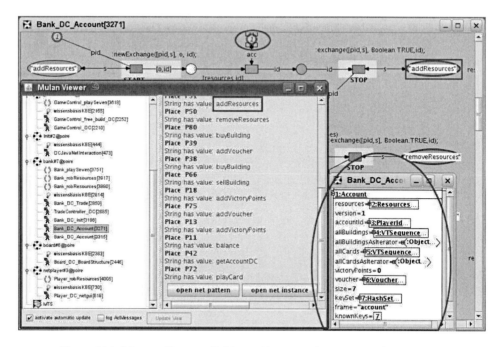

Figure 16.1: Mulan-Viewer linking to Renew token game and inspection.

Due to the fact that multi-agent systems in general and Mulan systems in particular are highly structured and loosely coupled, we are able to implement test beds for parts/areas of the system/processes. For decision components (interior processes, DCs) as well as for inter-agent interactions we have developed a technique that allows us to test them in a predefined setting independent of the rest of the system. The designed processes and nets are tested against dummy data or within a crafted multi-agent setup. Such component tests can be run either to detect bugs or to narrow the cause of some error condition down.

The tools presented in the following make use of the structure of a Mulan-based multi-agent system to present more abstract views of the system.

## 16.3.2 Mulan-Viewer

The Mulan-Viewer (see Carl (2003), Cabac et al. (2008d)) is particularly strong w.r.t. the requirements *linking information and artifacts*, as it is able to navigate any local or remote multi-agent system (dimension *coupling*) as well as entire platforms or internal items from an agent's knowledge base (dimension *scale*). The main components of the Mulan-Viewer are the platform inspector and the graphical user interface. An arbitrary number of platforms can be inspected both locally and remotely.

The user interface consists of two views: a MAS overview on the left and the detail view on the right (see Figure 16.1). The hierarchical structure of the multi-agent system is represented as a tree view. The levels of the tree view correspond directly to three of the four levels known from the MULAN model (the outermost level – system infrastructure – is missing). The message transport system agent (MTS) associated with each platform can be seen on the bottom left. If desired, messages can be collected and listed. The detail view allows inspection of chosen elements and provides integration with RENEW debugging facilities. It supports direct navigation to Petri net code (as well as net instances) of agents, protocols, decision components and knowledge bases. Additionally, all reactive protocols of an agent are listed so that breakpoints can be set directly from within the tool.

In Figure 16.1 the running instance of the net *Bank_DC_Account* from agent *bank#7* on platform *poire* has been opened in the detail view (right hand side of the MULAN-VIEW-ER) and can be seen in the background. The superimposed rectangles[2] indicate which elements from the detail view correspond to those in the inspected nets. In this case the string *addResources* shown in the detail view of the MULAN-VIEWER is contained by the place in question. The parts marked by superimposed ellipses[2] show how inspection levels can be nested: First the MULAN-VIEWER provides navigation (left hand side of the MULAN-VIEWER) to the desired agent and its protocols. Then the Petri nets can be inspected using RENEW. In the example the place on the top contains one token of type *Account*, which is inspected as UML object hierarchy (*token bag*).

We enhanced the MULAN-VIEWER with powerful (and additional) features (see Cabac et al. (2008)) for direct manipulation and control. These surpass RENEW's control and manipulation facilities by utilizing interfaces of the MULAN-imposed structure of the multi-agent system. The MULAN-VIEWER makes it possible to directly manipulate knowledge base entries (i.e. *hot data replacement)* and start (and stop) arbitrary (e.g. pro-active) protocols, decision components, agents and platforms. Additionally, a "new-protocol-wizard" supports the exchange of faulty protocols (or other nets) by new versions during runtime in a comfortable way.[3]

Thus a cohesion between inspecting, locating and fixing of bugs is achieved within the development tool support.

### 16.3.3 Mulan-Sniffer

The MULAN-SNIFFER (see Cabac et al. (2008d)) was inspired by the Jade Sniffer (2008); other related tools and approaches are the ACLAnalyser by Botía et al. (2004) and the sniffer in MadKit by Ferber et al. (2008). It uses (agent) interaction protocols (AIP) for visualization and debugging (see Cabac and Moldt (2005) and Poutakidis et al. (2002). The MULAN-SNIFFER focuses on analyzing messages sent by agents in a multi-agent system. Besides being portable (realized in *Java*) and modular (it has a complete plugin system), its key features are distribution, logging, analysis and visualization. The MUL-AN-SNIFFER is able to gather messages from both local and remote platforms. Messages can be selected using stateful or stateless filters. Basic filtering primitives (*from, to,* . . . ) are provided. More sophisticated filters may be added via the plugin system.

---

[2]Note that the original color of superimposed elements is red.
[3]Dynamic loading of nets is already supported by RENEW.

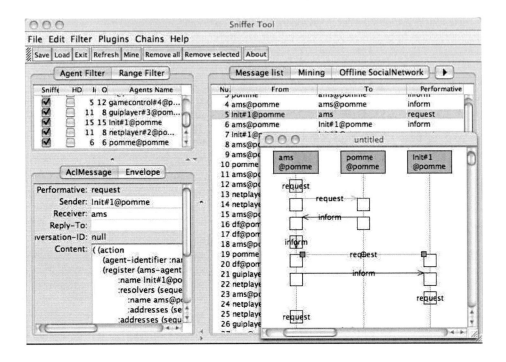

Figure 16.2: MULAN-SNIFFER UI with generated Sequence Diagram.

Offline filtering is also possible. *Mining-chains* can be used to apply arbitrary analysis algorithms to the messages (for examples see Cabac et al. (2006)). Apart from showing elementary statistics (total number of messages sent, received, etc.) each message can thoroughly be inspected. Moreover, Sequence Diagrams are auto-generated (in function of the filters applied) on the fly. More complex visualizations can – of course – be realized as plugins.

It is interesting to note that the Sequence Diagrams resulting from visualization can actually be re-used as Agent Interaction Protocol Diagrams. Petri net code stubs for agent protocols can be generated from these diagrams (see Cabac and Moldt (2005)). Thus, agent behavior can be defined by observing a running system turning user interaction (manually) into agent behavior or even allowing the agents to use these observations to adapt their own behaviors.

Figure 16.2 shows the MULAN-SNIFFER's main window. The MULAN-SNIFFER is in the course of sniffing the messages from a teaching project. The main window is divided in three major areas. The top-left one displays the agents known from sniffing into messages. Here, agents can be selected for simple filtering. The right area shows the *message list*. The currently selected message is displayed in detail in the bottom left area of the main window. Next to the message list tab one can select from a couple of viewer plugins already loaded. *Online SocialNetwork* (accessible via the arrow next to

*Offline SocialNetwork*) for example provides a visualization of the frequency of messages exchanged by pairs of agents. Additionally a part of the on-the-fly auto-generated Sequence Diagram is shown. Selecting a message arrow in the diagram will highlight the corresponding message in the message list and display the content in the message detail view (tabs: *AclMessage* and *Envelope)* and vice versa. The MULAN-SNIFFER uses the same interface of the platform as the MULAN-VIEWER for the collection of messages.

### 16.3.4 Components Tests

Decision components are implementations of agent-internal behavior. Since these processes are bounded by the agents, it is possible to construct component tests that can be executed *stand alone* (similar to unit tests). For this a setup procedure, offering data objects that can be processes, and manually executable test cases have to be defined. Erroneous models can thus be debugged *before* the agent system is executed.

The test for decision components can be defined in the same net and they can be performed on the fly at design time by starting a net instance of the decision component in the RENEW simulator. Test elements can remain in the net for documentation reasons and also for the possibility to be executed again, if the net has to be changed. The DC net components already offer some net components that are designed for this purpose (compare Figure 14.1).

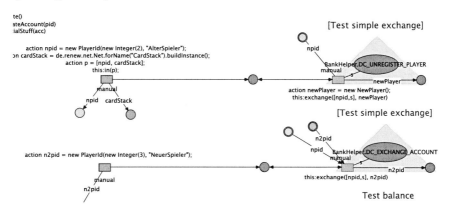

Figure 16.3: Component tests in *Bank_DC_Account* (net fragment).

Figure 16.3 shows a fragment of the *Bank_DC_Account*. The tested functionality is the de-registration of a player and the exchange of the account with another player in the case of a player leaving the game. The testing net components are distinguished through their different color scheme (blue net elements). Tests can be manually executed by firing the manual transition, which is conventionally distinguished by the orange color with the red frame (and defined through the inscription *manual*). The tests are individually setup through the transitions on the left.

For a similar testing possibility of interactions (i.e. interacting protocol nets) more effort has to be undertaken. Moreover, due to the nature of the interactions as communicating parts of the system the setup is more complicated and the test works only in a running MULAN system. However, it is possible to test interactions independently from other interactions. Thus, it is not only possible to construct the interactions independently but also valuable time is saved for the integration of the whole system by testing interactions individually. The tests are accomplished by test DCs. These are special decision components that offer the same interface as the real implementations but provide a setup and exemplary answers to requests.

Figure 16.4: Test component *Producer_DC_test*.

Figure 16.4 shows a simple DC test component that is generated automatically by the Use Case Plugin's generation feature. It shows the exemplary usage of tests components. By invoking the manual transition a new (standard) protocol (*simpleSend*) is instantiated pro-actively, which will send the message p to the addressee, in this case the agent itself. The alternative of launching test DCs or *normal* DCs is controlled by local (user-configured) and individual (per DC) properties settings, if the naming convention with suffix *_test* is followed. Thus a separation of debugged system setup from productive system setup is achieved.

# 16.4 Related Work

Several works have been done in the field of analyzing and debugging multi-agent applications.

## 16.4.1 Debugging in Multi-Agent Systems

Some of the described methods, techniques and tools apply visualization techniques to present information about the complex systems and most address a specific platform implementation.

### Van Liedekerke & Avouris

van Liedekerke and Avouris (1995) describe the need for tool support for multi-agent application development. They propose *Developer's Conceptual Models* (Perspectives), from which they directly derive views that are manifested as GUI workbench perspectives.

The presented system provides visualization covering most of the scale dimension. One main aspect is that the system receives, displays and offers information as an agent of the system. While the approach is modular, generic and abides by the agent-oriented paradigm, there are some drawbacks concerning debugging. Considering that all agents are autonomous entities, it is not guaranteed that operations that query or manipulate data or code are successful. Concerning the dimension of coupling, the architecture seems tempting in the way that the debugging capabilities are naturally remote, concurrent and autonomous. However, direct manipulation of running systems is not discussed.

### Ndumu, Nwana, Lee & Collis

Ndumu et al. (1999) tackle the "notoriously difficult task" of multi-agent system debugging by visualization (of several diverse perspectives of the system) and corroboration. They describe some control features of the system but do not emphasize on a coherent integration of the different tasks of detecting, locating and fixing bugs.

### Botía, Hernansáez & Gómez-Skarmeta

Botía et al. (2004) present an elaborated system (ACLAnalyzer) for Jade platforms that focuses on the analysis of ACL messages and the visual presentation of direct or inferred data. Their focus is on the communication level and presents overviews of whole agent organizations. Through this focus on the inferred system organization and the inter-agent communication (interactions) it becomes clear that the tool is mainly for analysis and visualization, while the manipulation features are restricted.

Botía et al. (2007) briefly investigate debugging of multi-agent systems in general and present a technique to visually cluster agents in highly populated agent systems.

### Lynch & Rajendran

Lynch and Rajendran (2008) propose an integrated development environment for multi-agent systems. Information about the system, system details and system control are communicated via messages and the focus lies on the gathering of commonly available information of heterogeneous systems. The agents volunteer the information. Although manipulation and control features are not excluded from the extensible architecture, their support within the basic implementation is limited.

### Lam & Barber

Lam and Barber (2004) take a similar approach of gathering information by modifying existing agent code so that the agents report their internal state to a central debugging component.

### Myers

Myers (2004) presents a thorough investigation into testing – mentioning debugging as associated to testing – and stresses the fact that it is a mistake to fix bugs in runtime code instead of in the source. In his opinion such an approach should be avoided. In contrast, we believe that for multi-agent systems (i.e. systems that include adaptive behavior) it is explicitly necessary to manipulate the state directly. Moreover, multi-agent systems actually provide meaningful technical constraints for such manipulations.

**Poutakidis, Padgham & Winikoff**

Poutakidis et al. (2002) focus on the debugging of interactions. They incorporate design artifacts that are developed during the design phase with the Prometheus methodology, i.e. AUML Interaction Protocols, for error detection during runtime. This is a highly specialized approach that is able to find sets of possible erroneous interactions. Errors include mis-sent messages (wrong address) and deadlocks. Such errors are easily and directly detectable in process-oriented multi-agent systems, such as MULAN.

## 16.4.2 Contributions

The first implementation of the MULAN-VIEWER has been proposed and done by Carl (2003). Its original intention was to provide inspection capabilities for the highly structured and complex hierarchical multi-agent applications built with the MULAN/CAPA framework. Initially, it provided inspection of the knowledge bases' contents, display of messages and simple navigation, i.e. opening a net instance for a selected element.

Schleinzer[4] and I extended the navigation capabilities and the expressiveness of detail views. A view for decision components was also added that lists the contents of places in the net instance. Thus, it is possible to observe status information directly in the MULAN-VIEWER. Together with the net component for the exchange channel interfaces the interface names are displayed. Several simple features for the control of the system entered the MULAN-VIEWER, such as buttons for starting agents, platforms, etc.

Schlüter (2008)[4] extended these controlling features in his bachelor's thesis – under my co-supervision – with several manipulation features. These are the manipulation of knowledge base entries (*hot data replacement*), setting of breakpoints in reactive protocol nets, manual invocation of protocols and decision components, display and reexamination possibilities for initial messages that were not understood and – most notably – the possibility to exchange protocols at runtime with altered (debugged) version (*hot code replacement*).

I have done the original conceptualization for the MULAN-SNIFFER. Together with Denz, I supervised the first prototypical implementation of the MULAN-SNIFFER on the basis of the AIP Diagram Plugin and Agent Interaction Protocol Diagrams by the students Heitmann[4] and Plähn[4]. The on-the-fly construction of Sequence Diagrams during execution and the supply of a message log were the first goals and the original reason for the implementation.[5] I included the linking of messages selections in different views of message lists, i.e. simple message list and sniffed Sequence Diagram.

---

[4]Heitmann, Schleinzer, Schlüter and Plähn are students, who participated in the AOSE projects between 2005 and 2007.

[5]Although the MULAN-VIEWER provides a simple message logging and inspection, the extensibility and the messages representation are quite limited and filtering is nonexistent.

I designed the net components and the approach for the stand-alone DC components testing and I proposed and enforced the usage of DC test components.[6] Both simple approaches of testing have been successfully and extensively applied in the later AOSE projects (Settler 5 and 6) and have added to the understanding of the system. It has especially accelerated the integration tasks, since many simple errors have been eliminated beforehand.

## 16.5 Summary

This chapter examines the process of debugging multi-agent systems from a practical point of view. We base the requirements for debugging of multi-agent systems on three orthogonal dimensions (*scale, coupling, activities*) which span the field of debugging. Requirements cover gathering, processing and displaying information as well as control and manipulation features of the debugging system.

| Observable objects | Viewer | Sniffer | RENEW | Comp. Tests |
|---|---|---|---|---|
| agents on platforms | ++ | − | + | − |
| agent state | + | − | ++ | − |
| protocols of agents | ++ | − | + | ++ |
| protocol state | ○ | − | ++ | + |
| transferred messages | + | ++ | ○ | + |
| interactions | − | ++ | − | ++ |
| communication infrastructure | − | + | − | + |

Table 16.4: Overview of tools and their capabilities in respect to dimension *scale*.

We present the concrete tool set to debug MULAN-based multi-agent systems and point out the particular strengths of each tool with respect to the requirements. Table 16.4 summarizes the features of the debugging tool set for MULAN with respect to the dimension of scale. The MULAN-VIEWER focuses on presenting the system structure – including agent internals – and provides control and manipulation features. The MULAN-SNIFFER observes the system by gathering, visualizing and mining agent messages externally. RENEW provides visual and interactive debugging features for the underlying Petri net code. Together all three form a comprehensive debugging tool set to locate and fix bugs within a MULAN-based multi-agent system. Component tests make it possible to detect and locate bugs in a reproducible manner.

---

[6]Note that components tests are used for DC testing, while test components are DCs that are used for interaction testing.

# 17 Monitoring and Analyzing Agent Interactions

In this chapter, we present an approach towards the application of process mining techniques to the analysis, design and validation of multi-agent interactions. In particular, we pursue the goal of reconstructing models of agent interaction protocols from sample interactions. Our approach is integrated into the FIPA-compliant, Petri net-based agent platform MULAN/CAPA.

The chapter is organized as follows: Section 17.1 provides a brief introduction to agent interaction analysis and process mining. Section 17.2 positions the process mining techniques in the field of software engineering. In Section 17.3 we present our approach towards analyzing agent interactions by means of process mining, where Petri nets build an important intermediate representation. In Section 17.4 we discuss our prototypical implementation of a tool for interaction monitoring, debugging and validation. The concept of mining chains implemented through net components is introduced in Section 17.5. In Section 17.6 we review existing work on agent interaction analysis and introduce process mining as an advanced analysis technique. Finally, Section 17.7 concludes the chapter with a discussion of the results reached so far and of possible future research.

## 17.1 Context

The concept of multi-agent systems (MAS) has gained increasing importance in computer science during the last decade. MAS research considers systems as aggregations of goal-oriented, autonomous entities (agents) interacting in some common environment (see e.g. Rölke (2004)). Since no or only minor central control is exposed on the agents, a coherent global system behavior emerges merely from their cooperative or competitive interactions.

The design, implementation and validation of MAS still remains a demanding task. Petri nets are frequently applied for modeling agent behavior due to the typical combination of formal conciseness and visual clearness as well as the possibilities of displaying and formally analyzing concurrent systems (Rölke 2004). Petri nets also support the verification and validation of MAS, since formal methods can be applied to assess liveness and safety properties of such models.

Unfortunately, the applicability of formal verification techniques is limited to simple and often practically irrelevant classes of MAS (see Edmonds and Bryson (2004)). Furthermore, such techniques can only be applied in a confirmative fashion, i.e. to verify (or falsify) previously posed hypotheses about a system's behavior. Agent-oriented software engineering (AOSE), however, is primarily an experimental process (see Uhrmacher

(2000)) consisting of prototypical design, simulation, observation and a-posteriori analysis in order to explore the system's behavior. Since the observation of even simple MAS might produce large and complex amounts of data (see Sanchez and Lucas (2002)), data mining has occasionally been proposed as supporting technique for such analysis (see e.g. Nair et al. (2004) or Remondino and Correndo (2005)).

To aid the understanding of dynamic processes – in particular interactions – in MAS, it seems straightforward to apply techniques from *process mining* originally developed in the domain of business process intelligence (see e.g. Herbst (2001) or van der Aalst and Weijters (2004)). These techniques seem especially appropriate in Petri net-based AOSE due to their ability to reconstruct concurrent Petri net models from execution traces. This leads to a number of potentially interesting applications during the AOSE development cycle.[1] (1) In the *system analysis phase*, process mining can be employed to aggregate behavior or interaction traces of relevant agents from the real system to Petri net models that flow into the design phase. (2) In the *design phase*, process mining seems to be a promising approach to integrate adaptability into Petri net-based agents by providing them with the ability to learn executable models of behavior from the observation of other agents' interactions. (3) In the *validation phase*, process mining can be used to aggregate large amounts of trace data observed from the running system. Those models can be visualized, formally analyzed or compared to design models to validate the system's behavior. Process mining might also support the detection of unforeseen, implicit interaction patterns emerging at runtime.

## 17.2 Process Mining in Software Engineering

The literature review shows that process mining can add to several stages of a software engineering life cycle. Figure 17.1 shows a selection of possible applications of process mining in the context of software development from the early to the late stages. The presented development cycle is very generic and borrows the software engineering disciplines from the Rational Unified Process (see Jacobson et al. (1999)).

In the context of Petri net-based software engineering, specific advantages become apparent: In the design phase process mining supports the understanding of a real system's structure and behavior. Process models mined from the real system form a straightforward basis for the (semi-)automated implementation of the Petri net-based software. In debugging, process mining adds valuable support when applied to large traces of a running system. In validation and testing, traces observed from the running software (or abstract Petri net models reconstructed from these traces) can (semi-)automatically be compared with the specification by means of conformance analysis techniques (see e.g. van der Aalst et al. (2005)). During the operation of the software system, process mining is suitable to support the monitoring and online optimization. It requires the mined Petri nets to be fed back into the running system.

In an agent-based context (as provided by our MULAN architecture) further integration of process mining stands to reason: Software agents can achieve a form of adaptability by inferring behavioral information from *watching* other agents act. Thus, they are able

---

[1]Similar applications of general data mining to MAS are discussed in (Remondino and Correndo 2005).

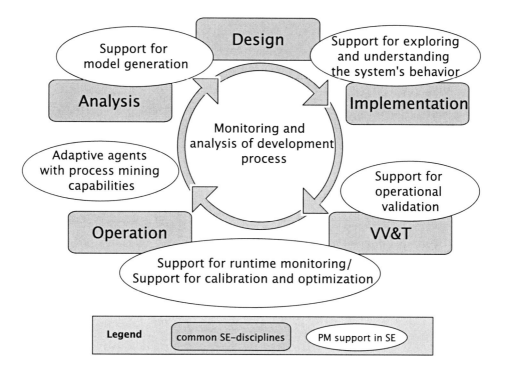

Figure 17.1: Overview of process mining activities in software development processes.

to construct a model of the behavioral patterns that are usual or useful in the system's environment. Furthermore, the use of the multi-agent system metaphor as a common abstraction for the software as well as for the development team (compare with Chapter 8 and Cabac (2007)) and process makes it possible to handle the mining of constructed processes and the mining of software development processes within the same conceptual framework.

The broad applicability of process mining to software engineering is due to the genericness of the techniques, which can be applied to several types of log data (for a related discussion in the context of change mining see Günther et al. (2006)). On the one hand, this includes traces of operational software systems, where the focus is either put on the behavior of single software components or on interactions including multiple objects or agents (see also Dustdar and Gombotz (2006)). On the other hand, process mining techniques can be applied to data recorded during the execution of real world processes to gain information about the processes supported by the software under development as well as about the development process.

Especially for distributed systems process mining can add valuable information for debugging and monitoring. However, software developers have to be able to apply the techniques easily without much overhead during the development phases, and the techniques have to be tightly integrated in the usual workflows and tools. In our work we propose to apply process mining techniques through a component-based approach that allows the developer to construct complex mining algorithms by joining components together to form a data-flow network.

## 17.3 An Approach towards Agent Interaction Mining

Though the similarities between the analysis of multi-agent interactions and the research field of process mining have recently been recognized in the literature (see above), the integration of process mining into practical methods and tools for AOSE is still in its infancy. In the following, we present our approach towards analyzing agent interactions with process mining techniques.

### 17.3.1 Embedding of Mining Techniques

Our approach towards Agent Interaction Mining (AIM) is integrated into a larger framework for Process Mining in (Agent-Oriented) Software Engineering. This framework covers several analysis perspectives related to the four conceptual levels of MULAN: (1) the *decision perspective* focusing on decision models encoded in an agent's knowledge base, (2) the *internal control perspective* regarding the processes running within a single agent, (3) the *external control perspective* concerned with multi-agent interactions, (4) the *structural perspective* focusing on (static) platform and MAS structures and (5) the *multi-level perspective* regarding relations between the perspectives mentioned before.

On our way to applying mining techniques to the analysis of MAS on multiple levels, we choose the *external control perspective* as a starting point. From the observation of message traffic, we proceed *bottom up*, i.e. we try to reconstruct basic interaction protocols in the first step. Through the recursive application of mining techniques to the results of the previous level, we aim to proceed to hierarchical protocols and higher level dynamical and structural patterns.

### 17.3.2 Mining Techniques

The task of AIM at the protocol level is formulated as follows: Given a message log recorded during the execution of a MAS, find the unknown set of interaction protocols involved in the generation of this log. This task can be divided into several subphases depicted in Figure 17.2. Generally, we consider the FIPA ACL message attributes `performative`, `sender`, `receiver` and some conversation control tags. By masking message content, we keep the following stages application-independent.

The first phase – log segmentation – is necessary because a log normally contains messages from several conversations, generated by multiple protocols. These messages must be sorted by assigning them to a *conversation* and by assigning each conversation to a *protocol type*. Given the information available in FIPA ACL messages (e.g. `conversation-id`) this segmentation is trivial.

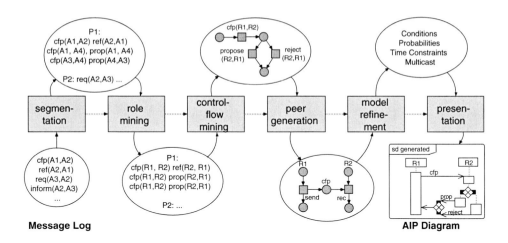

**Message Log**                                                                 **AIP Diagram**

Figure 17.2: A mining chain for agent interaction mining.

However, these tags are not excessively used on the CAPA platform and might generally prove to be too inflexible for detecting complex patterns of interaction. Therefore, we reconstruct conversations by *chained correlation* (van der Aalst et al. 2005) of messages based on the `in-reply-to` tag: Messages without this tag are assumed to start a new conversation. Other messages are appended to the conversation currently ended by a message with a corresponding `reply-with` tag. In doing so, we obtain 1 : 1 *conversation threads*. However, these might be part of a larger multi-party conversation that we reconstruct by merging all conversation threads sharing at least one `reply-with` or `in-reply-to` tag.

Assigning conversations to protocol types is a clustering task. For each conversation, we build a feature vector representing a *direct successor* relation of performatives.[2] Each vector component represents one possible succession of two performatives. It is assigned a non-zero value $a$ if this succession appears in the conversation and 0 otherwise. In regard to protocols with a typically branched control structure, combinations of performatives appearing near the start of a conversation are weighted stronger than those appearing at the end. Finally, we apply the *nearest neighbor* algorithm of Dunham (2003) to cluster similar vectors based on the Euclidian distance.

The result of the segmentation phase are traces of conversations ordered by protocol types. In the second phase – role mining – we further abstract the messages by replacing names of sender and receiver agents with conversation roles. We currently apply a simple unification algorithm that binds agent names to role names in the order of their appearance in the conversation. However, this simple approach might fail in branched or concurrent protocols. Alternatively, we consider using a role detection mechanism based on sets of sent and received performatives similar to the approach described by Vander-

---

[2]A similar metric is used in a preliminary approach by Vanderfeesten towards detecting conversation roles (Vanderfeesten 2006).

feesten (2006).

In the third phase – control flow mining – we collect the abstracted conversation traces of each protocol type and try to induce a model of the protocol's control flow. Interaction protocols such as those specified in Agent UML might contain concurrent, hidden and duplicate tasks. Therefore, the algorithm by Herbst (2001) seems to be a good choice at first sight. However, this algorithm requires an activity-based log, while the message log is event-based.

Based on ideas from Herbst (2001) and Schütt (2003), our preliminary process mining technique consists of two stages – automata inference and concurrency detection: First, we reconstruct a deterministic finite automaton (DFA) from each set of samples using the $k$-RI algorithm (see Angluin (1982)). The edges of the DFA are labeled with message performatives and sender/receiver roles. The $k$-RI algorithm can detect loops and duplicate tasks, but not concurrency. We therefore apply a modified version of the $\alpha$-algorithm to the DFA next. Based on the successor relation of labeled transitions, the algorithm detects hints for concurrency in the DFA's structure.

Control flow mining results in an overall Petri net model of each protocol. This model can be split straightforwardly into protocol templates for every conversation role. Each of these peers corresponds to one life line in an AgentUML Agent Interaction Protocol Diagram (AIP, see Cabac et al. (2003)), that might be used to visualize the mining results. Another possibility is to refine the reconstructed model by inferring temporal relations between messages with techniques described by van der Aalst and Weijters (2004). Yet another possibility is to apply the C 4.5 decision tree learning algorithm (Dunham 2003) to reconstruct branching conditions from message content attributes as proposed in (Herbst 2001). The attachment of branching conditions to the protocol templates leads to executable MULAN protocols.

## 17.4 A Tool for Agent Interaction Mining

In this section, we present a prototypical tool and show an example for the application of our interaction mining techniques.

### 17.4.1 Monitoring Tool

To integrate process mining facilities into the CAPA platform, we developed a monitoring tool named MULAN-SNIFFER as a RENEW plugin (Cabac et al. 2005). The name indicates that the tool's functionality was derived from typical MAS debugging tools such as the *JADE Sniffer* (Jade 2005). The MULAN-SNIFFER monitors all ACL messages sent between agents on the platform during a simulation. The resulting message log is displayed textually as a list or graphically as a UML Sequence Diagram. Filters can be applied to select messages containing certain performatives, etc.

Figure 17.3 shows the user interface of the Sniffer with an observed message log. The messages in the diagram are color coded to ease the monitoring of the MAS. They can be inspected in the bottom left view of the Sniffer window. The upper left view shows a list of observed agents which can be sniffed or blocked. It also shows the numbers of

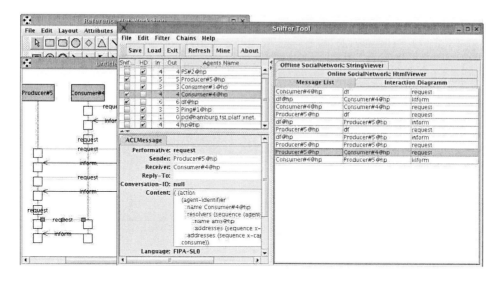

Figure 17.3: MULAN-SNIFFER GUI with observed interactions and RENEW GUI.

messages sent and received per agent. The tool makes it possible to observe changes in the diagram on the fly, i.e. when the message is sent.

The MULAN-SNIFFER differs from its 'ancestors' in two aspects that are important for our approach: (1) The recorded Sequence Diagrams are stored in the same format used by the MULAN design tools. They can therefore be edited and mapped to executable agent protocols. (2) More important, the *Sniffer* is a pluggable RENEW plugin (Cabac et al. 2005) that can be extended by plugins for process mining and filtering itself. Figure 17.4 depicts the MULAN-SNIFFER user interface with a table showing the communication frequencies as a simple example mining plugin.

It can be clearly observed in the simple example that one of the two Consumer agents is involved in a conversation with the Producer, while the other is not.

The interfaces for filtering and mining plugins are reminiscent of similar tools such as *ProM*[3] (see van Dongen et al. (2005)). Special emphasis is put on the *recursive* character of process mining algorithms: These algorithms operate on data and provide data for higher-level analysis. We therefore introduce the concept of *mining chains*. Complex process mining algorithms are constructed by combining basic building blocks in data flow networks as proposed by Jessen and Valk (1987). This visual modeling technique is frequently used in data mining tools (e.g. *WEKA*, see Frank et al. (2004)). The Petri net editor of RENEW builds an appropriate basis for editing mining chains.

---

[3]*ProM*: available at `http://prom.win.tue.nl/tools/prom/`

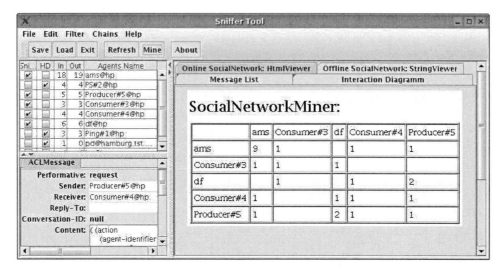

Figure 17.4: MULAN-SNIFFER with a table showing the communication frequencies.

## 17.4.2 AIM Plugin and Example

The example in Figure 17.5 shows a plugin that applies the algorithms described in Section 17.3.2 to the message log provided by the Sniffer. The messages partly result from multiple executions of a concurrent protocol simulating negotiations between a customer, a mediator and a service provider to allocate an order.

In Figure 17.5 the Sniffer UI can be seen (background) with a tree-view that shows the results of the log segmentation. Each tree node represents one identified protocol type with the respective conversations as children. On selecting a conversation, the associated messages are automatically highlighted in the Sequence Diagram view (see also Figure 17.3).

In the example, the samples belonging to the order allocation protocol were successfully separated from the surrounding 'noise', i.e. conversations executed during the registration of agents and the initialization of the platform. However, the performance of the clustering procedure strongly depends on a threshold determining cluster similarity. The window in the foreground shows the correctly reconstructed Petri net model of the order allocation protocol.

## 17.5 Net Components for Mining Chains

As part of our attempt to integrate process mining with AOSE, we have developed a set of net components for the modeling of process and interaction mining chains. These mining chains process large amounts of data observed during the execution of our multi-agent applications. For that reason the data has to be provided to the mining chain and the results have to be returned to the environment.

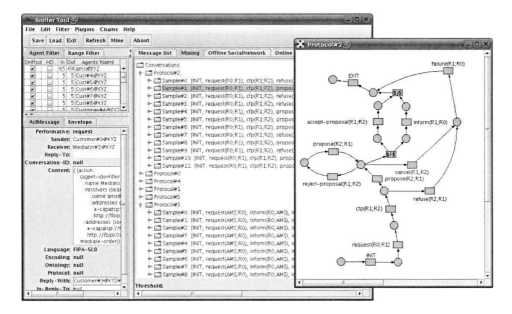

Figure 17.5: AIM Plugin of the MULAN-SNIFFER showing mined conversations.

## 17.5.1 Generic and Specific Mining Components

We identify as basic (generic) components for mining chains *sources*, *processors* and *sinks*. Figure 17.6 shows the generic mining components that can be used as templates to create specific net components.

Examples for the specific mining components are the interaction mining components shown in Figures 17.7 and 17.8. These net components can be interpreted as wrappers for implemented algorithms. A mining chain is composed of several net components and can also include sub-mining chains in a hierarchy of net instances. Also normal net elements can be used to add custom behavior.

## 17.5.2 Mining Chain

Figure 17.7 shows a mining chain for the mining of agent interactions from a message log. The message log is provided by the MULAN-SNIFFER (Processor: `SnifferMessageSource`) and processed by two processors to cluster the message list into different conversation types and instances. This intermediate result is visualized in the Sniffer and further processed in a complex processor (sub-net) for control flow mining shown in Figure 17.8.

The complex processor consists of two subsequent processors. From the provided log data these processors try to induce the control structure of the generating interaction protocol in a two-step procedure consisting of grammar inference and concurrency detection (see also Schütt (2003)). The resulting Petri net is finally displayed in the Sniffer. While a more detailed description of this preliminary mining technique can be found in (Cabac

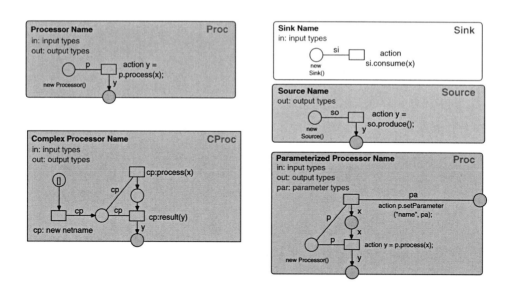

Figure 17.6: Generic mining chain components.

et al. 2006), the mining chain clearly depicts the basic structure of the implemented algorithm.

The generic mining components as well as the interaction mining components are realized as net components and they are integrated in RENEW as a plugin that makes the tools available to the modeler as palettes of tool buttons. Figure 17.9 shows the RENEW GUI with the two provided palettes of tool buttons.[4]

Generic mining components are used to provide templates for the specific and complex components (compare CProc in Figure 17.7). Specific components use the generic components as a wrapper for implemented processors, sources, or sinks.

The execution of the mining chain of Figure 17.7, the MULAN-SNIFFER and the resulting Petri net showing a representation of the mined interaction process are shown in Figure 17.10. In the back a running instance of the mining chain is displayed, at the top the Sniffer window shows the clustered messages, and in the front the resulting Petri net[5] is visible.

In our approach, thanks to the use of Petri net representation, we are able not only to implement pure sequential chains. We can also model chains that have a complex control-flow and the possibility of concurrent execution of processors exists. This is already shown in the example mining chain. Mining chains can also be included in agent

---

[4]Note that while the images on the buttons of the interaction mining components do not differ from the generic versions – in this early version of the plugin – it is still possible to identify the individual tools through the status line information while hovering over the tool button with the mouse pointer (compare Figure 17.9).

[5]Note that the layout of the net is beautified by hand for visual reasons, since the results of the implemented automatic layout algorithms are currently not satisfying.

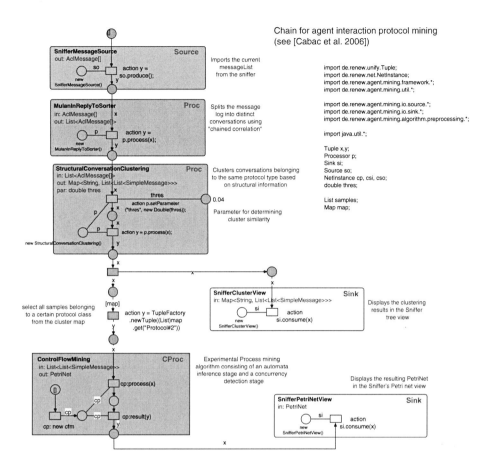

Figure 17.7: Example process mining chain for agent interaction mining.

protocols as they are used in the Petri net-based multi-agent system MULAN. By this means agents' adaptability could profit from the mining results by the possibility of analyzing agent interaction behavior on the ground of observed conversations.

In the analysis of interacting members of a cooperating group the approach of mining the interactions by the means of mining chains can lead to improved knowledge about processes, single tasks and their interconnections. This could lead to the possibility to improve processes on the ground of the mined results and identify mistakes like missing tasks.

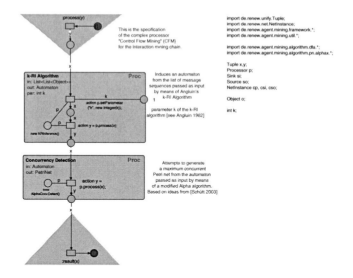

Figure 17.8: Definition of the complex processor for control-flow-mining.

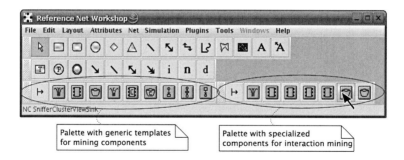

Figure 17.9: Renew GUI with the palettes for generic mining components and interaction mining components.

## 17.6 Related Work

Interaction analysis is currently an important topic in MAS research for the reasons mentioned above. In the following, we review related work on interaction analysis and introduce process mining as an advanced analysis technique.

### 17.6.1 Interaction Analysis in Multi-Agent Systems

Many frameworks for multi-agent application development include debugging tools that allow to monitor the message traffic on the agent platform. An example is the *Sniffer agent* integrated into the JADE framework (Jade 2005). This tool displays observed

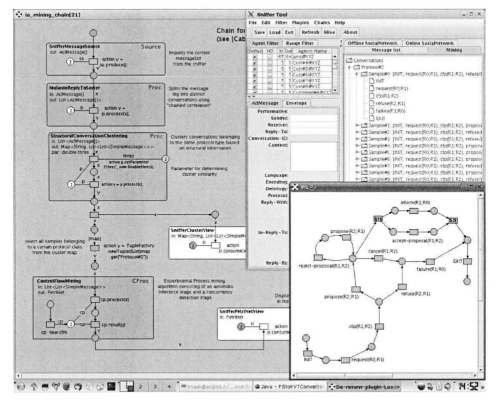

Figure 17.10: Screenshot of the execution of the interaction mining chain and the
MULAN-SNIFFER.

message sequences as UML Sequence Diagrams and provides basic filtering capabilities. Monitoring agent interactions leads to large amounts of data. Important behavior patterns are in danger to go unrecognized when the analysis is performed by hand. Therefore data mining techniques are increasingly applied in this context (see e.g. Remondino and Correndo (2005)).

### Nair, Tambe, Marsella & Raines

The algorithms for this task are mostly based on computational logic and stochastic automata: Nair et al. (2004) e.g. propose an approach towards team analysis in the domain of (simulated) robot soccer (*RoboCup*). They consider three complementary perspectives: The *individual agent model* is a situational decision model of a single agent represented by means of association rules. The *multiple agent model* represents agent interactions as a stochastic automaton. The *global team model* shows relations between team properties (e.g. ball possession time) and game results in a rule-based fashion.

### Botía, Hernansáez & Gómez-Skarmeta

Botía et al. (2004) focus on mining social networks at multiple resolutions from message logs using the *ROCK* cluster algorithm. In addition, their monitoring tool *ACLAnalyser* can automatically observe the execution of predefined interaction protocols on the JADE platform.

### Mounier

Mounier et al. (2003) present an approach towards *agent conversation mining* using stochastic grammar inference. Mining results are represented as a stochastic automaton, the edges of which are labeled with message performatives. The approach neglects concurrency and interaction roles.

### Hiel

Hiel (2005) applies extended Hidden Markov Models for the same task; also neglecting the aforementioned aspects. However, he suggests to improve the reconstruction of (concurrent) protocols by process mining techniques as a possible direction for future research.

## 17.6.2 Process Mining

Process mining (also referred to as *workflow mining*) is a subfield of data mining concerned with "method[s] of distilling a structured process description from a set of real executions" (see Maruster et al. (2002, p. 364)). The task is – given an *event log* recorded during process execution – to reconstruct properties of the generating processes. While most research is done in the area of *business process management* (see Herbst (2001)), other application domains such as the analysis of *web service interactions* (see Gombotz et al. (2005)) have recently been considered.

### Van der Aalst & al.

A large number of process mining techniques are available, that can be classified by the *perspective* that the analysis focuses on. The most prominent perspectives are control flow and organizational perspectives (see Van der Aalst and Wejters (2004)). The objective in the *control flow perspective* is to reconstruct the observed process' control structure – i.e. sequences, branches, loops and concurrency. The *organizational perspective* focuses on the "structure and the population" of the organization in which the processes are observed. This covers "relations between roles, [...] groups [...] and other artifacts" (Van der Aalst and Wejters 2004, Section 4.3). Tool support for process mining is increasingly becoming available. Aalst et al. developed the *ProM* process mining tool that is extensible through a plugin mechanism by mining, import, export and analysis plugins (see Van Dongen et al. (2005)).

**De Medeiros, Van Dongen, Van der Aalst & Weijters**

An often-cited mining technique for the control flow perspective is the $\alpha$-Algorithm:
From an event-based process log, this algorithm builds a concurrent Petri net model on
the basis of a *direct successor* relation. An extension of the algorithm can be proven
to reconstruct any net belonging to the class of *extended sound workflow nets* (see De
Medeiros et al. (2004)), but it cannot cope with noise, hidden tasks and duplicate tasks.[6]

**Herbst**

Herbst (2001) developed an algorithm for mining process models containing duplicate
tasks from activity-based logs. In an activity-based log start and end events of activities
can be identified, which eases the detection of concurrency.

**Ly & al. / Van der Aalst & Song**

Research on mining in the organizational perspective has so far focused on the reconstruction of *role assignments* (see Ly et al. (2005) and Van der Aalst (2004) and *social
networks* (see Van der Aalst and Song (2004)).

**Schütt**

Further tasks in process mining are *log segmentation* (i.e. the mapping of messages from
the process log to process instances and process classes) and *condition mining* (i.e. inference of branching conditions in the process model). Both are covered in an approach
by Schütt (2003).

**Gombotz, Baina & Dustdar**

Gombotz et al. (2005) apply interaction mining – i.e. the reconstruction of interaction
models from message logs, which covers aspects of both control flow and organizational
structure – to analyze the operation of web services at different levels (operation, interaction and workflow). One of the mining results is a so-called *web service interaction
graph* representing the relations of a particular web service and its neighbors.

**Van der Aalst**

Van der Aalst (2004) shows that the $\alpha$-algorithm can be used to mine Sequence Diagram-
like Petri net-structures from message logs. The approach is restricted to 1:1 interactions
and does not explicitly abstract from senders and receivers to interaction roles.

---

[6]A *hidden task* is a nameless activity not registered in the log. *Duplicate tasks* occur if the same
activity is executed under different preconditions.

### 17.6.3 Contributions

Together with Denz, I am the original author of the conceptualization of the tool set used for the analysis of agent interaction through observed messages: MULAN-SNIFFER and Mining Plugin. I have contributed to the development and furthered the extensibility of the MULAN-SNIFFER and investigated the possibilities of application of process mining within the PAOSE approach (compare with Figure 17.1).

I have also contributed to the integration of the mining functionality and the mining net components as plugins into the RENEW tool set. Furthermore, I have furthered the integration of ProM functionality into the RENEW tool set as plugin. I have improved the mining framework with yet other contributions. These are the possibility to extend the MULAN-SNIFFER with plugins, the linking of different message views' selected messages and the creation of a complex message filter for mobile agents that provides a migration path (compare with Cabac et al. (2009b)).

## 17.7 Summary

The MULAN / CAPA framework offers an integrated tool set supporting the development of Petri net-based MAS. It includes features for the specification, creation, documentation, monitoring and debugging of multi-agent applications. However, in concurrent, distributed and heterogeneous environments the analysis of multi-agent interactions is extremely difficult. Thus there is a need for elaborated techniques to handle large amounts of data. Process mining is one technique that can be successfully applied. The more abstract view of interaction mining allows to emphasize the desired perspectives (e.g. external control perspective) that are important for agent-based development and analysis (e.g. monitoring, debugging and validation).

This chapter describes how to embed interaction mining into agent-oriented software engineering. We have developed an approach to reconstruct interaction protocols from message logs, integrating and extending several process mining techniques. It allows us to structure message logs by means of clustering and to reconstruct non-trivial concurrent protocols. However, we have encountered several cases that the techniques cannot handle yet. Enhancing and validating them in greater detail is an important topic at issue. We have furthermore presented the MULAN-SNIFFER, a monitoring tool that is extensible by mining and filtering plugins. It is also applicable to many other FIPA-compliant MAS. This allows to monitor and mine in heterogeneous multi-agent environments and thereby evaluate our mining techniques in numerous real-world situations. Mining techniques could also improve the adaptability of Petri net-based agents, which can be exploited for improvements in the context of the *Socionics* project (see v. Lüde et al. (2009) and Asko (2005)).

# 18 Comparing Models

This chapter introduces a simple but efficient method that can simplify the task of the discovery of differences under certain conditions. To this means we exploit the graphical representation of the nets and transfer the problem of finding differences in the visual image of the Models. We also present an implementation of the method as plugin for RENEW (see Kummer et al. (2004) and Kummer et al. (2009a)), a multi-formalism tool, the graphical engine of which is based on JHotDraw (http://www.jhotdraw.org) and supports all kinds of modeling techniques (e.g.: Petri nets, Use Case Diagrams, Sequence Diagrams, Class Diagrams) and drawings (including import and export possibilities). Section 18.1 introduces the challenge of comparing diagrams. In Section 18.2 we describe the method, its implementation and integration within RENEW. Section 18.3 presents several examples to illustrate the method, the tool and the possible applications. Section 18.4 offers a comparison with other techniques and respective tools and the chapter is summarized in Section 18.5.

## 18.1 Context

During development of applications developers frequently encounter (and have to deal with) different and/or conflicting versions of model artifacts. Especially in shared projects, where modeling artifacts are shared through source code management systems (SCM) such as the Concurrent Versions System (CVS) or Subversion, conflicts frequently appear and have to be resolved manually by the developer. This is especially true for Petri net-based applications, since here the models are the code base of the system and thus treated as usual code with all attributes, such as collective code ownership. In the evaluation of the code (Petri nets) of other modeling artifacts the main problem is the identification of the syntactical differences or equalities. On the one hand, however, it is formally very hard to verify graph equality and even harder to determine the minimum of parts that are different. On the other hand, the graphical representation may contain valuable hints for the mentioned problems but may also differ without change in the syntax. The merging of changes is usually a manual task, even if only different parts of the nets have been modified. In contrast, when text-based source code is used, merging of non-conflicting concurrent changes is possible. To our knowledge no tool exists so far that manages the merging to some extent or even supports the developer in this task. Even if a string representation of the net code exists, this code is usually not processable by common tools such as *diff* (see Eggert et al. (2008)). This means that models in source code management systems are treated as binary files, even if the file representation of the diagram (model) is text-based, such as XML – as with SVG (Scalable Vector Graphics).

## 18.2 Discovery of Net Differences

The development of models within development groups frequently leads to conflicting models. Even if the system models are decomposable in many parts, still the problem persists – as with all source code – that within one design artifact (Petri net or UML diagram) several changes can occur concurrently and have to be merged. In this situation two tasks have to be performed. First, the differences have to be identified. Second, the changes have to be included. If conflicts occur in text-based source code, developers are supported by powerful tools and techniques, such as diff tools, versioning systems, etc. For models (Petri nets) these tasks usually have to be performed manually.[1] We believe that tool support for the discovery of net differences can accelerate the development of (net system) models significantly.

### Scenarios

We can distinguish at least two different scenarios in which the tool can be utilized: the *similarity check* and the *difference discovery*. In the similarity check a developer does not know whether two models (Petri nets) or two versions of the model (Petri net) share the same code (are syntactically/semantically equal but may differ visually). For text-based code there exist code beautifiers that manage to unify the style of code as a preparation for the differences tools. Restricted layout possibilities which could have the same effect as code beautifiers are usually too restrictive for model designers. Often model elements or text inscriptions have been moved in the diagram by another developer and this has been committed to the repository resulting in a conflict. If the models (or the model versions) contain only small differences (e.g. only one element has been moved) the ImageNetDiff[2] image will instantly show that the models are syntactically equal. The checking of the equality of the models is thus reduced to the checking of the graphically differing parts.

In the difference discovery the visual areas of the model that present differences can be easily spotted by the developer. Again, if small changes have been made in the model, such as the removal or the addition of elements, the ImageNetDiff image will directly and clearly show the differences. Removed objects are highlighted as red elements in the diff image and additions are highlighted blue. If this is not the case and if substantial changes have been made, at least the ImageNetDiff image points out which net areas are of concern to the developer and which parts have not changed.

### Technique

The tool (see also Cabac and Schlüter (2008)) makes use of the internal export function of RENEW and the ImageMagick (2009) tool kit. For the generation of the differences images in the format of Portable Network Graphics (PNG) or alternatively Encapsulated Postscript (EPS), the nets are first exported to the file system as images. Then the

---

[1]An alternative strategy is the avoidance of concurrent changes.

[2]The ImageNetDiff – sometimes also simply called *diff image* – presents the differences between two diagrams or nets. The functionality is provided by the Image Net Diff Plugin.

exported images are passed on as arguments to the imaging tool in order to compute the differences image, which will also be stored in the file system. The resulting image will feature light grayish drawing elements for the parts of the original images that are equal and two different shades of red for the additional and removed graphical parts. Finally, for the convenience of the user the image is displayed by RENEW once the computation of the differences image is completed. Sources of models that are to be compared can be either drawings (diagrams) opened within the editor of RENEW or files from the file system. Also command line commands exist that make it possible to quickly access the functionality of the plugin without loading the whole graphical editor of RENEW. On the command line it suffices to define the two comparing files as argument. Thus the tool can also be included in scripts. As a support for Subversion the tool is able to directly compare the current working version of a model with the locally stored code base file. This allows the developer to use the `renew diff <file>` command in the same manner as `svn diff <file>`. Especially if no (real) change has been done (i.e. involuntary saving of the model during inspection) the equality check can help to prevent superfluous check-ins. However, some limitations of the presented method exist that result from the used tools.

- For a flawless comparison the compared images must have the same size.

- The comparison cannot be customized.

- The color scheme is fix.

- The results for models in which all graphical elements have been moved are not yet satisfying because the images are compared coordinate pixel against coordinate pixel.

- However, a simple move of *all* elements does not have any effect on the result, since the images are clipped before export.

- There is no integration with the model representation in RENEW yet. Thus, the discovery of changes is supported but the knowledge has to be manually transferred to the model by the developer.

## 18.3 Examples

The presented method and tool are able to compare a broad variety of supported models and drawings. Here we present as an example the results of the tool for a Petri net model.

### 18.3.1 A Petri Net: The Mulan Knowledge Base

As an example for the presentation of the method we present a Petri net from the developing of multi-agent systems with MULAN: the knowledge base net of the MULAN standard agents presented in Section 4.3.2 (see Figure 4.10). The two nets differ – pragmatically – in the fact that they support two different property files formats: simple properties (as properties) and XML notation (for the KBE, Knowledge Base Editor). The net that supports the enhanced representation is built upon the simple version,

thus they are comparable. To find the similarities and differences of the implementation
we present fragments of both nets in Figures 18.1 and 18.2. The fragments show the
initialization of the net with the initial knowledge parts of the agent's interface to the
knowledge base and the interface that handles the initialization of decision components
(active knowledge). Figure 18.3 then shows a screenshot of the resulting difference image
(similar fragment).[3]

The developer's awareness is instantly attracted by the bright red and bright blue
net elements and inscriptions. One can see simple additions (manually highlighted in
the image by dashed squares) and also changes of the code / inscriptions (highlighted
through ellipses) that have been made. The image shows clearly that all of the old net
structure has been preserved. Only additional net elements and inscriptions have been
added and some inscriptions have been altered. In a scenario of a shared development,

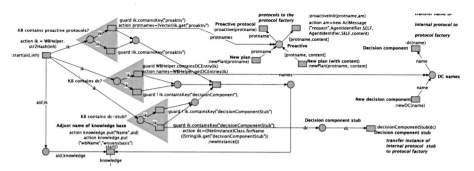

Figure 18.1: Knowledge base net template of a MULAN agent.

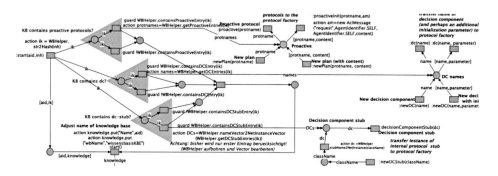

Figure 18.2: Enhanced knowledge base net template of a MULAN agent.

if a developer is confronted with a concurrent change of the net, which results in a
conflicting version of the net code, the tool can help the developer to decide whether
the code has been manipulated, the syntax not changed and/or if the changes have been

---

[3]The dashed squares and ellipses are added manually.

made in the same areas of the net. Thus, the manual act of merging the code or model can be significantly simplified and accelerated.

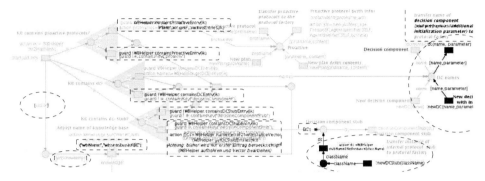

Figure 18.3: Screenshot showing differences of the two Petri nets.

## 18.3.2 Comparing (Embedded) Images

The tool is even able to show differences in (embedded) images. As a second example Figure 18.4 shows a (constructed) image (PNG, Image 1) and a minimally altered version (Image 2). Usually the difference is not even detectable. However the difference image to the right clearly shows the difference between the two images. In the PNG Image 2 the red square has been moved three pixels up and three pixels left. This possibility is not very surprising, since this is the original application domain of the ImageMagick *compare* tool. Note however, that the tool is able to cope with transparency as well.

Figure 18.4: Differences of embedded images (PNG).

## 18.3.3 Minimal Differences: A Sequence Diagram

As a large-scale model, we present a Sequence Diagram from a recent teaching development project of a multi-agent system. The model represents the initialization of a game. Here an agent sets up several agents necessary for the game to operate, such as supporting and player agents. We chose a large model because it best illustrates the use of the tool.

The scenario of the development process, here, is that the original model is the current head version in the Subversion repository. The developers have changed the models in

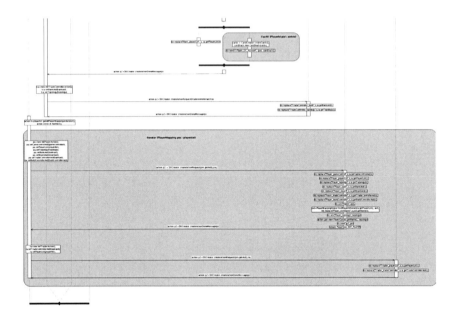

Figure 18.5: A Sequence Diagram for the initialization of a multi-agent system.

their checkouts (maybe some hours or days earlier). They want to know whether the diagram has changed and how. The command `svn status` will clearly show that the file has been changed. This however does not prove that the diagram has changed. They could look at both diagrams and decide manually if and where the change has occurred.

With the difference image the developers can clearly see and decide for sure that the *Player* role's activities have been changed. Moreover the image shows and proves that *all* other Roles' activities have not been altered.

## 18.4 Related Tools

### ImageMagick

ImageMagick (2009) provides with the *compare* tool a powerful, customizable tool that is able to compare images of all kinds and produce satisfying results of diff images as well as a metric that describes the difference found in a numeric value. While the original purpose of the tool is to measure differences in – for instance – photographic images against compressed versions of the same image, the tool works fine when applied to diagrammatic images.

### Graphviz

The excellent Graphviz (see Ellson et al. (2009)) framework provides – besides the incredible graph layout functionality – the tool *diffimg* to compare graphs. Resulting diff

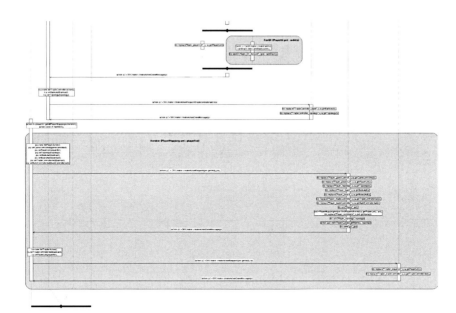

Figure 18.6: A minimally altered version of the Sequence Diagram (Figure 18.5).

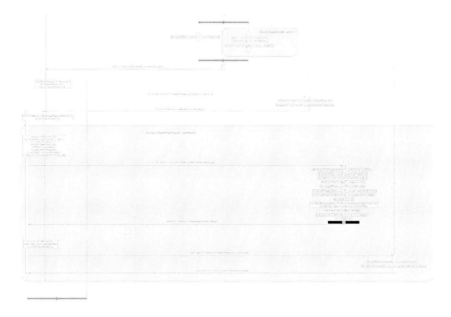

Figure 18.7: Diff image showing the differences between Figures 18.5 and 18.6.

images are in many cases satisfying. The tool produces monochrome (black & white) output, which shows the differences in the examined images as white areas. The rest of the image (graph, diagram) however is not represented in the diff image. It also remains unclear, which parts were removed or added.

**Perceptual Image Diff**

Perceptual Image Diff (`http://pdiff.sf.net`) compares images on the basis of the human visual system. The results for diagrammatic comparison are similar to the results of the tool *diffimg* (see above); the results for diagrams are poor.

# 18.5 Summary and Discussion

Although the approach is rather simple, the results are effective and surprisingly efficient. Developers of (Petri net) models have the means to visually check for differences in their graphical code through the presented tool support. Clearly a code beautifier for Petri nets and other models would considerably improve the results of the ImageNetDiff plugin. Net components (see Chapter 5 and Cabac (2009)) can impose a conventionalized structure upon Petri nets and could thus be utilized for this task.

The presented approach makes use of the graphical representation of diagrams such as UML diagrams or Petri nets, the export functionality to an image format and the processing of the images with the graphical framework ImageMagick. There are, however, several other possibilities to tackle the presented problem. One could compute equality of Petri nets on the grounds of the formal representation, including node and arc IDs, or develop a PNML (Petri net XML representation) diff tool.

The presented method and the tool leave room for many improvements. By choosing different color schemes and maybe also opaqueness in the diff images, the readability could still be improved significantly. However, since the used tool's main purpose of comparing images is not concerned with graph representations, it does not support this feature and a reimplementation or switch to another tool could – with some effort – produce better results. The interpretation of the graphically highlighted elements could lead to an integration of useful information within the Petri net editor in order to further support the merging of concurrent changes.

In principle, with the presented method, the results of image processing have to be re-transferred to the application domain. Alternatively, similar differences can be computed and presented to the developer on the direct analysis of Petri net structures. Here, additional information could support the process of matching elements in Petri net versions. For instance, ID-tagged net elements (in RENEW transitions and places have IDs) could be matched. However, this would not solve the problem of constructs that have different IDs but are syntactically equal. A method based on a Petri net (or model) representation is also less general than the presented method, which can be applied to other graphs such as UML diagrams.

# 19 API Documentation

This chapter presents Mulandoc, a prototype of an API documentation framework for MULAN applications. It is designed to be used in a similar fashion for MULAN applications as *Javadoc* is used for *Java* applications, and it addresses the fact that design artifacts in MULAN are Petri nets, i.e. diagrams. Additionally it takes account of the fact that the PAOSE process produces other design artifacts and includes them in the presentation of the applications' artifacts.

Mulandoc is integrated into the build process (as ant task) and automatically produces its output without the necessity of the developers' interference. The prototype presented here covers the models for overview, interactions, roles and agents. It presents the Coarse Design Diagram, Petri net and Agent Interaction Protocol Diagrams as images as well as knowledge bases as tables. The context is outlined in Section 19.1. In Section 19.2 we provide a brief description of the requirements for a documentation system in the context of PAOSE. Some related tools and possible alternatives are presented in Section 19.3 and Section 19.4 concludes this chapter.

## 19.1 Context

Each development process that produces design artifacts has to enable the developers to find necessary information in a fast and unobtrusive manner. The well-known *Java* API (application programming interface) documentation feature *Javadoc*[1] is able to generate clearly structured and navigable documents that are indispensable in nowadays development processes. In *Javadoc* documents are interconnected with links on all levels, indexes and overview documents exist that ease the orientation. *Javadoc* is quite static though and oriented towards *Java* code, which makes it difficult, if not impossible, to integrate other types of design artifacts or even other types of code.

## 19.2 Producing API Documentation

Mulandoc is meant to resemble the *Javadoc* API documentation – hence the name Mulandoc. After several attempts in the ongoing projects of agent application development that were either proprietary systems, hard to manually maintain or too unstructured and greedy to be useful, the requirements for a new documentation system were defined as follows.

- The system should be simple and easy to use.

---

[1]Javadoc, see http://java.sun.com/j2se/javadoc/.

- The system should be comparable to well-known systems, i.e. *Javadoc*.
- The system should be navigable, i.e. hypertext.
- The system should be extensible.
- The system should be automatic (ant task).
- Manual additions should be reduced to a minimum, if at all.

The result is a prototype of a hypertext (web-based) API documentation for MULAN. It is extensible and integrated into our environment as and *ant* task. Thus, it requires no effort and the generation can be automated, e.g. on a server where the documents can be made accessible for all participants. However, as it is still a prototype, not all artifacts are integrated in the generation of documentation.

The following figures show screenshots of the system for the Producer/Storage/Consumer (PSC) example presented in Chapter 21. Figure 19.1 shows the overview of the system API documentation in a web browser. The layout resembles the one from *Javadoc*. On the top, left side, the main categories (*agents, interactions, roles* and *coarse design*) can be accessed. Below is a list of all elements, which would be replaced by all elements belonging to a category. The exported image of the diagram is augmented with an image map that provides hyperlinks for the diagram element. The status-bar shows the destination: the *retrieve* interaction. Alternatively this kind of selection can be done via the elements list. An interaction (here *retrieve*) is represented by a list of all related

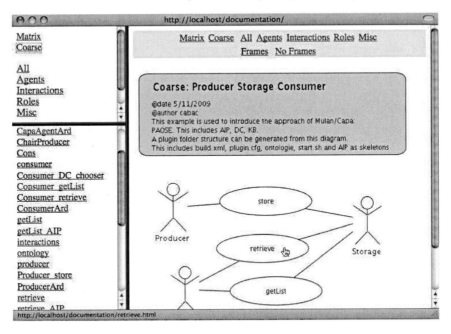

Figure 19.1: The Mulandoc overview: the Coarse Design Diagram with links.

artifacts. A click on one of the elements will open the artifact (diagram, table) in the detail view on the right. Figure 19.2 shows the *retrieve* AIP. The Petri nets belonging to the interaction can be accessed in the same manner as the AIP (see the URL in the status-bar). Figure 19.3 shows the protocol net *Storage_retrieve* in Mulandoc. The

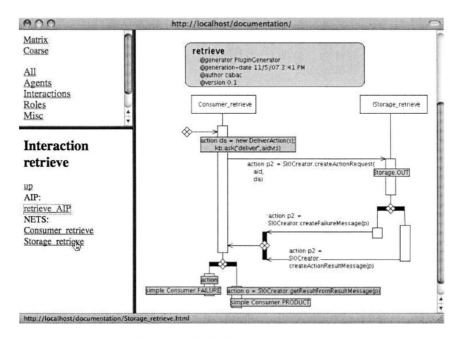

Figure 19.2: Mulandoc: the AIP *retrieve*.

Concept Diagrams are not included in the Mulandoc. Instead, they are included in the *Javadoc* representation as an extension to the package documentation for the ontology package. Figure 19.4 shows a screenshot of the Concept Diagram included in the generated *Javadoc* also supporting embedded links in the image. Alternatively to the Coarse Design Diagram in Figure 19.1 also a HTML table of the projects elements, not presented in the series of screenshots, can be displayed in the details view.

## 19.3  Related Work

### 19.3.1  Techniques

There exist several systems that allow to generate API documentations. They are usually designed for a certain programming language. Only few are able to work on several languages. Even if they support a set of languages, it is usually a small and fixed selection.

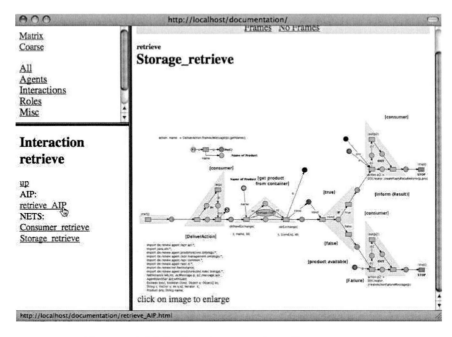

Figure 19.3: Mulandoc: the protocol net *Storage_retrieve*.

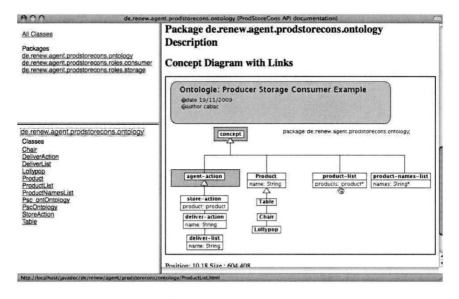

Figure 19.4: Including the Concept Diagram in the *Javadoc* package overview.

254

**JavaDoc**

*Javadoc* (`http://java.sun.com/j2se/javadoc/`) is extensible by doclets. These allow to customize the output. The input is restricted to *Java* code and cannot be extended to other languages.

**Doxygen**

Doxygen (`http://www.doxygen.org`) offers more flexibility regarding the programming language and is also able to generate diagrams from the source code – e.g. Class Diagrams – by employing dot. Several languages are supported (e.g. C,C++, Obective-C and *Java*) and in a limited way the system can be extended for other languages. The support does not however extend to graphical languages.

**XDoclet**

XDoclet (`http://xdoclet.sourceforge.net`) extends the idea of annotations not only for API documentation but also for the generation of code. This is described as attribute-oriented programming. It is restricted to *Java* code generation.

## 19.3.2 Alternatives

Mulandoc is not the first system that was created to gather documentation about the AOSE projects.

**SettlerDoc**

In the first Settler projects a proprietary system (specifically built for Settler) called Settler Doc was developed. It used PHP code and featured a JavaScript-based navigation that had to be manually maintained for each included element. *Javadoc* was included in the views. The huge amount of maintenance and the problem that the documentation was never up-to-date reduced the attractiveness of the system.

**SettlerDoc2**

With Settler Doc2 the attempt was made to achieve a generality. It was based on LaTeX and produced either PDF files or PostScript files. The system gathered all information and artifacts and strung them together into a large document. The structure of the produced output was unsatisfying, which made the document almost useless as documentation.

**NetDoc**

One remaining problem was the question of how to integrate comments for Petri nets and other diagrammatic artifacts. There exists no convention about how to comment Petri net models. The separation in in-line comments for the documentation of modeled elements and a part that describes the whole net or diagram is obvious. With NetDoc the net's description was moved to an external file that was structured and for which a special editor was created. The system docked its window to the window of the RENEW drawing. It was integrated in Settler Doc2 and also at first in Mulandoc. However, the biggest problem, besides the rough implementation, was that the descriptions resided in a separate file. In praxis most documents remained empty, i.e. the system was not accepted by the developers.

### 19.3.3 Contributions

My contributions to Mulandoc consist in the original conceptualization and definition of requirements for the project assignment. The first implementation was done by Meiners (2007). It used a simple text generation feature to write plain HTML text files, but provided a flexible architecture that made it possible to extend the system by additional project elements. Den, Lohmann and I (see Cabac et al. (2008b)) refactored the system to achieve a more flexible and also maintainable text generation feature. We included Velocity-based templates, introduced style-sheets for the HTML code, added support for knowledge base entries and improved the linking as well as navigation of the generated hypertext documents. Additionally, I extended the framework to generate image maps for the Coarse Design Diagrams. This allows hypertext navigation from the elements of the diagram to the target artifact documentation. I also added the inclusion of the Concept Diagram into the *Javadoc*'s package description of the ontology package.

Concerning the documentation of nets and diagrams in general, I included generic comment lines in the net component. The convention of how to write code is hard to follow. However, with the predefined generic comment lines for each net component, the comments can easily be manipulated and the generic comments also animated the developers to fill them with meaning. Apparently, it is easier to leave models uncommented than ignoring generic phrases. I also included the UML Note figure in the palette of the AIP Diagram Plugin, which can be used to annotate diagrams, nets or other images (compare with for example Figure 21.15).

I also discarded the need to describe each protocol net in an (external) description. Since the interaction is normally described through the AIP, it is more useful to have one detailed comment for the related AIP instead of distributed information in the AIP and in several protocol nets at the same time.

## 19.4 Summary

Mulandoc is a lightweight documentation system that automatically produces an API documentation for MULAN-based application. Although it is still in the state of a prototype, it is usable and leaves space for evolution through its extensible framework. It enables the developer to browse quickly through the models and other relevant artifacts of the system in the same manner as *Javadoc* does for *Java* code. The system makes full use of all design artifacts produced during the PAOSE development process.

# 20 Summary

In this part, techniques and tools for the analytical modeling of multi-agent systems are presented. In the context of multi-agent application development, analytical modeling means that the analytically produced models support the understanding and comprehension of the system. This includes the understanding of the system as a running program and as a specified system in the form of models and source code. The means of the analytical modeling is the explication of the models as diagrams. This diagrammatic model can then be *understood* by the observer and an understanding of the system thus achieved. As mentioned by Stachowiak (1973, p. 56), achievement of knowledge is achievement in models or through models. Thus, for the developers, it is only possible to achieve knowledge about the system, i.e. to understand the system, if they are able to build a model of the system.

The MULAN-SNIFFER explicates the conversations within a multi-agent system as Sequence Diagrams. On the ground of this visualization, the developers can achieve an understanding of the underlying processes in the system. They form a model, i.e. they create a mental model from the explicit model (compare with Section 2.2.2, Figure 2.3). Advanced techniques, such as process mining presented in Chapter 17, may reduce the model if the original amount of information or its representation cannot be explored efficiently. This form of abstraction is especially valuable in the case of complex dynamic systems.

The MULAN-VIEWER does not provide an explication of the system's structure as diagrammatic representation.[1] Instead, it uses the pragmatic approach of representing the hierarchical structure of the four layers of a MULAN application as tree list. Although this tree list representation is also an explication of the system's structure and, thus, supports the understanding of the system, it is just one of the main features of the tool. The MULAN-VIEWER derives its usefulness also from the possibility of inspecting the details of the system's elements. Here navigation between elements and linking of representation and related design artifacts add to the value of the tool. The controlling features of the MULAN-VIEWER turn the tool from an inspection tool to a multi-purpose tool that supports debugging activities, i.e. locating and fixing of errors (bugs).

Both tools manage to close the gap between the observation of the running system and the design artifacts, i.e. models and source code. The MULAN-VIEWER's advanced debugging abilities allow to inject new data and models on the fly (hot data/code replacement). The MULAN-SNIFFER produces Sequence Diagrams that can be used to construct Agent Interaction Protocol Diagrams in order to define new interaction protocols from observed behavior in the system.

---

[1]Although it can be argued that the tree (*JTree*) that represents the system's structure in the MULAN-VIEWER can be interpreted as graph.

The inspection of the system's description (specification) as diagrams/source code and the management of these artifacts is an essential part of system engineering. One of the most frequently done activities is the comparison of different versions of artifacts. For text-based languages, powerful tools exist that handle most of the tasks (finding differences and merging different versions) automatically or semi-automatically. Exactly the great advantage of diagrams – their diagrammatic representation – hinders a similar treatment for diagrams. The presented technique of comparing diagrams on a visual level with the Image Net Diff Plugin supports the developers, who handle diagrams such as UML diagrams (or alike) and Petri nets, in performing the main task, i.e. the finding of differences. The generation of the diff image is a form of explication of the model for the developer to understand the difference of the compared diagrams. For the documentation support during development, it is essential that the documentation should be up to date. Thus a lightweight and fast supporting system that needs as little maintenance as possible seems the only feasible solution to support the developers by their tasks of developing without producing too much distraction.

The techniques and tools, presented in this part, support the developers of MUL-AN-based applications within the PAOSE approach in understanding and managing the system and the system's artifacts. Moreover, they are valuable and essential instruments in the PAOSE approach.

# Part IV

# Example Applications

In order to demonstrate the modeling techniques and the supporting tools, this part presents a small teaching example, Producer/Storage/Consumer. It is described in detail in Chapter 21 where its execution is also demonstrated.

Additionally, this part presents the AOSE projects, teaching projects held between 2001 and 2008. The goal was to develop multi-agent applications on the basis of MUL-AN/CAPA. Two different systems have been built in those years, the Settler game and the agent-based workflow management system (WFMS). The Settler game was six times the topic of the projects and the WFMS twice.

In the context of these projects, the PAOSE approach as well as the modeling techniques and supporting tools presented in this work were developed and evaluated. The AOSE projects and a comparative evaluation are presented in Chapter 22.

# 21 Producer / Storage / Consumer

This chapter demonstrates the application of the presented modeling techniques for a small teaching example. It can be regarded as an advanced *'HelloWorld'* example application for MULAN. The Producer/Storage/Consumer example (PSC) is the extended version of the original Producer/Consumer example of Section 4.4.

It is useful to demonstrate the techniques on a small scale, where all details are still quite comprehensible. Thus we will go into detail by describing all developed artifacts of the complete development process. We will skip the requirements though, since they are not in the focus of this work and since the task definition is simple and clear. The original P/C example is extended by adding a storage, in which the producer can store *things* and from which the consumer can (a) get a list of all the names of the *things* available and (b) retrieve an item. This leaves us with three roles and three interactions.

We will start with the coarse design diagram in Section 21.1, from which several design artifacts are generated. This code base contains the Agent Interaction Protocol Diagram skeletons, the ontology file skeletons, the skeleton for the R/D Diagram, example DC nets and several other artifacts necessary to build and run the system. The ontology of the example is provided in Section 21.2 as Concept Diagram and as Protégé model. Then the interactions are presented in Section 21.3. The roles and the role-specific agent-internal behavior are modeled in Section 21.4. The modeling of decision components relies solely on elements native to reference nets, with the exception of ontology concepts and class constants. However, a more efficient implementation with *Java* can be easily achieved. Finally, in Section 21.5 the execution of the example is investigated in brief by using the tools for the analysis of multi-agent applications presented in Chapter 16 and 17, i.e. MULAN-VIEWER and MULAN-SNIFFER. A summary is provided in Section 21.6.

## 21.1 Coarse Design Diagram

The Coarse Design Diagram is modeled in a straight forward way from the task descriptions. It contains three roles (actors): *Producer*, *Consumer* and *Storage*, as well as three interactions (cases): *store*, *retrieve* and *getList*. Figure 21.1 shows the diagram elements of the PSC example. The connections define the participants in a given interaction and span the application matrix for roles and interactions. Participants of the *store* interaction are obviously *Producer* and *Storage*. For the *retrieve* and *getList* interactions the participants are *Consumer* and *Storage*.

The matrix is also displayed as an adjacency matrix (Table 21.1) generated from the diagram. This form of representation of the matrix is sometimes of advantage when the diagram gets crowded. Not surprisingly the table contains three roles as well as three interactions and each interaction has two participants.

> **Coarse: Producer Storage Consumer**
>
> @date 5/11/2007
> @author: cabac @version: 0.3
> This example is used to introduce the approach of Mulan/Capa: PAOSE.
> This includes AIPs, DCs, KBs.
> A plugin folder structure can be generated from this diagram.
> This includes build.xml, plugin.cfg, ontology, start.sh and AIPs as skeletons

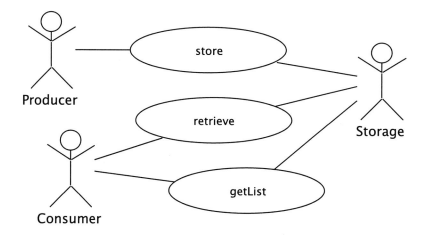

Figure 21.1: The Coarse Design Diagram of the Producer/Storage/Consumer example.

|  | Consumer | Producer | Storage |
|---|---|---|---|
| store |  | × | × |
| retrieve | × |  | × |
| getList | × |  | × |

Table 21.1: Generated matrix table from diagram.

Now it is time to setup our example system (PSC). The Use Case Plugin conveniently prepares the whole project. During generation the name of the project and the location in the file system is queried by dialogues. The given name is *ProdStoreCons*, while the location is the default MULAN development folder. Although the latter is not strictly necessary, it is convenient since the default MULAN folder contains already all dependent configuration files, such as ant tasks, properties and targets. Listing 21.1 shows the generated artifacts.

```
./build.xml
./etc/plugin.cfg
./src/de/renew/agent/prodstorecons/agents/projects.xml
./src/de/renew/agent/prodstorecons/agents/PSC.mas
./src/de/renew/agent/prodstorecons/agents/RolesDependencies.mad
./src/de/renew/agent/prodstorecons/agents/startKBE.sh
./src/de/renew/agent/prodstorecons/interactions/getlist
./src/de/renew/agent/prodstorecons/interactions/getlist/getList.aip
./src/de/renew/agent/prodstorecons/interactions/retrieve
./src/de/renew/agent/prodstorecons/interactions/retrieve/retrieve.aip
./src/de/renew/agent/prodstorecons/interactions/store
./src/de/renew/agent/prodstorecons/interactions/store/store.aip
./src/de/renew/agent/prodstorecons/PSCPlugin.java
./src/de/renew/agent/prodstorecons/roles/consumer
./src/de/renew/agent/prodstorecons/roles/consumer/Consumer_DC_test.rnw
./src/de/renew/agent/prodstorecons/roles/consumer/ConsumerHelper.java
./src/de/renew/agent/prodstorecons/roles/producer/Producer_DC_test.rnw
./src/de/renew/agent/prodstorecons/roles/producer/ProducerHelper.java
./src/de/renew/agent/prodstorecons/roles/storage/Storage_DC_test.rnw
./src/de/renew/agent/prodstorecons/roles/storage/StorageHelper.java
./src/ontology/PSC.pins
./src/ontology/PSC.pont
./src/ontology/PSC.pprj
./testing/start.shn
./testing/startCapa.rnw
```

Listing 21.1: Generated files for the example from Figure 10.5.

# 21.2 Ontology

For the sake of the example's generality, the ontology is defined in both possible ways. For completeness both are presented. Figure 21.2 depicts the ontology as a Concept Diagram.

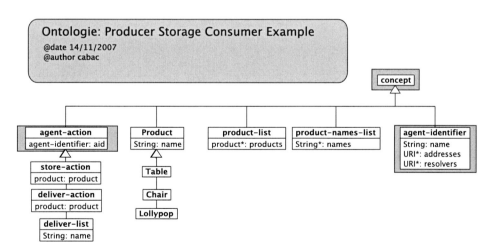

Figure 21.2: The ontology for the PSC example as Concept Diagram.

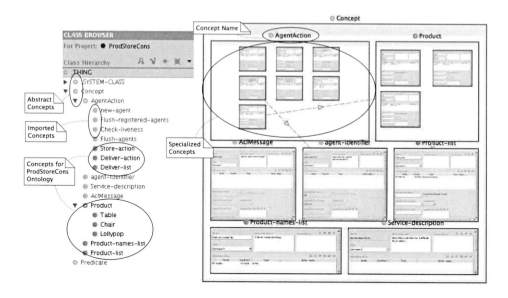

Figure 21.3: The ontology in Protégé and as Jambalaya tree-map.

Figure 21.3 shows a screenshot of the Protégé user interface (concepts view) and the tree-map of a part of the ontology produced with the Jambalaya plugin. The elements in the models are the same and the produced *Java* classes are compatible with each other. Note that general elements, such as *concept*, *agent-action* and *agent-identifier*, are imported in both models. In the Concept Diagram they can be identified by the surrounding gray box, while Protégé fades out the dots in front of imported concepts to distinguish these elements.

Note that the example's original design has been done when the ontology generation from Concept Diagram has not been available. Thus, the model had to be manually transferred to Protégé.

## 21.3 Interactions

The diagrams that specify the interactions are the Agent Interaction Protocol Diagrams (AIP), which are generated as skeletons from the Coarse Design Diagram. The skeletons contain only a descriptive box at the top and for each participating role a role descriptor. Thus, the tasks consist in designing the interactions *store*, *getList* and *retrieve*.

### 21.3.1 Interaction: store

The store scenario functions as follows: the *Producer* sends a message to the *Storage*. For the first interaction we assume that the *Storage* that has published its store service is also always capable of doing so. This simplifies the interactions that can be modified later on in order to react to unexpected behavior. The *Producer* 'knows' which product it produces.

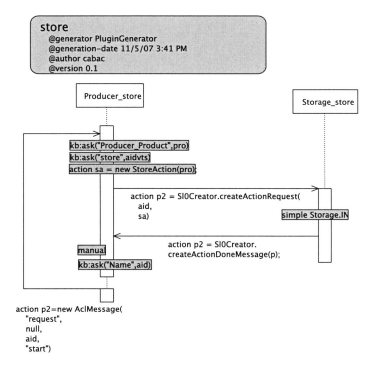

Figure 21.4: AIP: *store*.

Figure 21.4 shows a possible solution to the *store* interaction. The *Producer* starts this interaction pro-actively. The first tasks consist in retrieving the product the *Producer* produces and a list of agents that offer the *store* service from the knowledge base, where it is conveniently stored as initial knowledge. The product is wrapped into a *store-action* using the constructor of the *StoreAction* class (compare with Section 21.2). The resulting *agent-action* is again wrapped to form a request message *p2* (performative). The message is received by the *Storage* and added to the stock, which is managed by a decision component that offers the interface *Storage.IN* (see Section 21.4.3).[1]

After storing the product, the *Storage* sends an acknowledgment as reply to the *Producer*. The *store* protocol net of the *Producer* then waits for a *manual* interaction with the developer before it restarts the *store* protocol by sending a message to itself that

---

[1]Note that the actual interface name *store_in* is held in a helper class (Storage) as String constant. By defining the interface names as constants it is possible to check the correctness (type-safety) at compile time. Through the use of RENEW the developers actually get a dynamic syntax check at design time. Note also that the name of the helper class is pure convention and that at the time of design the convention *StorageHelper* did not exist.

satisfies the message-protocol mapping for *store* – in this case a simple action request with the content *start*. In order to determine the correct receiver, the knowledge base is queried for the name of the agent. Alternatively, the standard agent-identifier defined as constant *AgentIdentifier.SELF* could be used.

### 21.3.2 Interaction: getList

The interaction for the request to get the list of available products follows a similar course (Figure 21.5). Noteworthy are the dummy role descriptor and an alternative possibility

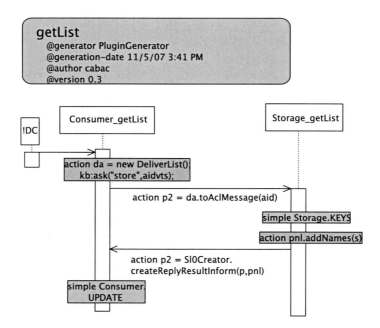

Figure 21.5: AIP: *getList*.

to produce action requests. The dummy role descriptor represents the call from the decision component (see Section 21.4.4), hence the name decision component. To be suppress generation for this element it is marked with an initial exclamation mark. For the construction of action requests all agent-action ontology classes provide a convenience method *toAclMessage(·)*.

### 21.3.3 Interaction: retrieve

The retrieve interaction is used by the *Consumer* to retrieve an offered *Product* from the *Storage*. With a given name the *Consumer* can order a product from the *Storage*. However, even though the *Storage* has offered a list of product names to the *Consumer* before, it is possible that the request for a product may fail. Thus, either a failure or a result message is sent back from the *Storage* to the *Consumer*. Either answer is processed accordingly by giving feedback to the decision component (interfaces *Consumer.FAILURE* or *Consumer.PRODUCT*).

Note that the initial message is not attached to any activation. Instead only a message join figure is used as an alternative to the dummy role descriptor plus activation.

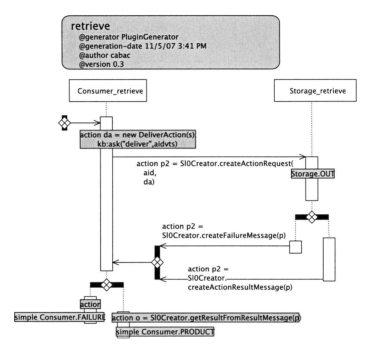

Figure 21.6: AIP: *retrieve*.

## 21.3.4 Protocol Nets

From the AIP interaction specifications Petri net skeletons are generated that are refined to achieve executable models. The *Storage*'s part of the *retrieve* protocol is presented in this section. The other nets are constructed in an analogous fashion.

### Storage_retrieve

The *Storage_retrieve* protocol net serves as example for the further development of interactions. Figures 21.7 and 21.8 show the generated skeleton and the refined model, which is executable code. To show the refinements in detail, we provide an image that shows the differences between the skeleton and the final model (Figure 21.9, removed parts red/new parts green) as image diff produced with the Image Net Diff Plugin (see Chapter 18).

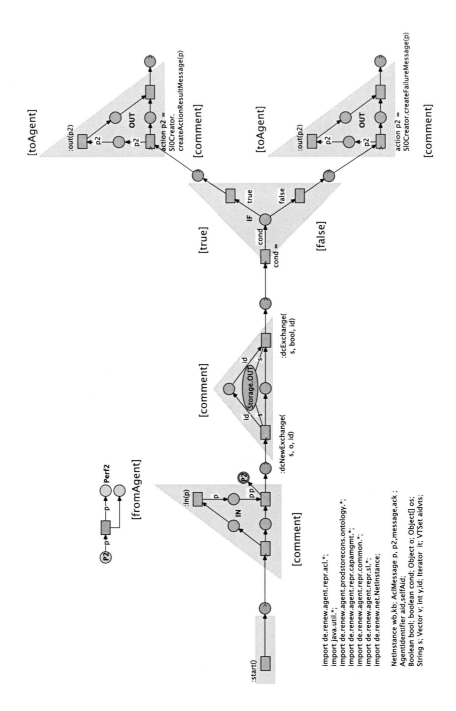

Figure 21.7: The generated skeleton *Storage_retrieve*.

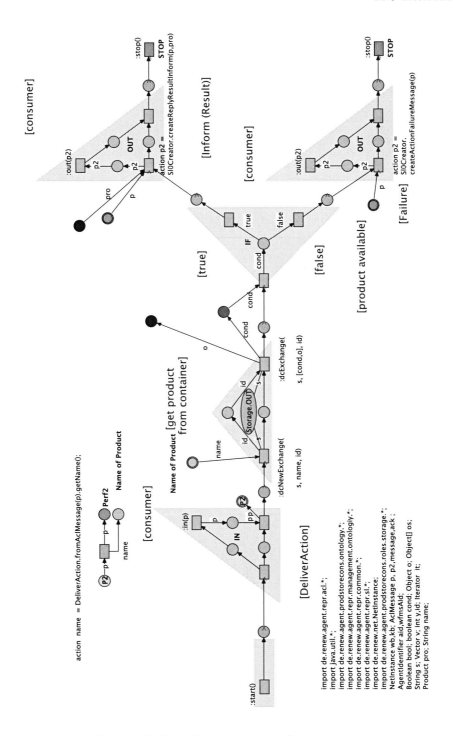

Figure 21.8: The refined protocol net *Storage_retrieve*.

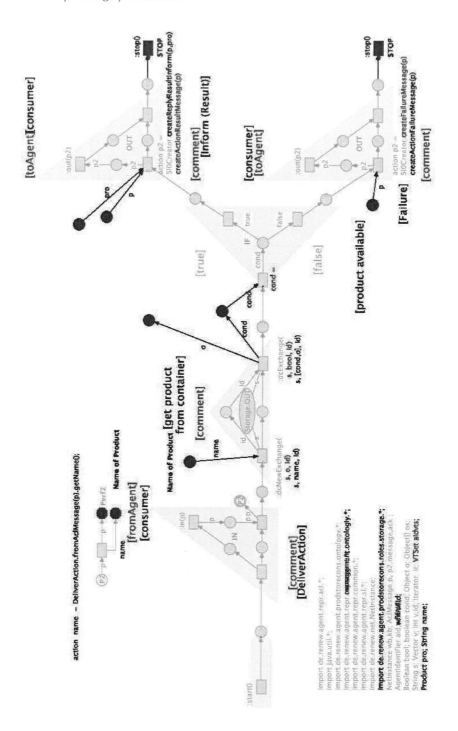

Figure 21.9: *Storage_retrieve*: diff of skeleton and refinement.

# 21.4 Roles

The agent roles define the organizational/structural aspects of the multi-agent application. Roles are directly derived from the Coarse Design Diagram and during generation of the initial project artifacts the folders for the role-dependent additional artifacts are generated. This includes a simple R/D Diagram skeleton.

## 21.4.1 Organizational Structure and Knowledge

The agent roles and the initial knowledge bases are defined using the R/D Diagram. Figure 21.10 shows the roles and services used and offered in the example. All elements are collapsed to show only their names and stereotypes. Roles are *Producer*, *Consumer* and *Storage*. Services *deliver* and *store* are both offered by the *Storage* and each is used by one of the other agent roles. All agent roles are instantiated as (CAPA) agents (see Section 21.4.5).

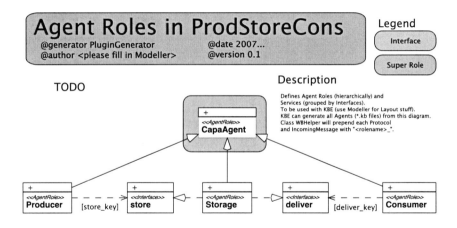

Figure 21.10: The R/D Diagram for the PSC example (folded elements).[2]

In the version of the diagram, in which all elements are expanded, several details are revealed. The *Producer* has four filled-in sections in its knowledge base. The product is given as an SL object in the state description section. The only required service is the *store* service. A list of agents, registered at the DF to offer this service, is retrieved and stored in the knowledge base under the key *store* during initialization of the agent with the role. The only protocol in the mapping is the *store* protocol. The name will be expanded to *Producer_store* during knowledge base initialization. It will be called as reaction every time when a start message is received. Initialization of the agent is done by the protocol *generalAgentSetup* (compare with the state description section of the *CapaAgent* in Figure 21.11), which is started pro-actively by every CAPA agent. This protocol

---

[2]The skeleton provides a list of hints how to proceed (*TODO*). The list is deleted, since done, the heading remained for possible hints in the future.

takes care of the registration of the agent at the AMS (agent management system) and of services at the directory facilitator (DF). It also takes care of the retrieval of required service suppliers. Since this initial DF lookup does not implement a subscription mechanism, the starting order of the agents (roles) is crucial.

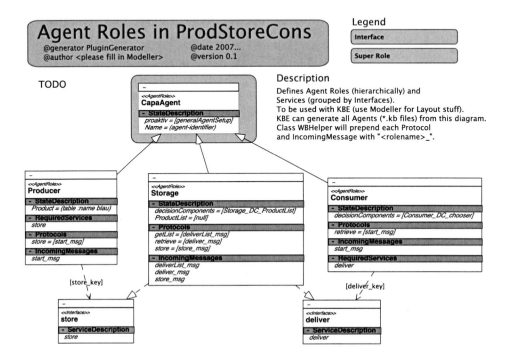

Figure 21.11: The R/D Diagram for the PSC (elements unfolded).

## 21.4.2 Internal Behavior

In our example the simple iteration of the *Producer_store* protocol is realized through a single manual transition in the protocol. For more elaborated functionality it is common and useful to define internal behavior as decision components as described in Chapter 14.

This can be regarded as an agent internal service offered to the communicative processes of the agents or as active knowledge. For the example this means that the *Storage* role needs to provide the storage functionality and the *Consumer* role has to provide a simple interface for the observer to control the interactions and observe the results.

## 21.4.3 DC: Storage_DC_ProductList

The *Storage* has to store *Products* – in our example these are SL objects. The proposed decision component internally stores the products in a simple list of tuples {[name, product]}. The functionality offered externally is: store a product in the decision component, get a list of all available products as names and retrieve a product that is in the list by providing the name of a product. The interface of the decision component is defined by the exchange channel names, provided as class constants: *Storage.IN*, *Storage.OUT* and *Storage.KEYS*. Internally, the functionality is provided by a list in place *MAP*. Figure 21.12 shows the interface and the internal functionality of the decision component as a scheme, i.e. it is not functional yet. Interfaces are defined through the combination of a place, which contains the name of the interface and a transition with a synchronous channel, i.e. up-link *exchange*. These elements are available as net components (compare with Figure 14.1). The interface transitions have a green color and are labeled *SIMPLE*, *START* or *STOP*.

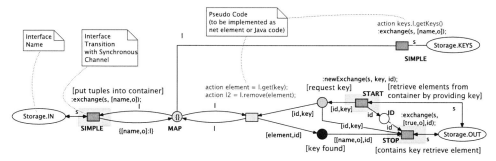

Figure 21.12: Decision component: *Storage_DC_ProductList* (abstract scheme).

The adding of a product is straight forward and atomic and the exchange channel can be an atomic *simple exchange* (compare with Figure 4.19). The retrieval of a product is designed to be asynchronous. And the proposed functionality, which is sketched as pseudo code has to be implemented. This can be done as *Java* code or directly as net code. In the following we opted to implement the functionality as Petri net code.

The retrieval of a product may fail, thus either the product is retrieved or an error is produced (compare with the interaction *retrieve* in Section 21.6). This results in an additional interface transition in the refined and executable model in Figure 21.13.

The retrieval of the list of keys uses an advanced version of a recursive channel chain similar to the model for the *flexible arc* (compare with Section 3.2.5, Figure 3.9). Thus, the extraction of the list of names from the list of tuples is atomic and the exchange channel can also be simple/atomic.

The extraction of a tuple from the list is not done in an atomic step, instead it is done in three steps. First the list is locked by the up-link call :lockList(), i.e. the list is moved from its original place (*MAP*). Then the list is searched atomically to retrieve a matching tuple. If one of the element matches, the tuple is removed (*[key found]*) from the list and the remaining list is repacked (channel :t(·,·)) and put back into the place *MAP*. If none of the elements matches (*nothing found*), the list is put back and no element is extracted. Depending on the outcome an appropriate answer is given through the call-back channel of the initial request.

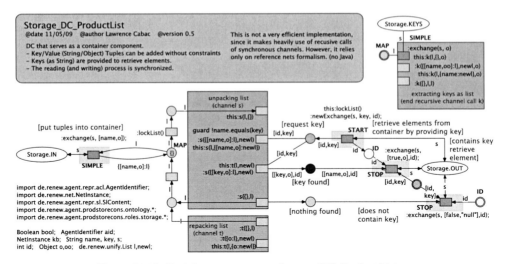

Figure 21.13: Decision component: *Storage_DC_ProductList*.

## 21.4.4 DC: Consumer_DC_chooser

For the *Consumer* we want to construct a simple user interface in order to control and observe the processes and their outcome. Figure 21.14 shows a decision component, with which the developer is capable of requesting the list of available products (*[proactive getList]*).

The updated list is put into the central place *LIST* and at the same time the list is extracted by a flexible channel into the place *KEYS*. With the adjoining manual transition a key can be selected and a product requested. The result is presented at the bottom of the net in either of the two big places. This can be either a possible error message on the left side (red place) or the received products on the right side (green place). To be able to test the interaction with impossible arguments the list can be initialized with arbitrary keys (*[manual Tests]*).

## 21.4.5 Agents

The last model that is missing for the example is the agent model. This model is, however, not modeled explicitly as diagram in the example. This is due to the fact that each agent owns exactly one role. Four agents are defined through their initial knowledge bases. They are *Cons* (role *Consumer*), *Store* (role *Storage*), *TableProducer* (role *Producer*) and *ChairProducer* (role *Producer*). The definition of agent types is directly done in the KBE. The produced artifacts are the merged agent role descriptions (ARD, see Section 11.4) as XML files (Extensible Markup Language).

The following Tables 21.2, 21.3 and 21.4 summarize the knowledge base files; entry types are omitted. The representation of the contents have been transformed into a table layout for better readability. Note that the special entry *Name* is set during deployment of the agent. The agents *Cons* and the two *Producer* agents do not have any reactive

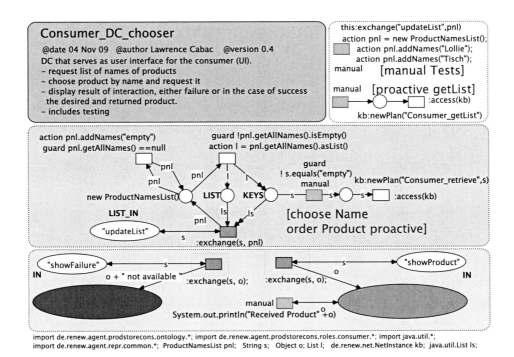

Figure 21.14: Decision component: *Consumer_DC_chooser*.

behavior, apart from the (pseudo-) pro-active behavior triggered by the *start* message. The *Store* agent, in contrast, has to react to the requests according to its offered services. This agent can be attributed with the stereotype *service agent*.

**Cons**

**IncomingMessages**

request;;;start;        retrieve

**Protocols**

retrieve        start_msg;

**RequiredServices**

deliver_key        deliver;;

**StateDescription**

| decisionComponents | Consumer_DC_chooser; |
| Name | ; |
| proactive | generalAgentSetup; |

Table 21.2: Knowledge base entries of the *Cons* agent.

**Store**

| StateDescription | |
| --- | --- |
| ProductList | null; |
| decisionComponents | Storage_DC_ProductList; |
| Name | ; |
| proactive | generalAgentSetup; |

| IncomingMessages | | |
| --- | --- | --- |
| request;((action (agent-identifier) (store-action)));FIPA-SL0; | | store |
| request;((action (agent-identifier) (deliver-action)));FIPA-SL0; | | retrieve |
| request;((action (agent-identifier) (deliver-list)));FIPA-SL0; | | getList |

| Protocols | | ServiceDescription | |
| --- | --- | --- | --- |
| store | store_msg; | store_key | store;; |
| retrieve | deliver_msg; | deliver_key | deliver;; |
| getList | deliverList_msg; | | |

Table 21.3: Knowledge base entries of the *Store* agent.

**TableProducer**

| Protocols | |
| --- | --- |
| store | start_msg; |

| StateDescription | |
| --- | --- |
| Product | blue; |
| Name | ; |
| proactive | generalAgentSetup; |

| RequiredServices | |
| --- | --- |
| store_key | store;; |

| IncomingMessages | |
| --- | --- |
| request;start; | store |

**ChairProducer**

| StateDescription | |
| --- | --- |
| Product | yellow; |
| Name | ; |
| proactive | generalAgentSetup; |

| IncomingMessages | |
| --- | --- |
| request;start; | store |

| Protocols | |
| --- | --- |
| store | start_msg; |

| RequiredServices | |
| --- | --- |
| store_key | store;; |

Table 21.4: Knowledge base entries of the *Producer* agents.

## 21.5 Observation of the PSC Example

The example is started by invoking an instance of RENEW with the provided start script
(`testing/start.sh`), which sets up the environment, such as the net path and the class
path. After starting a CAPA platform and launching the agents manually, a user can

interact with the system through the manual transitions in protocol nets or decision components. Alternatively, the models can be executed step by step or breakpoints can be set to control the execution. The system can be observed and the execution controlled by using the MULAN-VIEWER or by observing the token game of the Petri net instances. Figure 21.15 shows the executed system in the MULAN-VIEWER. Agents are displayed as nodes including the net agent icon ⬚ and the name of the agent, which consists of its given name, unique ID and the platform name on which the agent has been created. Besides the administrative agents (platform, ams and df) here (only) three other agents named according to their roles are displayed in their hierarchical structure, represented as a tree. The tree also displays the agent's internal elements as nodes (knowledge bases ♟, protocol nets ◗ and decision components 🐠). On the right side the details of the selected element can be inspected.

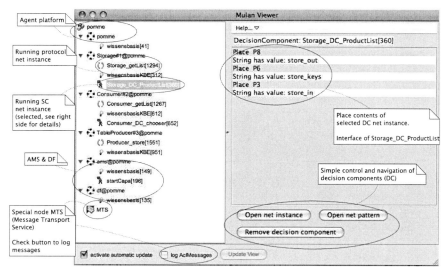

Figure 21.15: The executed example observed with the MULAN-VIEWER.

Advanced observation of agent conversations is done with the MULAN-SNIFFER. Figure 21.16 displays a screenshot of the MULAN-SNIFFER's user interface together with the sniffed messages as Sequence Diagram and a Petri net resulting from the process mining functionality. The main window of the MULAN-SNIFFER offers three views: the agent list, the message view (bottom left) and the details view. The agent list offers information about number of sent and received messages and the possibility to set inclusion or exclusion filters. In the screenshot administrative agents are disabled, while the example's agents are enabled for observation. The message view displays part of a selected message, showing performative, sender, receiver, content, etc. of the message. The selected message is highlighted in all views as well as in the diagram to the right.

The details view offers several tabs (e.g. for a list of the observed messages). In the screenshot the result of the mining process as clustered conversations is displayed in the mining tab. The mined protocols deduced from the sample conversations can be

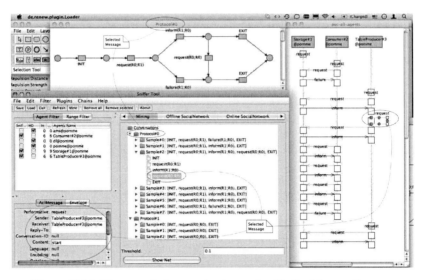

Figure 21.16: The executed example observed with the MULAN-SNIFFER.

converted into a process description, in this case a Petri net (*Protocol#0*) shown at the top. The net has been beautified through a computer assisted manual process. Here one can see the usual process of a request protocol-like flow. A deeper inspection shows that the store interaction and the retrieve interaction have been clustered as one protocol. This is not surprising, since both are simplified request protocols. Note that the manual restart of the *Producer_store* – by calling the own agent with the *start* message – results in the alternative final request (*request(R0,R0)*), which shows the same sender and receiver. One of these messages is selected in the MULAN-SNIFFER. Alternatively, the observer can also select a sample entry or even a protocol entry in the presented tree to highlight all related messages in the diagram.

## 21.6 Summary

This chapter presents the Producer/Strorage/Consumer (PSC) example in detail and at all stages of development covered by the presented modeling techniques of the PAOSE approach. As any *HelloWorld* example the usefulness of PSC lies in its clearness and the possibility to present a self-contained example as an introduction for a beginner. In addition to the presentation of the final artifacts, all design artifacts are presented. However, the usefulness of modeling those simple processes as abstract models, seems to be exaggerated. The full value and power cannot be experienced on such a small scale. The power of the approach and the usefulness of the produced models can only be valued, if the target system is a complex system. Especially if many developers cooperate in the construction of a complex system, possibly in a distributed setting, the utilization of the produced design artifacts is indispensable for communication and coordination within the development group.

# 22 Projects

This chapter presents the AOSE projects Settler 1 to 6 and WFMS 1 & 2. An outline of the history of the projects shows the development of the systems and that of the PAOSE approach. We will concentrate on the modeling techniques since they are in the focus of this work. Many other works have been nevertheless achieved in the context of the projects and the PAOSE approach, and some of them are briefly mentioned.

The latest version of the Settler application is presented. The focus lies on the produced models and the modeling in terms of system design. However, only a selection of the models will be presented because of their amount and size.

In Section 22.1 the context of the AOSE projects is presented and their objectives are discussed. Section 22.2 presents the projects and an historical outline and provides a selection of design artifacts for the Settler project. Section 22.3 briefly presents the systems that support the team during development with all kinds of functionalities, such as communication, project organization and sharing of teaching material. An evaluation and a discussion of the projects are provided in Section 22.4. Section 22.5 presents a list of works done in the context of the projects. Section 22.6 summarizes this chapter.

## 22.1 Context

For the development and evaluation of a Petri net-based agent-oriented approach, it is necessary to find an objective that matches the general setting requirements as well as the resources and possibilities of participants. On the one hand, we intend to realize in a developed multi-agent application (as an application of distributed artificial intelligence, DAI) a number of attributes. They are listed in the following:

**Distribution** The system should be distributed over a network of platforms.

**Concurrency** The system should allow concurrent behavior of agents, where possible.

**Social behavior** Agents in the system should cooperate or compete with other agents, negotiation should be included.

**Interactivity** Human actors should be able to interact with the system.

**Planning** Automatic agents should behave in a comparable manner as that of human actors (artificial intelligence).

On the other hand, in the frame of a teaching project (at the university), the students have to be able to achieve the goals of the project in a given time, usually short. There also has to be a special kind of motivation for students, as they are not employed, i.e. the motivation should come naturally to the participating students. Additionally, one has to take two other things into account. The first is that the students have to be taught the approach from the fundamentals to the very special details, which is very time consuming but has the advantage that all students start at the same level. The second point is that one has to give them the room to find the topic for their term papers and the possibility to finish them.

An interactive multi-user game is an ideal target that meets the combination of given DAI background and motivational requirements, as mentioned above. Here cooperation, competition, negotiation as well as concurrency and distribution are inherent attributes of the system. Additionally, the experience shows that students are generally eager to commit themselves in such a topic.

The second application domain in the AOSE projects, an agent-based distributed workflow management system (WFMS), meets the first set of requirements for a teaching project. However, the motivation of the students for the subject is somewhat minimal. One can make out several reasons for this. One of them is that the development of a middleware does not show the progress of the system and the students cannot identify with the targeted system. Another one is that in a teaching-intensive setting, the participants have to get acquainted with the paradigm, the framework, the modeling techniques, the tool set, etc. The necessity to become familiarized with another – completely new and different – topic seems not very appealing for the participants.

The first objective of the projects is to construct a distributed, agent-based application (here Settler or WFMS). The scenario for the Settler game is clearly set by the rules of the well-known board game *The Settlers of Catan*.[1] The game should support human players as well as automatic players.

The requirements and intention of the WFMS lie more in the area of joining different software engineering disciplines. Reese (2009) presents the details regarding the WFMS conceptualization, design and implementation. Here, since this is not the focus of this work, we will not go into the details of the requirements analysis.

Besides the direct objective in form of the application scenario, we have other objectives concerning the long-term development of the approach or the teaching aspects. The second objective of the projects are the further development of the approach in general as well as the modeling techniques and the supporting tool set in particular. In a project setting, the agent framework can also be further evaluated and tested. Thus, the project serves as evaluation ground for many purposes and the intensive application of framework tools and techniques has furthered the improvements of all underlying frameworks and tool sets, i.e. RENEW and plugins as well as MULAN/CAPA and extensions and variations.

The third objective of the projects is to provide the context in which the students can find a topic for their theses and finish them successfully. Here a multitude of theses (diploma, bachelor and dissertations) have evolved from the AOSE projects.

---

[1]Description of the game and rules can be found online at http://www.catan.com.

# 22.2 Settler and WFMS

Up to 2009, the AOSE project with the focus on the development of Settler has had six repetitions. While the first project and its results can be regarded as proof of concept for the MULAN frameworks applicability, the later projects focused on the improvements of the system, the approach (processes and techniques) and supporting tools.

In each project, several – but not all – design and implementation artifacts were transferred from the preceding project. This offered many advantages and also some disadvantages. Advantages are, for instance, the possibility to develop other aspects of the game. Disadvantages include the dragging along of legacy code. With Settler 5 a cut was made and the game was completely redesigned on the ground of the elaborated PAOSE approach, including Coarse Design Diagrams, R/D Diagrams, Agent Interaction Protocol Diagrams, the RemoteDC as GUI adapter and the explicit modeling of the ontology with Concept Diagrams. The generation of the ontology was first achieved with Protégé (Settler 5) and with the availability of the FS Ontology Generator Plugin directly from Concept Diagrams (Settler 6). Only GUI classes were transferred which had to be completely recoded so that they would adapt to the new ontology, and all code had to be translated from German to English.

## 22.2.1 A Brief Project History

The following list presents some of the main achievements.

### Settler 1 (2001)

The Settler 1 project can be regarded as a proof of concept. Here many aspects of the approach, the modeling and the general conceptualization were experimentally explored. There was no explicit ontology. All communication was string-based, which led to frequent failures because of unchecked typos. The TCP/IP communication for the inter-platform communication – and thus also for the playing of the game on more than one computer – was added during the project (Duvigneau 2002). The abstract modeling was reduced to a minimum. Actually, the only abstract model is a communication diagram shown in Figure 22.1

### Settler 2 (2002)

One improvement in Settler 2 was the introduction of net components. This provided advantages in structured Petri net models, an acceleration of development and an improvement of readability. The template-based net components also made it easier to learn how certain issues in modeling can be addressed through provided example solutions. Without the need to concentrate on the details, more energy was put into the design of the system. Overview of the interactions was given by an early prototype of the AIP Diagram Plugin. First AIPs were rough and of only little informative power, due to inexperienced modelers. Furthermore, the first domain-specific ontology objects were coded for an application in the MULAN context. The classes were manually coded

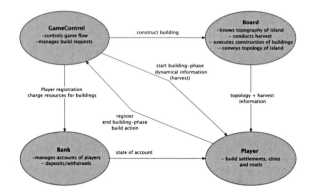

Figure 22.1: Modeling agents and communication in Settler 1.[2]

by numerous people and the management of concepts (i.e. registration at the parser) had to be done by the developers. Thus the communication was getting type-safe, reducing syntax errors/mismatches, but there was neither overview of the classes, nor explicit modeling. The amount of ontology classes is hard to determine. In the configuration file 54 classes are registered and in the specialization hierarchy 69 concepts are available. Settler 2 also introduced simple trading for the game.

### Settler 3 (2003)

Settler 3 was the first really playable version of Settler. A rudimentary GUI for the initialization exists. Remote players can connect to the game if names and IP-addresses of the *game-control* agents are available. The number of ontology concepts increased to 111 (or 112, see above). The explicit modeling of the ontology become a necessity. At least some of the concepts were for the first time (semi-automatically) generated and included in the source repository.

### Settler 4 (2004)

A full fletched GUI for the initialization of the game replaced the rudimentary one. The choice of different boards and local and remote players were possible to be defined at start time. The game concept of harbors entered finally the implementation. However, the advanced trading did not work correctly in all possible ways.

### WFMS 1 (2005)

The first WFMS project was the first original design from scratch since Settler 1. This and the underestimation of the complexity of the envisioned system resulted in only a reduced implementation. A rudimentary encapsulation of the already existing workflow

---

[2]Diagram adapted from Duvigneau (2002, p. 141).

engine by Jacob (2002) was able to execute workflows and dispatch activities. It is difficult to describe the system itself because it was discontinued, i.e. it is not executable anymore. Problematic, in retrospect, were the absence of role concepts (in implementation) and the lack of organizational modeling. These were topics already addressed. However, the tools and techniques were not ready for production. Last but not least, the technical framework, which included the existing workflow management system designed by Jacob (2002), had not been adapted for the project setting beforehand. This hindered the whole project.

## WFMS 2 (2006)

The second approach was avoiding most mistakes of the first WFMS project. The coarse design was for the first time done with a Use Case Diagram syntax by using a very rudimentary prototype of the Use Case Plugin. This helped to find an approach to the system and to communicate the ideas about how the system should be built. Also the KBE (KBE) was available for the first time. Although the experience with the tool and the proposed modeling technique was non-existent, the possibility to design the knowledge bases and to have an additional overview of all roles in the system added to the clearness of the system's model.

Reese et al. (2006) provided an overview of the envisioned architecture. Figure 22.2 shows the proposed architecture and the embedding of the system in the provided tool set/framework.

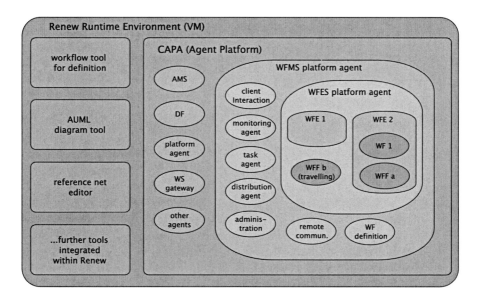

Figure 22.2: The architecture of an agent-based workflow management system.[3]

---

[3]Diagram adapted from Reese, Offermann and Moldt (2006, p. 83).

Several other artifacts have been presented in this work as examples for the modeling techniques. For instance the Coarse Design Diagram in Figure 10.2, the R/D Diagrams in Section 11.4 and fragments from the ontology e.g. in Figure 12.2.

Baggendorf and Jander (see Cabac et al. (2007a)), two of the developers provided their own vision of the system and presented it in their term paper.

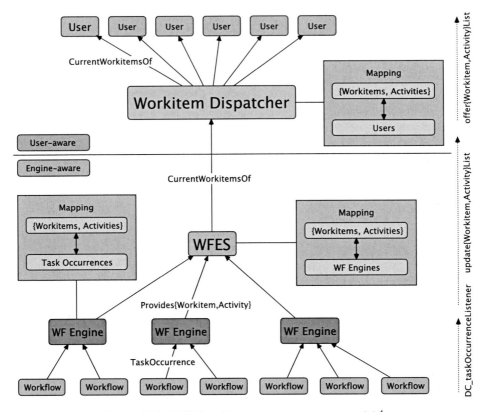

Figure 22.3: WFMS architecture as component model.[4]

The image shows the different agents of the WFMS. User agents are placeholders for user of the system. The technical part of the WFMS (*Engine-aware*), consists in a *workflow enactment service* agent, which manages several *workflow engine* agents. These last ones execute the workflows (which can actually also be agents). The open workitems are offered to the *user* agents by the *workitem dispatcher* agent, who is also responsible for the assignment of activities.

The model shows nicely that the bottleneck of the system lies in the interface between the engine-aware and the user-aware side. The tight connection between WFES and WIDispatcher is also observable in the R/D Diagram in Figure 11.6.

---

[4]Diagram adapted from Cabac et al. (2007a, p. 39).

**Settler 5 (2007)**

Settler 5 is a complete recode in English with the exclusive usage of ontology concepts. The development followed rigorously the PAOSE approach. All presented modeling techniques were applied (Coarse Design Diagrams, Concept Diagrams, R/D Diagrams, Agent Interaction Protocol Diagrams and DCs) and net components were used for all protocol nets and all decision components. For the first time manual tests for interactions and decision components were used to accelerate the integration.

Also for the first time the ontology was designed exclusively with Concept Diagrams (manually translated to Protégé). Mulandoc was available for the first time too, which proved valuable later in the project.

The organizational structure was also designed for the first time with experience (from the WFMS) as R/D Diagram.

An issue occurred during development that prevented the system – at first – to be used. The excessive use of ontology concepts in communication and for internal storage led to a slowdown of communication. Some of the communication objects were structures, which contained more than 1500 elementary and compound ontology concepts. The problem was later solved by an efficient implementation of the classes.

**Settler 6 (2008)**

This is the first project, in which the ontology generation was done directly from the Concept Diagrams with the FSOntologyGenerator Plugin provided by Teuber (see Cabac et al. (2009)). One major task that involved the redesign of a substantial part of the system was the redesign of the initialization. This was necessary to be able to introduce new players dynamically into games. For this, a lobby was also introduced, which offered open games to players without a game. The exchanging of players on the fly was introduced into the game scenarios and the trading interaction was fixed (p2p, p2b, 4–1 and harbors (3–1, 2–1)).

## 22.2.2 Models of the Settler MAA

This section presents the models of the Settler application (version 6) only in brief, given the high number of models and their size. We only focus on some aspects that highlight the design, the process and the application of the earlier presented techniques. For a detailed description of the complete development procedure see Chapter 21 and for a selection of the complete diagrams, of which some fragments are shown in this chapter, see Appendix C. It is however not possible to present the complete set of diagrams even in the appendix because of their large number.

**Coarse Design**

The coarse design starts as a process of collective brainstorming and discussion. The system coarse organization, the roles and the interactions are identified and denominated. This denomination process is closely linked to the design of the system's ontology (see the following section). In agent systems, where self-reflectivity is a desired feature, the roles and interactions might enter the ontology as concepts so that agents can *reflect* about their own status or interactions.

The roles and interactions are plainly listed on a blackboard and discussed, and the lists are directly entered into a Coarse Design Diagram on-the-fly during discussion. The result of a first approximation is presented in Figure 22.4. The result is further refined –

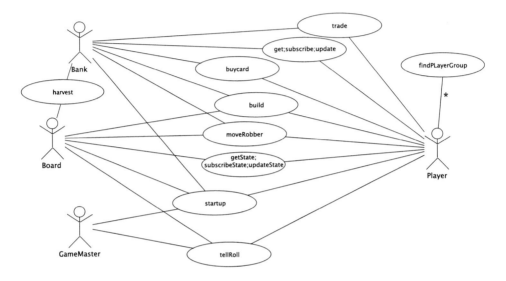

Figure 22.4: *On the fly* Coarse Design Diagram as result of group discussion.

either in group discussions, in smaller groups especially assigned to this task or by single managing participants –in order to achieve a full overview design of the system (compare with Figure C.1).

## Ontology

A first approach to the concepts in the system is presented in Figure 22.5. It is the result of a group discussion of required concepts, actions and predicates on the ground of the game instructions. In this phase of discussion a blackboard is an appropriate medium to support immediate feedback and frequent changes. The following columns are a copy of the blackboard.

| Actions | Concepts | Predicates |
|---|---|---|
| - moveRobber (Board) | - Field = Hexagon | - is CurrentPlayer (Player) |
| - Set Field (GameMaster) | - Edge = 2 Fields | - isGameOver (Board) |
| - InitGame (Portal) | - Vertex = 3 Fields | - isWinner (Player) |
| - JoinMe (Portal) | - Resource (= Grain, Ore, Wood,...) | - canBuild (Player, Vertex/Edge, Building, Road) |
| - getState (Board) | - DevelopmentCard (5 kinds) | - canAfford (Player, Building, Street, Card) |
| - buyCard (Bank) | - Building (=Settlement, City) | |
| - endMyTurn (GameMaster) | - Road | - isBeingBlocked (Field) |
| - KickMe (Portal) | - Harbor (=Vertex) | - isFree (Vertex/Edge) |
| - offerTrade (MarketPlace) | - Player | |
| - build (Board) | - Board | |
| - chargePlayer(Bank) | - DiceRole ([2,12]) | |
| - addRes | | |
| - addCard | | |

Figure 22.5: Blackboard photo of an initial approach.

The initial elements of the discussion that helped all participants to orient themselves are transferred to the Coarse Design Diagram and further specified and elaborated. This is done by a group of developers responsible for the consistency of the ontology. Special care has to be taken that duplicates, homonyms and synonyms do not enter the ontology. This is not always a trivial task. However, the ontology also grows with the further development of roles and interactions, and requests for new concepts or slots are frequently made. The responsibility of the ontology group is to add new concepts and spread the information among the developers that – for instance – a desired concept already exists with another name.

Just like interface design in object-oriented approaches, ontology design has to be done with extreme care. Especially since the other groups develop roles and interactions at the same time, a change (not an addition) in the ontology usually means refactoring for the affected groups.

**Roles**

In the Settler 5 project the system was built from scratch. The roles are defined after the coarse design in the R/D Diagram. At their creation they start with no contents except for their names. After a more elaborate version of the Coarse Design Diagram (almost as refined as in Figure C.1), the following roles were thus created: *Bank*, *Board*, *BuildController*, *Dice*, *GameController*, *Init*, *Player* and *Trader*. Soon, on the ground of requests from several role groups, some more agent roles entered the system: *TradeController*, *TradeInitiator*, *CurrentPlayerListener*, *JavaGuiPlayer* and *NetGuiPlayer*. Some of these, such as *Dice* and *TradeInitiator*, were later discarded. In Settler 6 the two roles *Portal*, *JavaPlanner* and *PlayerManager* entered the system and the *JavaBDIPlayer* was created during the work for the bachelor's thesis of Brin (2008).

Since the objective of the Settler game is to play a game and since the setup of the game agents may be static over the whole execution of the system, there was no need to imple-

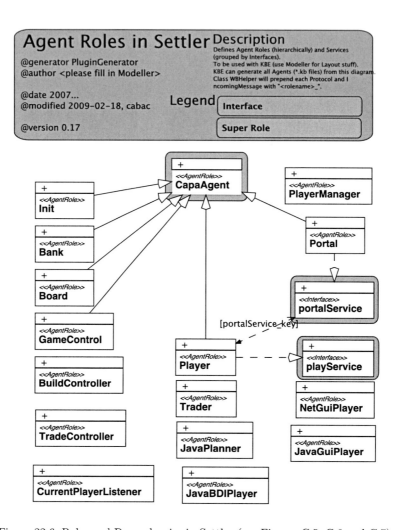

Figure 22.6: Roles and Dependencies in Settler (see Figures C.5, C.6 and C.7).

ment a dynamic lookup strategy with offered services and subscribed services. Instead the lean approach was taken that a setup agent initializes the whole system. This has also the advantage that this agent is the only one that needs to be started. Once started and provided with all the needed information, the agent deploys the system (agents) and initializes the game by handing the responsibility of control to the *GameController*. Thus no service needs to be specified, with the exception of the *PlayService* offered by a *Player* who wants to participate in a game. In Settler 6 the *Portal* offered a lobby for players to sign-up for offered games resulting in the *portalService*.

The resulting R/D Diagram is presented in Figure 22.6.[5] The system's organizational structure is rather simple, since there are almost no explicit services and thus no explicit service dependencies. Implicitly, the services and the acquaintances are provided by the *InitAgent*, which plays the *Init* role.

So far only roles (and services) have been names. Furthermore, the content of the role's knowledge bases remains to be defined. This is done directly in the KBE using the R/D Diagram. Figure 22.7 shows a screenshot of the KBE, displaying the project browser on the left, a part of the R/D Diagram in the center, an outline of the elements in the diagram on the right and the contents of a selected knowledge base entry at the bottom.

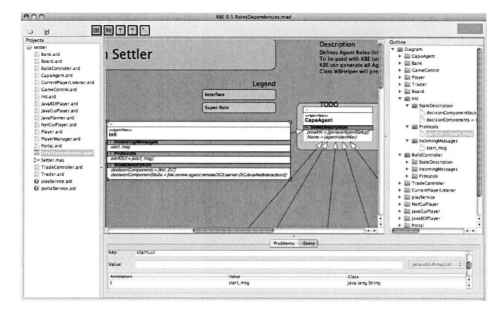

Figure 22.7: Screenshot of Settler R/D Diagram in the KBE.

In the screenshot the Init role is expanded and a protocol entry is selected. The entry is defined by the key *startGui*, which is the name of a protocol and the trigger for this protocol, the *start_msg*.

**Interactions**

Interactions are specified with Agent Interaction Protocol Diagrams, used to generate code structures of protocol nets. For the interactions that are defined in the Coarse Design Diagram, skeletons of AIPs are prepared for the developers' convenience. Here

---

[5]Please note that multiple specialization is not supported by the KBE. Thus agents can only have one role that is a *CapaAgent*, the other roles can be regarded as *abstract* roles, with which alone an agent cannot be initialized. Also super roles cannot be initialized.

the participating roles are already included and the developers can concentrate on the interaction design.

As an example for an interaction designed with an AIP, we present the *joinGame* interaction, depicted in Figure 22.8 as Agent Interaction Protocol Diagram.

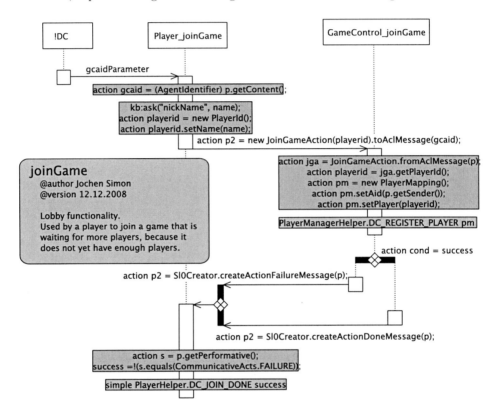

Figure 22.8: The *joinGame* interaction.

The scenario can be described as follows. A Player decides to join a game. This is done pro-actively, i.e. the human player uses its user interface to tell the place-holder agent to join the game, indicated in the diagram by the DC. The decision is expressed by choosing a game controller that has registered its game at the portal. The place-holder agent sends a message (*JoinGameAction*) to the addressed game controller, which contains the desired nick name and a player id. The *GameController* extracts the information from the received message and tries to register the new player at its game. If this fails, a failure message is sent back. If it succeeds, an acknowledgment is sent back. The player's joinGame protocol part then hands the information on to the responsible DC, i.e. in the case of a human player, to the GUI.

Although the underlying procedure seems simple, the given example clearly shows that numerous details need to be considered.

## Internal Behavior

In the Settler game several different types of internal behavior can be observed. The most obvious one is the possibility of human interaction, usually done by a graphical user interface (GUI). Here the generic DC adapter *RemoteDC*, presented in Section 14.3.2, is used for the connection of a *Java*-based user interface. The same interface is also used for the connection of an external deliberation system provided by Brin (2008). The alternative is the Petri net-based user interface prototype depicted in Figure C.11.

Another implementation is that of the *service* agents. The agents playing the roles *Bank* and *Board* are basically providing a service to the other agents that is resource management. In both cases a mere storing of resource information in the knowledge base – a simplified approach – would cause the protocol implementations to be extremely complex. Thus, the accounts of the bank and the board representation are implemented as decision components. This can be regarded as active knowledge, thus the DCs function as an extension of the knowledge base in providing storage of information, while implementing at the same time specific operations on the artifacts.

Similarly, the *GameController* offers the service of controlling the game. However, this is more like controlling the overall process, which can be expressed by the game round. Figure 22.9 shows the part of the *GameControl_DC* that represents the round of the

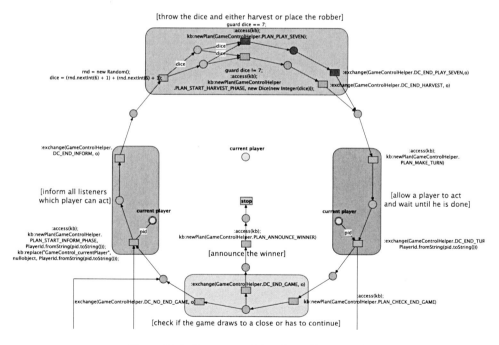

Figure 22.9: Fragment of the *GameControl_DC*.

game, consisting of four phases: (1, pink) informing about whose turn it is, (2, orange) announcing the dice result and performing harvest of robber, (3, blue) requesting one player to act and (4, yellow) checking conditions for the end of the game. The cyclic arrangement for such an iterating process seems obviously appropriate. It is somehow unconventional and the design took quite a while and a lot of care.

**Agents**

The agents that are specified for the game are the *InitAgent, BoardAgent, GameControl-lAgent, BankAgent, PortalAgent* and possibly a choice of the *PlayerAgents*. Figure 22.10 displays the KBE's MAS view, which provides the agent model, i.e. mapping of agents to roles.

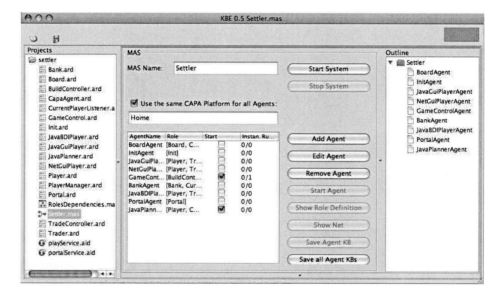

Figure 22.10: The agent model defined in the KBE.

## 22.2.3 Deployment

At startup of the game, the *InitAgent* is automatically deployed and, as described in Section 22.2.2, the *startGui* protocol is initially started, providing the GUI displayed as screenshot in Figure 22.11. In the GUI a user can choose from several options: adding players, selecting administrative agents and selecting from several different board designs.

After the choice is made, the *InitAgent* sets up all the other agents and provides acquaintances.

The running game offers two board representations as GUI. One is for observation only, for instance when observing automatic planner playing the game, or if an administrator wants to observe the game in which players from remote hosts participate. The second

Figure 22.11: The GUI of the *InitAgent* for the game setup.

board representation is integrated in the interactive user interface of the *JavaGuiPlayer* presented in Figure 22.12.

The GUI shows the board on which roads, settlements and cities may be built. In the screenshot two players participate, the *JavaGuiPlayer* (red) and an instance of an automatic player (yellow), whose planner is implemented in pure *Java*.

To the right the players resources are displayed as account information, informative messages are displayed underneath and in the lower right corner a chat window for internal player communication. On the left bottom the control field enables the user to choose from several actions grouped into tabs according to the context. Buildings are built by clicking on the board.

## 22.3 Tools for the Team Process

According to the *multi-agent system of developers* metaphor presented in Chapter 8 and the application matrix of roles, interactions and terminology presented in Section 8.2.3, the developers have been divided into groups, each responsible for one or more of the interactions, of the roles or for the ontology. The development of the system was thus done concurrently and distributed in time and space – although frequent meetings were conducted each week.

The flow of information is high and the need to communicate is immense. This can only be partly accomplished during the meetings. Moreover, the need to provide a *space* for information – to be stored and to be found – is equally high. In order to support the most asynchronous communication, we employ several IT-based systems that support the processes, the communication, the documentation and the teaching/learning aspects of the projects.

### 22.3.1 SCM

The longest in use and indispensable tool is a source code management system (SCM). In the course of the AOSE projects, we used at first CVS (concurrent versions system) and made the transition to Subversion in Settler 5. The use of an SCM is essential to the management of code in a collaborative and distributed development. Although this seems

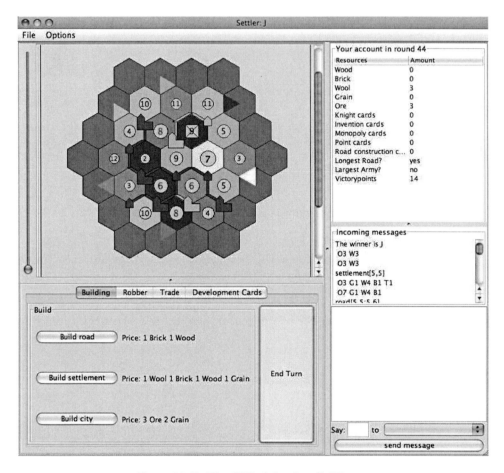

Figure 22.12: The GUI of the *JavaGuiPlayer*.

trivial, we would like to stress the fact that we employ the SCM for more than just source code management. In fact, we include all design artifacts into the management system. Thus, diagrams become first-order concept of the development. However, this is only possible if the artifact is represented in a manner that is compatible with the management system. A system, for instance, that produces binary blobs that include all artifacts in one archive – as for instance a zip archive – is not adapted for concurrent manipulation. A single textual representation for each artifact is in this case more adapted. Ideally, also the possibility to merge automatically non-conflicting concurrent changes would be of great advantage, but for graphical representation this is difficult, if not impossible. At least, the manual task of merging concurrent changes or checking for differences can be supported as presented in Chapter 18.

## 22.3.2 CommSy

CommSy[6] is a web-based system that resembles a minimal groupware oriented towards teaching/learning. The access to the system is provided by the University of Hamburg as a service for all members. The main advantages are the light-weight, unobtrusive interface, the availability and the simple setup of a new project room. With CommSy learning/project groups can organize themselves in an autonomous way. The main functionality provides easy support for group communication through various means and the sharing and organization of teaching materials or other. CommSy also offers online discussion and calendar management. Additional features are an internal wiki, a presentation web page and a chat room.

## 22.3.3 Trac

Trac[7] is a minimalist approach to web-based software project management. It provides an issue tracking system and a wiki. The advantages of an issue tracking system are substantial. It was used for the first time in the Settler 6 project in 2008 with success and eagerly resorted to by the students and organizers. An outstanding feature is the connection with the SCM repository. The issues descriptions and comments can link directly to the code, thus accelerating the navigation in the code. The integrated wiki also provides the possibility to link to programming artifacts and was used to host the short manuals (howtos) for the tools available in the PAOSE context. It does not, however, replace the CommSy system, since it does not allow the group organization or material sharing. Neither does it provide a communication support other than the email notification for relevant issues.

## 22.4 Evaluation and Discussion

The evaluation of the development process and the examination of the evolution of the approach are tasks that are not easily done. Although they are not in the focus of this work, in order to understand the impact of the modeling techniques on the developed system and on the development system, the context and the environmental constrains have to be considered.

## 22.4.1 Metrics

In order to grasp the complexity of the system (Settler 6), Table 22.1 lists numbers extracted from a repository checkout and from the running game.

A typical setup of the test to extract the presented numbers of firings and instantiations is to play the game with two players, either a human player (*Java* GUI) against *Java* planner or two planners competing against each other.

---

[6]CommSy – Community System: information and software available at `http://www.commsy.net`
[7]Trac is available at `http://trac.edgewall.org/`.

| Number of design artifacts | # |
|---|---|
| *Java* classes (no GUI) | 92 |
| *Java* classes (GUI) | 103 |
| Generated *Java* classes | 172 |
| RNW / protocol nets and DCs | 190 |
| AIP / interactions | 55 |
| Agent roles | 17 |
| Agents | 12 |
| Concepts in ontology | 144 |

| Runtime (simulation) | # |
|---|---|
| Firings | > 60,000 |
| Net instances | > 1,900 |

| Number of Petri net elements in nets | # |
|---|---|
| TransitionFigure | 3799 |
| PlaceFigure | 6412 |
| NetComponentFigure | 1145 |
| VirtualPlaceFigure | 1422 |
| ArcConnection | 10436 |
| Number of synchronous up-links | 1661 |

Table 22.1: Metrics of Settler 6

A game of two planners competing with each other lasts approximately two minutes. The system's size can be described by the number of created net instances divided by the average size of the nets. Thus, a typical system contains approximately $38,000^8$ transition instances. Many of the firing steps involve several of the transition instances through synchronization.

## 22.4.2 Quantitative Evaluation

An object of investigation concerning the approach is the efficiency of the methods applied. A very rough measure is the counting of the produced code. In the case of PAOSE this is even more vague, since the Petri net models have to be included in the measure. The question arises, how these numbers compare to conventional code? Since it is not easily answerable – if at all – we leave the reader with the remark that this consideration has to stay in mind.

Table 22.1 lists the number of artifacts and the lines of code within these artifacts. It is separated into *Java* classes (excluding code for the GUI[9]; extension *j* or *java*) and

---

[8]This number is probably a little bit too high, since many *often* used interactions contain less transitions than the average of approximately 20 transitions per net.

[9]Including the code for the GUI would approximately double the lines of code in the source; for Settler 6 for instance, the lines of code (*src-j*) including GUI is: 30412.

Petri nets (RENEW Drawings, RNW; extension $r$)

| # | S1 | S2 | S3 | S4 | W1 | W2 | S5 | S6 |
|---|---|---|---|---|---|---|---|---|
| src-j | 63 | 121 | 181 | 246 | 12 | 22 | 88 | 92 |
| gen-j | 1 | 1 | 2 | 5 | 62 | 71 | 121 | 172 |
| java | 64 | 122 | 183 | 251 | 74 | 93 | 209 | 264 |
| src-r | 68 | 86 | 123 | 143 | 62 | 94 | 110 | 188 |
| sum | 132 | 208 | 306 | 394 | 136 | 187 | 319 | 452 |
| **LOC** | | | | | | | | |
| src-j | 8788 | 15110 | 22687 | 32480 | 1513 | 3340 | 13745 | 15863 |
| gen-j | 0 | 0 | 72 | 208 | 9467 | 11767 | 19939 | 24959 |
| java | 8788 | 15110 | 22759 | 32688 | 10980 | 15107 | 33684 | 40822 |
| src-r | 18719 | 43229 | 65780 | 83685 | 23352 | 67370 | 63185 | 99195 |
| sum | 27507 | 58339 | 88539 | 116373 | 34332 | 82477 | 96869 | 140017 |
| ont-j | 0 | 5001 | 7085 | 7810 | 0 | 0 | 0 | 0 |
| ont-r | 0 | 0 | 0 | 0 | 0 | 365 | 1378 | 1267 |

Table 22.2: Files and lines of code in the AOSE projects.[10]

A distinction between manually coded artifacts (source, *src*) and generated code is also made. Last, for the matter of completeness, we also list the artifacts concerning the ontology (*ont*). Note that *Java* ontology classes (*ont-j*) are included in the number of *Java* source code classes, since they are manually coded. In contrast, the ontology artifacts (*ont-r*, the Concept Diagrams are also RENEW drawings) are not included in the count of Petri net source code drawings (*src-r*) because they contain the initial artifacts, from which the ontology classes are generated and are thus included in the generated *Java* classes (*gen-j*).

To estimate the evolution of the approach, Figure 22.13 presents the differences of the numbers for the lines of code between the projects divided by the number of participants of the projects for each category of code.[11]

The differences are only considered if the project is a continuation of the predecessor. Settler 1 to 5 and both WFMS are considered new starts. Again such a graphic has to be well-considered, since it is not possible to tell whether the differences in line of code reflect the actual work that has been done. This can be true, but it can also be that during the project the whole code of the predecessor project has been eliminated. However, the experience shows that code that is working will not be touched by the *next generation* of developers, if it is not necessary. We can thus presume that the graphic comes close to a real estimation of code produced per person in the AOSE projects.

---

[10]For comparison RENEW 2.2 releases lines of code: *Java*: sources 107,820 lines (915 classes) plus generated 17,146 lines (12 classes).

[11]$loc(p) - loc\_pre(p)/persons\_in\_project$: The number of participants have been determined from the registered members in CommSy (s1 34, s2 54, s3 49, s4 50, w1 62 , w2 43 , s5 42, s6 36) with the exceptions of those of Settler 1 to 2, which have been determined from the history of the CVS repository.

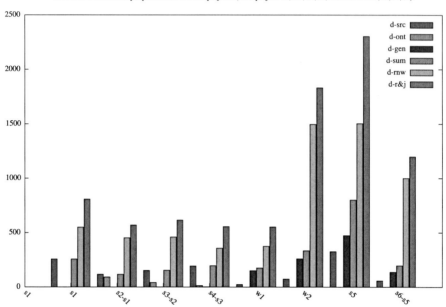

Figure 22.13: Growth of lines of code per person in the AOSE project.[12]

## 22.4.3 Discussion

The first projects that extensively applied all techniques for the development within the PAOSE approach were WFMS 2 and Settler 5. The goals of those projects were to design the complete system from scratch. This means that for Settler 5 the goal was to construct a system able to compete with a system that has been growing over four years and which was further elaborated in several diploma theses.

Comparing the process of development with the other projects is hard. However, the following list provides background information that can clarify several points.

### Settler 1 to 4

The projects Settler 1 to 4 were working on a system that evolved over several years. Functionality was added and old code was kept as legacy code. This resulted in duplicated functionalities; for instance the abstract board representation (not GUI) existed three times in Settler 4, i.e. the hexagon existed as original part of the board model, as SL

---

[12]Table and histogram are generated directly from the sources of the project repositories. The script that produces the table, the data file for the histogram and the gnuplot (available at `http://www.gnuplot.info/`) script to generate the diagram is available at `http://www.informatik.uni-hamburg.de/TGI/cabac/resources/`

communication object and as planning object. However, many technical problems were solved and advances in concepts were made.

## WFMS 1

WFMS 1 was an ambitious project that failed for several reasons; the goal of the project was vague, the conceptual preparation chaotic and the tool/modeling support limited.

## WFMS 2

WFMS 2 benefited from the experiences made in the preceding project; the steps of approach were clearer and the tool support was – for the first time – available from the beginning. Coarse Design Diagrams were used for the first time and so were R/D Diagrams and the KBE. The planners that resided as singletons inside the knowledge bases were conceptually generalized to become decision components. They quickly turned out to be the original conceptual focus for the role development. Moreover, the project was supported by numerous experienced developers that supported the participants and worked on advanced features, such as mobile agents.

## Settler 5

Settler 5 had completely different preconditions. The supporting team was small, but the students seemed to be motivated, since they could build the system from scratch without having to look into existing code. This left space for imagination and the group dynamics was distinctive. In this project the full set of modeling techniques and supporting tools were used. Additionally, the SCM system was modernized from CVS to Subversion. The code generation feature for the Coarse Design Diagrams especially left time to experiment with several setups and was also extremely useful to generate exercises. The ontology was for the first time designed with Concept Diagrams and, although the generator feature was not finished, this improved the design of the system and the overview of the developers over existing concepts. The discussions about new or changing concepts evolved to the crucial design activities. Still, process support was critical. In an ad hoc decision a CommSy category (*Tasks*) was transformed into a tracking system substitute, which worked rather badly.

Another goal in Settler 5 was to translate the whole remaining code of the GUI[13] from German to English, including source code, source comments and user interface language. This part was actually more time consuming than expected and lead to the situation that the GUI was not available for the already growing system. In fact, this lead to the construction of a prototype Petri net GUI, which is fully functional if not very ergonomic. It was realized as a decision component and it is presented in the appendix. The interface part of the net is presented in Figure C.11. The controller part of the net is not presented in this work.

---

[13]GUI classes were the only classes that were reintroduced into the code base of Settler 5. However, the code was completely recoded.

## Settler 6

Settler 6 introduced the issue tracking system *Trac*. This suggestion of improvement came from the students, and although many of them were concerned about the fact that yet another web-based tool was introduced – besides all the other tools – it was well accepted and it integrated itself smoothly. This project, though, suffered a little from the vast amount of code that had to be examined. Here, the documentation artifacts Coarse Design Diagram, Concept Diagram, AIPs and R/D Diagram were of great help. And so was the API, which was generated with Mulandoc, which was used for quick skimming – even during group discussions.

## 22.4.4 Qualitative Evaluation

The most striking observation about the numbers presented above is the increase of productivity in the three last projects. However, there is no possibility to judge from the numbers, which are the reasons for this increase of productive output. Thus, for the evaluation of the projects, the processes, the modeling techniques and the produced results, we have to have a qualitative evaluation.

The settings of all projects are comparable. The students that participated in the projects for the first time, which was the majority of participants, were inexperienced in the topics of Petri net modeling and agent-oriented software engineering. Thus, a large part of the project time was spent teaching concepts, basics, techniques and tools. In terms of evaluation this means that in average the conditions regarding the participants were comparable.

In each project some advanced students, who had already participated in on of the previous projects functioned as tutors for the new ones and also participated in the project work, just like the organizers. This is also comparable in all projects, even in the first one.

The projects were different in that some of them were a continuation of the previous year's project and some were starting as a new project. The time spent in analyzing and understanding the system that is to be continued is not insignificant. A continuation of the project also has more difficulties in providing the motivation for dedicated participation. It seems that starting from scratch offers an opportunity to improve the eagerness in teaching.

In the continuation of a project, a good documentation of the project is very valuable. The Settler 2, 3 and 4 projects relied on the term papers and theses for good documentation. In Settler 6 the documentation with Coarse Design Diagrams, Concept Diagrams, Agent Interaction Protocol Diagrams and the navigable hypertext of Mulandoc helped during the analysis phase. The amount of work that has to be done before a productive stage is reached, however, is immense for a system the size of Settler 5.

On the ground of the absolute numbers we can state that Settler is a mid-size system. The size is according to the numbers comparable to a system like RENEW (released), although we do not estimate the quality comparable. While Settler has a strong prototypical character, RENEW is a productive system that has evolved over a history of releases. Nevertheless, the amount of code produced in the Settler projects and also in the WFMS projects is not marginal. This is especially true if one considers that (1) much time in the projects is devoted to teaching and that (2) the students devote a part of the time to the preparation of their term paper. The teaching phase of the projects lasts approximately a third of the time. It consists of the introduction of the PAOSE approach, the MULAN concepts, the reference nets formalism and the tool set including RENEW as well as other supporting and development tools.

The approach has evolved on all levels. The processes and the guidance have been improved. Also the modeling techniques and the related tool set have been improved. The techniques and applied methods have grown and have been further improved over the projects. The approach evolved from an ad hoc approach that produced nice and effective results from experienced modelers to a systematic approach that focuses on the design and not on details of implementation, as it was the case in the first Settler projects.

Especially striking are the acceptance of modeling techniques and net component principles. These are the means for a systematic approach of Petri net-based AOSE from the technical and from the conceptual viewpoint. Throughout the projects I learned that the techniques were not only accepted by the participants but also quickly absorbed by the development system. The preconditions – in my opinion – for a successful acceptance are a lightweight appearance of the technique as well as an appropriate and ergonomic tool integration. This acceptance can also be observed when examining the large number of theses and term papers that have been produced in the context of the AOSE projects. In almost all of them one can find the techniques presented in this work to express the issues at stake, most notably the techniques and concepts that were early developed: net components and AIPs. Examples for this are the works of Duvigneau (2002), Rölke (2004), Reese (2009) and Wagner (2009b).

The projects and the context of the multi-agent application development itself evolved to form a dynamic environment, from which many ideas, works and solutions emerged. The processes behind this dynamic community are communicative, cooperative ones. It seems that – at least for some of the participants – the organizational form constitutes a metaphorical multi-agent system, which exists beyond the limits of the projects time schedules.

## 22.5 Related Work

One of the objectives of the AOSE projects is to further the evolution of the approach, the concepts, the frameworks, the modeling techniques and the tool set. Several works that emerged from the AOSE projects were already mentioned in previous chapters.

### 22.5.1 Other Works in the Context of the AOSE Projects

A selection of other works that originated in the AOSE projects and furthered various aspects of the approach, the concepts or the tool set are listed in the following:

**Planning** Seegert (2005) implemented a planning framework as Petri net system that used net components for the generation of plans (protocol nets). These plans were instantiated on the fly and fed as behaviors into the agents. He has also provided a planner for the settler game as prolog implementation.

**Teams** Wester-Ebbinghaus (2005) provided a team model for the coordinated team planning in the context of the AOSE projects. He implemented a planner for Settler that was realized in *Java*.

**BDI Planning** Brin (2008) realized an adapter to use the *Jadex* deliberation engine as back-end for a MULAN agent and implemented another planner in *Jadex* for the Settler game.

**Plugin Systems** The question, how dynamically reconfigurable system architectures can be designed have been investigated not only on the ground of agent systems but also in a more down-to-earth fashion. Here a conceptual model has been presented for a topic not thoroughly discussed yet in the research community although it is a hot topic in development. This is also the foundation for the dissertation of Duvigneau (2009).

**Holonic MAS** Schleinzer (2007) implemented a variation of CAPA which allows agents to act as platforms that host agents.

**Plugin-Agents** Schleinzer et al. (2008) presented the conceptual extension of the two concepts agent systems and plugin systems. The integration of both concepts offer interesting constellations. An agent that could extend a proprietary extension-point in addition to all the agent features offers a reliable and secure communication link.

**Agent-Plugins** The opposite possibility to make agents dynamically decomposable offers other fascinating possibilities, which were discussed during the progress of Schleinzer's diploma thesis (2007). The external behavior of an agent is determined through its interface. If the interface of an entity can change – e.g. by plugging in another one – then the type of the entity can change as well. Thus, a protocol that needs to act autonomously or pro-actively in a certain setting could be transformed into an agent and continue to behave in its original function as well.

**Mapa** Müller (2009b) implemented a variant of CAPA that is capable of visualizing the mobility of agents in a MAS infrastructure given as an infrastructure net.

**AgentIDE/Toolplatform** In this work I have presented the metaphor of multi-agent systems for the construction of software systems and for the organization of project teams. In fact, the metaphor also applies to the development process itself. One of the mid-term goals are to provide an integrated development environment that is designed in this fashion as well. The goal of the work done together with Markwardt (Lehmann et al. 2005)[14] is a multi-agent application that is an IDE for the development of multi-agent applications that supports a team of metaphorical *agents* in settings of distributed and concurrent development (MAS of developers).

---

[14]Name changed.

**AgentWFMS** The WFMS (Reese et al. 2008) was the foundation for the vision of several levels of integration of a process infrastructure into an agent framework by Reese (2009). This idea has been picked up by Wagner (2009b).

## 22.5.2 Contribution

I have participated in all mentioned projects, first as student, later as organizer. I contributed to the development of the board agent, the GUI, the *Java* planner, the WFMS user, the R/D Diagram designs, the ontologies and many other parts. I provided the tools for the modeling techniques and I also provided the installation and administration of supporting tools, such as the COMMSY, the Trac, the repositories (CVS, Subversion). Furthermore, I provided a full-fletched installer (on the basis of AntInstaller, see `http://antinstaller.sf.net/`) for the project setup, which automated and thus eased the complete setup of the development environment for the participants.

I was the main organizer of the Settler 5 project and in this project, for the first time, the principles, methods and the approach together with the modeling techniques were in the focus of the project. I designed, implemented and provided (together with Schleinzer) the CentralDF as MULAN platform service for Settler 5 (and 6). A central DF collects information of registered local DFs and offers the distribution of service lookup information in a centralized fashion. Without a global registry for services (like a central DF), it is impossible to execute real distributed systems.

## 22.6 Summary

The AOSE projects are the context for many activities in the context of Petri net-based Agent-Oriented Software Engineering (PAOSE). One objective is the development of concurrent and distributed systems with the framework MULAN/CAPA using the PAOSE approach. Another objective is the evolution of the approach, its methods, principles, modeling techniques and supporting tool set.

The applications developed in the series of projects evolved from pure proof of concept studies to applications that were usable. The game was playable from late stages of Settler 3. The WFMS 2 worked in milestone 1 and milestone 2. However, the milestone 3 was not reached (compare with Reese (2009) and Wagner (2009b)). Apparently, the complexities of the systems were underestimated by the organizers. But concurrent and/or distributed systems are complex ones. The experiences show that it is possible to construct these complex systems on the basis of the presented Petri net-based software engineering approach after the paradigm of multi-agent systems. Moreover it shows that even inexperienced developers can accomplish the tasks of developing concurrent and distributed systems.

# 23 Summary

This part presents examples of the application of the modeling techniques used in the PAOSE approach. The Producer/Storage/Consumer example in Chapter 21 provides a profound and detailed description of all aspects related to the modeling with the presented PAOSE modeling techniques. The whole development process is covered, starting with the coarse design over ontology, interaction and role design to the agent specification (agent model). The covered modeling techniques are: the Coarse Design Diagrams, the Concept Diagrams, the R/D Diagrams and the Agent Interaction Protocol Diagrams. The presented supporting tools are: the Use Case Plugin (including code generation), the FS Plugin (for the drawing of Concept Diagrams and the FS Ontology Generator Plugin for the generation of ontology classes), the KBE (including the generation of the knowledge base specifications as XML representation) and the AIP Diagram Plugin (including the generation of Petri net code skeletons). The modeling of decision components is done in Petri net directly.

Chapter 22 presents the series of AOSE projects Settler 1 to 6 and WFMS 1 & 2. Here several aspects are of interest. The development of the applications is the driving force that triggers the need to develop the concepts, the approach, the modeling techniques and the tool set to meet the challenges of the development of complex, distributed and concurrent systems.

The history shows that the approach evolves and through its development in many works (theses and term assignments) the complexity of applications that can be built on the basis of the framework MULAN/CAPA with the PAOSE approach has increased.

*23 Summary*

# Part V

# Conclusion

# 24 Summary, Discussion and Outlook

Petri nets make it possible to model systems that allow for concurrency and distribution. However, the expressiveness of models, constructed with simple P/T nets, is limited, and complex systems are not manageable. Here high-level Petri net formalisms show their advantages. In addition to coarsening/refinement, these techniques provide other powerful abstraction mechanisms – most notably folding/unfolding – and also inscription languages, which further increase the expressiveness.

Nets-within-nets (see Valk (1998) and Köhler (2004)) also provide a nesting of elements through token refinement that on the one hand enables developers to modularize their systems and on the other hand leaves room for dynamically changeable structures. On top of that, reference nets (see Kummer (2002)) provide a reference semantics for nets-within-nets, instance creations and synchronous channels for inter-object communication/synchronization. In this formalism arbitrary, changing and growing structures can be modeled. The reference semantics offer an intuitive integration of concepts such as references and net instances, borrowing several of those concepts from object-orientation (e.g. instances and dynamical binding). Additionally, the full power of the *Java* programming language is accessible through the inscription language. Systems designed in reference nets can be efficiently executed and comfortably constructed in Renew (Reference Net Workshop, see Kummer et al. (2009a)).

However, the organization of such dynamical systems is a challenge to the developers. To address the system's structural organization, several approaches have been taken. From the early approach of structuring as Object Petri Nets (see Moldt (1996), modeled in colored Petri nets) derives the reference model Mulan (Multi-Agent Nets, Rölke (2004)). Mulan provides a highly structured approach presented in four layers of nesting: the *MAS infrastructure*, the *platform*, the *agent* and the agent-internal components (*knowledge base, factory, protocols* and *decision components*). Capa (see Duvigneau et al. (2003)) extends the reference model to provide efficient FIPA-compliant communication.

The conceptual and technical framework, together with associated supporting tools, enables the construction and execution of concurrent and distributed software systems following the multi-agent paradigm based on Petri nets. The Paose approach (Petri net-based Agent-Oriented Software Engineering, see Moldt (2006b)) ties this framework together with modeling techniques, modeling tools, methods, principles, resources management, etc. to provide a systematic approach of developing Petri net-based multi-agent applications. Paose additionally provides the conceptual means as think tool (German: *Denkzeug*, see Moldt (2005)) and considers the context of development as well as the specific target application.

This work focuses on the modeling techniques and the respective supporting tools for the development of Mulan-based applications. The modeling techniques form a central part of the PAOSE approach. The supporting tools are the means for the integration of the modeling techniques into the development process.

## 24.1 Summary

This work presents modeling techniques and tools for the development of Petri net-based multi-agent applications. These include abstract modeling techniques, such as Coarse Design Diagrams, Dependency Diagrams, R/D Diagrams, Concept Diagrams and Agent Interaction Protocol Diagrams, as well as concrete modeling patterns implemented as net components for reference nets. Furthermore, a model of the development process (approach) is presented, which is described by its guiding metaphor (*the multi-agent system of developers*), its abstract process definition and a project setting.

**Introduction** outlines the context of this work, defines its objectives and motivates the approach. The context is given by three fields of computer science. These are Petri nets, agent-orientation and software-engineering.

**Part I: Multi-Agent Systems and Reference Nets**

In this part I present the foundation of concepts, techniques, frameworks and tools relevant for the development of the PAOSE approach for the development of multi-agent applications on the basis of MULAN/CAPA. This part deals with modeling in general as well as modeling in software engineering. Other topics are agent technology, the formalism of reference nets, the MULAN/CAPA framework[1] and the concept as well as application of net components. An overview of modeling techniques in other methodologies is also provided.

**Abstractions, Models and Views** gives an introduction into the field by defining the basic concepts of models, abstractions and views. These are the main abstract concepts throughout the whole work. The chapter recapitulates the notions and definitions given by Moldt (1996) and Laue and Liedtke (2000).

**Reference Nets and Renew[2]** introduces the reference net formalism and the Reference Net Workshop. The modeling technique of reference nets is the formalism in which the MULAN reference model is designed. It provides powerful basic (elementary) concepts for the construction of complex, distributed, concurrent and encapsulated systems. RENEW is the simulator and editor for reference nets. In RENEW the modeled systems can be executed effectively and efficiently. It can thus be described as both the implementation of a semantically precise formalism/simulator and as a runtime environment (RTE, sometimes also called virtual machine, VM) for the execution of a concurrency-aware modeling technique.

---

[1] Reference nets and RENEW form the conceptual and technical foundation for MULAN/CAPA.

[2] This chapter is a revised version based on Chapter 3 of my diploma thesis (2003).

My contributions to the development of RENEW include – besides testing and bug-fixes – advancements in the usability, improvements of the framework, efforts in the production and provision of the releases. An important contribution is the elaboration of the conceptual modeling of the plugin architecture together with Duvigneau (see Cabac et al. (2005) and also Duvigneau (2009)). I am the original designer of more than ten plugins for RENEW (some of which are officially released, compare with `http://www.renew.de`). I have also actively participated in the construction and design of several more plugins.[3]

**Mulan**[4]  is the central chapter of this part. At first, agent technology and agent-oriented software engineering are introduced. Then, the MULAN reference model is presented as a system of reference net models. The main concepts and notions regarding agents and the agents' parts are discussed. The models are developed from an abstract model to a concrete executable system (implementation) and the development of MULAN agents is sketched.

My contributions to the MULAN reference model are the introduction of the concept of decision components (DC) and the redesign/elaboration of several Petri net models. The obviously missing parts of agent-internal processes that could be designed similarly to the way protocols are modeled manifested themselves in several usages of crutches: protocols as long-running, interaction-spanning and agent-controlling, non-communicative processes or a planner interface as an extension in the knowledge base. The introduction of the decision components cleared this conceptual confusion and the integration of the decision components as emancipated parts in the agents on the same level as knowledge base and protocols lead to an improved, more powerful reference model. This included the improvement and clarification of the agent-internal communications. Another aspect that resulted from the fact that DCs entered the agent net is the conceptualization and development of a holonic agent system. The discussion included the question whether the agent parts (protocols, knowledge base, decision components, factory) should reside in one place only (unstructured approach) or each type on its own place (structured approach), with a clear separation and defined communication structure. This resulted in CAPA 2 by Schleinzer (2007).

Other contributions to the framework are the development of a central DF (directory facilitator), without which it would be impossible to locate CAPA instances on the network and improvements of the models in functionality and readability.

**Net Components**  presents the concept of net components. The idea for such a pattern-based approach originated from the need of structuring capabilities for protocol nets (see Cabac (2002)). The concept, which has proved itself to be capable of many other applications, has been improved and generalized. It is not only used to construct protocol nets – and thus accelerate the construction of multi-agent systems – but it also allows to generate Petri net models from Agent Interaction Protocol Diagrams, thus lending a

---

[3]I also adopted several plugins, which I maintain but currently do not actively advance in development.

[4]This chapter is based on Cabac (2003), Section 4.3. However, it is completely revised and reflects the changes and development that the framework has undergone since 2003.

formal transformational semantics to these diagrams. Several sets of net components have been developed and proposed. However the further improved original net components for protocol nets were so useful and successful that nearly all original protocol nets (31/37) have been (re-)designed with net components. Other works have also been built on the concept of net components, such as by Moldt and Rölke (2003) and Braker (2004).

The net component concept and the tool support as well as several sets of net components have been originally designed and developed by me. The tool and the technique have constantly been enhanced and the general approach of the tool framework made it possible to generalize the concept so that it is applicable to other modeling techniques, e.g. components for Use Case Diagrams. The framework thus additionally allows rapid prototyping of modeling techniques. In fact, the basis of the Net Components Plugin has been re-designed in order to be extensible on the ground of the RENEW plugin system/ concept. It can thus easily be extended by sets of net components as repositories. For the first time it is also possible to construct plugins exclusively by using net drawings or other drawings. By doing this we are able to dynamically plug-in, plug-out and re-plug-in different versions of the plugin while RENEW is running.

The Net Components Plugin has also been the first plugin to be integrated into the plugin system as an original plugin, i.e. it was the first plugin that added new functionality to RENEW. As such it also served as prototype and test case for the development of the RENEW plugin system.

**Modeling Techniques for OO and AO**[5]    lays the foundation for the diagrammatic modeling with a concise introduction of the Unified Modeling Language (UML). UML is an example of a modeling language that supports a multitude of views by a large set of modeling techniques to describe different aspects of a modeled system. Each view can be supported by one or more techniques, which focus on the modeling for this exact view. Each modeling technique offers the possibility to create either structural or behavioral models. I presented the most commonly used representatives of both categories: the Class Diagram and the Sequence Diagram.

The Agent Unified Modeling Language (AUML) is an approach to extend the techniques of UML for the needs of agent-oriented modeling. One of the most important contributions is the extension of expressiveness of Sequence Diagrams. In AUML they are called Interaction Protocols.

The presented object-oriented modeling techniques and descendants are opposed with several agent-oriented modeling techniques. Gaia, one of the most influential agent-oriented methodologies, is presented as a prototype of a methodology. Gaia does not prescribe a syntax or a technique set, but leaves instead room for interpretation. Finally, this chapter presents several modeling techniques used within several selected methodologies. The description of the modeling techniques focuses on the modeling techniques that are equivalent to the UML Class Diagrams and Sequence Diagrams.

The presented agent-oriented methodologies borrow from the industry standard of modeling UML. However, they also claim that the modeling with pure UML is not enough for multi-agent system construction.

---

[5]The parts about UML and AUML of this chapter are based on Cabac (2003), Chapter 2.

## Part II: Constructive Modeling and the Design Process

The elements that are missing in order to bridge *all* chapters of Part I are a development approach and the modeling language for MULAN/CAPA-based multi-agent applications. The modeling language, i.e. a set of modeling techniques, the supporting tool set and the parts of the PAOSE approach necessary to understand the utilization and application of the techniques are presented in this part.

**Multi-Agent System: A Guiding Metaphor**   introduces the guiding metaphor for the development process and the development team that is applied in the PAOSE approach. The metaphor is the *multi-agent system*. The multi-agent system concept, especially in the strongly formalized form of MULAN, which defines a highly structured architecture with strong concepts – in parts borrowed from the underlying reference net formalism – offers strong orientation for developers and other participants (such as users) of the development process. Thus, the multi-agent system metaphor is not only applied to the organization of the artifact (developed system) but also to the organization of the participating developers (development system).

For those who have incorporated the highly formalized form of a social organization as the foundation of their implementation, i.e. the developers, it is easy to re-transfer those concepts back to a social organization, i.e. their environment, as a development team. But also for participants not formally acquainted with the formalized way, it is possible to find guidance in the metaphor, since the original model for the formalization is the social organization of society.

My contributions in this field are the promotion and elaboration of this guiding metaphor (see Cabac (2007)), i.e. the explication of this model[6]. In fact, it is a rather strong guiding metaphor because of its formalization, its high structure and its generality for human organizations.

**Models for the Development of MAA**   describes the development process and its integration in the agent-oriented framework. Additionally, the application matrix with its three dimensions – structure, behavior and terminology – is presented. The modeling techniques, which are presented in detail in the other chapters of this part, are introduced.

The views of the modeling techniques map directly to the dimensions of development and are related to the parts of agent in the MULAN reference model. Additionally, the overview is presented. All four views are supported by modeling techniques.

My contributions in this context are the introduction and the design of the modeling techniques as well as their integration into the development process. Only if the views can be combined to form a composed system, the approach can be successful. I have also contributed to the systematic approach by defining the process alignment that ensures the compatibility of views, processes and artifacts. One of the main aspects here is the integration of concurrency into the design/development process. This has mainly been achieved through the application matrix and the tight definition of interface connections between dependent development fragments.

---

[6]The guiding metaphor is, just like any other metaphor, also a model (compare with Definition 2.1).

**Coarse Architecture of MAA**  introduces the Coarse Design Diagrams. These are diagrams that represent the organizational structure of the system, which is structured as two dimensions of the organizational matrix as roles and interactions. Coarse Design Diagrams borrow their syntax from UML Use Case Diagrams but use a different semantics. Actors represent roles and use cases represent interactions. This modeling technique is lightweight, intuitive and can be used to quickly sketch the organizational form.

The technique is supported by the Use Case Plugin for RENEW, which integrates the modeling technique into the development environment for MULAN applications. Although the modeling technique is simple, it is possible to generate the project's code bases from the diagrams directly and easily. The generator uses the Velocity template engine and produces numerous artifacts. It eases the setup for the project's code base and shortens this task significantly. I am the author of the Use Case Plugin, which offers the technique and integrates the tool support into RENEW.

**Organizational Structures of MAA**  describes the modeling of organizational structures in multi-agent systems. Two techniques are presented that have a slightly different focus. The first one are the Dependency Diagrams, which offer the modeling of relations between agents/roles and services. The outstanding feature of this approach is the integration into the system as round-trip engineering system. It is backed up by the Knowledge Round-Trip Plugin, which can construct agent descriptions (initial knowledge bases) and is also capable of extracting (analysis) the models from given implementations.

The second technique are the R/D Diagrams, which model the same aspects for the construction of multi-agent applications. The focus lies on the definition of knowledge base description in a comfortable way, while introducing an elaborated back end of the system based on an XML knowledge base representation. Tool support is provided by the Knowledge Base Editor (KBE). The unique feature in this tool is the technical integration of the role concept into the framework.

I was the technical supervisor for Dirkner's diploma thesis (2006), the objective of which was the development of the technique and the Knowledge Round-Trip Plugin (see also Cabac et al. (2006c) and Cabac et al. (2008c)). The development of the KBE was originally done by Klenski and Willner (2007). I participated in discussions and did some of the first testing of the tool and of the technique. One of my contributions is the integration of service dependencies in the same manner as for Dependency Diagrams (see also Cabac and Moldt (2009)). I have also taken care of the maintenance and the development of some improvements to the tool.

**Modeling Agent Ontologies**  presents the modeling of ontologies with Concept Diagrams within the agent context. Concept Diagrams are Class Diagrams that are reduced to model these agent ontologies. The modeling of Concept Diagrams is provided by the FS Plugin[7] and is thus done directly in RENEW. The generation of ontology classes from the diagrams is provided by the FS Ontology Generator Plugin developed by Teuber, which is documented as term assignment under my supervision (see Cabac et al.

---

[7]Information about the FS formalism is provided by Wienberg (2001)

(2009)). It uses the Velocity template engine for the generation of classes from predefined templates.

I have been the first who employed Concept Diagrams for the modeling of agent ontologies in the PAOSE context. The manual task of translating these models into Protégé models led to the idea to integrate the two techniques/frameworks.

**Modeling Interactions** presents the modeling of agent interactions with Agent Interaction Protocol Diagrams. These are a variation of the Interaction Protocols proposed originally in the AUML context. The syntax is adopted from AUML, the semantics is defined as transformational semantics through the translation into Petri nets. The technique is supported by the AIP Diagram Plugin that provides not only the drawing capabilities but also the generator feature that translates the diagrams into Petri net skeletons.

I am the author of the AIP Diagram Plugin as well as the designer of this interpretation of the modeling technique and have presented an early version of the techniques and of the tool in (Cabac 2003) and (Cabac and Moldt 2005).

**Modeling Agent-Internal Behavior** presents the modeling of agent-internal processes, which are – unlike protocol nets – not responsible for the communication. These are the decision components. The general concept of decision components is explained and a standard implementation is presented, which offers an advanced adapter, called Remote-DC, to attach other *Java*-based code.

I have participated in the introduction of the decision components as a generalized concept on the ground of the planner and I have promoted their integration as (first-order) members of the parts of the MULAN agents. The original simple implementation of the RemoteDC has been enhanced substantially by me and the redesign of the RemoteDC Plugin to the second version was co-supervised also by me and carried out by Rathjen (see Cabac et al. (2008b)). Furthermore, I have proposed the usage of DCs as prototypical GUI implementation and have contributed to their modeling (e.g. see Figure C.11 and following).

**Part III: Analytical Modeling of Multi-Agent Systems**

The modeling support for the construction of systems is presented in the preceding part: Constructive Modeling and the Design Process. However, to construct distributed, complex, coordinated and executable systems one needs to understand the processes and the inter-relations of its parts. In this work this process of extracting information of the system's structure and its processes is called analysis, and analogously the extraction of models from the system is called analytical modeling. This analytical modeling supports the developer's understanding of the system's nature.

I present several means to gather and display information to the developer from (a) the running system by observation and testing, (b) the aggregation of information during observation (from the outside), (c) the improvement of comparing models (diff for models) and (d) the gathering and presentation of the development-related information in a central hyperlink document structure, in order to provide an application programming interface (API).

**Monitoring and Debugging** analyzes the debugging processes of multi-agent applications. The investigation of debugging in the distributed, concurrent context of multi-agent systems leads to a classification of debugging regarding three dimensions: *scale*, *activities* and *coupling*. Due to the distributed, concurrent and emergent nature of multi-agent applications it becomes clear that debugging these systems has many aspects in common with conventional debugging, but many aspects are not recognized and are also not important in conventional debugging approaches. In this investigation, debugging of multi-agent systems encompasses – from the conceptual viewpoint – the conventional debugging approaches and extends these approaches by adding new techniques for the crucial aspects in multi-agent system debugging.

Two tools, designed as plugins for RENEW, are presented that demonstrate how advanced and conventional debugging features can be introduced for the development of MULAN applications.

My contribution in this area lies in the investigation and classification of all aspects of debugging in the context of multi-agent systems. My contributions in the tool set are the extension of the functionality of the MULAN-VIEWER (originally designed and developed by Carl (2003)) by detailed inspection techniques, the introduction of advanced navigation in the sources as well as executed models together with Schleinzer (some of the advanced features were presented by Cabac et al. (2008d), Cabac et al. (2009a)). I have also improved and extended the controlling features of the plugin to achieve a tool for the centralized control of the system together with Schlüter (2008). Thus the MULAN-VIEWER has become more than just a viewer and the name only remains for historical reasons. The second tool, the MULAN-SNIFFER, is a direct advancement of the Agent Interaction Protocol Diagrams. It has been envisioned in a twofold way as a visualization of the messages passing the platform's MTS (message transport service) – i.e. a visual message log – and as a collection of tools for message analysis that can be performed by advanced extensions. The original conceptualization was done by Denz (formerly Knaak) and me, the first prototypical implementation by Heitmann and Plähn (compare with Cabac et al. (2006d)). At time of construction the usefulness of the MUL-AN-SNIFFER surpassed the MULAN-VIEWER, which is capable of inspecting messages in a much simpler fashion. However, with the introduction of the navigation and controlling features, this has been compensated over time, and both tools have their advantages and unique application area.

**Monitoring and Analyzing** presents our approach of analyzing the communicative behavior of agents. We use process mining techniques to extract information about the behavior of agents that can be deduced from the traces of their communication. In the context of multi-agent systems this approach is particularly useful because of the distributed and concurrent nature of the system. Also the possibility of extracting behavior patterns automatically from observing other agents can lead to adaptable agents. The goal of this project, which is a joint work with Denz (see Cabac et al. (2006b), Cabac et al. (2006d) and Cabac and Denz (2008)), is to gather and provide a set of mining algorithms, that can be applied and combined easily by building mining chains on the basis of net components. So far a prototypical implementation and an example application exist.

My contribution in this project lies in the conceptual framework, the infrastructure support, the introduction of the Petri net-based net components for mining processors and the integration of techniques and tools, while Denz offers the expertise in mining techniques and integrated the ProM framework into our Mining Plugin, which extends the MULAN-SNIFFER.

**Comparing Models**  presents a simple but somehow useful technique that allows for the finding of differences in models – Petri nets, UML-like diagrams or even simple images. The approach is similar to the well-known diff tools used for the tracking of changes in text files. However, in contrast to text-based diff tools the presented technique can only be used interactively. Nevertheless, the technique considerably facilitates the handling and comparison of diagrams and net code.

My contribution is the conceptualization and development of the technique and the tool as RENEW plugin, while the idea originated during a discussion with Schlüter.

**API Documentation**  presents Mulandoc, an API documentation tool for MULAN applications that is meant to resemble the *Javadoc* API documentation – hence the name Mulandoc. After several efforts in the ongoing projects of agent application development that were either proprietary systems, hard to manually maintain or too unstructured and greedy to be useful, the requirements for a new documentation system were defined as follows: The system should be simple, similar to existing systems in use, produce a navigable hypertext and be extendible. The result is a prototype of a hypertext API documentation for MULAN applications that is simple enough to be useful and has a good acceptance due to its completely automatic generation.

My contributions in this matter consist in the original conceptualization and definition of requirements for a project assignment. The first implementation by Meiners (2007) used simple text generation of plain HTML text files, but provided a flexible architecture that allowed to extend the system by new project elements. A re-factoring by Den, Lohmann and me (compare with Cabac et al. (2008b)) resulted in the inclusion of Velocity-based templates, the introduction of style-sheets for the HTML code, an extension of the produced element documentation for knowledge base entries and an improvement of linking as well as navigation. I also extended the framework with the generation of image maps that provide hypertext navigation for the images of the Coarse Design Diagrams. Thus, the Coarse Design Diagrams were integrated into the generated document structure.

**Part IV: Example Applications**

This part presents examples of the application of the modeling techniques by showing the diagrams designed during three projects.

**Producer / Storage / Consumer**   The Producer/Storage/Consumer example presented in this chapter is displayed so as to show every detail of the modeling process from Coarse Design Diagram over Agent Interaction Protocol Diagrams, R/D Diagram, Concept Diagram all the way to the executable Petri nets as protocol nets and decision components. This is a typical introduction to the approach and the modeling with the presented models. By applying the diff feature of the Image Net Diff Plugin, the differences between the generated skeletons for protocol nets and the resulting executable models are shown explicitly. Thus the efforts for the necessary refinement to achieve an executable system are made explicit by visualization.

**Projects**   The Settler and WFMS projects (compare also with Reese et al. (2003)) are large scale models that have been developed with mid size teams. The projects have also been the test bed for the proposed techniques as well as for the PAOSE approach. The presented version *Settler 6* results from a complete reimplementation of the system using all presented techniques. The recoding was done in parts as proof of concept and in parts to get rid of relics and legacies from older projects, such as hand-coded ontology classes.

## 24.2 Discussion

In computer science one of the challenges is to cope with the complexity of software system development. A profound understanding of the developed systems is the essential precondition for the developers to handle the construction of software. During development, modeling is the means to further the understanding of software systems. However, if the developed systems are concurrent and distributed systems, i.e. complex ones, then the comprehension of these systems is neither trivial nor can it be assumed to be complete. For the individual participant as well as for the development team the acquisition of knowledge about the system is not an atomic task, it is a process that is interleaved with the development process. During development the knowledge about the system increases with the growing system, and there often emerge circumstances during development that cause the developers to revise their views. The understanding of the system is, furthermore, a collective process to which the individuals can contribute. In order to make this collective and dynamic process possible, systematic approaches have to be taken, information about the system has to be gathered as models and this information also has to be made available to all participants by making the models explicit. In software development these explicit models are usually diagrams.

The Unified Modeling Language (UML) is the standard for software system modeling in object-oriented approaches. However, it does not support the modeling of the essential attributes of multi-agent systems in an adequate way. In the agent-oriented community it is understood that UML alone, which is inherently interconnected with object-orientation, does not suffice for the modeling of multi-agent systems. Nevertheless, the advantages of the elaborated techniques are obvious. In addition to techniques specific to agent-orientation, the techniques of UML are used as supplements in this context – either directly or with modifications.

In the context of multi-agent application development with reference nets, numerous tools, techniques, systems, frameworks and principles converge to form an environment of execution and development. With reference nets, a formalism following the nets-within-nets paradigm of Valk (1998) and the efficient virtual machine RENEW, Kummer (2002) and Wienberg (2001) laid the foundation for the possibility to build large-scale, concurrent system models. Rölke (2004) and Duvigneau (2002) provided a reference model for multi-agent systems and a framework for the modeling and implementation of multi-agent systems – i.e. distributed, concurrent and adaptable systems – on top of RENEW and the formalism of reference nets. What is missing is an approach for the development of multi-agent applications on top of the middleware, here the framework MULAN/CAPA. Although many agent-oriented methodologies exist, they do not take into account the special features that are already included in this framework, i.e. the formal method of Petri nets, the process-oriented viewpoint, the strong focus on concurrency and distribution as well as their support. PAOSE (see Moldt (2006b)) fills the gap by providing an approach that does not only support concurrency and distribution for the developed system, but also focuses on the integration of concurrency and distribution in other aspects of the development, i.e. the development process, the development team organization and the development tool set. PAOSE also includes sociological theories and acknowledges the context of software systems as socio-technical systems.

However, without a clearly defined development process and without guidance, the power of the framework sketched above is not exploitable. Especially in a teaching setting, where students still learn how to approach the problems during development and have to improve their modeling and design capabilities, a well-defined process description is of importance. Here the clear structure of the matrix organization – provided by the PAOSE approach – helps the individuals and the team to succeed in their goals. It reflects the system organization of the development team, and it is accompanied by the intuitive, universal and easily acceptable guiding metaphor: the *multi-agent system of developers*.

This work provides the first coherent presentation of the PAOSE approach, although several aspects are only briefly sketched due to the focus of this work. In this context, I present a set of modeling techniques and supporting tools for the PAOSE approach and a suitable guiding metaphor for the development of MULAN-based multi-agent applications. The modeling techniques are specifically designed for the construction of MULAN applications and the supporting tools are integrated into the development environment. However, the techniques presented here can also be transferred to other frameworks. I also present analytical techniques to extract information from the developed system's resources as well as the executed system together with their respective tools.

For the modeling with Petri nets, a means to achieve better models is the utilization of net components. As in many areas, the investment needed for the design of a suitable set of patterns is high, but the payback during large-scale system development shared over participants and time is immense.

Throughout the development and elaboration on techniques and tools I employed an incremental approach. Incremental approach means that models of a technique were at first used without specific tool support, then step-by-step the technique as well as the tool support were improved.

Starting from several proposals for each modeling technique, a subset is pre-selected and a candidate chosen. Then, if accepted, a first implementation of a simple supporting tool for the drawing of models in the specified technique (although maybe not mature yet) is provided and further improved. The tools are directly integrated into the development environment and instant feedback results in new improved versions. The generation features that provide code skeletons for models or design artifacts are included into the tools. This approach of small steps of development together with immediate feedback and further improvements of the techniques as well as step-by-step integration of advancements in tool support has demonstrated itself to be especially fruitful to achieve not only adequate modeling techniques but also techniques that possess a high acceptance among developers.

The results of this thesis are embedded in the above discussed context. By providing the modeling techniques for the PAOSE approach together with the integration of the tool support into the development environment, I managed to substantially improve the development of MULAN-based applications on the conceptual as well as on the technical level.

On the conceptual level, the modeling techniques improve the quality of the development process. The structure and systematics of the PAOSE approach are improved and the development of multi-agent applications is accelerated. By making several concepts of the PAOSE approach explicit, such as the underlying guiding metaphor, I provide a clear and fundamental access to the approach. The understanding of the complex approach and the integration of individuals into the development organization is eased.

On the technical level, the quality of the constructed systems is improved. Moreover, the abstract models add to the clear structure of the multi-agent applications and to their documentation. The concrete models are structured through the pattern-based concept of net components. Their construction, utilization and adaptation is accelerated as well. Additionally, the possibility to extract explicit representation from the systems, which focus on the objectives of the developers, has also added to the understanding of these systems.

The presented modeling techniques together with the tool integration are the means for the support of the constructive design of Petri net-based multi-agent applications. The understanding of complex systems during development is supported by the analytical modeling. In both cases the means are the explicit representation of the models. Thus, the modeling techniques and their conceptual as well as technical integration into the framework presented in this work adequately support the development of systems with the PAOSE approach.

## 24.3 Outlook

In the context of this work many other questions in the field of Petri nets and multi-agent systems came up. Several of them directly arise from this work, some are related. In the following I present them in the context of the ongoing work.

## Paose

The PAOSE approach has evolved over the last years to form an elaborated and comprehensive approach for the development of software systems on the basis of Petri nets following the agent-oriented paradigm. It can be described as a radical and ambitious approach. Similar to, for instance, extreme programming (see Beck and Andres (2005)), in which *best practices* are taken to extremes, in the PAOSE approach the principles and concepts are similarly treated. However, also conventional methods and techniques are included, when useful. Since PAOSE positions Petri nets as the central aspect for conceptual approaches and also for system design, the approach can be described – in analogy to extreme programming – as I would phrase it as *extreme netting*. Daniel Moldt is the originator and coordinator of the efforts undertaken in this field, which is the topic of his ongoing research. In this context, there are still questions that remain open and several aspects that are considered *common sense* still need to be made explicit. The explication of the guiding metaphor is one step towards a comprehensive description of the approach. Open questions that have not yet found sufficient answers are (but are not limited to) an adequate project management, the integration of the development environment and communication support in the development team. The important question of how the approach can be lifted to levels that meat industrial requirements is addressed in a currently ongoing project.

## Decision Components

Youngest elements of the MULAN reference model, the decision components are – although well-supported through the RemoteDC Plugin and its framework – not supported by an abstract modeling technique. On the one hand, several approaches exist, which have been tried. Agent Interaction Protocol Diagrams, for instance, have been used to generate parts of the decision components as skeletons. This seems a worthwhile approach, especially since the decision components have entered the AIPs in many models. An extension of the generation feature for a restricted set of decision components can be integrated. However, the decision components have a large variety of structures. A support for all kinds of decision components would be difficult, if possible at all. On the other hand, the construction of decision components is well-supported. The DC Components Plugin provides structuring of decision components, on which ground the models can be constructed and maintained. For the description of the abstract RemoteDC interface, an abstract model or an integration into one of the presented modeling techniques would be desirable.

## AgentIDE

The techniques and tools presented in this work are integrated in the PAOSE approach. They can be seen as a part of a larger vision of an integrated development environment (IDE) for MULAN-based applications. However, for such a cause, a tight integration of tools have to be provided, and also other aspects besides modeling, debugging and code generation have to be considered. Among them are aspects like project management, integrated communication support, resource management, workflow management and build process management. Although many aspects are covered in our project settings – mostly through external tools (e.g. Trac, `http://trac.edgewall.org/`; COMMSY, `http://www.commsy.net`) – there exists no tight integration in the PAOSE approach. The dissertation of Kolja Markwardt covers several of the mentioned aspects. In this course he develops the *Process-Oriented Tool Agents for Team Organization* system. Previous joint work resulted in several publications, e.g. see Lehmann et al. (2005) and Markwardt et al. (2008). The diploma thesis of Matthias Güttler is also located in this context. He examines the project management in the AOSE projects and evaluates appropriate tool support, i.e. Redmine, `http://www.redmine.org`, as an alternative to Trac.

## Mobility

Mobility is a natural aspect in multi-agent systems. In MULAN-based systems, the modeling of mobility is intrinsic. In her diploma thesis, Eva Müller provides a variation of CAPA that makes the agent distribution in the multi-agent system infrastructure level (compare with the abstract MULAN model in Figure 4.3, layer 1) explicit. For this visualization she employs the token game of the Petri net model. Her enhancement offers a rich representation of the underlying agent system. In this context previous joint work already resulted in a publication (see Müller (2009b)).

Another possibility is the modeling of agent paths through the infrastructure network of platforms. A prototypical filter for the MULAN-SNIFFER exists that makes use of the fact that agents are transmitted as messages. The result is a Sequence Diagram that displays the migration history of agents. It is very similar to proposals made by Kosiuczenko (2002) for the modeling of mobility with Sequence Diagrams. The approach can be extended to achieve a Migration History Diagram by including, for instance, *contains* relation presentation in the diagram. These diagrams can then be used for the planning of routes, for the optimization of migration paths and also in multi-agent-based simulation.

The realization of agent mobility in the context of MULAN is another aspect that has to be further investigated. The objective here is to extend the modeled mobility (see above) to a real agent mobility beyond platform borders across real machines. In the context of the WFMS projects, experiments were conducted that showed prototypically the feasibility of an implementation of mobile Workflow agents (i.e. agents that are/represent a workflow). Although the integration of real mobility and the comfortable usage are not yet completed, the conceptual basis has already been made by Reese (2009) (see also Wagner (2009b)). Her notion of the mobility of workflow agents is comparable to the notion of migrating processes described by Kunze (2008). The life cycles for mobile workflow agents by Reese (2009, Figure 5.13, p. 178) is very similar to the one of migrating processes by Kunze (2008, Figure 5.5, p. 148).

## Organization-Orientation

A general trend in the agent research & development community is the search for the possibility to integrate the management of organizational structures into the frameworks currently in use. Additionally, research concerning flexible, dynamic organizational structures and their governance at runtime has begun to draw interest. These governance structures dynamically allow to re-organize and adapt the organization of multi-agent systems. More recent research follows the trend that organization theory already followed decades before, namely the explicit distinction of different levels and modes of organizational action. In this context, the dissertation of Matthias Wester-Ebbinghaus extends the reference model MULAN to higher levels. In his model, organizational units are nested inside each another, resulting in a multi-level organized system. For instance, a multi-agent system representing a company can be nested in a market, which again is nested in a society. Each level has its own set of rules, processes and governing entities. In Wester-Ebbinghaus and Moldt (2008), a concrete proposal for a reference architecture for organization-oriented software systems is presented. It is envisioned to be built on top of multi-agent systems, which Wester-Ebbinghaus calls a transition from multi-agent to multi-organization systems. How this transition can actually be realized is sketched in Wester-Ebbinghaus et al. (2008). In particular, a prototypical case study has been conducted on the basis of the organizational model for multi-agent systems: SONAR (see Köhler-Bußmeier et al. (2009)). An integration of the sketched architectures is yet to be done. However, in the future PAOSE has to follow the shift from the agent metaphor to the more abstract metaphor of organization. This has already been sketched by Wester-Ebbinghaus and Moldt (2006) under the term *organization-oriented software engineering* (OrgOSE).

### Agent Language

The development of an agent language on the basis of Feature Structure Nets (see Wienberg (2001)) seems tempting. The externalized handling of ontology concepts in *Java* classes can, on that ground, be integrated into the formalism. As additional benefit, the ontology would become flexible, i.e. changeable at runtime. Although this restriction does not exist in the MULAN/CAPA framework itself, the taken approach by representing the concepts as ontology classes relies on the statically compiled *Java* classes. An unsupported use of SL messages is also possible but hardly manageable in large scale.

### Unit Theory

The unit theory is an approach that aims at a flexible model of system units. Based on Petri nets and their principles, it allows to model flexible structures. Structures are changeable at runtime in unit templates as well as unit instances. The theory defines several basis operations on units, such as the removing or the adding of a unit. A first examination and prototypical implementation was done by Tell (2005), and Hewelt's diploma thesis deals with a conceptual approach and an implementation with Petri nets that facilitates the Net Components Plugin's functionality (see also Hewelt and Wester-Ebbinghaus (2009)).

### Plugin Systems

The multi-agent paradigm can be seen as a general approach of looking at matters. In order to apply the concepts to other areas, it is possible to reduce the capabilities of the agents, platforms or systems to achieve sound models for other paradigms. Thus a plugin system can be regarded as a restricted form of agents. Autonomy has to be restricted to achieve reliability. Life cycle management or service relationships, on the contrary, are already available in multi-agent systems. Extension relationships (e.g. as with extension points in Eclipse, `http://www.eclipse.org`) can be realized as proprietary communication channels. Some considerations have been published in this direction (see Cabac et al. (2005), Cabac et al. (2006a) and Schleinzer et al. (2008)). On the ground of this previous work Duvigneau (2009) provides in his dissertation a deep insight into the conceptual modeling of plugin systems with Petri nets. Although his work does not integrate agent technology, the root of his considerations lies in agent-related concepts and is closely linked to the MULAN framework. The plugin-agent concepts – i.e. agents that may function as plugins in certain context – are not mature yet and an implementation that provides a multi-agent system, in which agents can act as plugins – although this has already been conceptually and prototypically done with RENEW and MULAN – is not available.

### Agent-Based Workflow Management System

Based on the WFMS projects, Reese (2009) discusses in her dissertation the construction of a middleware framework on top of a multi-agent system as a generalized process infrastructure. The presented WFMS is one step towards the goal of a distributed, hierarchical, mobile and cooperative workflow engine. Several joint publications have resulted from this cooperation (see Reese et al. (2006), Reese et al. (2007), Reese et al. (2008)). In order to make the WFMS framework serviceable, the ease of use has to be improved. For a middleware it is not enough to have proven its academic feasibility, instead it also has to be possible to build, to deploy and to manage workflows in an easy, economic and ergonomic way. The integration of workflows and agents presented by Reese (2009) is also the conceptual foundation for the work done in the dissertation of Markwardt (see above). Wagner (2009b) provides a prototypical implementation of Reese's concept.

### Service-Oriented Architectures

In the same way as with plugin systems, service oriented architectures can be regarded as restricted forms of multi-agent systems. The focus lies on the distribution of systems and service management. Similar principles are applied to, for instance, service composition, service propagation, service broking and service orchestration. In the wider context of this subject, the dissertation of Jan (Ortmann 2010) deals with the formalization of such architectures as a formalism for RENEW. For this, he provides a prototypical plugin and formal verification.

In this context, Tobias Betz wants to provide – in the course of his diploma thesis – web-services for agents on the basis of web-service-conform communication. The approach involves a translation between SOAP messages (Simple Object Access Protocol) to ACL messages (Agent Communication Language).

## Simulation / MABS

Obviously, Renew can be employed as a simulation engine. The token game, itself, is a simulation of the execution. Strümpel (2003) augmented Renew's simulation mode for timed Petri nets with stochastic measures and evaluated the feasibility of this approach (see also Strümpel (2001)). She compared her presented framework for Petri net-based simulation with the Desmo-J framework (see Page et al. (2000) and Page and Kreutzer (2005)).

The simulation of dynamic and distributed systems on the basis of Mulan/Capa is still at a very early stage. A customized version of Mulan was used by Franz et al. (2007) to simulate a decentralized container terminal. This work showed the feasibility of using the Mulan reference model for the simulation by extending the framework with features such as timing measures and stochastic evaluation. In this matter a general integration of simulation support could extend the field of application. Here, Desmo-J offers highly interesting possibilities.

## Holonic Multi-Agent System

The conceptual and practical work of Schleinzer (2007) on a holonic redesign of Mulan/Capa resulted in an effective prototype. The field of application has not been exploited since. It is possible that in combination with simulation of multi-agent systems (see above) and/or with the visualization of mobility (see above) new application areas can be opened for the holonic framework.

## Security

An omnipresent topic is the security of systems. Especially open, distributed and mobile systems have to address security as a first-order concept. The dissertation of Till Dörges addresses security in the context of agent-orientation and Mulan/Capa. He wants to provide security patterns on the basis of Petri nets. Some work has already been published in this direction (see Horvath and Dörges (2008)).

Also in the direct context of Mulan/Capa, security matters have to be addressed. A direct integration of security features, on the conceptual as well as on the technical level, is desirable. This includes secure communication as well as matters of trust and reliability.

## MAS Metaphor

The multi-agent system metaphor is a strong metaphor. In the context of Paose it draws its power from the highly structured and formalized reference model Mulan. The metaphor can be further exploited. In agent-orientation it is the metaphor that is applied to the developed system. In Paose it is also applied to the development system (i.e. to organization and communication). For example, the application can be further extended to the development process and to the development support (i.e. the development environment, compare with the work of Markwardt, see above). The usefulness of each application has to be examined, and means to apply the metaphor have to be found. Nevertheless, in analogy to the object-oriented modeling techniques, which are not accepted by the agent-oriented community, other principles and dogmas that result from conventional paradigms should also be challenged. This could lead the development further into the direction of agent-orientation.

### Net Components

Net components are a means to structure Petri net models. They ease the construction and improve the readability of the models by providing patterns as templates. This approach is extensible to other areas of Petri nets modeling. Here new sets of net components have to be designed. The MULAN Net Components are well-established and have evolved in several iterations. The other sets are still in development and there is room for improvement.

On the side of tool support the net component integration could be further improved. As pointed out in Section 5.4.2 a collapsing (hiding) functionality would enable to further reduce the complexity of modeled system representation by hiding the complexity. For this matter, however, substantial changes have to be made to the technical framework so that the backwards compatibility can be ensured. In this context, also more conceptual foundations have to be provided in order to allow for usability.

### Debugging of MAS

The debugging and testing of multi-agent systems is not thoroughly addressed yet, in the literature as well as in implementations. Visualization has been proposed by many authors and it is useful for debugging. Process Mining is a young and quickly growing research field, which draws much attention. It is applicable to multi-agent systems and it has proven its feasibility. However, these techniques should be handled with care and farsightedness. Techniques that are able to observe actors in a multi-agent system can be used for the observation of individuals in societies. This does not imply that research should not be done in this direction, but it should be done responsibly and consciously.

In order to be able to build multi-agent applications, it is essential that powerful debugging techniques and tools are available for the developers of these systems. The techniques have to be able to directly address distribution and concurrency.

In this context, also testing has to be improved. The inclusion of automatic unit tests would increase the development speed, improve the reliability of systems and speed-up the refactoring of systems.

### Process Mining

Process mining can also be used with multi-agent systems in other contexts than debugging (see Chapter 17). Most interesting is that mining techniques can provide the possibility to introduce a kind of adaptability and social behaviors for agents into the framework. Through mining, an agent can infer new behavior patterns from observed conversations of surrounding agents. For this, on the technical as well as on the conceptual side, the algorithms have to be exploitable. However, the integration of PRoM features into the MULAN/CAPA framework has reached – up to now – only a prototypical level.

### Verification

Verification has not been the topic of this work. Nevertheless, in the context of multi-agent systems, as in the context of other complex systems, the necessity for verification is evident. The process view, as provided by Petri nets, can offer the possibility to introduce verification for such systems. In this context, Lehmann (2003) (now Markwardt) provides a framework for the automatic evaluation of Interaction Protocols. The interactions are described as workflow nets, which are the ground for the verification. Fundamental work in the field has been done by Köhler (2004) (definitions for object net systems), Farwer (2000) (object nets and logics) and Ortmann (2010) (extension of workflow nets).

### Multiple Formalisms

RENEW is able to execute multiple formalisms and is additionally also able to mix several formalisms in a simulation. This multi-formalism feature, which in version 2.2 is only supported for compiled net systems (shadow net systems), opens the field for new research. The effects that result from combinations of formalisms are not discussed yet. Especially in large scale models the reduction of expressiveness of parts of the system – e.g. reducing MULAN protocol nets to (communicating) workflow nets – could lead to possibilities to include verification for these parts.

Several formalisms are provided with the RENEW release, i.e. *Java* reference nets, P/T nets, bool nets, Feature Structure nets (see Wienberg (2001)). Other formalisms exist as prototypical implementations, e.g. workflow reference nets (see Jacob (2002) and Jacob et al. (2002)), scheme nets (see Delgado Friedrichs (2007)) and service description nets (compare with Ortmann (2010)). A candidate formalism that still awaits an integration is the formalism of algebraic nets (see e.g. Reisig (1991) and Stehr et al. (2001)).

## 24.4 Closing Statement

In order to be able to integrate the attributes typically provided by Petri net systems, such as concurrency and distribution, into software systems, it is not enough to simply construct systems by ad hoc modeling. We also need to build good models and we have to provide a systematic approach of reaching that goal. In the outlook of his dissertation, Olaf Kummer (2002) repeats this necessity – already stated by Daniel Moldt (1996) – that an adequate development approach for software systems built on Petri nets is essential.

> Petri spricht in diesem Kontext [einen Zugang zu Petrinetzen zu vermit-teln] auch von einer Kommunikationsdisziplin der Modellierung. Auch Mod-ellierung muß diszipliniert, also nach einen [sic] vorgegebenen Schema gesche-hen. In der Softwaretechnik zeigt sich, daß objektorientierte Programmierung nicht mehr allein steht, sondern durch einen objektorientierten Entwurf nach einer objektorientierten Analyse unterstützt wird. Auch für objektorientierte

Petrinetze wird eine an diese Technik angepaßte Entwicklungsmethode erforderlich sein, wie bereits in [Moldt, 1996] betont wird.

(Kummer 2002, p, 415)

Petri also talks in this context [of providing an access to Petri nets] of a communication discipline of modeling. Modeling has to be executed with discipline, i.e. following a predetermined procedure/plan. In software engineering the notion emerges that object-oriented programming is not isolated anymore. It is accompanied by object-oriented design and object-oriented requirements analysis. Also for the technique of object-oriented Petri nets, an adequate development approach will be required, as already stressed by [Moldt, 1996].

(Kummer 2002, p, 415, translation)

In the context of Petri net-based software development, the new set of modeling techniques improves the development of MULAN-based multi-agent applications. As a central part of the PAOSE approach, the presented work thus paves the way for a comprehensive and elaborated approach capable to integrate concurrency and distribution as first-order concepts.

# References

AAMAS (Ed.) (2002). *The First International Joint Conference on Autonomous Agents and Multiagent Systems, AAMAS 2002, July 15-19, 2002, Bologna, Italy, Proceedings.* ACM.

Agentcities (2005). Agentcities.
http://web.archive.org/web/20061129130425/www.agentcities.org/.

Angluin, D. (1982, July). Inference of reversible languages. *Journal of the ACM 29*(2), 741–765.

Asko, P. (2005). Acting in social contexts. http://www.informatik.uni-hamburg.de/TGI/forschung/projekte/sozionik/.

AUML (2004). Agent UML. Webpage. http://www.auml.org/.

Balzert, H. (1982). *Die Entwicklung von Software-Systemen: Prinzipien, Methoden, Sprachen, Werkzeuge*, Volume 34 of *Reihe Informatik*. Mannheim Wien Zürich: BI Wissenschaftsverlag. Unveränderter Nachdruck 1989.

Beck, K. and C. Andres (2005). *Extreme Programming Explained: Embrace Change.* Boston: Addison-Wesley.

Bergenti, F., O. Shehory and A. Sturm (2003, February). Agent-oriented software engineering. In M. Luck, W. van der Hoek, and C. Sierra (Eds.), *AgentLink easss 2003*, pp. 125–158. AgentLink.

Bergenti, F., M. Gleizes-Pierre and F. Zambonelli (Eds.) (2004). *Methodologies and software engineering for agent systems: the agent-oriented software engineering handbook.* Multiagent systems, artificial societies, and simulated organizations. Boston [u.a.]: Kluwer Academic.

Booch, G. (1993). *Object-Oriented Design* (2. ed.). Benjamin/Cummings Redwood City, CA.

Booch, G., J. Rumbaugh and I. Jacobson (1999). *The Unified Modeling Language User Guide: The ultimate tutorial to the UML from the original designers.* Addison-Wesley Object Technology Series. Reading, Massachusetts: Addison-Wesley.

Botía, J. A., J. M. Hernansaez and F. G. Skarmeta (2004). Towards an approach for debugging MAS through the analysis of ACL messages. In *MATES 2004. Proceedings*, Volume 3187 of *LNCS*, pp. 301–312. Springer.

Botía, J. A., J. M. Hernansáez and A. F. Gómez-Skarmeta (2007). On the application of clustering techniques to support debugging large-scale multi-agent systems. In *PROMAS 2006. Revised and Invited Papers*, Volume 4411 of *LNCS*, pp. 217–227. Springer-Verlag.

Braker, M. (2004, March). Workflowpetrinetze: Hierarchisierung mittels Netzen-in-Netzen. Diploma thesis, University of Hamburg, Department of Computer Science, Vogt-Kölln Str. 30, D-22527 Hamburg.

Bratman, M. (1987). *Intention, Plans and Practical Reason.* Cambridge: Harvard University.

Braubach, L., W. Lamersdorf, A. Pokahr and J. Sudeikat (2004). Evaluation of agent–oriented software methodologies - examination of the gap between modeling and platform. In *Agent-Oriented Software Engineering V, Fifth International Workshop AOSE 2004,* pp. 126–141.

Braubach, L., A. Pokahr, D. Bade, K.-H. Krempels and W. Lamersdorf (2005, 8). Deployment of distributed multi-agent systems. In F. Z. Marie-Pierre Gleizes, Andrea Omicini (Ed.), *5th International Workshop on Engineering Societies in the Agents World,* pp. 261–276. Springer-Verlag, Berlin.

Braubach, L., A. Pokahr and W. Lamersdorf (2005). *Software Agent-Based Applications, Platforms and Development Kits,* Chapter Jadex: A BDI Agent System Combining Middleware and Reasoning. Birkhäuser Book.

Braubach, L. (2007, 1). *Architekturen und Methoden zur Entwicklung verteilter agentenorientierter Softwaresysteme.* Ph. D. thesis, Universität Hamburg, Fachbereich Informatik, Verteilte Systeme und Informationssysteme.

Braubach, L. and A. Pokahr (2009, November). Jadex. website. `http://vsis-www.informatik.uni-hamburg.de/projects/jadex/`.

Brin, E. (2008, April). Das Belief Desire Intention-Modell und dessen prototypische Verwendung im Rahmen des Siedler V-Projektes. Bachelor's thesis, University of Hamburg, Department of Informatics, Vogt-Kölln Str. 30, D-22527 Hamburg.

Cabac, L. (2002). Entwicklung von geometrisch unterscheidbaren Komponenten zur Vereinheitlichung von Mulan-Protokollen. Bachelor's thesis (equiv.), University of Hamburg, Department of Computer Science.

Cabac, L. (2003, December). Modeling agent interaction protocols with AUML diagrams and Petri nets. Diploma thesis, University of Hamburg, Department of Computer Science, Vogt-Kölln Str. 30, D-22527 Hamburg.

Cabac, L., D. Moldt and H. Rölke (2003, June). A proposal for structuring Petri net-based agent interaction protocols. In W. van der Aalst and E. Best (Eds.), *24th International Conference on Application and Theory of Petri Nets, Eindhoven, Netherlands, June 2003,* Volume 2679 of *Lecture Notes in Computer Science,* pp. 102–120. Springer-Verlag.

Cabac, L. and D. Moldt (2005, January). Formal semantics for AUML agent interaction protocol diagrams. In *Agent-Oriented Software Engineering V: 5th International Workshop, AOSE 2004, New York, NY, USA, July 19, 2004. Revised Selected Papers,* Volume 3382 of *Lecture Notes in Computer Science,* pp. 47–61. Springer-Verlag.

Cabac, L., M. Duvigneau, D. Moldt and H. Rölke (2005). Modeling dynamic architectures using nets-within-nets. In G. Ciardo and P. Darondeau (Eds.), *Applications and Theory of Petri Nets 2005. 26th International Conference, ICATPN 2005, Miami, USA, June 2005. Proceedings*, Volume 3536 of *Lecture Notes in Computer Science*, pp. 148–167.

Cabac, L., M. Duvigneau, M. Köhler, K. Lehmann, D. Moldt, S. Offermann, J. Ortmann, C. Reese, H. Rölke and V. Tell (2005a, March). PAOSE Settler demo. In *First Workshop on High-Level Petri Nets and Distributed Systems (PNDS) 2005*, Vogt-Kölln Str. 30, D-22527 Hamburg. University of Hamburg, Department of Computer Science.

Cabac, L., N. Knaak, D. Moldt and H. Rölke (2006). Analysis of multi-agent interactions with process mining techniques. In *Multiagent System Technologies. 4th German Conference, MATES 2006 Erfurt, Germany. Proceedings*, Volume 4196 of *Lecture Notes in Computer Science*, Berlin Heidelberg New York, pp. 12–23. Springer-Verlag.

Cabac, L., M. Duvigneau, D. Moldt and H. Rölke (2006a, June). Applying multi-agent concepts to dynamic plug-in architectures. In J. Mueller and F. Zambonelli (Eds.), *Agent-Oriented Software Engineering VI: 6th International Workshop, AOSE 2005, Utrecht, Netherlands, July 21, 2005. Revised Selected Papers*, Volume 3950 of *Lecture Notes in Computer Science*, Berlin Heidelberg New York, pp. 190–204. Springer-Verlag.

Cabac, L., N. Knaak and D. Moldt (2006b, May). Applying process mining to interaction analysis of Petri net-based multi-agent models. Technical Report 271, University of Hamburg, Department of Informatics.

Cabac, L., R. Dirkner and H. Rölke (2006c, June). Modelling service dependencies for the analysis and design of multi-agent applications. See Moldt (2006a), pp. 291–298.

Cabac, L., N. Knaak and D. Moldt (2006d). Net components for the modeling of process mining chains. In D. Moldt (Ed.), *Proceedings of the 13th Workshop Application and Tools for Petri Nets. AWPN'06*, Number FBI-HH-B-267/06 in Report of the Department of Informatics, Vogt-Kölln Str. 30, D-22527 Hamburg, Germany. University of Hamburg, Department of Informatics.

Cabac, L., M. Duvigneau and H. Rölke (2006e, June). Net components revisited. See Moldt (2006a), pp. 87–102.

Cabac, L., T. Dörges, M. Duvigneau, C. Reese and M. Wester-Ebbinghaus (2007, June). Application development with Mulan. See Moldt, Kordon, van Hee, Colom and Bastide (2007), pp. 145–159.

Cabac, L., B. Teuber, Y. Küstermann, J. Kuhlmann, L. Schneider, M. Baggendorf, K. Jander and M. Meiners (2007a). Entwicklung eines agentenbasierten workflow management systems. online, http://www.informatik.uni-hamburg.de/TGI/paose/wfms2-booklet.pdf. German, project documentation and three term papers.

Cabac, L., M. Duvigneau, C. Reese, T. Dörges and M. Wester-Ebbinghaus (2007b). Models and tools for Mulan applications. In H.-D. Burkhard, G. Lindemann, R. Verbrugge, and L. Varga (Eds.), *Multi-Agent Systems and Applications V. Fifth International Central and East European Conference, CEEMAS'07, Leipzig. Proceedings*, Volume 4696 of *Lecture Notes in Computer Science*, Berlin Heidelberg New York, pp. 328–330. Springer-Verlag.

Cabac, L. (2007). Multi-agent system: A guiding metaphor for the organization of software development projects. In P. Petta (Ed.), *Proceedings of the Fifth German Conference on Multiagent System Technologies*, Volume 4687 of *Lecture Notes in Computer Science*, Leipzig, Germany, pp. 1–12. Springer-Verlag.

Cabac, L., M. Duvigneau, D. Moldt and B. Schleinzer (2007c). Plugin-agents as conceptual basis for flexible software structures. In *Multi-Agent Systems and Applications V. Fifth International Central and East European Conference, CEEMAS'07, Leipzig. Proceedings*, Volume 4696 of *Lecture Notes in Computer Science*, Berlin Heidelberg New York, pp. 340–342. Springer-Verlag.

Cabac, L. and N. Knaak (2007, June). Process mining in Petri net-based agent-oriented software development. See Moldt, Kordon, van Hee, Colom and Bastide (2007), pp. 7–21.

Cabac, L. and T. Dörges (2007, June). Tools for testing, debugging and monitoring multi-agent applications. See Moldt, Kordon, van Hee, Colom and Bastide (2007), pp. 209–213.

Cabac, L., D. Moldt and J. Schlüter (2008, September). Adding runtime net manipulation features to MulanViewer. In *15. Workshop Algorithmen und Werkzeuge für Petrinetze, AWPN'08*, Volume 380 of *CEUR Workshop Proceedings*, pp. 87–92. Universität Rostock.

Cabac, L., T. Dörges, M. Duvigneau, D. Moldt, C. Reese and M. Wester-Ebbinghaus (2008a). Agent models for concurrent software systems. In R. Bergmann and G. Lindemann (Eds.), *Proceedings of the Sixth German Conference on Multiagent System Technologies, MATES'08*, Volume 5244 of *Lecture Notes in Artificial Intelligence*, Berlin Heidelberg New York, pp. 37–48. Springer-Verlag.

Cabac, L., P. Totzke, N. Worch, J. Schlüter, T. Rathjen, E. Brin, T. Feldhaus, H. Schulz, F. Jodeit, T. Kipp, S. Seeland, J. Knocke, J. Den, N. Lohmann, M. Hewelt and D. Ortmann (2008b). Development of a multi-agent application in the context of Paose /Mulan. online, `http://www.informatik.uni-hamburg.de/TGI/paose/settler5-booklet.pdf`. English/German, project documentation and three term papers.

Cabac, L. and J. Schlüter (2008, September). ImageNetDiff: A visual aid to support the discovery of differences in Petri nets. In *15. Workshop Algorithmen und Werkzeuge für Petrinetze, AWPN'08*, Volume 380 of *CEUR Workshop Proceedings*, pp. 93–98. Universität Rostock.

Cabac, L., R. Dirkner and D. Moldt (2008c). Modeling with service dependency diagrams. In D. Moldt, U. Ultes-Nitsche, and J. C. Augusto (Eds.), *Proceedings of the*

*6th International Workshop on Modelling, Simulation, Verification and Validation of Enterprise Information Systems, MSVVEIS-2008, In conjunction with ICEIS 2008, Barcelona, Spain, June 2008*, Portugal, pp. 109–118. INSTICC PRESS.

Cabac, L., T. Dörges and H. Rölke (2008d, June). A monitoring toolset for Petri net-based agent-oriented software engineering. In R. Valk and K. M. van Hee (Eds.), *29th International Conference on Application and Theory of Petri Nets, Xi'an, China*, Volume 5062 of *Lecture Notes in Computer Science*, pp. 399–408. Springer-Verlag.

Cabac, L. and N. Denz (2008, November). Net components for the integration of process mining into agent-oriented software engineering. *Transactions on Petri Nets and Other Models of Concurrency I (ToPNoC) 5100*, 86–103.

Cabac, L., B. Teuber, J. Simon, T. Betz, S. Lühders, N. Wilzek and H. Ahrens (2009). Extending a multi-agent application in the context of Paose /Mulan. online, `http://www.informatik.uni-hamburg.de/TGI/paose/settler6-booklet.pdf`. English/German, project documentation and three term papers.

Cabac, L. and K. Markwardt (2009). Modeling the system organization of multi-agent systems in early design stages with coarse design diagrams. In D. Moldt, U. Ultes-Nitsche, and J. C. Augusto (Eds.), *Proceedings of the 7th International Workshop on Modelling, Simulation, Verification and Validation of Enterprise Information Systems – MSVVEIS 2009, In conjunction with ICEIS 2009, Milan, Italy, May 2009*, Portugal, pp. 109–118. INSTICC PRESS.

Cabac, L. (2009, June). Net components: Concepts, tool, praxis. See Moldt (2009), pp. 109–118.

Cabac, L., T. Dörges, M. Duvigneau and D. Moldt (2009a, September). Requirements and tools for the debugging of multi-agent systems. In L. Braubach, W. van der Hoek, P. Petta, and A. Pokahr (Eds.), *Multiagent System Technologies. 7th German Conference, MATES 2009, Hamburg, Germany, September 9-11, 2009. Proceedings*, Volume 5774 of *Lecture Notes in Artificial Intelligence*, Berlin Heidelberg New York, pp. 238–247. Springer-Verlag.

Cabac, L. and D. Moldt (2009, June). Support for modeling roles and dependencies in multi-agent systems. In M. Köhler-Bußmeier, D. Moldt, and O. Boissier (Eds.), *Organizational Modelling, International Workshop, OrgMod'09. Proceedings*, Technical Reports Université Paris 13, 99, avenue Jean-Baptiste Clément, 93 430 Villetaneuse, pp. 109–118. Université Paris 13.

Cabac, L., D. Moldt, M. Wester-Ebbinghaus and E. Müller (2009b, September). Visual representation of mobile agents – modeling mobility within the prototype MAPA. See Duvigneau and Moldt (2009), pp. 7–28.

Carl, T. (2003, August). Evaluation und beispielhafte Erweiterung einer referenznetzbasierten Agentenumgebung. Bachelor's thesis (equiv.), University of Hamburg, Department of Computer Science.

Cervenka, R. and I. Trencansky (2007). *The Agent Modeling Language - AML, A Comprehensive Approach to Modeling Multi-Agent Systems.* Whitestein Series in

Software Agent Technologies and Autonomic Computing. Birkhäuser Basel. DOI: 10.1007/978-3-7643-8396-1.

Christensen, S. and N. D. Hansen (1992, April). Coloured Petri nets extended with channels for synchronous communication. Technical Report DAIMI PB–390, Computer Science Department, Aarhus University, DK-8000 Aarhus C, Denmark.

Cossentino, M. and C. Potts (2001, September). PASSI: a process for specifying and implementing multi-agent systems using UML. `http://www-static.cc.gatech.edu/classes/AY2002/cs6300_fall/ICSE.pdf`.

Cossentino, M. a. (2005). *From Requirements to Code with the PASSI Methodology*, Chapter 4, pp. 79–106. In Henderson-Sellers and Giorgini Henderson-Sellers and Giorgini (2005).

Costello, R. B. (Ed.) (1996). *Webster's College Dictionary*. New York: Random House.

CPN Tools (2010, January). Computer Tool for Coloured Petri Nets. online. `http://wiki.daimi.au.dk/cpntools/`.

Dam, K. H. and M. Winikoff (2003). Comparing agent-oriented methodologies. In P. Giorgini, B. Henderson-Sellers, and M. Winikoff (Eds.), *AOIS*, Volume 3030 of *Lecture Notes in Computer Science*, pp. 78–93. Springer.

de Medeiros, A., B. van Dongen, W. van der Aalst and A. J. M. M. Weijters (2004). Process mining: Extending the α-algorithm to mine short loops. BETA Working Paper Series, WP 113, Eindhoven University of Technology.

Delgado Friedrichs, F. (2007, September). Referenznetze mit Anschriften in Scheme. Diploma thesis, University of Hamburg, Department of Informatics, Vogt-Kölln Str. 30, D-22527 Hamburg.

DeLoach, S. (2005). Engineering organization-based multiagent systems. In *Software Engineering for Large-Scale Multi-Agent Systems (SELMAS)*, Volume 3914 of *Lecture Notes in Computer Science*, pp. 109–125. Springer Verlag.

Dewey, J. (1980). *Art as Experience*. New York: Perigee Books, The Berkley Publishing Group.

Dirkner, R. and A. Lehning (2005). Grundlagen des Round-trip Engineerings in der agentenorientierten Softwareentwicklung am Beispiel von Interaktionsdiagrammen und Mulanprotokollen. Bachelor's thesis, University of Hamburg, Department of Informatics, Vogt-Kölln Str. 30, D-22527 Hamburg.

Dirkner, R. (2006). Roundtrip-Engineering im PAOSE-Ansatz. Diploma thesis, University of Hamburg, Department of Informatics, Vogt-Kölln Str. 30, D-22527 Hamburg.

Dunham, M. H. (2003). *Data Mining: Introductory and Advanced Topics*. Upper Saddle River (NJ): Prentice Hall.

Dustdar, S. and R. Gombotz (2006). Discovering web service workflows using web services interaction mining. *International Journal of Business Process Integration and Management (IJBPIM)*.

Duvigneau, M. (2002, December). Bereitstellung einer Agentenplattform für petrinetz-basierte Agenten. Diploma thesis, University of Hamburg, Department of Computer Science, Vogt-Kölln Str. 30, D-22527 Hamburg.

Duvigneau, M., D. Moldt and H. Rölke (2003). Concurrent architecture for a multi-agent platform. In F. Giunchiglia, J. Odell, and G. Weiß (Eds.), *Agent-Oriented Software Engineering III. Third International Workshop, Agent-oriented Software Engineering (AOSE) 2002, Bologna, Italy, July 2002. Revised Papers and Invited Contributions*, Volume 2585 of *Lecture Notes in Computer Science*, Berlin Heidelberg New York, pp. 59–72. Springer-Verlag.

Duvigneau, M. (2009). *Konzeptionelle Modellierung von Plugin-Systemen mit Petri-netzen*. Dissertation, University of Hamburg, Department of Informatics, Vogt-Kölln Str. 30, D-22527 Hamburg, Germany.

Duvigneau, M. and D. Moldt (Eds.) (2009, September). *Proceedings of the Fifth International Workshop on Modeling of Objects, Components and Agents, MOCA'09, Hamburg*, Number FBI-HH-B-290/09 in Bericht, Vogt-Kölln Str. 30, D-22527 Hamburg. University of Hamburg, Department of Informatics.

Edmonds, B. and J. Bryson (2004). The insufficiency of formal design methods - the necessity of an experimental approach - for the understanding and control of complex MAS. In *AAMAS*, pp. 938–945.

Eggert, P., M. Haertel, D. Hayes, R. Stallman and L. Tower (2008). Gnu diff utilities. online. `http://www.gnu.org`.

Ehrler, L. and S. Cranefield (2004). Executing Agent UML diagrams. In N. R. Jennings, C. Sierra, L. Sonenberg, and M. Tambe (Eds.), *Proceedings of AAMAS'04*, pp. 906–913. IEEE Computer Society.

Ellson, J., E. Gansner, Y. Hu, Y. Koren, S. North and A. Bilgin (2009). Graphviz homepage. online. AT&T Research, `http://www.graphviz.org`.

Farwer, B. (2000). *Linear Logic Based Calculi for Object Petri Nets*. Vogt-Kölln Str. 30, D-22527 Hamburg: Logos Verlag, ISBN 3-89722-539-5, Berlin.

Ferber, J. (1999). *Multi-Agent Systems: An Introduction to Distributed Artificial Intelligence*. Harlow [u.a.]: Addison-Wesley.

Ferber, J., O. Gutknecht and F. Michel (2003). From agents to organizations: An organizational view of multi-agent systems. In P. Giorgini, J. P. Müller, and J. Odell (Eds.), *Agent-Oriented Software Engineering IV, 4th International Workshop, AOSE 2003, Melbourne, Australia, July 15, 2003, Revised Papers*, Volume 2935 of *LNCS*, pp. 214–230. Springer-Verlag.

Ferber, J., O. Gutknecht and F. Michel (2008, January). MadKit. `http://www.madkit.net`.

FIPA (2001a, August). FIPA Contract Net Interaction Protocol. `http://www.fipa.org/specs/fipa00029/XC00029F.pdf`.

FIPA (2001b, August). FIPA Interaction Protocol Library Specification. `http://www.fipa.org/specs/fipa00025/XC00025E.pdf`.

FIPA (2002). *FIPA Request Protocol Specification* (Version 2002/12/06 ed.). FIPA.

FIPA (2009, December). Foundation for Intelligent Physical Agents. `http://www.fipa.org`.

Frank, E., M. Hall, L. E. Trigg, G. Holmes and I. H. Witten (2004). Data mining in bioinformatics using Weka. *Bioinformatics 20*(15), 2479–2481.

Franz, T., S. Voß and H. Rölke (2007). Market-Mechanisms for Integrated Container Terminal Management. In *6th International Conference on Computer Applications and Information Technology in the Maritime Industries – COMPIT'07*, pp. 234–248.

Gamma, E., R. Helm, R. Johnson and R. Vlissides (1995). *Design Patterns: Elements of Reusable Object-Oriented Software*. Reading: Addison-Wesley.

Gertchikova, O. (2004, June). Generating messages in Petri nets from messages in AIP diagrams. Bachelor's thesis (equiv.), University of Hamburg, Department of Computer Science, Vogt-Kölln Str. 30, D-22527 Hamburg.

Girault, C. and R. Valk (2003). *Petri Nets for Systems Engineering — A Guide to Modeling, Verification, and Applications*. Berlin: Springer Verlag.

Gombotz, R., K. Baina and S. Dustdar (2005). Towards web services interaction mining architecture for e-commerce applications analysis. In *International Conference on E-Business and E-Learning*, Amman, Jordan. Sumaya University.

Gumm, D. (2008). *A Model of Distributed Requirements Engineering: Understanding Interdependencies*. Ph. D. thesis, University of Hamburg.

Günther, C., S. Rinderle, M. Reichert and W. M. P. van der Aalst (2006). Change mining in adaptive process management systems. In R. Meersman and Z. Tari (Eds.), *On the Move to Meaningful Internet Systems 2006. Proceedings, Part I*, pp. 309–326.

Harel, D. and R. Marelly (2003). *Come, Let's Play, Scenario-Based Programming Using LSCs and the Play-Engine*. Springer-Verlag. ISBN: 978-3-540-00787-6.

Henderson-Sellers, B. and P. Giorgini (Eds.) (2005). *Agent-Oriented Methodologies*. Hershey, London, Melbourne,Singapore: Idea Group Publishing.

Herbst, J. (2001). *Ein induktiver Ansatz zur Akquisition und Adaption von Workflow-Modellen*. Ph. D. thesis, University of Ulm.

Hesse, W. and H. C. Mayr (2008). Modellierung in der Softwaretechnik: eine Bestandsaufnahme. *Informatik Spektrum 31*(5), 377–393. `http://dx.doi.org/10.1007/s00287-008-0276-7`.

Hewelt, M. and M. Wester-Ebbinghaus (2009, June). United – a Petri net based framework for modeling complex and adaptive systems. See Moldt (2009), pp. 207–226.

Hiel, M. (2005, May). Learning interaction protocols by overhearing. Master's thesis, Utrecht University.

Hitz, M., G. Kappel, E. Kapsammer and W. Retschitzegger (2005, September). *UML@Work: Objektorienteierte Modellierung mit UML 2* (3. ed.). dpunk Verlag.

Hofstede, A. H. M. T. (2005). Yawl: yet another workflow language. *Information Systems 30*, 245–275.

Horvath, V. and T. Dörges (2008, May). From security patterns to implementation using Petri nets. In B. D. Win, S.-W. Lee, and M. Monga (Eds.), *Proceedings of the Fourth International Workshop on Software Engineering for Secure Systems, SESS 2008, Leipzig, Germany, May 17-18, 2008*, pp. 17–24. ACM.

Huget, M.-P. and J. Odell (2004). Representing agent interaction protocols with agent UML. In J. Odell, P. Ciorgini, and J. P. Müller (Eds.), *Proceedings of the Workshop on Agent-Oriented Software Engineering at the Conference on Autonomous Agents & Multi Agent Systems (AAMAS'04)*, New York. (also in this collection).

Iglesias, C. A. and M. Garijo (2005). *The Agent-Oriented Methodology MAS-CommonKADS*, Chapter 3, pp. 46–78. In Henderson-Sellers and Giorgini Henderson-Sellers and Giorgini (2005).

ImageMagick (2009). Imagemagick homepage. online. `http://www.imagemagick.org/`.

Jacob, T., O. Kummer, D. Moldt and U. Ultes-Nitsche (2002, August). Implementation of workflow systems using reference nets – security and operability aspects. In K. Jensen (Ed.), *Fourth Workshop and Tutorial on Practical Use of Coloured Petri Nets and the CPN Tools*, Ny Munkegade, Bldg. 540, DK-8000 Aarhus C, Denmark. University of Aarhus, Department of Computer Science. DAIMI PB: Aarhus, Denmark, August 28–30, number 560.

Jacob, T. (2002). Implementierung einer sicheren und rollenbasierten Workflowmanagement-Komponente für ein Petrinetzwerkzeug. Diploma thesis, University of Hamburg, Department of Computer Science, Vogt-Kölln Str. 30, D-22527 Hamburg.

Jacobson, I., M. Christerson, P. Jonsson and G. Övergaard (1992). *Object-oriented Software Engineering; A Use Case Driven Approach*. Wokingham, England: Addison-Wesley.

Jacobson, I., G. Booch and J. Rumbaugh (1999). *The unified software development process: UML; The complete guide to the Unified Process from the original designers*. Addison-Wesley object technology series. Reading, Mass.: Addison-Wesley.

Jade (2005, June). Java Agent Development Framework. `http://jade.cselt.it`.

Jade Sniffer (2008, January). The sniffer for Jade. online documentation. `http://jade.cselt.it/doc/tools/sniffer/index.html`.

Jennings, N. R. and M. J. Wooldridge (1998). Applications of intelligent agents. In N. R. Jennings and M. J. Wooldridge (Eds.), *Agent Technology: Foundations, Applications and Markets*, Berlin Heidelberg New York, pp. 3–28. Springer.

Jensen, K. (1996). *Coloured Petri Nets* (2nd ed.), Volume 1. Berlin: Springer-Verlag.

Jessen, E. and R. Valk (1987). *Rechensysteme: Grundlagen der Modellbildung*. Studienreihe Informatik. Berlin Heidelberg New York: Springer-Verlag.

Juan, T., A. R. Pearce and L. Sterling (2002). ROADMAP: extending the Gaia methodology for complex open systems. See AAMAS (2002), pp. 3–10.

Kindler, E. (1997). A compositional partial order semantics for Petri net components. In *Application and Theory of Petri Nets 1997, Proceedings, volume 1248 of LNCS*, pp. 235–252. Springer-Verlag.

Klenski, M. and A. Willner (2007). Graphische Informationsmodellierung für Mulan-Agenten. Diploma thesis, University of Hamburg, Department of Informatics, Vogt-Kölln Str. 30, D-22527 Hamburg.

Köhler, M., D. Moldt and H. Rölke (2001). Modelling the structure and behaviour of Petri net agents. In J. Colom and M. Koutny (Eds.), *Proceedings of the 22nd Conference on Application and Theory of Petri Nets 2001*, Volume 2075 of *Lecture Notes in Computer Science*, pp. 224–241. Springer-Verlag.

Köhler, M., D. Moldt and H. Rölke (2003). Modelling mobility and mobile agents using nets within nets. In W. van der Aalst and E. Best (Eds.), *Proceedings of the 24th International Conference on Application and Theory of Petri Nets 2003 (ICATPN 2003)*, Volume 2679 of *Lecture Notes in Computer Science*, pp. 121–139. Springer-Verlag.

Köhler, M. (2004). *Objektnetze: Definition und Eigenschaften*, Volume 1 of *Agent Technology – Theory and Applications*. Berlin: Logos Verlag.

Köhler, M., D. Moldt, H. Rölke and R. Valk (2005). Linking micro and macro description of scalable social systems using reference nets. In K. Fischer, M. Florian, and T. Malsch (Eds.), *Socionics: Sociability of Complex Social Systems*, Volume 3413 of *Lecture Notes in Artificial Intelligence*, pp. 51–67. Springer-Verlag.

Köhler-Bußmeier, M., D. Moldt and M. Wester-Ebbinghaus (2009). A formal model for organisational structures behind process-aware information systems. Volume 5460 of *Lecture Notes in Computer Science*, pp. 98–115. Springer-Verlag.

Koning, J.-L., M.-P. Huget, J. Wei and X. Wang (2002). Extended modeling languages for interaction protocol design. *2222*, 68–76.

Kosiuczenko, P. (2002). Sequence diagrams for mobility. In S. Spaccapietra, S. T. March, and Y. Kambayashi (Eds.), *ER*, Volume 2503 of *Lecture Notes in Computer Science*, pp. 147–158. Springer-Verlag. http://dx.doi.org/10.1007/b12013.

Kruchten, P. (1995). Architecture blueprints - the 4+1 view model of software architecture. In *TRI-Ada Tutorials*, pp. 540–555. http://doi.acm.org/10.1145/216591.216611.

Kummer, O. (2001). Introduction to Petri nets and reference nets. *Sozionik Aktuell 1*, 1–9. ISSN 1617-2477.

Kummer, O. (2002). *Referenznetze*. Berlin: Logos Verlag.

Kummer, O., F. Wienberg, M. Duvigneau, J. Schumacher, M. Köhler, D. Moldt, H. Rölke and R. Valk (2004, June). An extensible editor and simulation engine for Petri nets: Renew. In J. Cortadella and W. Reisig (Eds.), *Applications and Theory of Petri Nets 2004. 25th International Conference, ICATPN 2004, Bologna, Italy,*

*June 2004. Proceedings*, Volume 3099 of *Lecture Notes in Computer Science*, Berlin Heidelberg New York, pp. 484–493. Springer.

Kummer, O., F. Wienberg, M. Duvigneau and L. Cabac (2009a, August). Renew – the Reference Net Workshop. Available at: `http://www.renew.de/`. Release 2.2.

Kummer, O., F. Wienberg, M. Duvigneau and L. Cabac (2009b, August). *Renew – User Guide (Release 2.2)*. Hamburg: University of Hamburg, Faculty of Informatics, Theoretical Foundations Group. Available at: `http://www.renew.de/`.

Kunze, C. P. (2008, April). *Kontextbasierte Kooperation: Unterstützung verteilter Prozesse im Mobile Computing*. Dissertation, University of Hamburg, Department of Informatics, Vogt-Kölln Str. 30, 22527 Hamburg, Germany.

Laka, W. (2007, December). Ausbau einer Infrastruktur für offene agentenorientierte Anwendungen im Kontext von Capa und OpenNet. Diploma thesis, University of Hamburg, Department of Informatics, Vogt-Kölln Str. 30, D-22527 Hamburg.

Lam, D. N. and K. S. Barber (2004). Debugging agent behavior in an implemented agent system. In *PROMAS 2004. Revised and Invited Papers*, Volume 3346 of *LNCS*, pp. 104–125. Springer.

Laue, A. and M. Liedtke (2000, September). Zustands- und prozeßorientierte Modellierung im Rahmen der Systemspezifikation. Diploma thesis, University of Hamburg, Department of Computer Science, Vogt-Kölln Str. 30, D-22527 Hamburg.

Lehmann, K. (2003, October). Analyse und Bewertung von Agentenprotokollen auf Basis von Petrinetzen. Diploma thesis, University of Hamburg, Department of Computer Science, Vogt-Kölln Str. 30, D-22527 Hamburg.

Lehmann, K., L. Cabac, D. Moldt and H. Rölke (2005, September). Towards a distributed tool platform based on mobile agents. In *Proceedings of the Third German Conference on Multi-Agent System Technologies (MATES)*, Volume 3550 of *Lecture Notes in Artificial Intelligence*, pp. 179–190. Springer-Verlag.

Lehner, F. (1995a). *Grundfragen und Positionierung der Wirtschaftsinformatik*, Chapter 1, pp. 1–71. In Lehner et al. Lehner, Hildebrand and Maier (1995).

Lehner, F. (1995b). *Modelle und Modellierung*, Chapter 2, pp. 72–164. In Lehner et al. Lehner, Hildebrand and Maier (1995).

Lehner, F., K. Hildebrand and R. Maier (Eds.) (1995). *Wirtschaftsinformatik – Theoretische Grundlagen*. Wien: Hanser Veralg.

Lilienthal, C. (2008). *Komplexität von Softwarearchitekturen*.

Lippert, M., A. Schmolitzky and H. Züllighoven (2003). Metaphor design spaces. In *Extreme Programming and Agile Processes in Software Engineering*, Lecture Notes in Computer Science, pp. 33 – 40.

Ly, T., S. Rinderle, P. Dadam and M. Reichert (2005, September). Mining staff assignment rules from event-based data. In *Workshop on Business Process Intelligence (BPI), in conjunction with BPM 2005*, Nancy, France.

Lynch, S. and K. Rajendran (2008). Providing integrated development environments for multi-agent systems. In *MATES 2008. Proceedings*, Volume 5244 of *LNCS*, pp. 123–134. Springer.

Mack, J. (2001). *Softwareentwicklung als Expedition: Entwicklung eines Leitbildes und einer Vorgehensweise für die professionelle Softwareentwicklung.* Ph. D. thesis, University of Hamburg, Department of Computer Science.

Markwardt, K., D. Moldt and C. Reese (2008). Support of distributed software development by an agent-based process infrastructure. In *MSVVEIS 2008*.

Maruster, L., A. Weijters, W. van der Aalst and A. van den Bosch (2002). Process mining: Discovering direct successors in process logs. In *ICDS: International Conference on Data Discovery*, Volume 2534. Lecture Notes in Computer Science. http://dx.doi.org/10.1007/3-540-36182-0.

Meiners, M. (2007). Mulandoc. Technical report, University of Hamburg, Department of Informatics.

Moldt, D. (1996, August). *Höhere Petrinetze als Grundlage für Systemspezifikationen.* Dissertation, University of Hamburg, Department of Computer Science, Vogt-Kölln Str. 30, D-22527 Hamburg.

Moldt, D. and H. Rölke (2003). Pattern based workflow design using reference nets. In W. van der Aalst, A. t. Hofstede, and M. Weske (Eds.), *Proceedings of International Conference on Business Process Management, Eindhoven, NL*, Volume 2678 of *Lecture Notes in Computer Science*, pp. 246–260. Springer-Verlag.

Moldt, D. (2005, August). Petrinetze als Denkzeug. In B. Farwer and D. Moldt (Eds.), *Object Petri Nets, Processes, and Object Calculi*, Number Report of the Department of Informatics FBI-HH-B-265/05, Vogt-Kölln Str. 30, D-22527 Hamburg, pp. 51–70. University of Hamburg, Department of Computer Science.

Moldt, D. (Ed.) (2006a, June). *Proceedings of the Fourth International Workshop on Modelling of Objects, Components, and Agents. MOCA'06*, Number FBI-HH-B-272/06 in Report of the Department of Informatics, Vogt-Kölln Str. 30, D-22527 Hamburg, Germany. University of Hamburg, Department of Informatics.

Moldt, D. (2006b). PAOSE: A way to develop distributed software systems based on Petri nets and agents. In J. Barjis, U. Ultes-Nitsche, and J. C. Augusto (Eds.), *Proceedings of The Fourth International Workshop on Modelling, Simulation, Verification and Validation of Enterprise Information Systems (MSVVEIS'06), May 23-24, 2006 – Paphos, Cyprus 2006*, pp. 1–2.

Moldt, D., F. Kordon, K. van Hee, J.-M. Colom and R. Bastide (Eds.) (2007, June). *Proceedings of the International Workshop on Petri Nets and Software Engineering (PNSE'07)*, Siedlce, Poland. Akademia Podlaska.

Moldt, D. (Ed.) (2009, June). *Petri Nets and Software Engineering, International Workshop, PNSE'09. Proceedings*, Technical Reports Université Paris 13, 99, avenue Jean-Baptiste Clément, 93 430 Villetaneuse. Université Paris 13.

Mounier, A., O. Boissier and F. Jacquenet (2003). Conversation mining in multi-agent systems. In *Proceedings of the CEEMAS 2003*, pp. 158–167.

Mulyar, N. A. and W. M. P. van der Aalst (2005). Patterns in colored Petri nets. BETA Working Paper Series WP 139, Eindhoven University of Technology, Eindhoven.

Myers, G. J. (2004). *The art of software testing* (2 ed.). Hoboken, NJ: Wiley & Sons.

Nair, R., M. Tambe, S. Marsella and T. Raines (2004). Automated assistants for analyzing team behaviors. In *Autonomous Agents and Multi-Agent Systems 8*, pp. 69–111.

Ndumu, D. T., H. S. Nwana, L. C. Lee and J. C. Collis (1999). Visualising and debugging distributed multi-agent systems. In *Agents*, pp. 326–333. http://doi.acm.org/10.1145/301136.301220.

Oberquelle, H. (1981). Communication by graphic net representations. Report of the Department of Informatics IFI-HH-B-75/81, University of Hamburg, Department of Computer Science, Vogt-Kölln Str. 30, D-22527 Hamburg.

Odell, J., H. V. D. Parunak and B. Bauer (2000). Extending UML for agents. In G. Wagner, Y. Lesperance, and E. Yu (Eds.), *Proc. of the Agent-Oriented Information Systems Workshop at the 17th National conference on Artificia l Intelligence*, pp. 3–17. http://www.jamesodell.com/ExtendingUML.pdf.

Odell, J., H. V. D. Parunak and B. Bauer (2001). Representing agent interaction protocols in UML. In P. Ciancarini and M. Wooldridge (Eds.), *Agent-Oriented Software Engineering*, pp. 121–140. Springer, Berlin. http://www.auml.org/auml/supplements/Odell-AOSE2000.pdf.

Odell, J. and M.-P. Huget (2003, July). FIPA Modeling: Interaction Diagrams. Working draft, Foundation for Intelligent Physical Agents. http://www.auml.org/auml/documents/ID-03-07-02.pdf.

Oestereich, B. (2001). *Objektorientierte Softwareentwicklung, Analyse und Design mit der Unified Modeling Language*. (5. ed.). Oldenbourg Verlag.

OMG (2003). Object management group. http://www.omg.org/.

Ortmann, J. (2010, February). *Höhere Petrinetze als Modellierungstechnik für dienstbasierte Geschäftsprozesse*. Dissertation, Vogt-Kölln Str. 30, 22527 Hamburg, Germany. submitted.

Padgham, L. and M. Winikoff (2002a). Prometheus: a methodology for developing intelligent agents. See AAMAS (2002), pp. 37–38.

Padgham, L. and M. Winikoff (2002b). Prometheus: A pragmatic methodology for engineering intelligent agents. In *Proceedings of the OOPSLA 2002 Workshop on Agent–Oriented Methodologies*, pp. 97–108.

Padgham, L. and M. Winikoff (2004). *Developing Intelligent Agent Systems: A Practical Guide*. Wiley Series in Agent Technology. Chichester [et.al.]: Wiley. isbn:0-470-86120-7, Pages 225.

Page, B., T. Lechler and S. Claassen (2000). *Objektorientierte Simulation in Java mit dem Framework Desmo-J.* Hamburg: Libri Books on Demand.

Page, B. and W. Kreutzer (2005). *The Java Simulation Handbook – Simulating Discrete Event Systems with UML and Java.* Aachen: Shaker.

Pavón, J., J. J. Gómez-Sanz and R. Fuentes (2005). *The INGENIAS Methodology and Tools*, Chapter 11, pp. 236–276. In Henderson-Sellers and Giorgini Henderson-Sellers and Giorgini (2005).

Petri, C. A. (2003, June). Net Modelling – Fit for Science? Booklet: Keynote Lecture Petri Nets 2003, Eindhoven University of Technology, Eindhoven, The Netherlands. At the 24th International Conference on Application and Theory of Petri Nets, ICATPN 2003.

Petrie, C. J., S. Goldmann and A. Raquet (1999). Agent-based project management. In *Artificial Intelligence Today*, pp. 339–363.

Pokahr, A. (2007, 1). *Programmiersprachen und Werkzeuge zur Entwicklung verteilter agentenorientierter Softwaresysteme.* Ph. D. thesis, Universität Hamburg, Fachbereich Informatik, Verteilte Systeme und Informationssysteme.

Poutakidis, D., L. Padgham and M. Winikoff (2002). Debugging multi-agent systems using design artifacts: The case of interaction protocols. In *Proceedings of AAMAS-02*, pp. 960–967. http://doi.acm.org/10.1145/544862.544966.

Reese, C., M. Duvigneau, M. Köhler, D. Moldt and H. Rölke (2003, February). Agent–based Settler game. In *Proceedings of Agentcities Agent Technology Competition (ATC03), Barcelona, Spain.* Agentcities.NET.

Reese, C. (2003). Multiagentensysteme: Anbindung der petrinetzbasierten Plattform CAPA an das internationale Netzwerk Agentcities. Diploma thesis, University of Hamburg, Department of Computer Science, Vogt-Kölln Str. 30, D-22527 Hamburg.

Reese, C., S. Offermann and D. Moldt (2006). Architektur für verteilte, agentenbasierte Workflows. In M. Schoop, C. Huemer, M. Rebstock, and M. Bichler (Eds.), *Service-oriented Electronic Commerce im Rahmen der Multikonferenz Wirtschaftsinformatik 2006 (MKWI 2006)*, Volume P-80 of *Lecture Notes in Informatics (LNI) - Proceedings*, Bonn, pp. 73–87. Gesellschaft für Informatik: Köllen Druck+Verlag GmbH.

Reese, C., M. Wester-Ebbinghaus, T. Dörges, L. Cabac and D. Moldt (2007). A process infrastructure for agent systems. In M. Dastani, A. El Fallah, J. Leite, and P. Torroni (Eds.), *MALLOW'007 Proceedings. Workshop LADS'007 Languages, Methodologies and Development Tools for Multi-Agent Systems (LADS)*, pp. 97–111.

Reese, C., M. Wester-Ebbinghaus, T. Dörges, L. Cabac and D. Moldt (2008). Introducing a process infrastructure for agent systems. In M. Dastani, A. El Fallah, J. a. Leite, and P. Torroni (Eds.), *LADS'007 Languages, Methodologies and Devel-*

*opment Tools for Multi-Agent Systems*, Volume 5118 of *Lecture Notes in Artificial Intelligence*, pp. 225–242. Revised Selected and Invited Papers.

Reese, C. (2009). *Prozess-Infrastruktur für Agentenanwendungen.* Dissertation, University of Hamburg, Department of Informatics, Vogt-Kölln Str. 30, D-22527 Hamburg.

Reisig, W. (1982). *Petrinetze - Eine Einführung.* Berlin: Springer-Verlag.

Reisig, W. (1991). Petri nets and algebraic specifications. *Theoretical Computer Science 80*, 1–34.

Reisig, W. (1997, October). *Elements of Distributed Algorithms: Modeling and Analysis with Petri Nets.* Springer-Verlag New York.

Remondino, M. and G. Correndo (2005, June). Data mining applied to agent based simulation. In Y. Merkuryev, R. Zobel, and E. Kerckhoffs (Eds.), *Proceedings of the 19th European Conference on Modelling and Simulation*, Riga, pp. 374–380. SCS-Europe.

Rölke, H. (1999). Modellierung und Implementation eines Multi-Agenten-Systems auf der Basis von Referenznetzen. Diploma thesis, University of Hamburg, Department of Computer Science.

Rölke, H. (2004). *Modellierung von Agenten und Multiagentensystemen – Grundlagen und Anwendungen*, Volume 2 of *Agent Technology – Theory and Applications.* Berlin: Logos Verlag.

Rumbaugh, J., M. Blaha, W. Premeralani, F. Eddy and W. Lorensen (1991). *Object-Oriented Modeling and Design.* Englewood Cliffs, New Jersey 07632: Prentice Hall.

Russell, S. and P. Norvig (1995). *Artificial Intelligence a Modern Approach.* AI. Prentice Hall.

Sanchez, S. M. and T. W. Lucas (2002). Exploring the world of agent-based simulations: Simple models, complex analyses. In E. Yücesan, C.-H. Chen, J. L. Snowdon, and J. M. Charnes (Eds.), *Proceedings of the 2002 Winter Simulation Conference*, pp. 116–126.

Schleinzer, B. (2007, December). Flexible und hierarchische Multiagentensysteme – Modellierung und prototypische Erweiterung von Mulan und Capa. Diploma thesis, University of Hamburg, Department of Informatics, Vogt-Kölln Str. 30, D-22527 Hamburg.

Schleinzer, B., L. Cabac, D. Moldt and M. Duvigneau (2008, 5.–7.November). From agents and plugins to plugin-agents, concepts for flexible architectures. In *New Technologies, Mobility and Security, 2008. International Conference, NTMS '08, Tangier, Morocco. Electronical proceedings*, pp. 1–5. IEEE Xplore.

Schlüter, J. (2008, October). Accelerating the debugging process within a development environment for multi-agent systems: Extending tool support for Capa. Bachelor's thesis, University of Hamburg, Department of Informatics, Vogt-Kölln Str. 30, D-22527 Hamburg.

Schumacher, J. (2003, October). Eine Plugin-Architektur für Renew – Konzepte, Methoden, Umsetzung. Diploma thesis, University of Hamburg, Department of Computer Science, Vogt-Kölln Str. 30, D-22527 Hamburg.

Schütt, K. (2003). Automated modelling of business interaction processes for flow prediction. Master's thesis, University of Hamburg, Department for Informatics.

Seegert, V. (2005). Untersuchung von Planerkonzepten für Mulanagenten. Diploma thesis, University of Hamburg, Department of Computer Science, Vogt-Kölln Str. 30, D-22527 Hamburg.

Shehory, O. and A. Sturm (2001). Evaluation of modeling techniques for agent-based systems. In *Agents*, pp. 624–631.

Silva, C. T. L. L. and J. Castro (2002, 11). Modeling organizational architectural styles in UML: The tropos case. In O. Pastor and J. S. Díaz (Eds.), *Anais do WER02 - Workshop em Engenharia de Requisitos*, pp. 162–176.

Sommerville, I. (1996). *Software Engineering* (5. ed.). International computer science series. Wokingham: Addison/Wesley.

Stachowiak, H. (1973). *Allgemeine Modelltheorie*. Springer-Verlag.

Stehr, M.-O., J. Meseguer and P. C. Ölveczky (2001, December). Rewriting logic as a unifying framework for Petri nets. In H. Ehrig, G. Juhas, J. Padberg, and G. Rozenberg (Eds.), *Unifying Petri Nets*, Lecture Notes in Computer Science (Advances in Petri Nets). Springer-Verlag.

Strümpel, F. (2001, July). Exemplarische Evaluierung von Ansätzen zur Modellierung ereignisorientierter Simulationsszenarian anhand von Petrinetzen und DESMO. Bachelor's thesis (equiv.), University of Hamburg, Department of Computer Science, Vogt-Kölln Str. 30, D-22527 Hamburg.

Strümpel, F. (2003). Simulation zeitdiskreter Modelle mit Referenznetzen ("simulation of time-discrete models with reference nets", in german). Diploma thesis, Faculty of Informatics, University of Hamburg.

Sturm, A. and O. Shehory (2003, July 03). A framework for evaluating agent-oriented methodologies.

Tell, V. (2005, March). Grundlagen für die prototypische Umsetzung eines Multiagentensystem basierten Leitmodells. Diploma thesis, University of Hamburg, Department of Computer Science, Vogt-Kölln Str. 30, D-22527 Hamburg.

Uhrmacher, A. M. (2000). Agentenorientierte Simulation. In H. Szczerbicka and T. Uthmann (Eds.), *Modellierung, Simulation und Künstliche Intelligenz*, Ghent, pp. 15–45. SCS-Europe.

UML (2003a, October). UML 1.5 Specifications.
`http://doc.omg.org/formal/2003-03-01.pdf`.

UML (2003b, October). UML 2.0 Specifications.
`http://doc.omg.org/formal/2005-07-04.pdf`.

UML (2005, Juli). Unified modeling language: Superstructure. `http://doc.omg.org/formal/2005-07-04.pdf`.

UML (2009, December). UML Resource Page. `http://www.uml.org/`.

UML Q & A (2009, December). OMG-UML Questions and Answers. `http://www.omg.org/gettingstarted/uml_qa.htm`.

v. Lüde, R., D. Spresny and R. Valk (2003). Rationalität und organisierte Anarchie oder: James Bond im Garbage Can. In R. v. Lüde, D. Moldt, and R. Valk (Eds.), *Sozionik: Modellierung soziologischer Theorie*, Volume 2 of *Reihe: Wirtschaft – Arbeit – Technik*, pp. 9–45. Münster - Hamburg - London: Lit-Verlag.

v. Lüde, R., D. Moldt and R. Valk (2003). *Sozionik: Modellierung soziologischer Theorie*, Volume 2 of *Reihe: Wirtschaft – Arbeit – Technik*. Münster - Hamburg - London: Lit-Verlag.

v. Lüde, R., D. Moldt and R. Valk (Eds.) (2009). *Selbstorganisation und Governance in künstlichen und sozialen Systemen*, Volume 5 of *Reihe: Wirtschaft – Arbeit – Technik*. Münster - Hamburg - London: Lit-Verlag.

Valk, R. (1987). Nets in computer organisation. In W. Brauer, W. Reisig, and G. Rozenberg (Eds.), *Petri Nets: Central Models and Their Properties, Advances in Petri Nets 1986, Part I, Proceedings of an Advanced Course, Bad Honnef, September 1986*, Volume 254 of *Lecture Notes in Computer Science*, pp. 377–396. Springer-Verlag.

Valk, R. (1995, June). Petri nets as dynamical objects. In G. Agha and F. D. Cindio (Eds.), *Workshop Proc. 16th International Conf. on Application and Theory of Petri Nets, Torino, Italy*.

Valk, R. (1998). Petri nets as token objects - an introduction to elementary object nets. In J. Desel and M. Silva (Eds.), *19th International Conference on Application and Theory of Petri nets, Lisbon, Portugal*, Number 1420 in Lecture Notes in Computer Science, Berlin Heidelberg New York, pp. 1–25. Springer-Verlag.

van der Aalst, W. M. P., A. P. Barros, A. H. M. ter Hofstede and B. Kiepuszewski (2000). Advanced workflow patterns. In O. Etzion and P. Scheuermann (Eds.), *Cooperative Information Systems, 7th International Conference, CoopIS 2000, Eilat, Israel, September 6-8, 2000, Proceedings, CoopIS*, Volume 1901 of *Lecture Notes in Computer Science*, pp. 18–29. Springer-Verlag.

van der Aalst, W. M. P., A. H. M. ter Hofstede and A. P. Barros (2000a). Workflow Patterns. `http://is.ieis.tue.nl/research/patterns/download/wfs-pat-2000.pdf`.

van der Aalst, W. M. P., K. M. van Hee and R. A. van der Toorn (2002). Component-based software architectures: A framework based on inheritance of behavior. *Science of Computer Programming 42*(2-3), 129–171.

van der Aalst, W. M. P. and A. H. M. ter Hofstede (2002, August). Workflow patterns: on the expressive power of (Petri-net-based) workflow languages. In *Proc. of the Fourth International Workshop on Practical Use of Coloured Petri Nets and the CPN Tools, Aarhus, Denmark, August 28-30, 2002 / Kurt Jensen (Ed.)*, pp.

1–20. Technical Report DAIMI PB-560. http://www.daimi.au.dk/CPnets/workshop02/cpn/papers/Aalst.pdf.

van der Aalst, W. M. P. (2004). Discovering coordination patterns using process mining. In L. Bocchi and P. Ciancarini (Eds.), *First International Workshop on Coordination and Petri Nets (PNC 2004)*, pp. 49–64. STAR, Servizio Tipografico Area della Ricerca, CNR Pisa, Italy.

van der Aalst, W. M. P. and M. Song (2004). Mining social networks: Uncovering interaction patterns in business processes. In *Proceedings of the 2nd International Conference on Business Process Management*, Potsdam.

van der Aalst, W. M. P. and A. J. M. M. Weijters (2004). Process mining: a research agenda. *Computers in Industry 53*(3), 231–244.

van der Aalst, W. M. P., M. Dumas, C. Ouyang, A. Rozinat and H. M. W. Verbeek (2005). Choreography conformance checking: An approach based on BPEL and Petri nets. Technical Report BPM-05-25, BPMcenter.org.

van Dongen, B. F., A. K. A. de Medeiros, H. M. W. Verbeek, A. J. M. M. Weijters and W. M. P. van der Aalst (2005). The ProM framework: A new era in process mining tool support. In *ICATPN*, pp. 444–454. http://prom.win.tue.nl/tools/prom/.

van Hee, K. M. (1994). *Information Systems Engineering: A Formal Approach*. Cambridge: Cambridge University Press.

van Liedekerke, M. H. and N. M. Avouris (1995). Debugging multi-agent systems. *Information and Software Technology 37*, 103–112.

Vanderfeesten, M. (2006). *Identifying Roles in Multi-Agent Systems by Overhearing*. Master's thesis, Utrecht University. in preparation.

Wagner, G. (2005). *Towards radical agent-oriented software engineering processes based on AOR modelling*, Chapter 10, pp. 277–316. In Henderson-Sellers and Giorgini Henderson-Sellers and Giorgini (2005).

Wagner, T. (2009a, September). A centralized Petri net- and agent-based workflow management system. See Duvigneau and Moldt (2009), pp. 29–44.

Wagner, T. (2009b). Prototypische Realisierung einer Integration von Agenten und Workflows. Diploma thesis, University of Hamburg, Department of Informatics, Vogt-Kölln Str. 30, D-22527 Hamburg.

Weiß, G. and R. Jakob (2006). *Agentenorientierte Softwareentwicklung: Methoden und Tools (Xpert.press)*. Secaucus, NJ, USA: Springer-Verlag New York, Inc.

Wester-Ebbinghaus, M. (2005, November). Spezifikation eines Teamworkmodells für Mulan-Agenten. Diploma thesis, University of Hamburg, Department of Computer Science, Vogt-Kölln Str. 30, D-22527 Hamburg.

Wester-Ebbinghaus, M. and D. Moldt (2006, September). Auf dem Weg zu organisationsorientierter Softwareentwicklung. http://www.informatik.uni-hamburg.de/TGI/publikationen/public/data/2006/Wester+06/Wester+06.pdf.

Wester-Ebbinghaus, M., M. Köhler-Bußmeier and D. Moldt (2008). From multi-agent to multi-organization systems: Utilizing middleware approaches. In A. Artikis, G. Picard, and L. Vercouter (Eds.), *International Workshop Engineering Societies in the Agents World (ESAW 08)*.

Wester-Ebbinghaus, M. and D. Moldt (2008). Structure in threes: Modelling organization-oriented software architectures built upon multi-agent systems. In L. Padgham, D. C. Parkes, J. Müller, and S. Parsons (Eds.), *7th International Joint Conference on Autonomous Agents and Multiagent Systems (AAMAS 2008), Estoril, Portugal, May 12-16, 2008, Volume 3*, pp. 1307–1310. IFAAMAS.

WfMC (2005). Workflow reference model. `http://www.wfmc.org/standards/docs/tc003v11.pdf`.

Whitestein Technologies (2009). Cham, Switzerland. `http://www.whitestein.com`.

Wienberg, F. (2001, January). *Informations- und prozeßorientierte Modellierung verteilter Systeme auf der Basis von Feature-Structure-Netzen*. Dissertation, University of Hamburg, Department of Computer Science, Vogt-Kölln Str. 30, D-22527 Hamburg.

Wikipedia – Leitbild (2010, June). Leitbild (Unternehmen). (online). `http://de.wikipedia.org/wiki/Unternehmensleitbild`.

Wikström, K. and A. Rehn (2002). Playing the live jazz of project management. online. `http://www.reformingprojectmanagement.com/docs/playing-the-live-jazz-of-project-management.pdf`.

Willmott, S., M. Beer, R. Hill, D. Greenwood, M. Calisti, I. Mathieson, L. Padgham, C. Reese, K. Lehmann, T. Scholz and M. O. Shafiq (2005). Netdemo: opennet networked agents demonstration. In M. Pechoucek, D. Steiner, and S. Thompson (Eds.), *AAMAS 2005. Proceedings (Industry Track)*, pp. 129–130. 2 individual demos: (1) CAPA: The CAPA Mobile Chat Agent & Web Services Gateway Agent and (2) Settler: AgentBased Settler Game.

Wooldridge, M. and N. R. Jennings (1995). Intelligent agents: Theory and practice. *Knowledge Engineering Review 10*(2), 115–152.

Wooldridge, M., N. R. Jennings and D. Kinny (2000). The Gaia methodology for agent-oriented analysis and design. *Autonomous Agents and Multi-Agent Systems 3*(3), 285–312.

Zambonelli, F., N. R. Jennings and M. Wooldridge (2003, July). Developing multiagent systems: The Gaia methodology. *ACM Transactions on Software Engineering and Methodology 12*(3), 317–370.

Züllighoven, H. (2005, October). *Object-Oriented Construction Handbook*. dpunkt Verlag/Copublication with Morgan-Kaufmann. ISBN 3-89864-254-2.

*References*

350

# Acronyms

**ACL** Agent Communication Language

**ACM** Association for Computing Machinery

**ADEPT** Advanced Decision Environment for Process Tasks

**AGR** Agents Groups Roles

**AI** Artificial Intelligence

**AID** Agent Identifier

**AIM** Agent Interaction Mining

**AIP** Agent Interaction Protocol Diagram (.aip)

**AMS** Agent Management System

**AO** Agent Orientation

**AOM** Agent-Orientated Modeling

**AOSE** Agent-Oriented Software Engineering

**API** Application Programming Interface

**ARD** Agent Role Descriptions

**AUML** Agent UML

**BDI** Beliefs Desires Intentions

**Capa** Concurrent Agent Platform Architecture

**CD** Concept Diagram

**CDD** Coarse Design Diagram

**CPN** Colored Petri Nets

**CVS** Concurrent Versions System

**DAI** Distributed Artificial Intelligence

**DC** Decision Component

*Acronyms*

**DD** Dependency Diagram

**DESIRE** Design and Specification of Interacting Reasoning

**DF** Directory Facilitator

**DS** Distributed Systems

**Ed.** Editor

**Eds.** Editors

**EPS** Encapsulated Post Script

**FIPA** Foundation for Intelligent Physical Agents

**GIT** Distributed Version Control System

**GUI** Graphical User Interface

**HTML** Hypertext Markup Language

**HTTP** Hypertext Transfer Protocol

**ID** Identifier

**IDE** Integrated Development Environment

**IEEE** Institute of Electrical and Electronic Engineers

**IP** Internet Protocol

**J2SE** Java 2, Standard Edition

**JADE** Java Agent Development Environment

**JAR** Java-Archive (.jar)

**JDK** Java Development Kit

**KB** Knowledge Base

**KBE** Knowledge Base Editor

**LNCS** Lecture Notes in Computer Science

**LOC** Lines of Code

**MAA** Multi-Agent Application

**MadKit** Multi-Agent Development Kit

**MAS** Multi-Agent System

**ML** Metalanguage

**Mulan** Multi-Agent Nets

**NC** Net Component

**OO** Objekt Orientation

**OOSE** Object-oriented Software Engineering

**OMG** Object Management Group

**OSGi** Open Service Gateway Initiative

**Paose** Petri net-based/Process-oriented AOSE

**PDF** Portable Document Format (.pdf)

**PDT** Prometheus Design Tool

**PHP** PHP: Hypertext Preprocessor

**PMS** Plugin Management System

**PNG** Portable Network Graphics

**R/D** Roles & Dependencies

**Renew** Reference Net Workshop

**RMI** Remote Method Invocation

**RMIT** Royal Melbourne Institute of Technology

**RNW** Renew-Petri net Drawing (.rnw)

**SCM** Source Code Management System

**SL** Semantic Language

**SVN** Subversion Version Control System

**SWE** Software Engineering

**TCP** Transmission Control Protocol

**TGI** Theoretical Foundations of Informatics
(Theoretische Grundlagen der Informatik)

**UI** User Interface

**UML** Unified Modeling Language

**VM** Virtual Machine

**WfMC** Workflow Management Coalition

**XML** Extensible Markup Language

**YAWL** Yet Another Workflow Language

**blob** binary large object

**ca.** circa

**e.g.** for example

**et al.** and others (et alii)

**etc.** and so on (et cetera)

**ff.** and following pages

**p.** page

**pp.** pages

**vs.** versus

**w.r.t.** with respect to

# Glossary

## A

**Agent**  There are many different points of views on what an agent is. In this work an agent can be seen as a generalization of an object. This is the software engineering view on it. Agents have several characteristics: they communicate, they are pro-active, they have (limited) knowledge of their environment and they are autonomous. See Section 4.1.

**Agent-Oriented Software Engineering (AOSE)**  In the context of multi-agent systems, the →*Software Engineering* for the agent-oriented paradigm.

**Agent Platform**  An agent platform is a system on which agents can exist.

**AOSE**  See →*Agent-Oriented Software Engineering.*

**Approach**  A collection of systematic prescriptions of modeling techniques, methods, principles and proceedings that include the actions that lead to a →*Model /* system. An approach is a →*Model.* A guiding metaphor may offer guidance to the developers without explicitly name every detail. Compare with Figure 1.2 and →*Methodology.*

**Architecture**  An architecture defines underlying fundamental forms of system design.

**AUML**  Agent UML, agent unified modeling language.

## C

**Capa**  See →*Concurrent Agent Platform Architecture.*

**Communicative Act**  A communicative act is the basic element of the →*FIPA* agent communication language (ACL), which is following Searle's speech act theory. An →*Agent,* that sends a message, executes a communicative act. The receiver of the message is informed about something, requested to do something, ask something, etc. The communicative acts are categorized through the →*FIPA* in the form of →*Performatives.*

**Concurrent Agent Platform Architecture (Capa)**  A →*FIPA*-compliant implementation of →MULAN.

**Conversation**   A conversation in the context of →MULAN describes an →*Interaction*, i.e. a sequence (or scenario) of →*Communicative Acts* (messages). It can be regarded as an instantiation of an →*Interaction protocol* (or short →*Protocol*) used in the →*FIPA* specifications. In MULAN a conversation is usually held by two (or more) →*Agents*. Here the actual conversation is executed through the instantiated →*Protocol Nets*.

# D

**DC**   See →*Decision Component*.

**Decision Component (DC)**   A decision component defines the internal behavior of an agents. In contrast to →*Protocol nets*, decision components do not participate in inter-agent communication. They can be regarded as agent-internal services and are useful as adapters between agents and other software components, such as databases or graphical user interfaces (GUI). The interface of decision components is described in Table 4.5.

**Diagram**   A representation of a model expressed in a diagrammatic language (modeling technique). A diagram is a →*Model*. See also Section 2.2.

**Down-link**   A down-link in the context of →*Reference Nets* forms a →*Synchronous Channel* together with its counterpart the →*Up-link*. The down-link is annotated with the reference to the reference net containing the up-link.

# E

**Extensible Markup Language (XML)**   The Extensible Markup Language allows to hierarchically structure information as text. It is likewise readable for humans and machines and allows for automatic validation and transformation.

# F

**FIPA**   See →*Foundation for Intelligent Physical Agents*.

**Flexible Arc**   Flexible arcs are special arcs of the →*Reference Nets* formalism and can be used in →RENEW. They allow to move a variable amount of tokens from or to a place with one firing of a transition.

**Foundation for Intelligent Physical Agents (FIPA)**   The FIPA is an international organization that promotes and fosters specifications for the interoperability between →*Agents* and agent-based communicative infrastructures of various providers.

# I

**Implementation** (1) An implementation of a system coded in a programming language, i.e. a program.
(2) A concrete application of an abstract model.

**Interaction** An interaction is a process of communication between two or more agents. See also →*FIPA*-specifications, →*Interaction Protocols* and →*Agents*.

**Interaction protocol** The →*FIPA*-specifications use interaction protocols to describe the processes of →*Conversation* between two or more →*Agents*.

**Interface** An interface is a definition of methods, by which an artifact can be addressed. In *Java* an interface describes the public facade of a class and *interface* is also a keyword. The interface for →*Reference nets* is given by the signature of its →*Up-links*.

# K

**Knowledge Base** A knowledge base is the entity that holds the knowledge (sometimes also called beliefs) of an agent. In →MULAN the standard implementation of the knowledge base is a Petri net that encapsulates the agent's knowledge (see Section 4.3.2). The interface of the MULAN knowledge base is described in Table 4.2.

# L

**Life Cycle** The life cycle determines the state of a given artifact. It usually consists of initialization, operation, cleanup and eventually some other phases depending on the type of artifact. The →*FIPA* specifications defines the life cycle of an →*Agent* in terms of six phases: `unknown`, `initiated`, `active`, `waiting`, `suspended` and `transit`.

# M

**MAA** See →*Multi-Agent Application*.

**MAS** See →*Multi-Agent System*.

**Methodology** A collection of methods that can be applied (usually – in the context of software development) to construct, design, investigate or analyze software systems. The methods determine the techniques, principles and procedures to be applied.

**Model** A representation of a part of the world. See also Section 2.2.

**Multi-Agent Application (MAA)** A multi-agent application is a purposefully designed system of agents that act together in coordination to achieve a common goal.

**Multi-Agent Network**   A multi-agent network – or agent communication infrastructure – connects agent platforms to systems in which agents can interact with each other.

**Multi-Agent Nets (Mulan)**   The MULAN framework defines a multi-agent system (actually a platform) of a complete multi-agent framework based on →*Reference Nets*. MULAN is recognized as the reference implementation of a multi-agent system and can thus be interpreted as the concept behind agent-oriented software engineering with Petri nets or – due to its operational semantics – also as implementation. A →*FIPA*-compliant implementation is given through →CAPA. Chapter 4 gives an introduction to the MULAN framework.

**Multi-Agent System (MAS)**   A multi-agent system is a generic and ambiguous term that is used in the context of →*AOSE* in many different forms. It can describe an application or a framework which is constructed with agents that work in cooperation, coordination and/or competition. See also →*Platform*, →*MAA* and →*Multi-Agent Network*.

**Mulan**   See →*Multi-Agent Nets*.

# O

**Ontology**   An ontology defines concepts for the description of a system's parts (world representation) and the relationships between these concepts. In →*Software Engineering* the term is connected with a glossary, in database-driven design it is related to the entity/relationship model. In linguistics an ontology defines a closed area of concepts that form the language regarding one system. In this work an ontology is an explicit representation of all concepts in the system.

# P

**Performative**   The performative defines the intention of a →*Communicative Act*.

**Platform**   See →*Agent Platform*.

**Proactiv**   An →*Agent* acts out of its own intention.

**Protocol**   The term protocol is used ambiguously. See →*Interaction protocol* for FIPA agent interactions or →*Protocol Net* for agent role-specific parts of conversations modeled within →MULAN.

**Protocol Net**   A protocol net is the agent role-specific part of a conversation of agents, which is defined through an →*Agent Interaction Protocol* and is modeled (implemented) as a →*Reference net*. The interface of protocol nets is described in Table 4.4.

# R

**Reactiv**  An →*Agent* reacts to a message received.

**Reference Net Workshop (Renew)**  The Reference Net Workshop is both a simulator and a graphical development environment for →*Reference Nets* and other formalisms.

**Reference Nets**  Reference nets are object-oriented high-level Petri nets. The inscription language in reference nets is based on Java. Tokens can be colored and can even be active elements, such as objects or reference nets again. The formalism uses net instances, →*Synchronous Channels* (for the communication among nets) and token refinement to allow to build arbitrarily and dynamically structured systems. →RENEW.

**Renew**  See →*Reference Net Workshop*.

# S

**Semantic Language**  →*FIPA* language for agent communication.

**Simulation**  Within the Petri net community, simulation corresponds to the execution of net models. Execution and simulation can be used synonymously in this context.

**Software Engineering**  The research of the systematic approach of creating software.

**Synchronization**  Synchronization is a crucial mechanism in concurrent systems. Petri nets allow to model synchronizations in an elegant an intuitive way. However, these synchronizations are of a static nature, modeled as a transition. →*Reference Nets* allow to model dynamic synchronizations in Petri nets through →*Synchronous Channels*.

**Synchronous Channel**  A synchronous channel is formed for the firing of two (or more) transition dynamically at runtime during the simulation of a →*Reference Nets* system. At least one →*Down-link* and one →*Up-link* have to be involved in a synchronous channel. All involved transition are →*Synchronized* for this firing.

# U

**UML**  See →*Unified Modeling Language*.

**Unified Modeling Language (UML)**  The standard modeling language for object-oriented systems from the Object Management Group defines various types of diagrams that are used during object-oriented analysis and design.

**Up-link**  An up-link is in the context of →*Reference Nets* one of the two inscriptions for transitions, that form a →*Synchronous Channel*.

## X

**XML**     See →*Extensible Markup Language.*

# A About this Work

## A.1 Notation

This text conforms to the convention of text styles shown in Table A.1. This should give the reader some help about where or how he can find additional information about acronyms or proper names.

| Category | Style |
|---|---|
| Program code | Verbatim |
| Inscriptions from images | *Italic* |
| Persons | Initial Capitals |
| Names of tools | *Slanted* |
| Acronyms | CAPITALS |

Table A.1: Notations

Some names receive a special treatment, being displayed as small caps.[1] They are the names or the elements related to the Paose approach (e.g. Renew and Mulan).

## A.2 Used Tools

This work is written in LaTeX on Debian Gnu/Linux (http://www.debian.org) and Mac OS X (http://www.apple.com). All diagrams and images – with the exception of screenshots – are produced with Renew unless stated otherwise. Many of the diagrams produced with Renew are expressed in the modeling techniques that constitute the focus of this work. These techniques rely on supporting tools implemented as plugins for Renew. A list of plugins, which have been developed in the context of this work, is presented in Table B.2. Screenshots have been produced with *Grab, Kscreenshot* or *gnome-screenshot*. Annotated screenshots are again produced with Renew. ImageMagick was used for the conversion of images and as a processor for ImageNetDiff presented in Chapter 18. Other used tools and libraries that are not included in Renew (for text and/or code) are: *Eclipse, Xemacs, LaTeX, Velocity, Subversion, CVS, Git, Gnuplot* and *Ant*.

---

[1]Note that this style is not available in headings of in combination with the bold text style.

| Tool/System | Tasks |
|---|---|
| RENEW | Petri net development and execution diagram design |
| Grab Ksnapshot Gnome-screenshot | Screenshots |
| ImageMagick | image conversion |
| Eclipse | *Java* programming |
| *Java* JDK | *Java* Framework and VM |
| Xemacs LaTeX Ispell | text processing |
| Velocity | template generation |
| Subversion CVS Git | text/code versioning |
| Ant | build environment |
| gnuplot | histogram generation |
| Bash | scripting |
| grep sed nano fink | various |

Table A.2: Tools and systems used for the development of the presented work.

# B Implementations

## B.1 Lists of the Modeling Techniques and Plugins

Table B.1 lists the modeling techniques of the PAOSE approach. The plugins developed in the course of this work are listed in Table B.2 and in Table B.3.

| | |
|---|---|
| CDD | Coarse Design Diagram (Chapter 10) |
| DD | Dependency Diagram (together with Dirkner) (Section 11.2) |
| R/D | Roles/Dependencies Diagram (introduced dependencies, Section 11.4) |
| | *(original developers: Klenski and Willner (2007))* |
| CD | Concept Diagram (Chapter 12) |
| AIP | Agent Interaction Protocol Diagram (Chapter 13) |

Table B.1: List of PAOSE modeling techniques.

*Net Components Plugin*
- · basic NC functionality (extensible by plugins)

MULAN *Components Plugin*
- · NCs for protocol nets (NC extension)

*Use Case Plugin*
- · drawing of overview diagrams (coarse design) / use cases (NC extension)
- · including project generation

*DC Components Plugin*
- · NCs for decision components (NC extension)

*AIP Diagram Plugin*
- · drawing of Agent Interaction Protocol Diagrams
- · including protocol generation

*Image Net Diff Plugin*
- · adding diff functionality for drawing / diagrams

*FAPlugin*
- · plugin for the drawing of finite automata
- · example net PMS-based plugin

Table B.2: RENEW plugins that are developed by the author.

MULAN-VIEWER

---

- · main authors: Carl, Duvigneau, Schleinzer, Schlüter
- · further original conceptualization/development (navigation, debugging)
- · technical advisor for diploma thesis (Schleinzer)
- · technical supervisor bachelor's thesis (Schlüter) / maintenance

MULAN-SNIFFER

---

- · project assignment supervision for Heitmann and Plähn
- · original conceptualization (with Denz)
- · technical basis (AIPs), integration

*Mining Plugin*

---

- · authors: Denz, Cabac
- · original conceptualization (with Denz)
- · technical basis (net components), integration (redesign as plugin), maintenance

*Knowledge Round-Trip Plugin*

---

- · authors: Dirkner, Cabac
- · original conceptualization
- · technical supervision for diploma thesis (Dirkner)
- · maintenance, refactoring, redesign

*Knowledge Base Editor (KBE)*

---

- · authors: Klenski, Willner, Duvigneau, Wester-Ebbinghaus, Cabac
- · additional technical advisor diploma thesis (Klenski, Willner)
- · maintenance, redesign of the modeling syntax

*Ontology Generator Plugin*

---

- · authors: Teuber, Cabac
- · project assignment supervision for Teuber
- · based on Feature Structure Types, using Velocity
- · original conceptualization

*MulanDoc Plugin*

---

- · main authors: Meiners, Küster, Den, Lohmann, Cabac
- · original conceptualization / original re-conceptualization
- · technical supervision for the project paper of Meiners
- · additional features (image maps, coarse design diagram integration)
- · maintenance

*RemoteDC{1,2}*

---

- · authors: Markwardt (v1), Ratjen (v2), Duvigneau, Cabac
- · maintenance / refactoring / additional features (version 1)
- · project paper supervision for Ratjen
- · re-conceptualization for version 2 / redesign of interface net and stub

*Jadex Planner Integration*

---

- · bachelor's thesis co-supervision for Brin
- · refactoring / construction of JadexLibs plugin

Table B.3: Plugin and tools within the context of this work.

# C Modeling Settler

This appendix lists a set of models developed during the creation of the Settler system. These are the Coarse Design Diagram with the application matrix extracted presented in Section C.1, the ontology as three Concept Diagrams presented in Section C.2, the structure of the system as R/D Diagram in Section C.3, an exemplary interaction (*build*) in Section C.4 and some of the user interfaces, one implemented as a decision component net and the Settler board representation, presented in Section C.5.

## C.1 Overview: Coarse Design Diagram

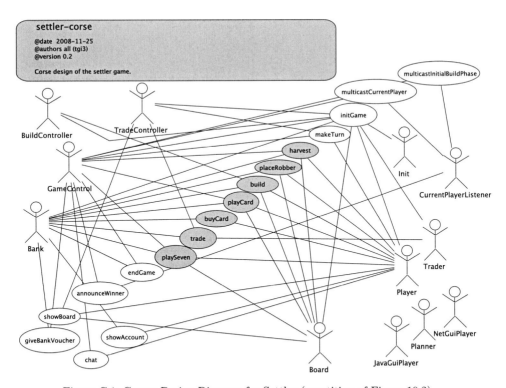

Figure C.1: Coarse Design Diagram for Settler (repetition of Figure 10.2).

## C.2 Ontology

The ontology of the Settler system is defined in three Concept Diagrams. They are pragmatically separated into (ordinary) concepts, agent actions and predicates. The layout of the diagrams have been modified to achieve a readable text size. The alternative Protégé model, which has been maintained for evaluation and backup reasons and models the exact same ontology, is not presented here.

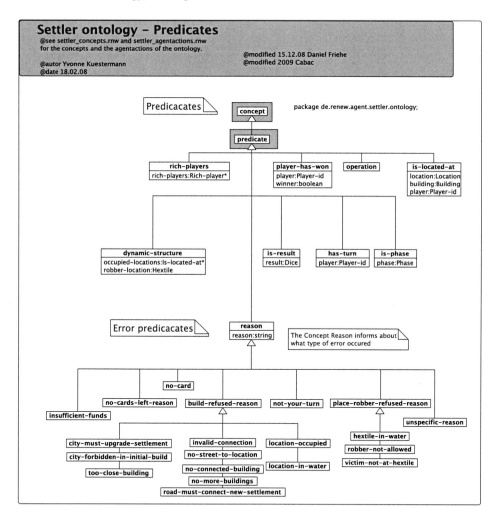

Figure C.2: Concept Diagram: ontology in Settler (predicates).

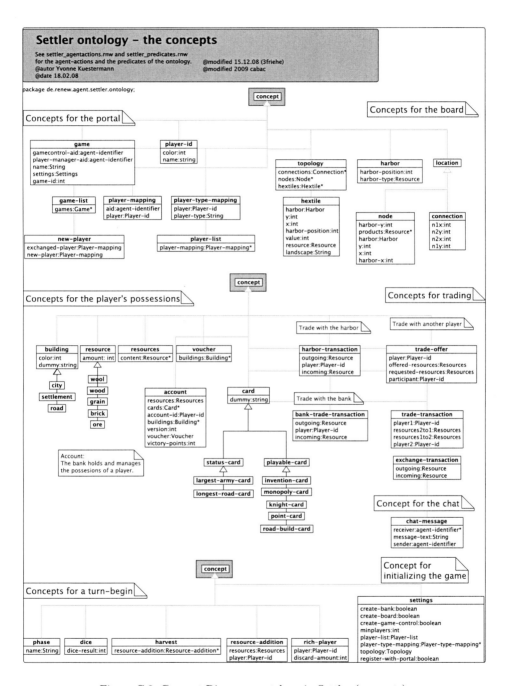

Figure C.3: Concept Diagram: ontology in Settler (concepts).

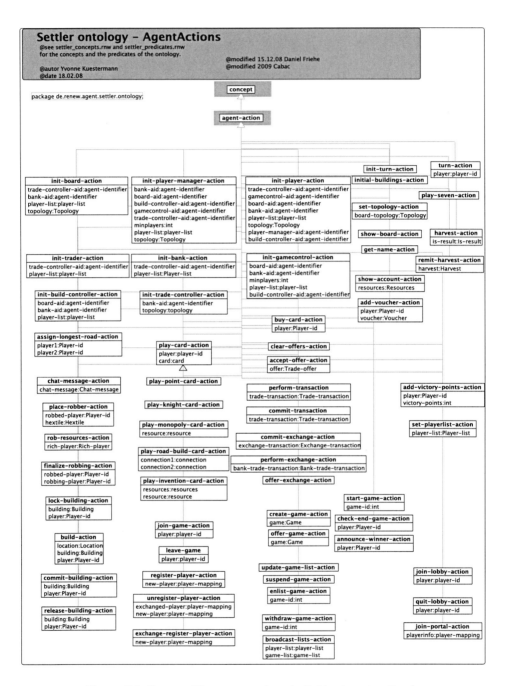

Figure C.4: Concept Diagram: ontology in Settler (agent actions).

# C.3 Roles and Dependencies

The initial knowledge bases of the Settler system are defined through a R/D Diagram, which is presented in Figure C.5 as an overview – with collapsed role and service descriptors – and in Figures C.6 and C.7 in the expanded version of the same diagram.

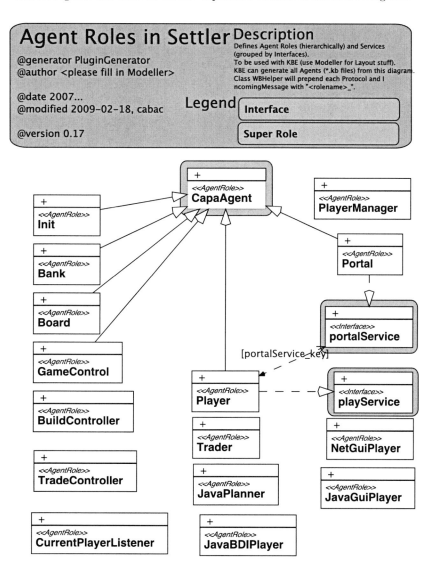

Figure C.5: Roles and Dependencies in Settler (nodes collapsed, reprise).

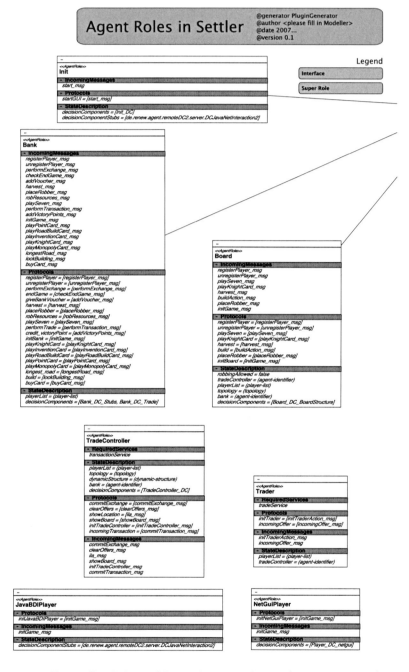

Figure C.6: Roles and Dependencies in Settler (expanded, part 1).

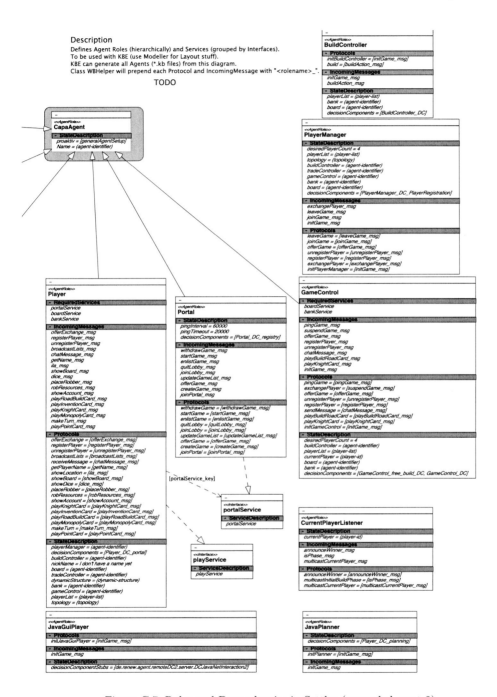

**Description**
Defines Agent Roles (hierarchically) and Services (grouped by Interfaces).
To be used with KBE (use Modeller for Layout stuff).
KBE can generate all Agents (*.kb files) from this diagram.
Class WBHelper will prepend each Protocol and IncomingMessage with "<rolename>_".
TODO

Figure C.7: Roles and Dependencies in Settler (expanded, part 2).

```xml
<?xml version="1.0" encoding="UTF-8" standalone="yes"?>
<Role relatedTo="" roleName="JavaGuiPlayer" xmlns="http://tempuri.org/XMLSchema.xsd">
    <StateDescription>
        <entry argTypes="java.lang.String" valueType="java.util.Vector">
            <comment/>
            <name>decisionComponentStubs</name>
            <value>de.renew.agent.remoteDC2.server.DCJavaNetInteraction2;</value>
        </entry>
    </StateDescription>
    <Protocols>
        <entry argTypes="java.lang.String" valueType="java.util.ArrayList">
            <comment/>
            <name>initJavaGuiPlayer</name>
            <value>initGame_msg;</value>
        </entry>
    </Protocols>
    <IncomingMessages>
        <entry argTypes="java.lang.String_java.lang.String_[Ljava.lang.String;_java.lang
            .String_java.lang.String_java.lang.String_java.lang.String_java.lang.String"
            valueType="de.renew.agent.repr.acl.AclMessage">
            <comment/>
            <name>initGame_msg</name>
            <value>request ;;;((action (agent-identifier) (init-player-action)));FIPA-SL0
                ;;;;</value>
        </entry>
    </IncomingMessages>
</Role>
```

Listing C.1: Generated ARD file for JavaGuiPlayer.

## C.4 Interaction: AIPs and Protocol Nets

As exemplary interaction, all artifacts of the *build* interaction are presented in the following. The interaction is specified as AIP. Figures C.8 shows the whole interaction protocol as an overview (with inscriptions reduced to keywords), while Figures C.9 and C.10 show the same AIP (enlarged) with all action and exchange inscriptions expanded. The interaction in short: the Player wants to build a building and sends a request to the BuildController, who asks the Bank and the Board whether the conditions are satisfied. An appropriate answer is sent to the Player and the Bank will also credit the victory points for the building.

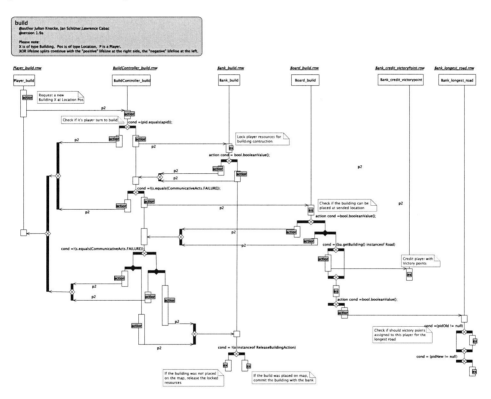

Figure C.8: Interaction: *build*.

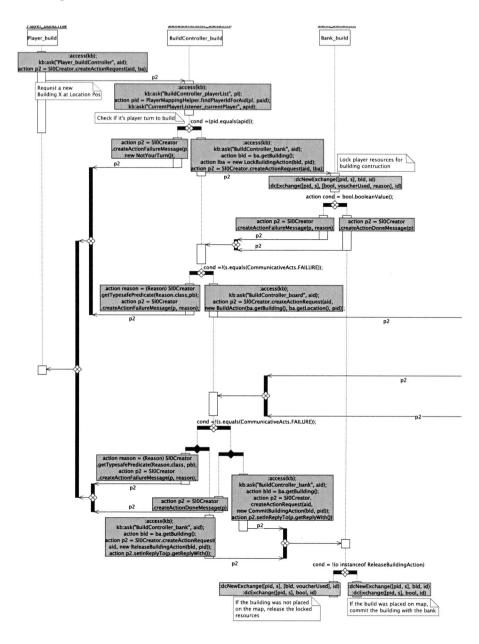

Figure C.9: Interaction: *build* (Part 1).

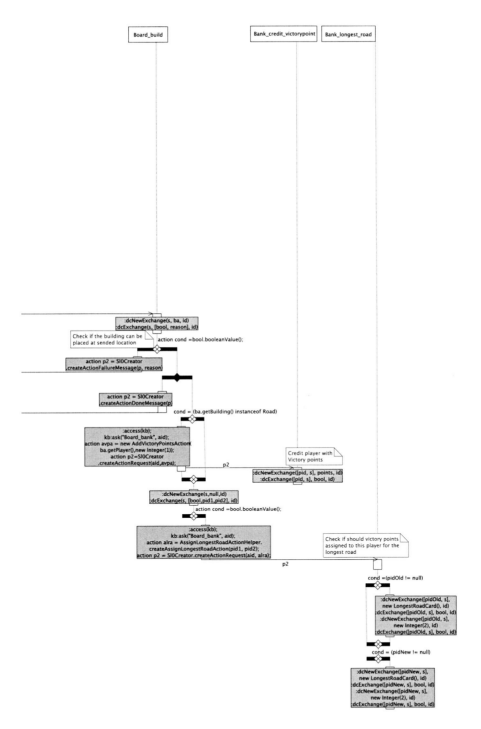

Figure C.10: Interaction: *build* (Part 2).

## C.5 User Interfaces

Figure C.11 shows the main interface part of the Petri net-based GUI for the Settler game, while the game is being played. All in Figure C.11 shown elements of the net, with the exception of the background, are manual transitions or virtual places. The virtual places display the contents of places in the controller cv part of the net (not presented here). Thus they function as output interface. Transitions are connected to the controller part via synchronous channels (down-links) and act as simple input elements.

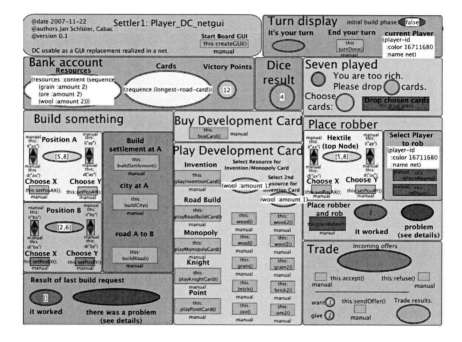

Figure C.11: Execution of *Player_DC_netgui* (interface part).

In the image the current account can be observed (in SL representation). The player owns two grain, two ore and two wool. Other displayed information is that he owns the longest road card, that he has won the game with 12 victory points, the last dice result was four and whose turn it is (as player-id). Note that on the left side two spinner widgets (*Position A,B*) are used to determine the position, where the building is to be built. The sending of the request is executed with the transitions next to the spinner. After the answer is received, the result of the request is presented in either one of the two places underneath as token or as message. In the net instance the last build action was to build a city on position 5,8 and that this was successful (see Figure C.12). Several other elements exist for other situations in the game, e.g. discarding guards when being robbed. The board is displayed in a separate window, the opening of which is triggered through a manual transition at the top of the net.

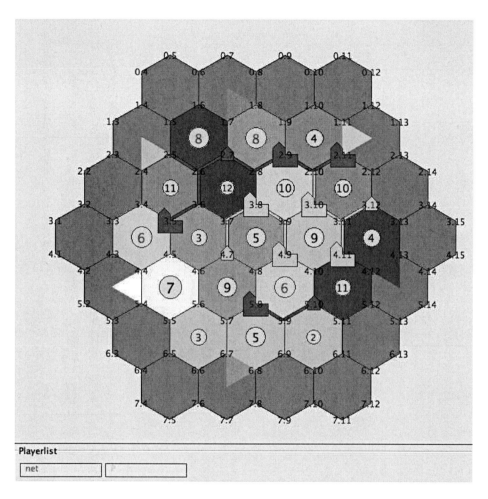

Figure C.12: The Settler board representation after the game of the NetGUI player is finished. Compare with state in the NetGUI in Figure C.11.